Clothing

A STUDY IN HUMAN BEHAVIOR

Clothing

A STUDY IN HUMAN BEHAVIOR

Mary Shaw Ryan

CORNELL UNIVERSITY

Holt, Rinehart and Winston, Inc.

New York,   Chicago,   San Francisco,   Toronto,   London

Preface

HOME ECONOMISTS in recent years have become increasingly aware of the importance of the social-psychological factors related to clothing. Concurrently, greater emphasis has been placed on these elements in clothing and textiles curriculums. *Clothing: A Study in Human Behavior* is a reflection of this emphasis and is designed to be a systematic survey of psychological and sociological investigations in which clothing has been one of the variables. It presents a critical evaluation of the knowledge in the area and the theories and hypotheses considered promising for future research.

Its collateral aim is to acquaint the reader with the research methods that have yielded this information. It is hoped in addition that the contents will serve as a stimulus to more research on the psychological and sociological aspects of clothing. The bibliographies at the ends of chapters have been assembled to reflect the full range of literature available on clothing behavior.

The book has been prepared as a text for the clothing and textiles curriculum wherever there is a specific interest in clothing as a form of human behavior. In its individual parts, the volume may have particular relevance for several courses in which the study of clothing is carefully defined. Part One is a conceptually organized introduction to the psychology of clothing. The instructor may also find it useful as reading for courses in design and selection of clothing. Part Two is concerned with consumer problems. The approach here is based primarily upon original theory. It is hoped that it will give new perspectives to research in this field and be valuable as supplementary material for courses in merchandising and buying. Part Three in its concentration on social-psychological implications of clothing for different age groups will perhaps be found appropriate for courses on clothing for the family. There has been a surge of research interest in child and adolescent psychology resulting in recognition of children and adolescents as differing from adults in values, interests, and attitudes, as well as in size and ability. In spite of the increase in knowledge about children and adolescents, the only attempts to organize and present social-psychological views of clothing for children and adolescents have been brief and superficial treatments. Part Three is therefore a step toward filling this gap. As the expected life span increases, we are finding many problems in gerontology which have taken on

v

new importance. The last chapter answers some of these problems in relation to clothing.

The author is greatly indebted to former students who have used and made helpful suggestions on various chapters. Many of their studies are cited in the text and credited to them. Colleagues and the administration at Cornell have been kind in giving encouragement. The author is especially grateful to Dr. Mary Wines of the University of Delaware, who read Part One and gave valuable criticisms. Her daughter, Adelaide, has been helpful in reading proof and offering suggestions. Particular appreciation also goes to Dr. Mary Lou Rosencranz of the University of Missouri who read the entire manuscript and aided by contributing her insightful and sympathetic reactions to the material. At the same time the author holds herself entirely responsible for whatever errors and misjudgments may have crept into her work.

The contributions of writers and publishers who very kindly allowed quotations and tables to be taken from their books and articles is indeed appreciated. Finally, most of all, the author is grateful to her husband, Professor Thomas A. Ryan, who supported her throughout the period during which the manuscript was written with his unfailing patience, encouragement, and constructive criticism.

M.S.R.

Ithaca, New York
December 1965

Contents

Clothing

A STUDY IN HUMAN BEHAVIOR

Part One

Social-Psychological Aspects of Clothing: General Considerations

OUR interest in clothing, the reasons we choose particular garments, the effects of clothing on behavior, and even the way in which we perceive clothing are all dependent upon social and cultural factors. As Dorothy Dickins says, "Clothing serves in the main a social purpose just as food serves in the main a health purpose." (4:346). If human beings were not reacting to other human beings in social situations, then there would be no felt need for clothing beyond, perhaps, the protection it offers from cold. Certainly there would be neither fashion nor change of fashion. There would be no desire to have one style of garment instead of another. Knowledge of the social-psychological aspects of clothing is, therefore, basic to the study of clothing.

The surprising fact is that only in comparatively recent years have specialists in the clothing field recognized the importance of social-psychological factors. Up until 1947 the emphasis was either upon construction and design of clothing or on the study of textiles; the significance of the contributions of the social sciences was barely acknowledged. In that year a group of home economists joined various representatives of the social sciences to explore areas of research interest relevant to both groups. This meeting stimulated both the social scientists and the textile and clothing specialists to think about the combined areas, and a large number of problems were suggested for research (2). The following year a psychologist, George Hartmann (6), who was one of the participants at this meeting was a principal speaker at a conference of college teachers of textiles and clothing and further stimulated thinking in the social-psychological aspects of clothing. During

2

the summers of 1949 and 1951 seminars on the "Development of Studies and Research in the Sociological Aspects of Clothing" were held at Michigan State College. Those attending these seminars considered the sociological, anthropological, and psychological theories which might explain clothing behaviors and considered research methods that promised to be productive in the area.

In the years since these first evidences of awareness of the importance of the social sciences to the study of clothing, interest has mushroomed. Each year there are more college courses, workshops, and individual lectures given on this topic; more and more graduate students combine work in clothing and the social sciences, and each year new reports of research prove that the social-psychological aspects of clothing are considered a vital part of the total field of textiles and clothing.

Research and theoretical speculation in the area in which clothing and the social sciences overlap contribute to social psychology as well as to the clothing field. The social psychologist is concerned with the interaction of people in their social and cultural environments. Clothing plays a double or triple role in social interactions. In reacting to another person the first step is forming an impression of him. Clothing plays a part, often an important part, in the way we perceive other people. Clothes affect the action of the wearer. They, in part at least, determine the role he plays in society. One of the simplest means of identifying certain groups is through clothing.

Although some psychologists recognized earlier than those in the clothing field that important problems existed in the social-psychological aspects of clothing, there has been relatively little research by social psychologists in which clothing has been one of the variables studied. In recent years there has been no marked increase in the number of such studies prepared by psychologists, while home economists working in clothing have accelerated their research interest in the behavioral aspects of clothing.

The first element to interest psychologists was the basic question: why do we wear clothes? Wundt, called the father of experimental psychology, and others such as Westermark, Dunlap, Sanborn (see Chapter 2), sought the reason. Each writer had his own theory. Some accepted the Biblical explanation of modesty; others thought that clothing was first worn as protection against the elements, insects, enemies, or supernatural forces; while others believed that it was adopted as a form of decoration or a symbol of excellence: the hunter or the warrior with his trophies. By the first quarter of this century the interest of psychologists in this speculation had died out; anthropology was developing as a separate field and this type of analysis became a function of its research.

At the same time, early in the twentieth century, interest was focused on self and the effects of clothing on the self. James (9) stated that self is identified with clothes. G. Stanley Hall and Flaccus (5) tried by means of a questionnaire to determine some of the effects of clothing on the self. Simmel (13) was interested in fashion and how clothing satisfies both the need to belong and to differentiate oneself from others. Dearborn (3) writing on the physiology and psychology of clothing enumerated the effects of clothing which he considered important. Many of the ideas of these early authors have been supported by later research, others still need to be investigated.

By the 1920s the psychologists were concerned with proving that their discipline was scientific and practical. Research concentrated on such problems as animal learning and the development of mental tests; any serious consideration of the self was abandoned. Problems in which clothing was a variable would have been looked upon as trivial and unworthy of experimentation. The clinical approach of Freud took exception to this. His psychoanalytical theories formed the basis for Flugel's book on the psychology of dress, still considered a classic. There were a few scattered studies which related to clothing. Wilheminia Jacobson (8) did an interesting research project in experimental esthetics which related to clothes, and Hurlock (7) and Barr (1) each did doctoral theses relating to fashion motivation. As interest in adolescent psychology developed a number of studies appeared such as Silverman's (see Chapter 13) which have either been concerned with psychological aspects of clothing for the adolescent or studies in which clothing has been one of the variables considered. For the most part, however, the areas of social psychology relating to clothing were ignored by the social scientists.

In the years since World War II social psychology has developed rapidly as a separate field. The importance of the concept of self has again been emphasized and a few social psychologists have recognized that clothing should be considered. In formulating theories, clothing is often given as an illustration of various laws or principles, but seldom has it been a part of experimental design. Clothing can be used, as a few studies have illustrated, as a means of proving or disproving certain fundamental laws and principles in social psychology. It offers a tangible and concrete means of measuring social-psychological changes. Kreober, an anthropologist, demonstrated this as early as 1919. He used measurements of certain dimensions of dress as a quantitative means of showing cyclic changes in styles. In recent years, the length of women's skirts as dictated by fashion and as worn on the streets was used as a means of studying how far man is willing to be pushed by leaders. Other social psychologists have mentioned fashion as a way of showing the American social structure and differentiating between status groups or as a means of identifying a cultural role. One of the few fairly large projects undertaken by social scientists concerning clothing was done at Michigan State University under the joint sponsorship of the Sociology and Anthropology and the Textile and Clothing Departments. Various parts of this project will be discussed in detail in later chapters.

In spite of the scattered studies by social scientists over the last sixty years and the advance made by home economists in clothing studies in recent years, one of the greatest needs now is to take a look at current social-psychological theories, to relate these to clothing problems, make predictions from them, and then test these predictions. Treece (14) has made a beginning in this direction by examining certain social-psychological theories and relating them to clothing. We need more such predictions with research projects designed to test these predictions.

Within the over-all view of the research and theories of the social-psychological aspects of clothing given in this book, two theories will be encountered again and again. The first of these is the role theory of interaction. Role is regarded as a pattern of attitudes and actions taken by an individual in social situations.[1] Basic to this theory is the notion of the self-concept. Role in this theory is the prime unit of interaction between persons. The specific role an individual plays at any given moment depends upon the situation and upon his concept of himself. Thus, an individual may play many different roles; at various times he may be the serious efficient business man, the club wit or the devoted father. The self as object of awareness is the unit which interacts with the role to lead to specific human behavior. Thus, the individual who thinks of himself as friendly attempts by his actions to appear friendly to others. Although research based upon this theoretical framework is just beginning, this theory seems to offer the most logical explanations. Clothing may influence the self-concept and so make the playing of a role easier, it may even determine whether a particular role is to be played.

---

[1] Definition based upon that of Sarbin, Theodore, "Role Theory" Chapter 6 in *Handbook of Social Psychology* Vol I (Gardner Lindzey, Ed.) Cambridge Mass.: Addison-Wesley Publishing Co. Inc. 1954.

The second theory which we will discuss in various contexts is that clothing is one of the means by which we bolster our self-esteem and seek acceptance from others. Thus, one might assume that those who have the greatest sense of security or self-confidence would have less interest in clothes than those who were less sure of themselves. In discussing socioeconomic status, we would theorize that those highest in the status scale would have less interest than those below, and that those who are moving (or want to move) to a higher status would show increased concern over clothing; in considering age differences we would state that the period of greatest concern in clothing would be during adolescence when there is the greatest concern over being accepted and approved by the group; in the specific situation we would expect that the individual would be more concerned in the social situation in which he was unsure of his acceptance than in the social situation in which he is with friends.

In Part One of this book we will discuss the social-psychological aspects of clothing in general: the part clothing plays in our perception of people; the wearer and why he chooses the clothes he does, and the ways in which clothing affects his behavior. In Part Two we will again be discussing the individual and his clothing behavior, but, this time we will focus our attention on the individual as a consumer, his motivations in the purchase of clothing, shopping behavior and satisfactions with garments. In Part Three we will examine the research and theories related to age differences in the psychological aspects of clothing.

Bibliography

1. Barr, Estelle De Young. A psychological analysis of fashion motivation. *Archives of Psychol.* No. 171, 1934.
2. Brasie, M., Brew, M. L., Fitzsimmons, C., Rankin, M., and Smart, R. C. Research areas of textiles and clothing. *J. of Home Ec.* 39(10), 1947, 620–624.
3. Dearborn, G. The psychology of clothing. *Psychol. Rev. Monogr.* 26(1), 1918, 1–72.
4. Dickins, Dorothy. Social participation as a criterion for determining scientific minimum standards in clothing. *Rural Soc.* 9, 1944, 341–349.
5. Flaccus, L. W. Remarks on the psychology of clothes. *Pedag. Sem.* 13, 1906, 61–83.
6. Hartmann, G. W. Clothing: personal problem and social issue. *J. of Home Ec.* 41(6), 1949, 295–298.

7. Hurlock, Elizabeth. Motivation in fashion. *Archives of Psychol.* No. 111, 1929.
8. Jacobson, W. An experimental investigation of the basic esthetic factors in costume design. *Psychol. Monog.* 45(1), 1933, 147–184.
9. James, W. *Principles of Psychology.* Vol. I. New York: Henry Holt and Co., 1890.
10. Langer, L. *The Importance of Wearing Clothes.* New York: Hastings House Publishers, Inc., 1959, 334p.
11. Rosencranz, Mary Lou. Social and psychological approaches to clothing research. *J. of Home Ec.* 57(1), 1965, 26–29.
12. Rosencranz, Mary Lou. Sociological aspects of clothing studied. *J. of Home Ec.* 42(3), 1950, 206.
13. Simmel, G. Fashion. *Internat. Quart.* 10, 1904, 130–155.
14. Treece, Anna J. *An Interpretation of Clothing Behavior Based on Social-pychological Theory.* Ph.D. Thesis, Ohio State Univer., 1959.
15. Warning, Margaret. Future Explorations in Home Economics: Clothing. *J. of Home Ec.* 52(8), 1960, 646–651.

Suggested for additional reference:

Roach, Mary Ellen and Eicker, Joanne Bubolz. *Dress, Adornment, and the Social Order.* New York: John Wiley & Sons, Inc., 1965, 418 p.

Chapter 1

First Impressions

*F*irst impressions play a very important part in the later social interaction between individuals. If a first impression is poor, it may create avoidance, or at least halt any effort for a further meeting, while if the first reaction is favorable, a pleasant stimulus toward a renewal of that encounter may evolve. In situations where individuals are introduced or accidentally meet, the interaction between them will be colored by the first impressions of each. Our treatment of another person will be cordial or cool according to our impression of him. Clothing, because it is one of the clues used by people in these first reactions, may therefore play a part in the actual selection of our friends and acquaintances.

Furthermore, the evaluations of each will be influenced by the clothes he is wearing and what he thinks his impression is upon the other. As you meet anyone you are not only forming impressions of him but you know he is forming impressions of you. You are aware of your own appearance and may have ideas of the way he will be perceiving you. This will influence your behavior toward him. For example, if you think you look sophisticated you try to play the role of a sophisticated person. If you are caught doing something you think is slightly ridiculous you may act the role of a clown or wit. The same will be true of the other person.

Perhaps the impression the other person makes on you or you make on him is completely erroneous. Whether it is or not, it nevertheless does influence the social interaction and should therefore be recognized as a part of the total situation.

While this seems to be complicated, clothing actually simplifies our perception of people or of the total situation. It often serves as a short-cut. We see at a glance that one man is a waiter and we know what action to take toward him and what to expect from him. Imagine how much more difficult it would be in any situation if everyone were dressed alike. For example, take the simple act of going downtown to shop. How would you know which man was the policeman? It might take considerable time and questioning to identify him if it were not for his uniform. It would take scrutiny of every face to distinguish your friends and acquaintances, while now often the clothing will be the only clue needed in a brief glance to tell you whether or not a person might be someone you should recognize. Because the waiter and the customer are dressed differently, you don't make a blunder by asking the customer to serve you. Similarly in any situation involving people the clothing may aid in enriching or clarifying the perception of the total situation.

The subject of first impressions is itself a broad subject. We can examine their accuracy, how they develop, their influence on later actions, the attributes of garments that give various impressions or what types of clothes "go with" or "should be worn by" certain "personality types."

In order to make our discussion more meaningful let us ask ourselves the following six questions and examine any research evidence which we have to help us to answer them.

1. Do clothes communicate something about the wearer to others, if so, do they always or just under certain conditions?
2. *What* do clothes tell others about the wearer?
3. Is there agreement among observers or does everyone see a person in a given costume differently? If there is agreement is it within a small homogeneous group, a given culture, a given age group, or do all perceive him in the same way?
4. How accurate are our impressions, that is, do our impressions agree with the "real" characteristics of the person? Are some more accurate than others?
5. What qualities or attributes of clothing determine our impressions?
6. How do these impressions develop?

1. Do Clothes Communicate Something about the Wearer to Others?

This question might be phrased: In reacting to persons do we perceive more than the physical characteristics of each, and, if so, is clothing one of the

cues which we use? This is not only the most basic question in our discussion of the part clothing plays in the perception of people but also the
easiest to answer.

It is obvious from our daily experiences that we do perceive other persons as having certain personality characteristics, or classify them according
to status, age, or occupational groups, with nothing more than their physical
appearance as clues. Psychologists, for many years have been interested in
this phenomenon. Most of the early studies were concerned with the degree
of accuracy of such perceptions, but some studies have been made of the
process itself. Asch (1) has shown how impressions of personality are organized by giving groups of students two lists of discrete qualities said to
belong to a person. The lists were identical except for one word. In one
series the words in both lists were: intelligent, skillful, industrious, determined, practical and cautious. One of the lists also included the word
warm and the second list the word *cold*. The subjects were instructed
to write sketches of the person described and also to indicate on a check
list the trait terms which best fitted the impression they had formed. The
group which had the list including *warm* formed quite different impressions
than those whose list included *cold*. In each case the total list of adjectives
was interpreted so that the impression was a unified, consistent and meaningful whole for the subject. In checking the list of traits the group who
had *warm* in their original list were much more likely to check *generous,
happy, humorous, popular,* while the group who had cold in their list
checked the opposite. On the other hand the two groups were alike in that
their impressions. Changing one descriptive word changed the total im-
they checked important, serious, strong, and honest as being consistent with
pression in some ways and not in others. Other key words were used in
place of *warm* and *cold* and were found to have less effect upon the total
impression. These were assumed to be characteristics which were less central.

It is highly probable that in perceiving another person clothing may
give clues which serve, as did the adjectives *warm* and *cold* in Asch's
study, to organize the impression into a logical whole. It may be that some
aspects of clothing, say appropriateness, may affect the total impression
more than other aspects such as color. A most interesting and worthwhile
series of experiments could be carried out using Asch's study as a basis
for formulating hypotheses. The difficulty with such a study would be the
number of variables. For this reason, pictures rather than actual persons
would probably allow for greater control.

Unfortunately, clothing has not been one of the variables in this sort
of experiment or in any dealing with the process of impression formation.
We know neither how nor to what extent clothing affects the formation
of impressions of people. We do have evidence, however, from a number
of studies and pilot investigations that clothing is one of the clues used

in perceiving persons and that impressions vary with variations in clothing.

As a class exercise, over 50 girls in a class in clothing selection were asked to bring in written descriptions of one or more strangers they had seen over a holiday. There had been no previous discussion and no further instructions were given before the holiday. The girls brought back descriptions of physical appearance, but also descriptions of the age, interests, socioeconomic level, personality traits as they saw them. Each of the students described at least one characteristic beyond the physical aspect of the individual, and some gave very detailed descriptions of personality, the socioeconomic background and the type of life of the stranger they were describing. It might be added parenthetically here that a number of the students later met the people they had described and about half thought they had been quite accurate in their descriptions while the rest changed their opinions. We will discuss accuracy of impressions later, however.

Jacobson (14) had models stand before her classes. The students were asked to write down their impressions of the models and also how well acquainted they were with each. Over 9000 responses made by 116 girls were analyzed. The impressions described the intelligence, the psychological, as well as the physical characteristics, even with models who were unknown to the judges.

Another piece of evidence that we do perceive more than just physical aspects when we see an individual is given by Lehtovaara,[1] who obtained over 1000 first impressions formed by 338 different people. In general the conclusions indicated that first impressions are almost always formed and that they are usually formed rapidly with a high degree of certainty in feeling. In other words, people not only see others as having certain characteristics but they are confident that they are seeing correctly and that their judgment is accurate.

These studies indicate that we do perceive more than the physical characteristics and in each study there is the implication that the impressions are formulated because of the appearance of the subjects. There is no proof, however, that the impressions would have varied if the clothing had been varied.

In the following studies we have more direct evidence of the part that clothing plays in forming impressions.

Hoult (11), Douty (8), and Rosencranz (21) each showed respondents pictures rather than living models. Hoult used photographs of actual people. The heads and bodies were photographically exchanged so that the same head appeared on differently clothed bodies and different heads were judged on each of the clothed bodies. Posture was kept constant in so far as possible.

---

[1] A. Lehtovaara, First impressions. *Studia, Psychol. Paedogog.* Lund. 2, 1948, 123–152.

The judges found no difficulty in checking on a number of characteristics such as intelligence and cooperativeness. Differences in judgment of personal characteristics were found to be related to the clothing. That is, the same head would be perceived differently when shown over differently clothed bodies. We have, therefore, evidence that the clothing was a factor leading to the perception of personal characteristics in the pictured persons. Douty did not exchange the heads and bodies in her photographs, but each of her 4 models was photographed in 4 different costumes and a control costume (smock). The projected photographs were rated by women who were divided into four judging groups. Each group rated each of the persons only once in an experimental costume. Two additional groups of judges rated the same costumes in terms of the women who would probably buy and wear them. Significant differences in the judges' ratings of social status and personal traits were found to be associated with changes in clothing. Thus, clothing was shown to have an influence on the judges' impression of the social status and personality traits of the subjects.

The respondents in Rosencranz' study were asked to tell about drawings of people. We will discuss this study in more detail later, but here it is interesting to note that the respondents were able to give detailed descriptions of the character, status, age, and so on of the people and to describe total situations. Each of the pictures had some incongruity in dress. The respondents noted this and referred to it in their descriptions.

In a number of classes as demonstration of methodology, my students have conducted small research studies. In one such study, 6 girls appeared twice before high school classes. One girl was dressed alike on the two occasions and the other 5 differently on the two occasions. On the second occasion which was approximately three weeks after the first the classes were told that some of them had misunderstood the instructions the first time and that therefore the test needed to be repeated. The classes were not informed that the models had changed their clothing. Both times the high school students rated the models on various personal characteristics. The girl who was dressed alike on the two occasions was judged to have the same personal characteristics both times, while those who were wearing different clothing were judged differently. The similar ratings for the girl who was dressed alike on the two occasions points to the reliability of the ratings. The dissimilar ratings for the girls who were dressed differently indicates that the ratings on personality traits were influenced by the subjects' clothing.

In other class demonstrations pictures have been used with the face covered or removed so that this variable did not effect the results. In every case the results have shown that the judgment of the person on the picture is influenced by the clothing.

The first part of our first question can then be answered in the affirmative.

Clothes do have a definite influence on the impressions or characteristics a person attributes to those he meets. That is, clothing tells the observer something about the wearer.

The second part of the question was "is this true at all times or just under certain conditions?" Hoult's study also gives us some evidence on this point. In his first experiment 13 students stood before 46 judges on two occasions. The models were *known* to the judges. On the first occasion 4 were secretly told to "dress up" for the second test and 4 were told to wear old and sloppy clothing, the remaining 5 were asked to dress exactly as they had before. No real changes occurred in the ratings given the men on the two tests. However, in later experiments, when judges were rating pictures of *strange* men, differences in clothing did lead to differences in ratings. These results would indicate that our perception of personality traits of people is influenced by clothing when we do not know them, but not when we are well acquainted with them. This you may have noticed in your own experience. You may see that a friend looks especially attractive or looks very sloppy on a given day, but you don't change your opinion of her character or of her status because of her appearance on that day. Whether the effect is just on the first impression and drops out immediately or whether clothing has an influence over several meetings has not been investigated.

Research investigating the development of judgments of people over a period of time and the factors which are most important at various stages is needed. This is not to say that the clothes of a family member or friend do not communicate anything to his family or friends. The way a friend is dressed may tell us the mood he is in, whether he is tired, or what he is planning to do next. For example, the graduate students who are also teaching assistants wear quite different types of clothing on the days they teach. If the male graduate student is wearing a white shirt, tie, and jacket or the girl high heels and a suit you do not need to question them, you know immediately that they are teaching on that day. The care with which a friend or member of the family has dressed, the colors, or even the particular garment chosen may indicate to the family or close friends something of the mood of the wearer. Whether the wearer is or is not known to the observer may not influence the fact of communication but it may influence what is communicated. We may note temporary differences in mood or activity, but we do not perceive the friend or family member as fundamentally changed in values, attitudes or personality traits because of his clothing.

The perception of a person varies, then, with the extent to which the viewer is acquainted with the subject. It also varies with the viewer himself and as we will see in the next section with his task at the moment or his situation.

The answer to our first basic question is that we do perceive people differently because of their clothing and grooming, but, this may vary with the viewer, his acquaintance with the subject and the situation in which he is perceiving the individual.

2. What Do Clothes Communicate to the Observer about the Wearer?

We have already suggested some characteristics communicated by clothing or in which clothing is one of the clues used. No one has attempted to compile an exhaustive list, but from research studies as well as from our own experience we can name many characteristics of individuals which may, at one time or another, be conveyed by clothing. Before we start to list the characteristics perceived as a result of clothing, we should understand that almost never would we perceive all of these characteristics on first seeing another person. The particular sorts of characteristics perceived will depend upon the interests and values of the observer, the situation and usually the task of the observer. Not only the sorts of characteristics perceived but also the amount perceived will vary with the observer's task and interests. Walking down the street we may only perceive that we are passing a mother and her child or a group of teenagers, but if we were interviewing a candidate for a job as receptionist we might decide from her appearance that she was neat, attractive, efficient, between twenty-five and thirty, well educated, possessing a sense of humor, and so on. While we might be wrong on many of these counts we would, because we were trying to decide whether or not to hire her, see these characteristics. You may have asked when you wanted service in a restaurant, "Which was our waitress?" When you were ordering, it was sufficient to identify her as the one to take your order, but if you were meeting her at a party you might notice much more.

In the following pages we will be listing, then, the characteristics which can or may be perceived about a person if the observer's task implies the perception of such characteristics or if it is appropriate to the situation.

We will start with some of the most obvious characteristics which are perceived and those which we know are influenced by clothing.

⌣ SEX ⌄

In almost every culture men and women dress differently and this is, of course, the first thing we notice. In our own culture besides obvious differences such as trousers versus skirts, pastel colors in contrast to darker, somber colors, simple tailored versus fancy ruffles, and so on, various authors have compiled lists of textures, lines and details which are associated with masculine and feminine garments. A small study carried out at Cornell, using forty-seven college women and fifty-three college men as subjects, listed the following factors in a shirt or blouse which made it appear masculine: loose fit, emphasis on shoulder width, stiff, coarse material, and one pocket on chest. The feminine image of a blouse or shirt seemed to include: sleeves blousy or full, less than full length sleeve, delicate look, decorations, neck treatment other than shirt collar.

We have only to look at historical costumes to realize that the particular attributes which are perceived as masculine or feminine vary with the period and the culture. Nevertheless, in each period and in each culture there are sex differences in clothing which are or were recognized when and where they were worn.

AGE

Although there seems to be less and less differentiation of age groups by clothing in our present culture, we still do differentiate the approximate age of an individual by the clothing as well as by the face, posture or figure. For example, I can look out of my window over the campus and distinguish the students from professors or from older visitors by the jackets or overcoats the men are wearing. In other cultures, to the observer, clothing indicates more definitely the age of the wearer. For example, in many cultures physical maturity is indicated by a change in clothing. The girls' clothes indicate that they are of marriageable age or the boys' attire indicates whether he is to be considered a man or a boy. In our grandparents' time also this was indicated by a shifting to long trousers or by putting up a girl's hair and lengthening her skirts. In India little girls are dressed in the Western manner, but when they reach maturity they are expected to wear the sari. In each of these cultures the approximate age of the wearer becomes immediately evident to the observer.

OCCUPATION

We have already given examples of identifying the occupation of the wearer by his uniform or type of clothing. We even use clothing terms to describe the type of job, for example we say "white collar worker." In some cases these are not only short-cuts helpful to the general public, as in the case of police uniforms, but also safety devices. In most construction jobs today, workmen who are trained and qualified for certain jobs wear helmets color coded to their job. Thus an electrician is differentiated from a steel worker. Other men on the job can then readily identify the man they need for the immediate task. In some cases the differences are subtle and although difficult to describe, are still recognized and used. For example, a man recently told me about his new secretary. He stated that she was a good worker and efficient. He went on to say that she even "looked like a good secretary" and that he was sure she dressed according to rules given her in secretarial school. He tried to contrast the difference between her dress and that of his own daughter in college, but he found that there was little which could be specified. Nevertheless both he and I were aware of differences.

In some organizations the rank of the worker is immediately obvious to

The influence of clothing on perception of occupation and socioeconomic level. Note that the faces are identical in both drawings, but in each the man in uniform is perceived as a doorman and the man in the topcoat as a well-to-do person.

others from his clothing. The laboring man will wear "work clothes," his foreman may wear a sport shirt, those higher in rank may wear white shirts or a white shirt and tie while those still higher may wear a jacket (see p. 66).

In some institutions or areas professional women may be differentiated from their secretaries by their clothing: the professional woman wears a suit while her secretary wears a skirt and blouse but no jacket and so their respective jobs are immediately recognized.

SOCIOECONOMIC STATUS

Although, as with age, there is at the present time less differentiation of socioeconomic status by clothing than there was in the past, it is still present.

Often in a given locality this is very pronounced. Because of her clothing a woman may be described as "from the country-club set," as a "suburban matron" or from a given section of the town. At one time the mink coat was the most obvious symbol of high socioeconomic status. Although it has lost some of this symbolism it is still looked upon as a mark of high status for many. In college a few years ago a cashmere sweater had much the same connotation.

Douty, as mentioned earlier (see p. 12), has given us research evidence of the perception of social status as affected by clothing. Each of the four stimulus persons in her study had a significantly different rating on this factor in the different costumes.

Veblen's theory of economic consumption was based upon the premise that people choose their clothing primarily to indicate their status to others. He explained dress and fashion as means of demonstrating that the wearer was in the leisure class and had no need to labor. The examples he gave were such items as the tight restricting corsets or the binding of the feet of the former high-class Chinese women. Both of these would prohibit a woman from working and so demonstrate to the world at large that this woman did not need to work. Other examples, such as jewels and furs, while not prohibiting work, demonstrated wealth.

Form and Stone (10) have noted that in the city symbols such as clothing are necessary to place and appraise social status of strangers and passing acquaintances. In the small towns where men know each other and have many contacts this is unnecessary. They interviewed 125 adults from three widely differing socioeconomic levels. All socioeconomic groups tended to use descriptions of clothing and mode of dress more often in appraising the "working class" than the other three social categories—"high society," "middle class" and "down-and-outers." "Images of appearance" were used least often in appraising the "middle class."

Stone has shown that "white collar workers appraised clothing in terms of its potential for favorably impressing the other people with whom they come in contact at work." (p. 4)

It can be stated with assurance, then, that socioeconomic status is often perceived directly from the appearance of the subject and that different judgments of social status are associated with changes in clothing.

MARITAL STATUS OR RELATIONSHIP TO OPPOSITE SEX

In Western cultures at the present time the engagement ring and the wedding ring are the only means by which marital status is indicated to the observer, but in other cultures there are often greater changes in dress. Even within our own culture certain groups have very precise symbols which tell others of the wearers' relationship to a member of the opposite sex. The students in a given high school may indicate to others whether or not they are "going steady" by the buckle on the back of "ivy league pants" being fastened or unfastened, by the girls' wearing the boy's sweaters, or by both having matching shirts, and so on.

MEMBERSHIP IN SPECIAL GROUPS OR ORGANIZATIONS

The jacket worn by the gang, the blazer worn by a specific school or a specific class in college, the athlete's letters on sweaters are all obvious examples of ways in which clothing announces to others the group with which the wearer is affiliated. The list could be expanded almost indefinitely from the Brownie or Cub Scouts to Mason's or Knights of Columbus, or to the such-and-such bowling league. In some cases not only membership in the group but rank in the organization is indicated by clothing items. Some uniforms or costumes are similar for members of an organization throughout the country or the world, while others are specific to a small defined group. Some are regulated by the group or members of the group such as the official pins or jewelry of a fraternity or other organization. Others are just what the "gang" wears such as the head gear of a certain clique at school.

The times at which these uniforms or specific garments are worn also varies. Certain uniforms for specific organizations are worn only for the official meetings of the organization while others may be worn whenever the individual so desires.

ATTITUDES, INTERESTS AND VALUES

We have been discussing, thus far, mostly specific or concrete facts about the individual communicated by clothing but there are also more abstract qualities such as the individual's values, interests and attitudes which may also be conveyed by clothing. The beatnik hopes, at least, that he is perceived as an individual who is above such trivial interests and values as those related to clothing. In a small study done by some of my students one hypothesis was: "The type of clothing a person wears for a given situation influences the way others will perceive his personal concept of himself, the values he places on personal appearance, and his concern over the opinion of others." The technique employed by Hoult was used. Pictures were made of 5 models each dressed in a different way. Photographically each head was placed on each body making 25 pictures. The models were unknown to the judges. Among a list of adjectives and descriptive phrases on the schedule were several relating to attitudes listed in the hypothesis above. The judges were given a schedule to fill out for each picture and were told they could check as many or as few adjectives or phrases as they felt were appropriate. The judges were 52 college women and 40 college men. The costumes were: (1) dungarees and sweat shirt, (2) skirt and white blouse, (3) housedress, (4) business type suit, and (5) black dress with large pin and many bracelets. Each of these was judged 5 times with 5 different heads. Although they were only to check a phrase or adjective if it seemed "appropriate" every phrase or adjective concerned with the attitudes or values of the subject was checked by some of the judges and the percentage of times each was checked varied with the clothing of the model.

Three phrases had to do with what the judge considered was the model's concern over other's opinions. One of these was: model is "concerned with other's opinions of her socioeconomic status." Only 8 percent of the models when wearing a house dress were checked on this item while 50 percent of those wearing the black dress were considered to be "concerned with other's opinions of her socioeconomic status." (See Table 1.)

Concern of S. as perceived by judges	Costume				
	Dungarees	Skirt and blouse	House dress	Suit	Black dress
	PERCENTAGE DISTRIBUTION				
Concern with SE	15	17	8	31	50
Concern with taste	22	21	15	37	38
Disregards opinion of others	26	11	61	7	5

table 1 Concern over others' opinions as shown by type of costume worn.

The judges' impression of the value which the models placed on clothing also varied with the type of garment the models appeared to be wearing (see Table 2).

These few examples are merely an indication that some values and attitudes may be expressed by clothing. No research has indicated other attitudes but many hypotheses on this subject might be formulated and investigated.

Perceived value placed on clothing by subject	Costume				
	Dungarees	Skirt and blouse	House dress	Suit	Black dress
	PERCENTAGE DISTRIBUTION				
Clothing *not* important	22	13	50	3	5
Clothing is asset	17	27	5	57	62

table 2 Judges' impressions of value of clothing to models.

MOOD

The perception of an individual's mood is often conveyed by the clothing he wears or his grooming. Although we make this as a categorical statement, we have only empirical evidence to support it. Frequently one hears someone say "don't you look gay and carefree in your light green." Remarks of this sort are common. Many times it is not the color of the costume, but the grooming or care with which the individual has dressed that gives the clue as to his mood. The individual who is "all spruced up" or "dressed up" is perceived as ready for a good time.

The individual who has been careless about his appearance we often believe is in a low mood, not caring what others think of him. Psychologists and psychiatrists report that they use grooming and apparent interest in appearance as a clue in the diagnosing of a psychiatric patient. When the patient tries to improve his grooming, the doctor considers the patient recuperating. When the patient is completely disinterested in his appearance then the doctor fears the patient is having a bad day.

Perhaps the most interesting use of color and type of garment to impart mood is found in costuming for the stage. Whether or not they always succeed, costumes are designed to set the mood of the scene, or of the play or opera as a whole.

PERSONALITY

When we speak of what clothes express or communicate or the impression of a person as influenced or determined by clothes personality traits are usually implied or mentioned. Many schemes have been developed for interpreting the personality of others from their appearance. Some of these have had wide popular acceptance and are even used by some companies in the selection of personnel. Although not based upon controlled research these schemes and articles are accepted and there is a common belief that appearance does indicate something about the personality of the wearer. Later we will examine the accuracy of perception of personality characteristics as judged by appearance and also whether or not there is agreement among observers. At this point we wish only to establish whether or not people do perceive others as differing in personality characteristics and if this is a function of the subjects' clothing and grooming. There is ample evidence that we do see people varying in personality traits and this is, partially at least, dependent upon the clothing of the person being judged.

A large body of research literature on this topic is available, most of which deals with the accuracy of such impressions. In all of the studies, the observers did form impressions of the personality characteristics of persons with the appearance of the subjects the only stimulus. Furthermore the observers usually gave their judgments with a high degree of certainty.

We will not attempt to review all of the research on the judgment of personality characteristics from appearance but confine ourselves to a few examples. We will take our examples from research initiated by researchers in the area of clothing since they have used clothing as a variable. In most of the work done by psychologists, they have used either the total appearance of the subject or have confined themselves just to faces.

Douty, in the study cited earlier (see p. 12), used a series of ratings of personal traits as well as ratings on social status. The exact trait names which she used are not listed, but the items were based upon the Yang-Yin classifications of Northrup. Thus, the scales had such adjectives as dynamic, assertive, self-assured or dignified at one end and gentle, receptive, delicate, submissive and warm at the opposite end. Differences in personal-trait scores were found to be significant for three of the four stimulus persons.

In the study also described earlier in this chapter in which photographically the heads of 5 girls were each imposed on 5 costumes, adjectives describing personality traits were included in the checklist. Certain adjectives were checked more frequently when the heads were attached to one costume as opposed to other costumes. For example, the pictures were checked as being more aggressive and vivacious when the costume pictured was either dungarees or the black dress. The models were judged irresponsible more often when pictured in the house dress than when pictured in any of the other costumes. The differences in general were greater between faces than between costumes for the personality traits. This is in contrast to the perception of socioeconomic status, education, occupation, and intelligence. All of these changed much more with the costume than with the face. In other words, these results show that clothing definitely is a factor in the perception of personality traits, although it may not be as important a factor as the individual's features or facial expression. It is highly probable that the importance of clothing in the perception of another person varies with the personality characteristics being judged. For example, we might depend on clothing as one of the most important clues in judging the efficiency or the aggressiveness of another person, but depend more upon the face or facial expression in evaluating the friendliness or shyness of that person.

It may be that for some personality traits clothing is never one of the clues used. In fact we do not even know whether all personality traits are or can be perceived immediately. Obviously this is another area in which more research is needed. All that we can say at the present time is that there is evidence to show that we do perceive personality traits of persons and that these perceptions sometimes vary with the clothing of the person.

STEREOTYPES —

Stereotypes are generally considered by psychologists as a classificatory concept. Thus all people of one race, nation, occupation, or other group are

Some present-day stereotypes of men. Each detached head seems appropriate for one of the headless figures drawn above or on the facing page

classified together as having similar characteristics and similar appearances. The more we know about individuals from these groups the more the stereotype breaks down. Social psychologists are interested in stereotypes in relation to prejudice and the factors which tend to either formulate or break down both the prejudice and the stereotype. This is not a part of our problem, we wish to simply point out here that stereotypes are nearly, if not always, pictured visually. The clothing, and grooming as well as the body build and coloring are a part of the stereotype. For example, the stereotype of a college professor is usually a pale, thin man with stooped shoulders, wearing glasses and dressed in shabby tweeds. This is as much a part of the stereotype as is the professor's scholarly characteristics or his absent mindedness. Similarly we tend to have a short-cut way of picturing many groups with which we are not familiar. For example, look at these facing drawings. You will probably have no difficulty in matching the heads with the bodies and as you do so you will doubtless identify the person depicted as one of a special group or "type." Along with the identification you can doubtless describe various characteristics of the person depicted—the socioeconomic level, age, occupation, personality characteristics, and perhaps even attitudes or values. Clothing and grooming are the principal variables in the pictures.

SUMMARY

We have found that in perceiving another person we form an impression which may include his age, socioeconomic status, group with which he is identified, occupation, and even his personality traits, values and feelings. Furthermore,

Note that as the appropriate head from the facing page is matched to the corresponding costume a term such as "business man" or "beatnik" seems accurate.

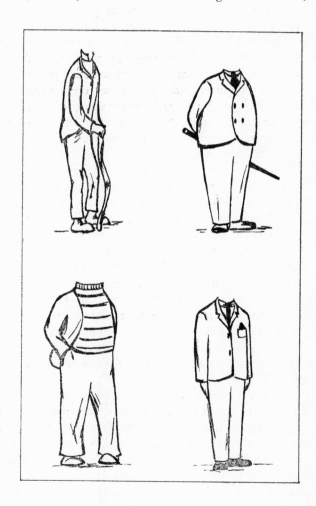

clothing and grooming may play an important part in the perception of all of these characteristics.

3. Is There Agreement among Observers on Impressions of People?

This question is perhaps the one with the greatest practical import. We wish to know if all people or certain segments of the population, assuming that the task is the same, will perceive a given subject in the same way. If a group of individuals selected from a particular segment of the population are asked to give their impression of the friendliness of a subject will they agree or disagree? If the judges are selected randomly from the total population will they agree or disagree? We are still not concerned with the accuracy of the impressions but simply whether judges agree. Supposing that a person gives the impression of being a prosperous and upright citizen and yet he is actually a pickpocket. If we find upon investigation that almost everyone who sees him agrees that he looks like a prosperous and upright citizen then we will wish to investigate further to see what makes him look this way. If, on the other hand, the impressions are not consistent then the task of looking for reasons would be completely impractical.

Common sense tells us that some impressions are the same for nearly everyone in a broad cultural group while others are consistent only for small subgroups. For example, almost all of the students in a given school might see a student as one who is "going steady" but those in another town or even adults in the same town might not see this. Almost anyone in our Western culture, or perhaps in the world, would identify a man as belonging to the armed services because of his uniform, but the details of ribbons and decorations would reveal much more to the person who had contact with the army or navy than they would to someone who has had no such contact.

Whether or not there is agreement among judges is a real problem only when we are concerned with the more abstract characteristics. For occupation, age, nationality, or belonging to specific groups, we can usually predict quite accurately that there will be agreement and how far the agreement will extend.

For the more abstract characteristics such as personality traits, and the interests or values of the subject, we are not able to make such predictions without research evidence. Unfortunately the research evidence on this point is relatively meager. Rosencranz (21) has shown that the total "clothing awareness" of the individual varies with the socioeconomic status of the observer. Those from a higher socioeconomic status had a higher clothing awareness score than did those from a lower status. Other variables related to socioeconomic level such as higher education, membership in more organizations, higher verbal intelligence and husband in a white-collar position were also associated with high clothing awareness. There were 82 women in her sample stratified according to the husband's occupation. The clothing-awareness score was measured by scoring responses to a series of seven pictures each of which showed some incongruity in dress. To obtain the clothing-awareness score the following were added:

1. Number of typewritten lines of clothing comments.
2. Number of characters for which clothing was mentioned.
3. Number of cards about which respondent said the clothing gave the idea for the story.
4. Number of clothing incongruities mentioned.
5. Number of themes expressed in relation to clothing.

She found no relationship between the age of the respondent and clothing awareness nor between clothing awareness and whether the respondent was from a rural or urban environment.

The results of this study imply that those of high socio-economic status use clothing as a clue in the perception of people more than do those of low socioeconomic status. There is, however, the possibility that given different pictures the results might have differed. The pictures were designed, we assume, by a person of high socioeconomic status. It may be that different clothing incongruities would be more evident and therefore elicit higher scores for those from low socioeconomic groups had the picture been designed by a member of this group. If this were true we would still have evidence that there is a difference between socioeconomic groups, the difference would be one of kind rather than of the amount of total awareness. Form and Stone (10) also found differences among socioeconomic groups—in one study in the degree of clothing awareness and in another study, in the extent to which clothing is considered useful in determining social status in others.

Neither of these studies deals directly with the problem before us. Is there agreement among observers in the *way* in which they perceive another person and does this vary with the clothing worn? In the study by Rosencranz, for example, in order to answer this question, we would need to know if there were consistent differences or similarities in the way in which the character in a given picture was perceived. For example, in viewing the illustration on page 26 I perceive the total situation as a group of college students before a college building. The girl in black, I see as an outsider probably one who has not been to college and does not know what is generally worn on a college campus. I imagine most respondents who had been or were well acquainted with college students would see it in the same way. Would those from a low socioeconomic group who were unacquainted with college perceive this picture in the same way?

In class demonstrations college girls have been shown pictures of people

FROM MARY L. ROSENCRANZ, CLOTHING SYMBOLISM. *Journal of Home Economics.* 54 (1), 1962, P. 18.

Do you think the girl in black belongs to the rest of the group?

from which the face has been eliminated. The pictures have been taken from the same magazine and posture controlled as far as possible. Results have shown that there is remarkable agreement on the perception of personality traits in such tests. These classroom trials have shown that within the particular group of students in a given college we do find agreement. However, this group is a fairly homogeneous group and we cannot predict from these results what would be found in a random sample.

In the pilot study described earlier (see p. 12) in which 5 subjects were rated on personality traits by high school classes at two different times there was a high degree of agreement among the judges on both occasions. Again the group of judges was fairly homogeneous. Within the particular group agreement was found but predictions cannot be made from this group to other groups.

Only one study seems to have tackled the problem of whether or not there is agreement in the perception of people as dependent upon clothing across cultures. Sherlock (23) compared Indian with American men in their perception of personality characteristics and mood, when the stimulus was a picture of an Indian woman dressed in different saris and in the same saris draped in various ways. Pictures of the Indian woman were taken against the same background and, insofar as possible, standing in the same position but in different saris. The saris also differed in color, in the manner of draping, and some were printed while others were plain. The face was hidden by a frame so that the model's facial features or expression would be eliminated as a variable. The judges were asked to rate the subject on a variety of adjective scales. These scales were made up of opposing adjectives with spaces between to indicate how closely the costume seemed to be related to the adjectives at either end of the scale as:

weak - - - - - - - - - - - - - strong

In general there were surprisingly few differences between the reactions of the American and the Indian judges. The Americans more often checked the neutral column and the Indian men tended to use the extreme ends of the scales but differences were not great. The mean responses of the two groups were in the same direction away from the neutral point over 92 percent of the time. The discrepancies in the few cases where they did occur were that the Indians tended to judge some of the pictures as active, excitable, and independent while the Americans were more apt to check passive, calm, and dependent. It may be that the American stereotype of the Indian woman would tend to make them perceive all Indian women as more passive, calm, and dependent. The Indians and Americans judged all of the 14 saris on the same side of the ugly–beautiful, expensive–inexpensive, quiet–loud, secure–insecure, and bad–good scales. In this study the agreements between the Americans and Indians were so "great that the conclusion can be made that judgments of personality, mood, and socioeconomic status of a person from his clothing are crosscultural," (p. 84) at least between a group of Indian and American male students in one university. Even here the results must be interpreted cautiously: the American men in this study were from a university where they often see Indian women in saris and the Indian men were studying in an American university. Other groups of American and Indian men might give different results.

Many of the studies on first impressions doubtless obtained data which could answer our questions concerning the agreement of observers. Since this has not been the objective of the studies the data has not been reported in a way which is helpful on this point. The question nevertheless is of great practical value both within and across cultures. Those working in or studying cultures other than their own need to recognize and understand the subtle differences which are taken for granted by those within the given culture. He also needs to know what impression he may be making on others by his own clothing. If all people react in the same way then the problem dissolves, but, where the reactions differ, they should be determined so that those planning to work in or study different cultural groups could be trained to perceive differences in others and to dress themselves so as not to offend others. The mistakes made by some of the early missionaries who went out from the United States illustrate this need.

The determination of consistency between observers in judging others by clothing is of practical value within as well as between cultural groups. The advertiser could predict with certainty the impressions the models in his advertisements would have on readers or on television viewers. Politicians, actors, and salesmen among others are dependent on the impressions they make on others.

This entire question could be approached from a different angle. We could ask the question: What is the influence of the viewer on the perception of others or how do individuals differ in their perception of a person, and does this differ with the clothing of the subject being viewed? The results should be the same whether we ask the question in this form or ask whether there is agreement among groups. However, when we ask about the influence of the viewer, we might be more likely to inquire into the personality, the values and attitudes, including prejudices, of the individual observer to see the effect of these on his perception of people. We know from other studies in perception that the values and interests of the viewer have an influence on what he perceives. It seems reasonable, therefore, to hypothesize that these would influence how he perceives people due to their clothing. Unfortunately we have no research evidence on this point at the present time.

4. How Accurate Are Our Impressions of People?

The accuracy of impressions is obviously going to vary with the characteristic being judged. We can assume a high correlation between judges' impressions of certain subjects' occupations and the actual occupations of those subjects. A policeman or a nurse will be correctly identified by practically any group, at least within the United States. Likewise the wearer of a group's uniform will be correctly identified as belonging to that group.

For other characteristics, the correlations would presumably be less high and depend upon the similarity between the judges and the subjects, or the extent to which the judge is familiar with the characteristic being judged. We might all recognize, by the uniform, a man as a member of the armed services, but differences between ranks might be apparent only to those who had been in the services or had friends or relatives in the service. An individual from a low socioeconomic level could, we assume, quite accurately judge whether given individuals were of a somewhat higher or lower socioeconomic level than he while at the same time he might group together or confuse all those who were of medium or high socioeconomic level. The opposite would be true of an individual from a high socioeconomic level. He might be able to distinguish socioeconomic groupings within the higher socioeconomic levels but not in the lower. Likewise in judging age, a thirteen-year-old boy might be able to distinguish accurately a twelve-year old from a fourteen-year old by his clothing but would not be able to tell a thirty-year-old man from one fifty years old.

When we come to the question of the accuracy of our perception of the intelligence and personality characteristics we have a great deal of research most of which has shown that the accuracy of such judgments are not much better than chance.

In the 1920s and 1930s there were many studies dealing with the accuracy of impressions of intelligence and personality characteristics when the appearance of the person being judged was the only information available to the judges. The general plan of such research was to present to judges either pictures or models and ask them to rate the subjects on one or more traits. The impressions were then compared with some independent criterion which was assumed to be valid. In some cases the criterion would be a test score, such as a measure of the subject's IQ when intelligence was being judged. In other cases the criteria might be the rating of those who were acquainted with the subjects. For example, pictures of a group of students might be judged on a number of characteristics first by their classmates and then by students in another school who were not acquainted with the subjects. The ratings by the classmates would in this instance be considered the criteria or the "true" measures of the characteristics of the subjects and the impressions of the strangers would be compared with these criteria as a measure of the accuracy of the second group's impressions.

In general the correlations of the judges' impressions and the independent criteria were extremely low. That is, there was little or no relationship between the judges' ratings of those acquainted with and those not acquainted with the subjects. Some studies have found the relationships no better than chance while others have found a slight correlation between the two.

These results showing little or only chance accuracy have been found time and again and have been reviewed in many beginning textbooks in psychology. In spite of this we perceive people as having certain personality traits with such a degree of certainty that we tend to disbelieve the research findings. Even personnel workers and others who are acquainted with the literature on the subject find themselves making judgments of intelligence or personality on appearance.

In attempting to find why we are not more accurate in forming impressions of intelligence and personality, research has shown some of the systematic errors involved and some of the characteristics of judges which increase or decrease accuracy. The judges who are similar to the subjects in respect to the characteristics being judged tend to be more accurate than those who differ from the subject in this respect. Several systematic errors have been identified which effect accuracy. One of these is the *halo* effect. This is the name given to the tendency for the rater to rate all traits as *good* when his general impression of the person is good and to rate the person as *bad* on all traits when his general impression is poor. Researchers have also found that there is a tendency to rate all individuals high on favorable traits. Perhaps we all have the golden rule so firmly imbedded in our way of reacting to others that we apply it in such instances. Another systematic error is the tendency to be logical within our own theoretical framework. Thus, if we believe that studiousness and seriousness are related then if we perceive a person as serious, we also perceive him as studious.

Clothing has not been one of the variables in any of these studies on the accuracy of the perception of personality traits. This is surprising since theoretically we might predict it to be one of the most important variables. We choose our own clothing and grooming and therefore we would expect this to reflect more accurately our personality traits than our physical features over which we have little control. It would be interesting to compare the accuracy of judgments of personality traits when the subjects were dressed in their own clothing and when dressed in some control garment. Our hypothesis would be that the accuracy would increase somewhat for certain traits but not for others. Since none of the studies has varied the clothing of the subjects we do not know whether this factor adds or detracts from the accuracy.

We do know that on occasion clothing is deliberately used to detract from the accuracy. In an article concerning burglars and burglaries Black points out that

The good burglar has the appearance to get into any of the best buildings in town, and he has the wherewithal to dress well. . . . If a good burglar is pointed out to the average citizen, the citizen's first reaction is bound to be, "But he doesn't *look* like a burglar," which is precisely the point. . . . On countless occasions, clerks in the best hotels have allowed burglars who didn't look like burglars to go straight upstairs.[2]

Another example of deliberately dressing to give the wrong impression is recounted in a book on counterespionage.

Impressions are fatal. You may take it for granted that the really clever spy will make an excellent impression. One of the world's most famous criminologists once stated that the person who had made the best impression on him had been a woman who had poisoned her children for the insurance money, and the one who had made the worst impression on him had been a famous philanthropist and reformer.[3]

We have seen that the accuracy of our impressions of people varies with the characteristic being judged. Under ordinary circumstances we may be relatively accurate in our perception of some occupations, probably make a better than chance estimate on socioeconomic level, but form little better than a chance opinion on personality characteristics and intelligence. Although we do know that clothing is one of the clues used in perceiving characteristics of unfamiliar people, we do not have any factual information on whether it adds or detracts from accuracy of judgment.

In spite of the fact that accuracy of perception of personality characteristics is very low, we should keep in mind that we nevertheless do perceive personality characteristics when we have only the appearance of subjects presented to us. Therefore the important problems for those interested in the effect of clothes on others is first to determine the extent of agreement among judges and secondly, where there is agreement, to determine the attributes of clothing and grooming which lead to various impressions.

5. What Qualities or Attributes of Clothes Determine Our Impressions of People?

For most of us this is by far the most fascinating question relating to first impressions. We would like a simple, definite set of rules which would

---

[2] Susan Black, "A Reporter at Large: Burglary I," *The New Yorker,* December 7, 1963, p. 112.

[3] Oreste Pinto, *Spy-catcher,* New York: Harper & Row, Publishers, 1952, p. 40.

tell us what colors, textures, and lines to wear to give a desired impression. Naturally, we think we have pleasant and attractive personality traits and we want others to notice them in us. It would be very reassuring to know definitely that if we wear certain colors and lines all who see us would know that we have these desirable traits.

Many authors in popular magazines and in textbooks have attempted to answer this felt need. They have described "personality types" relating these first to the physical coloring and build of the person and then listing colors, lines and textures appropriate for each type. We may find descriptions of the coquette, the dramatic type, the garçon, or the ingénue with appropriate clothes given for each. Some list as many as ten types while others divide everyone into just two. Some conceptualize types as either having or not having certain personality traits. Others recognize a continuum between opposing traits, that is, a person may be toward the aggressive end of the scale or the docile end. In almost every case the personal coloring and the body build are also given for each type. For example, the person described as very feminine, gentle, kind, and a clinging vine is assumed to be petite and blonde and she is told to wear pastel colors, dainty fabrics, ruffles, lace, and so on, while the masculine, forceful, dramatic person is described as large and brunette and one who should wear dark, bright colors, striking lines and rough textures. We will discuss in a later chapter the research dealing with the relationship between personality factors and body coloring and build. The question for us to attempt to answer here is: Are these rules valid insofar as attributes of garments give desired impressions? We further wish to ask how we determine whether or not they are valid.

It would seem on first thought to be relatively simple to design experiments in this area. We know it would be necessary to control all the variables except the one which we wished to study. Therefore, if we wished to determine the influence of the *color* of the costume on our perception of people we would have two identical models or pictures of one model. The background, posture of the model(s), expression, grooming, the style of the dress and the amount and kind of decoration all would need to be the same, and only the color of the garment varied. We would then have judges rate the individual (or pictures) dressed in the various colored dresses. Supposing we do all of this, managing to control all of the variables, and find that the model is rated as being more feminine when she is wearing pink than in other colors. This is probably what we predicted we would find. We could then say with relative assurance that all other things being equal that a woman will look more feminine in pink than she will in purple or brown or some other color.

There have been a number of research studies which have found positive

correlations between colors and mood-tones. Wexner (26) presented a class
of 94 college students with a series of eleven moods (exciting–stimulating;
secure–comfortable; distressed–disturbed–upset; tender–soothing; protective-
defending; despondent–dejected–unhappy–melancholy; calm–peaceful–serene;
dignified–stately; cheerful–jovial–joyful; defiant–contrary–hostile; and powerful–strong–masterful). The subjects were also presented with 8 stimulus
colors (red, orange, yellow, green, blue, purple, brown, and black). It
was found "that for each mood-tone certain colors were chosen to 'go
with' that mood-tone significantly more often than the remaining colors."
Red was chosen most frequently for exciting, protective and defiant moods;
blue for secure, tender and calm; black for despondent and powerful; orange
for disturbed; purple for dignified; and yellow for cheerful.

Murray and Deabler (18) repeated this experiment using groups which
varied in socioeconomic status, and also of neuropsychiatric patients. In
general the results agreed and the data again suggest that people do associate
colors and mood-tones. There were, however, significant differences between
the groups of subjects in their over-all responses which suggests that the
associations are, at least in part, learned, and that the groups involved in
such experiments should be considered. The "socioeconomic differences appeared to be more important in causing differential choice of colors to go
with mood-tones than were either mental health differences or differences
in geographical regions within this country" (p. 283).

It must be kept in mind that these experiments were concerned with
color per se and that we cannot generalize from colored paper to the colors
worn by a given individual. Furthermore, these colors were presented in
only one shade and one saturation and generalizations cannot be made
to other shades and saturations of a given hue. Just how practical or valuable is such information for one interested in clothing? We know that a
girl wearing pink and orange striped stretch pants would be perceived
quite differently from a girl wearing a full pink organdy skirt. Although
our research results might be reliable and valid we would still not have
solved the problem. We would need to study not just each color but each
value and chroma of each color, all combinations of these (including varying the amount of each color in the combination), and each of these with
types of garment, decoration, lines, and so on. This obviously is an impossible task. They are not attributes with known effects which can simply
be added together. A change in one variable may change the effect of all.

Even if we were able to do this in a reasonable length of time they
would become useless with changes in fashion. We certainly perceive the
person who is dressed fashionably as different from the person who is equally
well dressed but in clothes which were fashionable ten years ago. Even
the way in which we see color combinations varies over time. Some years

ago if anyone were seen wearing a combination of blue and green, or black and brown, or red and pink they would immediately have been classed as uncouth and having poor taste. Now we consider such combinations as sophisticated and not unusual.

Thus colors, color combinations, lines, textures and types of garments are all variables which affect each other and the effect of any or of any combination may change with time. Therefore any definite set of rules we can be sure is not the result of valid research, but is rather the opinion of the particular author.

This is disappointing for as we have said we would all like sets of rules which we knew to be reliable. While we do not have the rules we would like, we still do not have to depend upon random choice. We have seen in earlier sections that the perception of persons is influenced by the clothing of the model and there is evidence that, at least within homogeneous groups, there is agreement among judges. Our answer lies here. The people we are likely to meet and wish to impress are usually within relatively the same group as we; therefore, the chances are they will see a garment in much the same way that we do. If we are in doubt about our own judgment of a given garment, then friends or relatives can probably give us a better idea of how others will see us than could any given list of do's and don'ts. Also there are certain general findings which can be obtained from research and which can serve as general guide lines. Instead of using specific hues if we divide colors into broad general classes and compare the red end of the spectrum with the blue end, dark colors with light shades or saturated with grayed colors we generally find agreement among groups. The colors toward the red end of the spectrum tend to be exciting and the blues and greens quieting. Light colors tend to be more cheerful than dark colors and saturated colors more exciting and cheerful than grayed colors. These results again are primarily with colored paper rather than garments on a person and so are subject to the same objections given earlier.

There is the possibility that although other aspects of dress may change in fashion, the line direction may not be subject to fashion changes and this line may be expressive of certain personality traits to the majority of people. In almost any fashion the trim or the structural lines of the dress may be vertical, horizontal, diagonal or curved. Some authors in discussing how lines may express various personality traits have based their discussion upon the results of psychological experiments by Lundholm (16) and Poffenberger (19). In the first of these experiments the subjects were given a list of adjectives which are used to describe personality and were asked to draw lines which represented them. In the second experiment a group of 500 subjects were given the same list of adjectives and were also given the lines which the first group had drawn, and they were asked to match the adjectives to the lines. The results in both of these studies were similar and there was agreement which showed that there is feeling tone connected with pure lines which is perceived by the majority. These were simply lines drawn on paper and were therefore a great deal shorter than the lines in a dress would be. The assumption has been that the same feelings would hold true for lines in a dress, but this assumption has not been proven. The results from the studies on paper would make this, however, a logical hypothesis for future study. As a preliminary experiment in this field a study was planned at Cornell in which pictures rather than dresses themselves were to be used. An artist was hired to make pictures of models in particular dresses. The models were to be traced so that they would be identical as to facial features, size and posture. The color of all the dresses was to be the same. Four types of dresses—full and fussy, full and simple, slim and fussy, slim and simple—were to be made with each of the various types of lines—vertical, horizontal, diagonal and curved. The plan was to have subjects rate these pictures or to rank them in relation to the various adjectives given in the experiments quoted above. The experiment was never carried out because the artist had made minute changes in the model and in the coloring of both the dresses and the model so that any changes might have been due to line direction or to the changes in color and drawing, and, consequently, the results would have been inconclusive. The attempt to do a controlled study in this area has not been repeated. Perhaps a better way to attack this problem would be to use historical costumes, thus minimizing the effect of fashion. In any such experiment, it should be kept in mind that what is seen in a picture may not be seen on a full-sized, three-dimensional figure. Even more important, the characteristic posture and patterns of movement of the individual may be a very important variable. Until we have more definite information available, we hypothesize that there is a difference in feeling tone due to line direction, but this is still just a hypothesis and not proven.

We have discussed primarily the perception of personality traits in attempting to answer the question concerning the attributes of garments which serve as clues in our perception of people. In the perception of other characteristics the results are not as negative. In many instances the attributes of garments which prompt us to see the wearer in a given way are obvious. The attributes of garments which indicate the extremes of the socioeconomic scale—for example, rags versus furs, rich fabrics, and jewelry—are recognized by all. Likewise, the uniforms worn by certain occupational or membership groups are evident and need no experimentation or even enumeration.

Form and Stone (10) have given us a list of clues which white collar and manual workers use to identify the occupational affiliation of others. (See Table 3.)

Symbols, clues, and expressive items	White Collar Workers	Manual Workers	Totals
Type of garment			
Uniforms	50	24	35
Overalls, coveralls, aprons, work clothes	23	24	24
Suits, sport clothes, and tuxedoes	23	7	14
Fabric clues			
Marks on clothing—grease, paint, dust	27	21	24
Dirty or clean clothes	18	31	25
Good quality, expensive, or tailored clothes	18	21	20
Expressive clues			
Well dressed or dressed up ...	18	21	20
Neatly dressed or presentable .	9	14	12
Conservative vs. flashy and loud clothes	23	3	12
Other clues			
Shoes, adaptations to clothes (special pockets), trademarks, and other labels	27	3	14
Hands, dirty or clean	9	3	6
Tools of the trade: rulers, briefcase, etc.	9	—	4
Totals*	254	172	210
Number of respondents	22	29	51

* Some respondents identified more than one type of garment, symbol, or expressive item.

table 3 Percentage distribution of clothing symbols, clues, and expressive items used by Vansburg men to identify the occupational affiliations of others. From William H. Form and Gregory P. Stone, The Social Significance of Clothing in Occupational Life. *Technical Bulletin* 247, June 1955.

6. How Do These Impressions Develop?

In answer to this last question we have almost no concrete experimental evidence. We assume that the way in which we perceive people is learned and depends, then, upon our past experience. For example, if someone had seen only women teachers who wore suits and had seen few suits on others, then that individual would come to associate suits with teachers and would tend to classify everyone who wore a suit as a teacher. Further, if this same individual had met only teachers who were domineering, then he would further associate suits with a domineering personality and would perceive anyone who was wearing a suit as domineering. If it was not just this one individual but all the members of a town who had had experiences with domineering teachers who wore suits, then we would expect all the members of that town to perceive women in suits in the same way. This example is obviously very much simplified and exaggerated (as well as being untruthful, we hope). We never find that all the people in the same profession dress alike unless they wear a uniform, and we do not find everyone who wears a particular kind of garment or particular color as having certain personality traits or belonging to a certain group. Nevertheless, there are still some aspects of dress which we observe often enough in given individuals that cause us to form certain associations. For example, at the present time in the United States and many of the countries most closely associated with the United States men usually wear strictly tailored clothes with severely tailored lines and of neutral and dark colors. For the majority of people in this culture, straight severe lines then suggest masculinity while pastel colors and frills, because they have been seen on babies and women but rarely on men, suggest femininity. The study by Murray and Deabler described in the last section (see p. 33) supports the theory that such perceptions are learned because their groups responded differently to associations between colors and mood-tones. However, we have no experimental evidence which confirms this theory in relation to clothing as a clue in the perception of people.

Summary

We know that first impressions play a very important part in later social interaction between individuals. Our problem in this chapter has been to determine the part that clothing plays in the formation of first impressions. We have found that clothes do play a part, often an important part in the way in which we perceive an individual. Clothes may give us clues as to the sex, age, occupation, socioeconomic status, organization(s) to which the individual belongs, marital status, intelligence, values, attitudes, and personality of the subject. For some characteristics our perceptions have a high degree of accuracy but for others, such as personality characteristics, that accuracy may not be much more valid than chance opinion. The perception of certain characteristics determined by certain attributes of garments may be the same for all observers; others are similar for specific groups, while others are individually determined. Although we can list some specific attributes of clothes which give us clues for some characteristics, there are other perceived characteristics for which we do not know the garment attributes.

The entire field of perception of people as influenced by clothing and grooming is one in which more research is needed.

Bibliography

1. Asch, S. E. Forming impressions of personality. *J. of Abn. and Soc. Psychol.* 41, 1946, 258–290.
2. Bruner, Jerome S. and Tagiuri, Renato. The Perception of People. Chapter 17, 634–654 in Vol. II, *Handbook of Social Psychology* (Ed. Lindzey, G.). Reading, Mass.: Addison-Wesley Publishing Co., Inc., 1954.
3. Brunswik, Egon. *Systematic and Representative Design of Psychological Experiments.* University of California Press, 1947, pp.31–32.
4. Burtt, H. E. *Principles of Employment Psychology.* New York: Harper & Row, Publishers, 1942, 568p.
5. Byers, Margaretta and Kamholz, Consuelo. *Designing Women.* New York: Simon and Schuster, Inc., 1938, 276p.
6. Child, I. L. and Doob, L. W. Factors determining national stereotypes. *J. Soc. Psychol.* 1943, 17, 203–219.
7. Child, I. The judging of occupations, from printed photographs. *J. of Soc. Psychol.* 7, 1936, 117–118.
8. Douty, Helen I. Influence of clothing on perception of persons. *J. of Home Ec.* 55(3), 1963, 197–202.
9. Fleck, Henrietta. Focus on perception. *Pract. Forecast for Home Ec.* 9(7), 1964, 19, 48–49.
10. Form, W. R. and Stone, G. Urbanism, anonymity, and status symbolism. *Am. J. of Soc.,* 1957, 62, 504–514. For additional clarification see Stone, G. Appearance and the Self, Chap. 5 p. 86–118 in *Human Behavior and Social Processes.* (Rose, A. M. Ed.) Boston: Houghton Mifflin Company, 1962.
11. Hoult, T. F. Experimental measurement of clothing as a factor in some social ratings of selected American men. *Amer. Soc. Rev.* 19, 1954, 324–328.
12. Kelley, H. H. The warm-cold variable in first impressions of persons. *J. of Personality.* 18, 1950, 431–439.
13. Kittles, Emma Louise Holmes. The Importance of Clothing as a Status Symbol Among College Students. Ph.D. Thesis, Ohio State Univer., 1961.
14. Jacobson, Wilhelmina E. First impressions of classmates. *J. of Appl. Psychol.* 1945, 29, 142–155.
15. Langer, L. *The Importance of Wearing Clothes.* New York: Hastings House Publishers, 1959, 334p.
16. Lundholm, Helge. The affective tone of lines: experimental researches. *Psychol. Rev.* 28, 1921, 43–60.

17. Morton, Grace. *The Arts of Costume and Personal Appearance.* New York: John Wiley & Sons, Inc., 1943, 391p.
18. Murray, D. C. and Deabler, H. L. Colors and mood-tones. *J. Appl. Psychol.* 41, 1957, 279–283.
19. Poffenberger, A. T. and Barrows, B. E. Feeling value of lines. *J. Appl. Psychol.* 8, 1924, 187–205.
20. Rice, S. A. 'Stereotypes': a source of error in judging human character. *J. of Personnel Res.* 5, 1926, 268–276.
21. Rosencranz, Mary Lou. Clothing symbolism. *J. of Home Ec.* 54(1), 1962, 18–22.
22. Secord, P. F., Bevan, W. Jr. and Dukes, W. F. Occupational and physiogonomic stereotypes in the perception of photographs. *J. of Soc. Psychol.* 37, 1953, 261–270.
23. Sherlock, Ruth Lillian. A Cross-cultural Study of the Communicative Aspect of Clothing. M. S. Thesis, Cornell Univer., 1961.
24. Stritch, T. M. and Secord, P. F. Interaction effects in the perception of faces. *J. of Personality.* 24, 1956, 272–284.
25. Veblen, T. *The Theory of the Leisure Class.* New York: The Macmillan Company, 1912.
26. Wexner, Lois B. The degree to which colors (hues) are associated with mood-tones. *J. of Appl. Psychol.* 38, 1954, 432–435.
27. Wishner, J. Reanalysis of "impressions of personality." *Psychol. Rev.* 67, 1960, 96–111.

Chapter 2

Motivation
in
Clothing Choices

*T*he previous chapter discussed the influences of clothing on our perception of people. Let us turn now to the other side and discuss the wearer. Why do we dress? Why do we want new clothes? Why do some of us wear saris, some frilly dresses, and others slacks? Are we consistent in our choices? How does the society in which we live, our position in that society, our interests, attitudes, and values affect what we wear? These questions are all related to the broad topic of motivation.

By motivation or the *whys* of clothing we are referring to the general reasons in back of our clothing selection. We are not concerned at this point with the question of why we choose a specific yellow dress with a pleated skirt instead of a blue one with a straight skirt. We will discuss these more specific questions when we come to the section on consumer motivation and behavior. Unfortunately the term *motivation* has been used to cover questions related to why we choose a particular garment or why we choose a particular type of garment, as well as the more general questions concerned with the reasons for dressing as we do. While all of these questions doubtless are related it would clarify our thinking if we had words to differentiate the type of question with which we are dealing.

The general questions are more in line with the problems the psychologist usually classifies as *motivation*. Motivation is one of the most basic and fundamental problems in psychology. Theories and concepts concerning it have been put forth and discussed since the early days of psychology. However, the subject is so complicated and is so difficult to treat experimentally that a theory acceptable to everyone has not yet been developed. In fact, differences of opinion are probably greater here than in any other area of psychology because they run the gamut from explanations stressing the innateness of motives to those emphasizing environmental causes, from physiological explanations to those using external factors or the unconscious.

Nearly all of the basic psychological theories of motivation have been used as a basis for research or speculation to answer the "whys" of clothing.

Instinct Theories

One of the earlier theories of motivation was the instinct theory. Some psychologists felt that we act as we do because of innate instincts. The number of instincts hypothesized varied from one psychologist to another. It follows naturally from a theory which emphasizes the innateness of instincts as an explanation of behavior, that the explanation of why we choose particular clothing might be found by answering the question "Why were clothes first adopted?" One of the earliest problems in the psychology of clothing to receive attention from the psychologists and anthropologists was the question of why we wear clothes at all and why they were first worn.

There have been four principle theories set forth to answer the question of why people first adopted clothes. The first theory was the biblical one of *modesty,* that is, clothes were worn to cover nakedness and because of shame. This has been the most widely known and probably the most widely accepted theory. Wundt (30) was an early advocate of this theory. While everyone recognizes that we feel immodest when parts of our bodies which are usually covered are exposed, this theory has been disputed on the grounds that modesty is not the same in different cultures. A part of the body covered by those in one culture will be left exposed without any shame by those in a different culture. Whatever amount of clothing is in general use in a given culture seems modest to the people in that culture while any subtraction from the customary amount is felt to be immodest.

The second theory to explain the origin of clothes is the opposite of the first theory. It has been called the *immodesty* theory. Clothes were first worn, according to this theory, to call attention to the parts of the body covered. Westermarck (29), for example, wrote that in many cases covering was originally adopted as a sexual lure. There is no doubt that the parts of the body which are usually concealed do take on added attraction; for example, in our own culture when skirts were long, the fleeting glimpse of a feminine ankle was felt to be more intriguing by men than is the sight of the leg today. It is difficult, however, to conceive that primitive man who had been naked would realize that parts of the body would be more alluring if covered, and would for that reason cover parts of the body.

A third theory states that man first wore clothing as *protection*. There are various modifications of the theory. Some believe that clothing was worn as protection against the elements, others that it was worn as protection against insects and beasts, and still others as protection against enemies or against harm from supernatural forces. In regard to protection against weather, it has been pointed out that clothing originated in the tropics where there would be the least need for such protection, and that in areas where it is colder there are tribes which wear little or no clothing and yet do not seem to suffer greatly. Dunlap (9) was the principal proponent of the theory that clothing was originally adopted to protect the wearer from the bites of insects. He points out that in many areas the first clothing was dangling strips of hide or leaves which would tend to keep flies and other insects away from sensitive areas. Still others have felt that clothing was first worn as protection against the enemy or against supernatural forces. Those who hold to this theory note that in some tribes the first clothing was the hide and often the heads of beasts which were supposed to frighten the enemy. There are also those who believe that the first clothing was to protect the wearer from supernatural elements or as a charm to bring them luck, health, fertility, or some other desired state. The reasons given for holding this point of view are that many of the earliest forms of clothing were strings of shells or other ornaments and in many cultures these do have a significance in their religious beliefs.

The fourth and final theory of the origin of clothing is that it was one means of *esthetic expression*. This theory has been called the decoration or ornamentation theory. In support of this, Starr (25) says that while there are some tribes who do not have dress there is no tribe that does not have ornamentation of some manner. The ornamentation may take the form of dress, of jewelry, or of painting the skin or mutilating the body in some way. Decoration of the body by any of these means is considered by some to be simply a desire to create beauty. Others have felt that the basis was one of attraction of the opposite sex. Opponents of this theory have pointed out that many of the garments worn could not be called decorative by anyone, and some are not supposed to be seen by others and therefore cannot be worn for this reason. A theory allied to the decoration theory is that clothes were first worn for prestige reasons. The first individuals to wear clothing, according to this concept, were hunters who wore parts of animals as trophies. As the greatest hunter was the most admired member of the group the more trophies he wore the greater the respect shown him.

It may have been that more than one of these reasons was the cause of the origin of dress in various cultural groups and that one of these reasons was operating in one culture, another in another, or that none was the motive for the first wearing of clothing.

Psychologists for the most part have dropped instinct theories of motivation. As it became necessary to increase the number of instincts to explain behavior the theories became too unwieldy to be useful. It has taken somewhat longer for such theories to be dropped as an explanation of clothing behavior. We still find some writers going back to the question of why clothes were first worn in order to answer why we wear clothes now and why we wear certain styles of clothing. We have come to recognize, however, that there is little reason to assume that an answer to why clothes were first worn can enlighten us concerning clothing behavior today.

Drive or Need Theories of Motivation

As the term *instinct* fell into ill repute among psychologists, it was largely replaced by the concept of *drive* or *need*. Two groups of psychologists have used these terms. One, the behavior psychologists who use both terms in a carefully defined system. Their research has been primarily concerned with proving or disproving points in the theory by the behavior of rats in controlled laboratory situations. This theory has had little influence on studies of motivation in clothing selection.

Other psychologists or other social scientists have also used either the term *drive* or *need,* but have been much less rigorous in their definitions. They have used the terms interchangeably to mean anything the individual requires for health and adjustment. They may or may not imply an inherited characteristic.

The classification of motives which includes these drives or needs varies greatly from author to author. Since, however, many present-day psychologists hold some theory of this type, much of the research and discussion on motivation in clothing selection has either implicitly or explicitly used one of these theories as a basis for hypotheses.

As early as 1918 Dearborn (8) stated that "clothing at one time or another, in some people if not in others, protects us against various kinds of fear: (1) of ridicule, (2) of the estimation of poverty, (3) of the estimation of inefficiency or stupidity, (4) of numerous dermal discomforts, (5) of bodily internal discomforts, (6) of the estimation of immodesty, (7) of anxiety, (8) of the estimation of lack of self-respect, (9) of the estimation of a lack of good taste, (10) of obtrusiveness, (11) of an underestimation (real) at first impressions, (12) of homeliness or lack of the desired beauty" (p.51). His list of motives was based upon personal observation and speculation. It is interesting to compare this list with those based upon later research.

Research based upon the drive or need theories has for the most part used questionnaires which ask individuals why they like some clothes better than others, what they want their clothing to do for them, why they chose what they did, and so on. The questionnaire method of getting at these problems is by no means an ideal one. If the questions are specific, there is a danger of suggesting the answers. If the questions are not specific, the answers are often vague and unclassifiable. This vagueness is to be expected because individuals usually have not formulated for themselves their motives in selecting garments. The questionnaire method, however, is perhaps the best one we have as yet for obtaining such material from enough individuals to make the data reliable without consuming an inordinate amount of time.

Hurlock (17) sent a questionnaire on motivation in fashion to over 1400 people. Her subjects ranged in age from 16 to 51 with the greater number in the lower age group. The questionnaire was designed to discover why individuals follow fashion and at what period in life clothes are most important, as well as other factors not directly related to motivation. The questions on motivation were concerned with such factors as: whether individuals dressed to please their own sex or the opposite sex, dressed to appear prosperous, choose clothes to enhance their best features, and if modesty was a factor in their choice of clothing. It is evident that the hypotheses upon which these questions were based were primarily derived from need or drive theories of motivation, but with the instinct theory still an influence.

The results of this study are open to some question because it was undertaken before much of the methodology now employed in questionnaires was developed. There are a number of leading questions which suggest the answers, while other questions are so worded that the "proper" answer is evident. For example, one of the questions relating to the desire to appear prosperous is worded: "Do you always try to dress so as to appear prosperous? Yes. No." Because this question has the word *always* in it, there would probably be the tendency to check "No" rather than "Yes" even though the individual often, or under certain conditions, did wish to appear prosperous. Another question is worded: "(a) Do you follow fashions so as to appear equal to those having a higher social position than you? Yes. No. (b) Do you change your style of dress when your social inferiors copy it? Yes. No." In this question the tendency might be to answer "No" to both parts because of the implication of "social climber," which is frowned upon in our culture. The same criticism might also have been leveled at the question concerning the desire to appear prosperous. If the question had been worded in another way the results might have been different.

As a result of this questionnaire Hurlock found that more people dress for their own sex than dress for the opposite sex. Looking prosperous, Hurlock found, was not a motive in following fashion, while modesty and the desire to enhance one's own features were positive motives. Most of the individuals answering her questionnaire said that they chose their clothes to be inconspicuous rather than conspicuous. The question from which she obtained this last result again suggested the "correct" answer, however.

In every question related to age she found that approximately two-thirds of her group felt that clothing was of the greatest interest, was considered to be of the most importance, and had the greatest effect on happiness during adolescence. The other third felt that clothes were more important to them as adults than they had been as adolescents. Almost no one felt that clothes had been of the greatest importance during childhood.

In 1934 Barr (2) developed another questionnaire on motivation in fashion. Her emphasis was upon the "activity of choice." The questionnaire was designed to provide data upon such drives or motives as: the desire for conformity, economy, comfort, the tendency to be modest, the desire for self-expression (either in desire to express personality or desire to enhance physical self) and attitudes towards sex and femininity. The questionnaire was given to approximately 350 women between the ages of seventeen and fifty years with the majority of the women in the nineteen to twenty age group. Some of the women were interested in clothing as a profession while others were not.

In the few years between Hurlock's study and this study numerous articles were published on techniques of questionnaire construction. In Barr's study, therefore, care was taken in the wording of the questions to avoid any set answer and, wherever possible, suggesting an answer. Some of the questions were directed toward the type of motive, such as conformity, modesty or economy. Examples of such questions are:

When you are in the company of women [another question is for men] which of your dresses do you prefer to wear?

_____ the prettiest
_____ the simplest
_____ the most expensive
_____ one which looks most expensive
_____ the most dignified

and

Do you choose dresses (check as many as necessary)
_____ to make you look slender?
_____ to make you look tall?
_____ to make your shoulders look narrower?
_____ to bring out the color of your eyes?
_____ to make you look short?
_____ to make you look stouter?

_____ to set off your natural figure?

_____ to reveal your legs?

_____ to show your arms to the best advantage?

_____ to express your personality?

_____ to make you look distinctive?

_____ to make you look youthful?

_____ to make you look prosperous?

_____ to make you look dignified?

_____ to make you look competent?

There were other questions which sampled the knowledge of the subjects in reference to fashion. The hypothesis here was that those who had acquired the greatest fund of knowledge concerning fashion would be those who were most anxious to be in fashion and that, therefore, this would be a measure of depth of motivation. The questions attempting to measure knowledge of fashion were principally a sampling of the individual's knowledge of fashion terms. For example, one question asked. "What simple names would you give these colors?" There followed a list of 21 color names which were popular at the time the questionnaire was given out, such as "beige, chianti, new leaf, clair de lune." Another question was worded, "How would you describe the meaning of these words to someone who does not know?" Sixteen terms followed this question. Included in the list were: "bouffant, haute couture, decollete, ensemble, Directoire, godet, tailleur." The results of the questions on knowledge were correlated with the intensity of desire to be in fashion. The desire to be in fashion was measured by the question, "Do you feel it important to be in style? Check how important. _____ Very important. _____ Moderately important. _____ No importance at all." No relationship was found between the measures of knowledge and whether or not the individual felt it very important to be in style. This does not necessarily mean, however, that there is no correlation between knowledge acquired in the field of fashion and the strength of motivation in that area. In the first place, there is the possibility that the questions did not obtain the data which they were designed to obtain. For example, the question of the importance of being in style may not be a good measure of strength of motivation in that area. The phrase "to be in style" may mean different things to different people. Further, almost all of the individuals in the various groups checked that they felt either that it was moderately important or that it was very important, and only a very few checked that they felt it was of no importance, so that the question only differentiates between two degrees of importance. On the other hand, knowledge in the field may be related to other fashion motives. For example, those who have the greatest knowledge in the field may not feel that it is of great importance to be in style but to be in the lead and be ahead of the style for the majority; or they may want to conform only to a certain degree but show a good deal of individuality, and therefore check that being in style is moderately important rather than very important. In other words, some individuals may interpret the question so that the varying degrees apply to the word style rather than to the word importance. The results of this questionnaire, then, have neither proven nor disproven any relationship between knowledge of fashion terminology and the depth of motivation in fashion.

Barr's study did show which reasons were given by the greatest number of people for choosing garments. She found that the "desire to conform" was the most frequent or diffuse motive. Modesty was found to be a motive in some instances, but here also the desire to conform played a part. The desire to conform is again shown in the subject's preferences for designs and colors which make them appear more like the popular ideal of slenderness.

The most important conclusion from Barr's study seems to be that the majority of people choose clothing which will enable them to conform to the group. Further conclusions from this study are that most individuals are not motivated to look prosperous, neither do they especially care about looking dignified or competent. They do want to choose clothing which will make their figure most like the fashionable ideal, they want to bring out the best in their physical appearance, and they especially want to show enough individuality so that they feel they are expressing their own personality by their clothes.

Another attempt to find what drives or needs were responsible for the wearing of clothing was not a controlled research in any sense of the word. It is, however, another illustration of the wide acceptance of a drive or need theory as the basis for discussion and research in motivation in the selection of clothes. Thorndike (26) asked a group of psychologists what "wants" they thought clothing fulfilled, and the proportion of the clothing expenses used to fulfill each of these wants. The consensus of opinion from the psychologists was that the clothing bill was spent:

41 percent for protection against cold, heat, and rain
6¾ percent protection against animals and disease
12½ percent for approval of others
7 percent for self-approval
10 percent to gain pleasure in courtship and sex activities
8 percent for other social intercourse
6 percent for pleasures of vision
3½ percent to win mastery or domination over others
2 percent to win their affection

The most recent and most systematically organized research relating clothing behavior to a need theory of motivation is that of Creekmore (6). She based her hypotheses upon Maslow's theory of motivation as formulated in 1954 (he later revised the classification of needs). In this theory the needs, operating usually at the unconscious or preconscious level, occurred loosely in the following hierarchal order:

Physiological (food, air, water, sex, and so on)
Safety
Belongingness (or love needs, both giving and receiving)
Self-esteem
Self-actualizing (desire for fulfillment)
Cognitive (curiosity and learning)
Esthetic

Partial fulfillment of one need allowed another to emerge. Any behavior might be determined by several needs. Creekmore hypothesized positive relationships between certain aspects of clothing behavior, general values of the individual and relative fulfillment of these basic human needs. In addition to those enumerated by Maslow she added one additional need—the need for action.

To test her hypotheses she gave her sample of 300 college women three tests which were designed to measure: (1) basic needs, (2) general values, and (3) clothing behavior.

As a measure of basic needs she developed 56 statements. For each statement the respondent was asked to indicate whether she would be very likely, somewhat likely, 50/50, somewhat unlikely, or very unlikely to do the same thing in the stated situation or in a similar situation. Each need was balanced against every other need. A few sample statements with the need they were designed to measure are:

When Sarah moved to a new neighborhood she bought some amusing animal planters for her kitchen since most of her neighbors had a special interest in them. (Belongingness)
Joan chose pieces of furniture that she liked and would enjoy regardless of how they looked to others. (Self-actualization)
Susan would much rather study the illustrations in art books than read what was said about the artists. (Esthetic)
Mr. Green has never been sick, but regardless of the statistics, he carries two hospitalization policies, just in case. (Safety)
Anne didn't want her math teacher to know that she still didn't understand how to work the problems after he had explained them the second time. (Self-esteem)

General values were measured by the Allport-Vernon-Lindzey test of values. We will discuss this test in greater detail in the chapter dealing with clothing values (see Chapter 5).

The measure for clothing behavior consisted of a clothing-interest inventory of 130 items in the following 14 classifications:

Appearance
Status symbol
Management
Theoretical
Conformity
Tactual aspects
Modesty
Fashion
Experimentation
Tool use
Altruistic behavior
Construction
Symbolic meaning interest
No concern for clothing

The items consisted of such statements as:

I experiment with new and different types of make-up. (Experimentation)
Beautiful fabrics inspire me to think about what I could make from them. (Construction)
I choose most of my clothing in fabrics that are smooth and soft to touch. (Tactual)
I buy easy-care dresses and blouses for school. (Management)
I notice clothes that are expensive. (Status symbol)
When I feel blue I perk myself up with my brightest or warmest sweater. (Tool use)
There are some clothes I enjoy wearing because they express the way I feel about myself. (Symbolic meaning)

The respondents checked each of these statements on a scale from $1 = $ almost never to $5 = $ almost always. Scores were then obtained for each classification.

Although the majority of relationships hypothesized by Creekmore were not borne out by the experiment there were some significant relationships. The needs for belongingness and self-esteem were both related to the behavior items which referred to clothing as a status symbol. The need for self-esteem was also related to the use of clothing as a tool. Creekmore suggests that her instruments for measuring both needs and clothing behaviors might be improved and that with more valid instruments more positive relationships might be found. Furthermore, her sample was a homogeneous group that was not differentiated in needs or values as sharply as a random sample of the population.

Economic Theories

We have mentioned Veblen's theory of conspicuous consumption earlier (see p. 17). Although his theory was broader many of his illustrations were concerned with clothing. It has, therefore, often been quoted by authors writing about motivation in the clothing area.

This theory was probably the basis for certain questions in the studies given in the previous section. A number of questionnaires included questions on whether or not the individual dressed to look prosperous. The results of these direct questions were negative. That is, respondents said that appearing prosperous was *not* one of their motives in choosing clothing. The problem of the relative importance to the consumer of looking prosperous is still unsettled, however, since these questions might not give a true picture. They are open to the criticism given before, that is, individuals tend to give the answer they know is the accepted one. In other words, looking prosperous might be of greater importance to the individual than he or she would be willing to admit.

Hoyt (16) objected to the fact that Veblen emphasized this one motive and omitted discussion of others. With even this restricted emphasis, however, she shows how factors influencing consumption have so changed since the period in which Veblen was writing that this motive can no longer be considered important. The four influences which she feels tend to replace conspicuous consumption are:

1. "Admirable simplicity" which represents a mixture of motives but stress is on simplicity and casualness as exemplified in blue jeans, hatlessness, backyard suppers, and first names.
2. "Inconspicuous consumption" found especially in suburbia where the individuals tend to be in the same socioeconomic group. In such a situation everyone is supposed to live according to certain minimum standards but not to go beyond their neighbors in consumption.
3. The "Package," or trend for each family is to keep up to minimum standards but beyond this to stress one or several areas of consumption because of special interests or situations. Thus each family has a different pattern of consumption and uniformity is much less evident than formerly.
4. More children. In the past people said that they could not afford children because they felt the need to provide expensive goods and services. Now it is felt that larger families are more important to the child and family than specific goods or services.

Hoyt feels that the tremendous technological drive in our society possesses us almost as a religion and has replaced conspicuous consumption.

Another economist, Paul Nystrom has also written extensively on the motivation in fashion. He bases his theory of motivation on the drives or hungers as described in the preceding section but lists the specific drives which especially relate to fashion as: boredom or the tendency to become tired of sensations experienced constantly, self-assertion or the desire to be different, rebellion against convention (especially the conflict of youth with convention), companionship and imitation.

While there have been other economic theories of motivation they have not significantly influenced research in the area.

Psychoanalytical Theories of Motivation

There is also the psychoanalytical approach which concentrates upon one or two basic instincts or forces, the particular forces varying from one psychoanalytical theory to another. These forces are deep in the subconscious, and the ways in which they influence the individual can only be divined by deep probings or indirect measures, because they are kept submerged in the subconscious. For Freud, the founder of psychoanalysis, the basic drives were originally life and sex. Later he changed his theory of motivation and substituted the life and death forces, or instincts, with the sex instincts included in the life instincts. The life instincts had as their goals the preservation of the individual life and the species (in the original theory the ego instincts aimed at self-preservation and the sexual instincts aimed at preservation of the species), the death instinct was a compulsion to return to the inorganic state out of which living matter was formed.

The best known and most minutely analyzed of the life instincts are the sexual instincts. For many, this is, in fact, the distinguishing feature of psychoanalysis. Likewise the approach of the first psychoanalyst to the problem of motivation in dress emphasized the sexual instincts. Such psychoanalytical approaches are exemplified by Flügel (11) and Bergler (3). Flügel's point of view was that we are trying to satisfy two contradictory tendencies with clothes—to call attenion to, or display the body, and to hide the naked body. Clothes serve to cover the body and thus gratify the impulse for modesty, but at the same time they may enhance the beauty of the body and call attention to its various parts or symbolize the hidden parts; thus clothes, he believes, arouse sexual interest because they symbolize the sexual organs. Nearly all of the clothing items worn by men—shoes, tie, hat, collar, and even coat and trousers he feels are phallic symbols while the shoes, the girdle, garter, and most jewels he names as examples of female sexual symbols.

Flügel gave a series of radio talks on the subject of "Psychology of Clothing." In order to obtain some information on the validity of his theory he sent out questionnaires to listeners to his program. Questionnaires were returned to him by 132 men and women, and the data obtained from them are the basis for his report. The results are probably influenced by the talks which they had heard, but since the content of these talks is not reported, there is no way of knowing how much the results were influenced by this means. Another criticism of this study is that the questions were often so worded that the answers may have been suggested. He asked his respondents whether they felt pleasantly supported or strengthened by stiff or tight clothes or constricted and restrained by them. Whether they felt their clothing was too heavy, too warm or too thin and whether or not they enjoyed the feeling of air currents, sun, and so forth. All of these were obviously directed at investigating erotic sensations. Some of his respondents reported that they felt they got strength from tight clothes while tight clothes gave others a feeling of restraint. More of the respondents (especially the men) thought that clothes were too heavy rather than too thin.

Bergler (3) also considers that clothes serve a deep need and are a defense against man's unconscious fear of a woman's body. Because the woman's body is clothed, man can undress her body in his thoughts and thus protect the illusion of his masculinity or "hemanness" which in turn protects him against women. Bergler suggested that a large percentage of dress designers are homosexuals whose unconscious hatred—or deeper fear of—women is responsible for the absurdities in dress and for the constrictive and uncomfortable fashions. This obviously is a very extreme point of view accepted by few.

A more recent attempt to investigate motivation in the selection of clothing from the psychoanalytical point of view was made by Cobliner (5). Prestige or desire for social status emerged from his data as the most important factor in conforming to fashion. But on further analysis the role of status was not, he says, what it appeared to be. The real basis of conformity, he believes, is the desire to be attractive to the opposite sex. His questionnaire was given to only 18 students and therefore the results can only be taken as suggestive of further research. He does not give the questions which he used but states that most of them were indirect questions. Cobliner bases his statement that the real source of conformity seems to be the desire to be attractive to men on the grounds that the report stated that the girls at first did not like the "new look" but later liked it because it made them appear more feminine. He feels that this shows that they basically wanted to attract men, but they did not consciously recognize this desire. However, the fact that the girls may not have liked the "new look" at first but liked it later might be explained by the demonstrated fact that we learn to like the familiar. Any new style may at first appear strange and ugly, but after it has become generally accepted it is no longer felt to be ugly.

Although we may not agree with the conclusions Cobliner draws from this small study, there does seem to be merit in his suggestion that a technique other than the questionnaire be used. He suggests that a projective technique would be best. His reasoning is that the basic motives in choosing clothes are related to attraction of the opposite sex and that such a motive will not be admitted, or consciously recognized, and for this reason a questionnaire method is inadequate. A projective test might, on the other hand, reveal such a motive. These indirect techniques will be described in greater detail when we discuss consumer motivation.

Other Theories of Motivation

There have been many other theories of motivation which might be used as the bases for hypotheses in the field of clothing which thus far have not been used. For example, the field theories have not been discussed as a possible explanation for clothing behavior. Green[1] suggests that Lewin's theory (4), in which the force field in an individual's life space is the direct cause of behavior, might be one of the most useful theories to explain clothing behavior. All force fields act upon the individual in a given position at a given time with the demands imposed by the organism's tensions operative. The question related to clothing behavior for Lewin would not be "why does the person choose this particular garment" nor "why does he dress" but rather "what force fields are operating in his life space in relation to tensions about dress?" Although this approach perhaps offers greater flexibility in attacking the problems and gives general explanations it does not suggest specific hypotheses which might be tested in relation to clothing.

In recent years there has been a good deal of discussion of the cognitive approach to human motivation. Festinger (10) for example, has suggested the importance of cognitive dissonance as a motivating state.[2] Cognitive dissonance refers to relation between two cognitions which exist simultaneously for a person, but which do not fit together. When this happens the individual seeks to change one or the other so that they are reconciled. This is not considered by Festinger as a complete theory of motivation but as an additional need such as hunger. In certain clothing behavior cognitive dissonance offers an explanation of factors other theories fail to explain. For example a number of years ago in interviewing college students, we found that the majority of students, when they were in a situation for which they were inappropriately dressed, tried to keep in the background so as not to be seen. A very few reacted in just the opposite way—they tended to act like clowns and called attention to themselves. Finding themselves inappropriately dressed in a group situation created cognitive dissonance. The individuals saw that the group considered

---

[1] Mary E. Green. Unpublished paper.
[2] The author is indebted to Mary Wines for the suggestion that such theories of motivation might be useful in explaining some clothing behavior.

a certain type of clothing appropriate for the occasion, and realized that they were dressed differently. The majority solved the dissonance by withdrawing from the group or the attention of the group. The few who reacted in the opposite way apparently resolved the dissonance for themselves by forming a particular subgroup—the clowns or entertainers. This addition to existing theories of motivation should be kept in mind for it might aid in explaining certain clothing behavior which other theories fail to explain and also serve as hypotheses for future research.

Summary

None of the theories of motivation we have discussed have seemed to us an adequate explanation of clothing behavior. Perhaps the reason that they have proved to be inadequate is that they have been too simplified. Harms (14) has made this criticism of theories concerned with the origins of clothing. He believes that all dress is motivated by the environment—both physical and social. Dress is a means, he says, through which man can express his sense of belonging to the group and his subjective sentiments. Others have emphasized this dual nature of clothing; on the one hand, individuals may show by their dress that they belong to a particular group, class, sex, religion and on the other hand show their own individuality. This statement while valid is so broad that it is not particularly helpful in getting at the whys of clothing behavior.

If we are to come to an understanding of why we dress as we do we will need ultimately to formulate explicitly a theory or theories concerning motivations in clothing behavior, and put specific hypotheses based upon these theories to experimental tests. First, however, let us examine what evidence we can find on the various factors which influence us to dress as we do. In the following chapters we will discuss some of the factors and the research findings related to them.

Bibliography

1. Allport, G. W. The trend in motivational theory. *Amer. J. of Orthopsychiatry.* 23, 1953, 107–119.
2. Barr, Estelle. A psychological analysis of fashion motivation. *Archives of Psychol.* 171, 1934.
3. Bergler, E. *Fashion and the Unconscious.* New York: Robert Brunner, 1953, 305p.
4. Clawson, J. Lewin's vector psychology and the analysis of motives in marketing, in *Theory of Marketing* (Cox, R. and Alderson, W., ed.). Chicago: Richard D. Irwin, Inc., 1950.

5. Cobliner, W. G. Feminine fashion as an aspect of group psychology: analysis of written replies received by means of a questionnaire. *J. of Soc. Psychol.* 31, 1950, 283–289.

6. Creekmore, Anna M. *Clothing Behaviors and Their Relations to General Values and to the Striving for Basic Needs.* Ph.D. Thesis, Penna. State Univer., 1963.

7. Cunnington, C. *Why Women Wear Clothes.* Faber and Faber Ltd., London, 1941.

8. Dearborn, G. V. N. The psychology of clothing. *Psychol. Rev. Monogr.* 26(1), 1918, 1–72.

9. Dunlap, K. The development and function of clothing. *J. of General Psychol.* 1, 1928, 64–78.

10. Festinger, L. *A Theory of Cognitive Dissonance.* Stanford, Calif.: Stanford Univer. Press, 1956, 285p.

11. Flügel, J. C. On the mental attitude to present-day clothes. *British J. of Medical Psychol.* 9(Part 2), 1929, 7–149.

12. Flügel, J. C. *The Psychology of Clothes.* Hogarth Press, London, 1930, 257p.

13. Garma, Angel. The origin of clothes. *Psychoanalytic Quart.* 18, 1949, 173–190.

14. Harms, E. The psychology of clothes. *Amer. J. of Soc.* 44, 1938, 239–250.

15. Hartmann, G. W. Clothing: personal problem and social issue. *J. of Home Ec.* 41(6), 1949, 295–298.

16. Hoyt, Elizabeth. Consumers' motivation reconsidered. *J. of Home Ec.* 48(9), 1956, 681–684.

17. Hurlock, E. B. Motivation in fashion. *Archives of Psychol.* 111, 1929.

18. Jacobson, W. E. Human motives underlying fashion changes. *Practical Home Ec.* 14, 1936, 230–231.

19. Jacobi, J. and Walters, S. G. Social status and consumer choice. *Social Forces.* 36, 1958, 209–214.

20. Madsen, K. B. *Theories of Motivation.* Cleveland: H. Allen, 1961, 356p.

21. Nystrom, P. *Economics of Fashion.* New York: The Ronald Press Company, 1928, 521p.

22. Payne, Blanche. Psychological aspects of sewing. *Butterick Pattern Book.* Fall, 1949.

23. Schull, P. M. Notes sur certains aspects de la psychologie du costume. *J. de Psychologie Normale et Pathologique.* 39, 1946, 121–123.

24. Simmel, G. Fashion. *International Quarterly.* 10, 1904–05, 130–155.

25. Starr, F. Dress and adornment. *Pop. Sci. Mon.* 39, 1891, 787–801.

26. Thorndike, E. L. Science and values. *Science.* 83, 1936, 1–8.

27. Veblen, T. *The Theory of the Leisure Class.* New York: The Macmillan Company, 1912, 404p.

28. Warden, Jessie. Some desires or goals for clothing of college women. *J. of Home Ec.* 1957, 49(10), 795.

29. Westermarck, E. A. *The History of Human Marriage.* London: The Macmillan Company, 1921.
30. Wundt, W. *Elements of Folk Psychology.* New York: The Macmillan Company, 1916, 532p.
31. Young, K. *Social Psychology.* New York: Appleton-Century-Crofts, 1935, 680p.

Chapter 3

How Society Influences
Clothing Choices

*U*ndoubtedly, the most evident influence on choice of clothing is derived from the particular society or cultural group to which we belong. We have only to note the similarity of clothes in a given period of time or in a particular geographical location and the differences in clothing between ages and geographical areas to see this influence. Today women in India wear saris, in the United States dresses and suits, and in Polynesia the sarong. Looking at various periods rather than places, we see that in the United States at the turn of the nineteenth century women wore dresses of the empire style which were clinging and diaphanous with high waist lines, long slim skirts and little decoration. By the middle of the nineteenth century the skirts were voluminous and the costumes stiff with heavy fabrics and elaborate ornamentation. In the mid-twentieth century the dresses had skirts which were again slim with simple decoration but were short.

No history of costume is complete unless we know something of the society which wore that type of dress. Books or courses in psychology of clothing are often approached from the historical point of view with the emphasis upon the society and social changes which are reflected in dress. Since this phase of the psychology of clothing or history of costume has been covered in other books we will mention here only briefly some of the ways in which clothing reflects the society in which it is worn.

What in Society Influences Our Choices?

IDEALS

Political and religious ideals are reflected in the dress of a nation or religious group. In periods and countries under a monarchy the nobility are differentiated from the masses by their dress. Furthermore, the dress of subjects reflects the ideals of the ruler. In a democracy in which all men are conceived as equal there are no clear class distinctions in dress. The hero of the moment may be copied or fashions may be initiated from any group in the culture. For example, the sport shirt which is common for men of all social classes originated in the lower economic groups and spread to the higher. In time of war when there is need for seriousness, the dress becomes more subdued. In World War I when women first worked in offices and factories in large numbers, the dress of women became more masculine This reflected the seriousness of the times and the fact that women were doing what earlier had been considered man's work. This type of dress was also more practical for the working girl. In periods after wars when there is a shortage of men, women's dresses tend to become much more elaborate because there is more competition for the men remaining.

It has been pointed out by various authors that periods which have been characterized by looseness of morals and licentiousness have had this reflected in their clothing. At the other extreme, periods which have been prim and puritanical in their moral standards have produced costumes which we would describe by the same adjectives. The term *strait-laced* which originated as a description of binding or restricting by means of stays or bodice we commonly use to mean strict in manners or morals.

Almost every religion has influenced the clothing of its believers from the Moslems who thought it a sin for women to expose their faces, arms, or legs to the Mennonites of today whose simple unornamented clothing reflects their convictions. As we study the history of religions we find that many of the great religious reformers have been concerned with reform in dress as well as morals and beliefs.[1]

GENERAL CULTURAL DIFFERENCE

The general income level of a population will be visable in the patterns of dress of its members. Consequently, a society which has a large middle class will be differentiated in clothing patterns from one which has a large peasant class and a small wealthy class.

ATTITUDES TOWARD WOMEN

Buice (7) has shown that the attitudes of each age toward women and the ideal woman have influenced the women's sport clothes. During the eighteenth-

---

[1] Langer (33: Chap. 8) has many descriptive examples of the influence of religion on dress.

century when the fragile type was admired, there were no sport clothes and the same corsets that were used in other activities were worn for their only exercise—dancing or training in posture and graceful movements. Costumes for active sports came into being when women's rights and privileges became a political issue. Gym clothes became more masculine and more adaptable to active sports in the twentieth century when women were considered capable and free to take on many of the activities and responsibilities formerly assigned only to men. Although this discussion deals only with sport clothes a review of the costumes for other activities over this period shows that the attitudes toward women influenced not only sport costumes but costumes for all other occasions too.

ATTITUDES TOWARD CHILDREN

In ages and cultures in which children have been ignored, they have been dressed in few clothes or in cast-off clothing. When children have been considered miniature adults and have been expected to behave as adults their clothing has been designed in similar fashion. At the present time, with emphasis placed upon children and their needs and with the attitude that children should be given freedom of expression, their clothes have been created with children's activities and capacities in mind.

CURRENT EVENTS

Political happenings, the hero of the hour, world affairs, Olympic games, are all reflected in certain garments, fabric prints, or accessories. When a popular show is on we often see an influence in dress or hair styles, such as the poodle hair cut when *South Pacific* was a very popular musical. When there was a great deal of interest in the opening of the ancient tombs in Egypt, the clothes had ornaments or materials printed with designs of objects taken from King Tutankhamen's tomb.

TYPES OF ACTIVITY

An agrarian society or a fishing community will dress differently from an urban society. Anspach, as we will see later, has shown that democratic, active, sports-minded Americans can be identified by their casual dress.

TECHNICAL DEVELOPMENT

The technical advances and mechanical inventions of a period also influence the clothing of that period. The new synthetic fibers now on the market have changed our fashions. Because of ease in washing, there is no longer the sharp differentiation between a housedress and a dressy dress. Also, because of the ease of cleaning, the new fabrics may be in lighter colors. New dyes and new finishes also obviously influence the clothing of a people. New machines which allow mass production of garments have not only changed the types of garments but also the quantity an individual owns. The influence of the industrial revolution has often been mentioned as an important influence on the history of costume. The fact that modern heating methods allow our buildings to be as warm in winter as in summer and that we travel from building to building in cars has definitely influenced the types of clothing which we wear in winter—now our underwear does not vary from winter to summer, we may wear short sleeves in winter, our skirts may be short and our legs covered only by sheer hose. These would have been most uncomfortable in the years before central heating. The fact that a great deal of travel is done by plane where the weight of luggage is limited discourages the use of heavy and elaborate garments. The increased speed of transportation and communication have led to the rapid dissemination of fashion news and so to not only the quickening change of styles but to similarities in fashion in many parts of the world. The list of technical changes and their impact upon clothing could go on and on. These are merely a few examples of the more obvious technical developments which have influenced the types of clothing we wear.

CUSTOMS AND FOLKWAYS

Although fashions change from year to year, there are certain customs or folkways concerning clothing which, although they may change in time due to fashion, nevertheless prevail in any given cultural group over a long period of time. For example, one of the oldest customs concerning dress is that the later in the day, the more formal and elaborate our attire. This custom holds true for nearly every type of function: clothes are less formal for a wedding in the morning than they are for a wedding in the evening; we wear more formal clothes to a dinner party than we would to a luncheon; a matinee performance of an opera or concert requires less formal clothing than an evening performance.

There are customs or folkways relating to location as well as to time of day. Generally speaking the more urban the center the more formal the clothing. Almost any fashion magazine differentiates between town and country wear. This is true even when the type of occasion is the same. Thus we would dress more formally for luncheon in the city than we would in a small town.

How Society Governs Our Choice of Clothing

The means by which the society governs the individual's choice of clothing may be either direct through laws and rigid custom or indirect through example and more subtle social pressures.

LAWS AND RIGID REGULATIONS

In some cultures, rules concerning clothing have been inflexible and concerned every individual in the cultural group. Before Japan was influenced by Western culture, for example, Lafcadio Hearn (21) described the rigid regulations applying to every detail of life, including clothing, of the Japanese farmer. The types of sandals and even the material of the thongs of the sandals were strictly regulated. The bindings and ornaments of the hair were likewise fixed by law. In Rome when Roman culture was at its peak, there were laws governing the number of colors which members holding various ranks could wear. Queen Elizabeth I of England issued numerous decrees concerning the clothing of her subjects. In France during the Middle Ages the dress and the length of the veil were regulated according to the rank of the wearer. During the seventeenth century in the United States only the upper class might wear lace, silver and gold thread, slashed sleeves, embroidered caps, "bands & rayles," gold and silver girdles, hat bands, belts and ruffs (25). During World War II there were restrictions in clothing which while not binding regulated almost all clothing. The rules laid down at this time for designers and manufacturers are summarized by Chambers. (10: 76–85.)

Besides the government or royal edicts which have governed the people's clothing, religion has decreed the kind of habiliments to be worn by its believers (see p. 58).

The examples given thus far have been primarily taken from history, and it is tempting to assume that today, especially in our free and democratic countries, that there are no such regulations. Although it is true that today we do not find many examples of government or religion dictating what *all* its people will wear, yet we do find that both government and religion regulate to the smallest detail what certain of its members wear. The governments of all countries require certain uniforms of all army and navy personnel. The uniforms themselves are not only rigidly controlled but small decorations which serve as insignia of rank are firmly regulated. Imagine the scandal if a private in the army wore stars on his shoulder! An example of religion dictating the clothing to be worn by certain members of the group is the nun's habit or the priest's robe. In both these examples, from religious practices and from the armed services, the individual has a choice (except in certain periods in the armed services) in that he or she may or may not join the group which is required to wear the habit or uniform, but once that choice is made the individual has no voice in the selection of his clothing.

In many other cases the individual's clothing is not regulated all of the time but may be for certain occasions or under specific circumstances. Some churches for instance require that a woman cover her head whenever entering the church. For specific occasions such as the coronation of Queen Elizabeth II there are strict rules governing what those of each rank should wear. In this case, although the regulations were changed from those of the past because many in England could not afford the apparel formerly decreed, nevertheless the regulations were exact in the extent to which her subjects could deviate from the former regulations.

There are other restrictions which apply at the present time to all individuals at specific times and places. Some resort towns, for example, have laws governing street wear; there are public beaches which have regulations concerning beach wear; restaurants may refuse entrance to anyone who is not dressed according to a certain standard—for instance, a man may be refused admittance if not wearing a tie and jacket. Although these regulations apply to designated times there are more general rules which prohibit any individual in any public place from "indecent exposure."

Also there are large groups of individuals whose clothing is regulated because of their business or profession. Policemen, guards, doormen, bell hops, waiters and waitresses, service-station attendants, nurses, barbers, surgeons, beauticians, and ushers are familiar examples. The college professor in many universities is required to wear an academic costume for certain ceremonies and in some universities in England to wear them for teaching. His costume is rigidly controlled in that he must wear only the hood and cap and gown which he is entitled to wear because of the degree which he holds and the university from which he obtained the degree. In certain schools the students are required to wear school uniforms.

In some cases the general type of uniform or costume is standard throughout the civilized world while in other cases it is worn only by the employees of a given concern, or it may vary in detail from place to place. For example, the details of the policeman's uniform may vary from city to city, and the style of the nurse's cap depends upon the hospital from which she graduated but are similar enough to be recognized throughout most of the world. The costume of the airline hostess, doorman, waitress, salesgirl in a store, gasoline-station attendant, and many others are determined by the company employing the individual and regulations are laid down by the employer. In all of the cases in which the business or profession determines the costume, it is necessary for the individual to wear that costume only when on duty; at other times he has freedom of choice.

In other occupations the regulations are less detailed and sometimes not specifically verbalized but are nevertheless equally binding. The salesgirl in a dress shop or department store where uniforms are not worn is often expected to wear a dark dress, the salesclerk is expected to wear a jacket and often a white shirt. Collins (11) conducted an interesting study on the dress of salesgirls and secretaries and the way in which they are governed by the job.

There are other instances in which the regulations may not be written down or, even if written down, there is no direct and certain punishment for not following them. In the examples given above, the individual would be subject to punishment by the state or religion, would be fired from the job, or would be forbidden entrance. Legend and custom which have persisted concerning local costumes may be exactly as rigid and the costumes determined in as minute detail as any legal regulations, but in this case it is public opinion, belief in the legends, and pride in the cultural group which forces the individual to comply. This is true of many of the peasant costumes of Europe which today are worn principally at holiday time. Another example would be the plaids of the Scotch clans. A member of one Scottish clan is very proud of his tartan and would never wear the tartan of another. The plaids for the various clans are recorded and the times at which each is to be worn is also specified, but there are no rules which force the individual with threat of punishment to observe these traditions.

INDIRECT CONTROL OF INDIVIDUAL DRESS BY SOCIETY

In spite of all these examples of regulation and rigid custom, the majority of us seldom are forced by laws and rules to change or modify our apparel. Our society, nevertheless does govern how we dress. There is a desire on the part of every normal individual to feel that he belongs to a group and that he is accepted and has the approval of that group. Along with this desire to be accepted is the fear that if he differs from the group markedly in any respect, such as clothes, he will be criticized or ridiculed by the other members and perhaps even be rejected for these reasons.

The term *group* is used here in a very loose sense. It may at one time have a very broad connotation such as a nation or a particular age group. (A high school or college student, for instance, is recognized in almost any part of the United States by his clothing.) At other times, it refers to smaller groups to which the individual conforms. In one clique the garment which is in high style is accepted and those no longer in high style seem common and uninteresting—as does the person who wears them. In another group, even within the same city, the individual who is dressed in high-fashion clothes is considered queer and eccentric.

Society also limits the range of deviation from the norm which is acceptable. In certain groups, especially among adolescents, the individual has very little margin for individuality. In such a group all must dress almost alike to be acceptable. A few years ago in the local high school all of the girls wore sweaters or shirt-type blouses, skirts, white bulky socks and brown loafers. No girl would feel comfortable in colored socks. In other groups the range of acceptable deviation is much greater.

The Individual's Role and Its Influence on His Clothing

SOCIAL STATUS OR SOCIAL CLASS

In the chapter on the perception of people it was noted that the status of an individual was often perceived through his clothing. Again, discussing motivation we found that the advertising of one's status (or desired status) has been considered one of the strongest reasons for dressing as we do. In fact, some theorists have considered it the primary reason.

The topic of status and its influence on the clothes we choose and on our attitudes towards the importance of dress has received a good deal of attention lately, both from social psychologists and from those whose focus is on clothing. In research it has been both the primary variable under study and has also been one of the dependent variables with its effect noted.

Barber and Lobel (2) in analyzing the "fashion copy" in women's magazines over a twenty-year period reached the conclusion that although in our democratic system there is a certain similarity at all class levels, there are also important differences. Thus, there are no sharp breaks between various classes, but a continuum with a great deal of mobility within the continuum. Also, within this continuum they find class distinctions reflected in dress. The classes which they differentiate and the typical clothing for each class are as follows:

1. At the top of the American social class system are those families where lineage . . . (extends) back one or more generations . . . (high) present occupational position. These are the "old money" families with established pre-eminence of social status. At this top level there is very little need to compete . . . women may even maintain a certain independence of current changeful "fashion." Their quality clothes can remain roughly the same for several years. They can stress the esthetic functions of clothes somewhat at the expense of "fashion" dictates. At an extreme one many even be queer and eccentric in one's dress . . . the taste of these women is more British than French. . . . Advertisements appealing to this taste stress adjectives like "aristocratic," "well-bred," "distinguished."

2. In the social class just below the "old money" families we find most of the "high fashion," Paris conscious style leaders. . . . Their clothes symbols are related to wealth and high living rather than to family connection. Cosmopolitan, Parisian French styles express their values better than do conservative, British modes. . . . The recurrent symbols of prestige are sophistication and chic; the word "glamor" is never used, for "glamor" is "cheap." Especially they are cautioned against the *nouveau riche* sin of obvious ostentation. . . . That is, one must actually spend a great deal on clothes, but one must not appear to have done so.

3. In the middle and lower middle classes . . . fashion has a different meaning. There is a distaste for "high style," for what is "daring" or "unusual.". . . . "Respectability" is the standard, not "breeding" or "effect." Clothes are conservative but "smart" and "smart" is what everyone else in one's social class is wearing.

Using the distinctions described by Barber and Lobel as a basis we would predict that the highest socioeconomic group would assign less importance to clothing than the lower groups and that the next to the highest groups would assign the greatest importance. This hypothesis was generally confirmed in a study by Vener (50). He found a positive, although very low, correlation between the total socioeconomic status score and the individual's personal estimate of the importance of clothing.[2] One of the reasons that the total correlation was not higher was because the highest status groups did not show the highest estimate of clothing importance. He says "it appears that clothing decreases in importance in the highest status categories."

The Vener study was a part of a larger clothing project undertaken jointly by the departments of Sociology and Anthropology and Textiles and Clothing at Michigan State University. Stone and Form, the principal authors of this project, report the relationship between occupation and the social significance of clothing (17). Their division of occupation was simply two-fold, the white-collar workers and the manual workers. They found a number of differences between these two groups. In the first place, the white-collar workers placed more importance on clothing than did the manual workers (see Table 4) (17:12).

Clothing importance scale scores	White-collar occupations	Manual occupations	Total
Low (0–4)	38	71	56
High (6–10)	62	29	44
Total	100	100	100
Number of cases	52	55	107

table 4 Differences in the importance assigned to clothing by men employed in manual and white-collar occupations. From William H. Form and Gregory P. Stone. The Social Significance of Clothing in Occupational Life. *Technical Bulletin* 247, June 1955.

The differences were even greater when the questions dealt specifically with work clothes. The reasons given for clothing importance likewise differed for the two groups. Office personnel placed greater importance on contact with the public and making satisfactory impressions on others.

---

[2] Clothing importance was measured with a Guttman-type unidimensional attitude scale and social status with a modified Warner scale. The Warner scale for socioeconomic status includes occupational status, source of income, type of house, and educational level.

If norms governing work dress are violated, white collar workers are most concerned with the responses of audiences which are large, impersonal, and loosely organized, while manual workers are most concerned with the responses of their immediate work groups. Thus 70 percent of the office personnel (as opposed to 33 percent of the plant workers) were concerned about reactions to violations of clothing norms on the part of such reference groups as the general public, clientele, customers, professional or occupational societies, or the entire work force [p.35].

The manual workers emphasized more frequently the functional utility of their clothing and its durability.

Two thirds of the white-collar workers and two fifths of the manual workers felt that their mode of dress affected job advancement. The white-collar workers recognized the importance of clothing in making good impressions, "dressed up" when applying for their first employment much more frequently than did the manual workers. Men in the white-collar positions purchased more items of clothing and paid more per item than did men in manual jobs, and yet they more often had feelings of clothing deprivation.

In another part of this project the respondents were given stories and asked for their reactions. Two of the stories were concerned with violation of clothing norms. In one of these stories the respondents were told of a man who was consulting a lawyer for the first time. "The man arrived at the lawyer's office and was surprised to find him casually dressed in a faded sport shirt that hung out over an unpressed pair of slacks" [p.42]. The respondents were asked what they would have done in the man's place. Over two thirds mentioned disapproval of the lawyer's clothing. About one seventh would have refused to use his services; about the same proportion would try to learn more about him, make certain reservations before employing him or would have employed him despite the poor impression. "Thus, it appears that although two-thirds evaluate his *dress* negatively, two-fifths approve of *him* sufficiently to consider using his services [p.43]." The technique employed in this part of the project is interesting and may prove helpful in attacking some of the problems concerned with attitudes toward clothing.

Jasinski (29) considers that much finer divisions of occupational levels than that between white-collar and manual workers are shown by the way men dress for work. In one factory, the pattern was as follows:

Suntan trousers and shirts but no tie for inspectors; slacks and sport shirts for lead men; slacks, white shirts, and ties for assistant foremen; and the same, plus a jacket, for the foreman [p.38].

He says that such modes of dress are seldom formally established, in fact administration and workers alike often deny that they exist. Nevertheless,

*"You are now looking at a man whose appearance
says 'I do not travel with the herd.' "*

observation shows that they are maintained and that they are used to indicate "what behavior to extend and to expect from other individuals. Thus
a staff man can walk into the shop and readily identify the foreman of a
particular section if consistent dress codes prevail" [p.38]. Distinctive garb
may also increase group solidarity and, presumably, group morale. He gives
examples of employees trying to adopt the style of dressing of a higher-
status group and being compelled either by his group or his superiors to
revert to the garb appropriate to his actual rank in the organization.

Within hospitals we see similar divisions between the orderlies, interns, doctors, and surgeons or between the registered nurses, practical nurses, student nurses, and volunteer workers.

There are differences between status groups in their attitudes toward the importance of clothing and their awareness of clothing symbols as well as in the types of clothing worn. Rosencranz (43) has shown that women who were of the upper social class, belonged to a greater number of organizations, had a higher education level, a higher income, subscribed to more magazines, possess higher verbal intelligence, and had husbands in the white-collar occupational group scored higher on clothing awareness in her test than did those who were lower on each of these dimensions (see p. 23). The technique is a promising one which we hope will be used in further studies. For example, it would be valuable if we knew the qualitative differences between groups in their responses to such differences. Does one age or social-status group perceive a given person in a picture differently from another age or social status group?

RACE

In the studies discussed above various socioeconomic or occupational groups have been compared in their clothing behavior and attitudes or awareness. Kittles (31) compared Negro college students with the white college students on the importance of clothing as a status symbol, their utilization of clothing as a symbol of status and factors which affect clothing choices. Her sample consisted of 181 white college women and 200 Negro college women from two Southern segregated schools. A clothing-importance scale was developed from a series of 41 statements concerning attitudes toward clothing. Respondents were also asked to check whether they owned or would like to own certain high-status clothing items. Respondents were also asked the reason for not wanting to own items on the high-status clothing list.

Kittles found, contrary to her hypotheses, that the white students scored significantly higher on the clothing-importance scale than did the Negro students. The white students also owned more and desired to own more of the high-status clothing items.

The white students who participated in more social activities and who came from larger home towns had higher scores on the clothing-importance scale than did those who participated less and came from small home towns. The results were the opposite for the Negro students. These results are surprising, especially as she also found that the Negro group who were in the lowest-income group owned more high-status clothing items than did white students. As the income level went up for the Negro group, the number that owned high-status items relatively decreased and vice versa for the white group. It has generally been considered, as Kittles hypothesized, that Negroes place more emphasis on clothing than do white people in the

United States. The fact that Negro students in the lower-income group own more status items than the white students seems to support this belief but her results in general do not confirm it. Therefore it may be that income is a more important factor than race and since it is known that Negroes are more often in the lower-income bracket than are the whites this may account for the general impression that they put more emphasis upon clothes. However, the results for her Negro group as well as studies such as Stone and Rosencranz contradict this. Several other factors may have accounted for her results. The groups she was using were segregated schools. The Negro students may put less emphasis on clothes when they are in their own group, but if they were in an integrated college participating with white students they might put more emphasis on the importance of clothing. Finally her group, as a sophisticated college group, may be aware of this belief concerning Negroes' emphasis upon clothes and be self-conscious about it, therefore, in answering the questions they tried to give what they considered the most acceptable response. We hope that this interesting and well-planned study will be repeated on Negro and white students in integrated colleges. The results would answer some of the above questions.

Kittles did find differences between whites and Negroes in their reasons for assigning importance to clothing items symbolic of high status. White students wanted the items because they were "ego boosting" while Negro students tended to give reasons which suggested elevating themselves in the eyes of others. The Negro students relied on mass media for getting ideas for their clothes to a greater extent than did the white college students, while the white college students more often checked "watching what others wear." There were also differences between the Negro and the white students in respect to factors which affect their clothing choices. Negroes, more frequently than whites, checked "stores not conveniently located," "not enough exclusive styles," and "certain stores will not serve me," while whites checked "high prices" more frequently than Negroes.

SOCIAL MOBILITY

We have discussed the influence of the individual's present social status or socioeconomic level and his race upon his clothing behavior and attitudes. However it may not be the present position in society, but the desired position or the mobility that is the most important factor. Gates (19) investigated this problem. Mobility was measured by the difference in status score between the woman's husband and father. The status score was based upon a modification of the Warner scale. Levels of extrinsic reward orientation were measured by questions on (1) social status and prestige, (2) income, (3) job security, (4) social prominence, and (5) job promotion. Social mobility or movement in relation to the peer group was measured by asking the respondent to compare the education, financial attainment, and the prestige of the position of her husband with that of her high school and post high school peer group. She found no significant differences between the mobile and the nonmobile respondents in: preference for new fashions, reading of fashion magazines, preference for exclusiveness of stores or ownership of prestige items. The upward mobile respondents scored significantly higher in recommending the buying of clothing to conform, but lower in the desire to be well-dressed. The aspirationally upward mobile group owned significantly more prestige items than the concomitantly upward mobile group but did not vary in any of the preferences, attitudes, or behavior measured. Those with high extrinsic reward orientation owned more prestige items, ranked preference for exclusive stores higher, tended to have greater preference for new fashions, but were lower in fashion knowledge than those with low extrinsic reward orientation.

Thus, at least for the sample which Gates was using, the mobility from one status group to another seemed to have little effect on clothing behavior or preferences. However, her sample was limited to 88 women from two economic groups in a small city. Her research instruments and methodology were well planned. It is unfortunate that they have not been used with other groups.

COMMUNITY SIZE

Not only the social status within a community but the size of the community itself may be an influence on our clothing choices. In the past there was a recognizable difference between the clothing of the farmer, the small-town person, and the urbanite. This difference has broken down so that it is usually impossible to distinguish rural persons from urban persons when in the same situation. Nevertheless, several studies have shown that there is a difference in attitude toward and interest in clothing related to the size of the home town. In general, individuals from the city environment put greater emphasis upon clothing than do those from the country. This may be related to the fact that in the rural area or small town everyone knows everyone else and hence is not apt to judge on appearance while in the city strangers are coming into contact with one another and forming impressions based, at least in part, upon appearance. Another explanation might be that in the city there are greater shopping facilities and a larger array of clothes from which to make selections and that this stimulates greater interest. We will need further research to reach conclusions on the reasons for this difference.

Cultural Role

In any complex society there are a wide variety of cultural roles and each individual plays a number of these roles. Each sex, age, socioeconomic, occupational, and regional group has certain characteristic roles assigned to it by the culture and the individuals within the group tend to live up to the expectations of the society. We have seen how various social status and occupational groups can be differentiated by their choice of and their attitudes toward clothing. In turn the choice of clothing indicates to others the group or groups to which the individual belongs and thus helps to facilitate relations between individuals. When we perceive an individual as a member of a certain age, social status or occupational group we know how to react to him and what to expect of him.

Many specific examples of cultural roles might be given. The policeman is supposed to be the protector and be fearless, the marine tough and very brave, the nurse sympathetic and competent. Individuals in the uniform belonging to any one of these occupations or defense branches play the role which they believe is expected of them. Nuns attending the university one term were interviewed as an informal class project on the psychological effects of religious habits. They all felt that their habits had a great effect upon their actions as well as on the actions of others toward them. Knowing that people in general expected a nun to be sweet, gentle, dignified, and serious as well as deeply religious, their robes were a constant reminder to them to act in that way and to live up to people's expectations. Those interviewed felt that, although they had chosen a particular way of life which embraced this type of behavior, nevertheless, the fact that they wore habits which showed to the rest of the world that they had chosen this sort of life did influence the way in which they acted. Also, because it influenced the way in which others reacted to them, this in turn affected their actions.

It is not only in uniforms that we see the effect of clothing on the cultural role. We also see it in our everyday dress. Anspach (1) points out that American women with their many roles have adopted the classic functional type of dress which depicts the broad role of busy and ageless American women rather than particular roles of age or job.

Bush and London (8) have suggested that the differences in the modes of dress within a particular society are indicative of differences in social roles and self-concepts of members of that society, and changes in modes of dress in a society are indicative of the changing roles of members of that society. It follows from this that the greater or smaller the variability of clothing styles in a society the less or more well-defined are the social roles in that society. They illustrate these hypotheses by the wearing of knickers of the prepubescent boys when their role as boys was sharply differentiated from that of men and the disappearance of this distinguishing garment when the role of the boy was less clearly defined. The implication brought out here is not only that the role of the individual in society governs his clothing, but that the limits of permissible variation are defined by his role in that society. Another example of this same principle might be the housedress. In the early part of this century the role of wife and mother was primarily that of housewife. Her role was to take care of the material wants of the family—its food and clothing and the house. The particularly successful woman in this role was the one who was the best cook, kept the neatest house and was a good seamstress. Her costume was a housedress and was worn, at least in the morning, by the vast majority of women. The role of the wife recently has been changing. With the technical advances in food preparation and in various appliances for the home the wife may work outside of the home or take on many community responsibilities. She is expected, perhaps with the help of her husband, to feed her family good and nutritious meals, but, as this can be done by using packaged or frozen foods, it is no longer a matter of pride with her and neither she nor society considers it an important aspect of her role. If she is at home while the children are young, the family relationships occupy a more prominent position in her role. She now calls herself "homemaker" rather than "housewife." With the changing of the role we see a corresponding change in the dress of the wife. The housedress has all but disappeared. The young homemaker instead wears shorts or slacks or skirts, blouses, and sweaters, showing she is ready to be a companion to her children, or ready for work outside of the house.

The sex role is another example of a social or cultural role. Each society differentiates between jobs, specific ways of performing, and clothes for the sexes. Recently in our own culture many of these role expectations have broken down, as women have been accepted in jobs and take part in sports originally considered masculine. Men likewise have assumed tasks around the house, adopted hobbies and avocations formerly considered feminine and in their clothing slightly more feminine colors and styles have been introduced. Richards[3] hypothesized that an individual's preference for traditional behavior norms for each sex is related to their preference for traditional clothing norms.

It has been suggested that it is easier for a girl to learn her appropriate sex role than it is for a boy and that this is due, in part, to clothing. The little girl as she pretends or takes the role of mother is able to "dress up" in clothing which helps her to pretend and therefore teaches her something of her sex role. The little boy, however, can not "dress up" in his father's clothing and so does not have this advantage. We have no evidence to support this hypothesis.

One way of determining the relationship between cultural roles and clothing is to examine a number of cultures which vary in the degree of

---

[3] Louise Richards, *The Relation of Attitudes toward Sex-Role to Selected Clothing Attitudes in a Sample of 48 Male Graduate Students.* M.S. Thesis, Pennsylvania State Univers., 1960.

differentiation of a given role and see if this is accompanied by a change in clothing. Thomas[4] examined the initiation-into-adulthood rites of various cultures and related the emphasis put on these rites to the clothing worn during the ceremonies and to the change in clothing before and after these ceremonies.

Fashion and Fashion Changes

Fashions in the Western world are changing more rapidly today than they have at any time or place in history. This is in part due to the rapid technological changes which we have already noted, but it is also due in part to our flexible class system, to the growth of urban centers and to population mobility. Fashion changes slowly in rigid class or caste systems in which the individual has no prospect of changing his status. It also changes slowly in small stable communities where there is little interchange with new people and everyone knows everyone else, his family, and his reputation.

In considering fashion changes, we frequently use the term *fashion cycle*. This should not be interpreted to mean that what was once in fashion reappears as fashionable again and again after certain set intervals. It is true that at least some aspects of style do recur at various periods, but when we speak of the fashion cycle we mean something quite different. It refers to the gradual rise and fall of a particular fashion. When a style is first introduced it is followed by a few daring individuals. Presently their clothing is copied and the particular fashion is adopted by those people who are considered "smart" and "fashionable." Finally, it is accepted by large masses of people and the style thus reaches its peak. When it has been accepted by the majority of people then those who were the first to accept it change to a new fashion and the wave starts to drop off. If we plotted the number of individuals wearing a certain style on one axis and time on the other axis, we would find the results falling on a single wavelike curve similar to the curve of normal distribution. These fashion cycles vary as to their length, that is, as to the speed with which they rise and fall in popularity: some fashions may be taken by large numbers soon after they are introduced, while others do not reach their greatest popularity for many months or years. As first pointed out, by Ross[5] fashion is not progressive. Progress always follows the line of advantage and is always changing for the better, fashion on the other hand, moves in cycles and one cycle may have clothing which is less convenient, less adapted to the life of the times, or less beautiful than the preceding wave.

Although a single fashion, such as cincher belts, may follow the form

---

[4] Alice Thomas unpublished paper.
[5] E. A. Ross, *Social Psychology* New York: The Macmillan Company, 1908.

of a wave and be completely unrelated to any previous or following wave, there are also certain aspects of dress which change in fashion but which can be compared over long periods of time. For as long as women wear skirts, for example, the length of the skirts, the position of the waist line, and fullness of the skirt can be compared.

Kroeber (32) used fashion illustrations of evening gowns and measured the length of the dress, the length of the waist line, the depth and width of décolletage, the diameter of the waist and of the skirt. So that these measurements might be comparable for different fashion pictures, the total length of the figure was measured from the mouth to the tip of the toe and the rest of the measurements were expressed in relation to this figure. The total time range covered was from the year 1605 to 1936. He was thus able to plot the change in each of these dimensions in dress for over 300 years. The conclusions drawn were that each dimension of dress appears to have a more or less independent history but that some of the dimensions have periodic swings, which are fairly regular. The surprising features of these periodic swings from greatest to shortest length or breadth is the great length of the periods. The swings from the shortest skirt to the longest and back to the shortest, that is, one complete wave, were 144, 53, 109, and 94 years in length. On the average, then, it has taken about a full century for the complete wave to take place, which certainly does not indicate the rapid fashion changes which we have come to believe are typical of our culture. The change in basic silhouette is very gradual with minor fluctuations which, at the time, appear to be drastic changes. The implication of these results is that "the role of particular individuals in molding the basic dress style is slight. The influence of creative or important individuals is probably largely exerted on the accessories of transient mode" [p.148].

Another attempt to trace fashions by means of fashion illustrations and portraits over a long period of time was made by Young (53). She selected what seemed to be a typical dress for each of the 178 years in her study and classified them into the fundamental types of skirt form. She found that there were three basic skirt forms—tubular, bell-shaped and with back fullness. Each of these types she found predominated for approximately a third of a century. The bell shape predominated from 1725–1759, back fullness from 1760–1795, tubular 1796–1829, bell again from 1830–1867, back fullness 1868–1899, and tubular started again in 1900. If the same progression continued, then the bell shape should have predominated from the mid 1930s to the late 1960s when we would expect back fullness to be coming into fashion. Perhaps historical perspective will change our view but the tubular form still seems to have been predominate during the second third of the century. At the end of each cycle Young found that there was more emphasis upon the sleeves and the upper parts of the body than on the skirts, while at the beginning of the cycle there was more variation in the skirt silhouette with much less variation when the fashion was at its peak of popularity. This type of research is greatly needed, although there are difficulties in obtaining accurate measurements so that comparisons can be made. It is also difficult to determine how far one can generalize from a few pictures of a period.

FADS

Fads are related to the more superficial aspects of fashion; in clothing for example, fashion refers to the general style of the dress, the shape of the skirts, whether the material is simple or elegant, the amount of decoration, or the wearing of short or long coats. A fad usually is concerned with some minor detail of the costume, often some form of decoration, such as tying a scarf at the neck in a certain way, or wearing mismatched socks, specific types of inexpensive jewelry or jackets autographed by all one's friends. Fads usually develop much faster, last for a much shorter period, and die out much more rapidly than fashions. They usually do not spread as far nor to all groups, while fashion influences large cultural divisions. A fad may be followed only by a certain age group, by those in a certain community, by the boys or girls in a particular school, or even by the members of a certain clique in a specific school. It is more often followed by young people than by adults and is often looked upon by adults as being in poor taste. The same general rules for the rise and fall of fashion seem to hold true for fads. For over a quarter of a century Bogardus (6) asked 95 to 170 key people throughout the country to list fads as they observed them. If an item appeared on five lists he accepted it as a fad. He was thus able to see the areas in which fads occurred and to plot the length of the cycle. He found that more than half of the fads were women's dress and accessories and most survived less than six months.

Although we may know some of the reasons for the rate of change in fashions or fads we are very much in the dark as to why certain specific styles become fashionable and others do not. Many ideas are given us each year by the dress designers but only a relatively small percentage are accepted and become popular. The entire clothing industry from fabric manufacturer to clothing retailer can make or lose fortunes depending upon whether or not they have guessed correctly what will become popular. Likewise in fads, a certain accessory, such as the Daniel Boone hat in the 1950s may sweep the country and become a nationwide fad while many other items, even items having to do with the same event or hero, do not.

Jack and Shiffer (26) have given evidence to show that designers, if they are to be accepted, must keep within certain limits or they will not be followed. They measured the length of women's skirts for the years 1929 to 1947. The measurements were taken from pictures in selected magazines. The first series of measurements was taken from *Vogue.* The measurements in this series were supposed to indicate what the designers were dictating. The second series of pictures was taken from *Woman's Home Companion.* The third series was taken from photographs in *Life* and were supposed to reveal what the woman on the street was wearing. The problem was to see if the "woman on the street" did follow the "fashion dictators." Although the sampling technique and statistical analysis in this study have weaknesses, the evidence seems to support their hypothesis that the woman on the street will follow the dictates of the designers up to a certain point but then refuse to go beyond certain limits. In other words, when the designer tried to shorten clothes, the woman on the street would shorten her dresses, but there was a point beyond which she would not shorten them; when the designer indicated long dresses the woman on the street would lengthen her hem lines but would not go beyond a certain length. This study begins to help us determine why certain styles are accepted and others are not. We know that to be acceptable a fashion must keep within limits of what has been acceptable in the past. Other reasons may be found by studying fashion leadership.

FAD AND FASHION LEADERSHIP

Within any given group the acceptance or rejection of a fashion is probably dependent upon the acceptance or rejection of it by the leaders in the group. Katz and Lazarsfeld (30) found that fashion leadership varies with interest in clothing, gregariousness, and position in the life cycle. Fashion leadership was measured by the amount of advice given on clothing selection. As would be expected the woman who is more interested in clothing is more apt to be a fashion leader. Holding interest constant, however, fashion leadership varies with the individual's position in the life cycle. The probability of being a fashion leader is greatest for young unmarried women and then descends in the following order: wives with small families, wives with large families, and lastly matrons. Fashion leadership also increases with expanding gregariousness. The more gregarious the individual as measured by the number of organizations to which she belongs and self-estimate of number of acquaintances the more apt she is to be a fashion leader. Fashion leadership also varies with the social status. The lower-status group has fewer leaders than the middle and upper-status groups. However, the upper-status group does not have more than the middle status group. In fact among the most gregarious of the high-status group there is a *drop* in leadership. The hypothesis given to explain this is that gregarious and high-status individuals talk more about public affairs, charity work, and women's clubs and less about clothing, and secondly that it may not be considered good form in this group to ask for or give advice on taste in clothing.

An interesting study on fashion leadership was carried out by Janney (28). In a woman's college Janney had seven of the students observe the rise and spread of every fashion and fad. These girls reported the origin and development of sixty-seven clothing fads in the college. An analysis of these data showed that fads are originated by young women who are members of prestige-bearing cliques, and who are also leaders in other types of activities and are apparently popular with men. The fads may be confined to a particular clique and, when they are, the type of fad seems to be congruent to other types of social activity in which the clique engages. The overwhelming majority of girls do not originate fads but follow them within a period of several weeks. Those girls who are insensitive to fads are in general insensitive and unskillful in other types of social situations.

Summary

The type of clothing which we wear and the choices we make are first of all governed by the society or culture in which we live. The influence of the society may be in formal controls such as rules and regulations or may be informal as in customs or folkways or just what is accepted by the group. The controls both formal and informal may apply to all individuals in the society or just to specific groups such as those in a certain profession. Furthermore the controls may govern what the individual wears at all times, what he wears at work, or simply what he wears at a specific time or place.

The individual's place in society and his socioeconomic status also influence his clothing and the importance he places upon it. In general the higher the socioeconomic status the greater the emphasis upon clothes. This relationship apparently breaks down for the highest socioeconomic level. A theory which might explain this is that the members of the highest socioeconomic group because they are well established and socially secure do not feel the need of demonstrating their position by their possessions such as clothing. If this theory is true, then we would predict that the socioeconomically mobile and those oriented toward a higher socioeconomic status would place greater emphasis upon clothes than the nonmobile or those not interested in reaching a higher status. The only research which we have on this point does not confirm this hypothesis. From this theory we would also predict that Negroes, due to their subordinate position in American society would also put greater emphasis upon clothes. Although this was not found to be true in two segregated colleges, nevertheless, the reasons for assigning importance to clothes given by the Negro and white students seem to support this theory.

The influence which society exerts upon the individual in his clothing choices can perhaps be best explained by the role theory. In a complex society such as ours there are a wide variety of cultural roles. Each individual plays more than one of these roles and is aware of what others expect of him in each of them—expect in dress as well as behavior. The individual tries to live up to these expectations.

Bibliography

1. Anspach, Karlyne. The American in casual dress. *J. of Home Ec.* 55(4), 1963, 255–257.
2. Barber, B. and Lobel, L. S. "Fashion" in Women's clothes and the American social system. *Social Forces.* 31, 1952, 124–131.
3. Beaton, Cecil. *The Glass of Fashion.* Garden City, N.Y.: Doubleday & Company, Inc., 1954, 397p.
4. Bell, Q. *On Human Finery.* New York: A. A. Wyn, Inc., Publishers, 1949, 134p.
5. Bogardus, E. S., *Essentials of Social Psychology.* Chap. XIII. Los Angeles: University of So. Calif. Press, 1918.
6. Bogardus, E. S. Social psychology of fads. *J. of Applied Sociology,* 8, 1923, 239–243.
7. Buice, Mary E. The effects of social change on women's physical education costumes. *Pi Lambda Theta Journal.* 27(4), 1949, 239–245.
8. Bush, G. and London, P. On the disappearance of knickers: hypotheses for the functional analysis of the psychology of clothing. *J. of Soc. Psychol.* 51, 1960, 359–366.
9. Cannon, K. L., Staples, R. and Carlson, I. Personal appearance as a factor in social acceptance. *J. of Home Ec.* 44, 1952, 710–713.
10. Chambers, Bernice. *Fashion Fundamentals.* Englewood Cliffs, N.J.: Prentice-Hall, 1947, 501p.
11. Collins, June. *Symbolism in Occupational Life.* Unpublished talk at Cornell Univer.
12. Dickins, Dorothy. Social participation as a criterion for determining scientific minimum standards in clothing. *Rural Soc.* 9, 1944, 341–349.
13. Ditty, Donna. *Social-Psychological Aspects of Clothing Preferences of College Women.* Ph.D. Thesis, Ohio State Univer., 1962.
14. Eastman, Susan. Fashion's foibles. *American Dyestuff Reporter,* 42(1), 1953, 9–10 and 15.
15. Flügel, J. C. *The Psychology of Clothes.* London: Hogarth Press, 1930, 257p.
16. Form, W. H. and Stone, G. P. Urbanism, anonymity, and status symbolism. *Amer. J. of Soc.* 62, 1957, 504–514.
17. Form, W. H. and Stone, G. P. *The Social Significance of Clothing in Occupational Life.* Technical Bulletin 247, Michigan State Univer. Agricultural Exper. Sta., June, 1955.
18. Fox, M. S. Clothing and personal adornment as expressions of American life. *Art in American Life and Education.* 40th Yearbook. Nat. Soc. for Study of Ed. Bloomington, Ill.: Public School Publish. Co., 1941, 114–119.

19. Gates, Ruth E. *Clothing Behavior Associated with Types of Mobility, and with Extrinsic-Reward Orientation, Among a Specified Group of Non-Employed Wives.* Ph.D. Thesis, Penna. State. Univer., 1960.
20. Hall, E. T. *The Silent Language.* Garden City, N.Y.: Doubleday Company, Inc., 1959, 240p.
21. Hearn, L. *Japan: An Attempt at Interpretation.* New York: The Macmillan Company, 1904, 549p.
22. Hoffman, Adeline M. *Clothing Behavioral Factors for a Specific Group of Women Related to Aesthetic Sensitivity and Certain Socio-Economic and Psychological Background Factors.* Ph.D. Thesis, Penna. State Univer., 1956.
23. Holtzclaw, Katherine. Costume and culture. *J. of Home Ec.* 48(6), 1956, 401–404.
24. Hurlock, E. B. *The Psychology of Dress.* New York: The Ronald Press Company, 1929, 244p.
25. Iverson, Marion Day. Color in pilgrim and puritan dress. *Antiques.* 61, 1952, 240–241.
26. Jack, Nancy K. and Shiffer, Betty. The limits of fashion control. *Am. Soc. Rev.* 13, 1948, 730–738.
27. Jacobi, J. E. and Walters, S. G. Social status and consumer choice. *Social Forces.* 36, 1958, 209–214.
28. Janney, J. E. Fad and fashion leadership among undergraduate women. *J. Abn. and Soc. Psych.* 36, 1941, 275–278.
29. Jasinski, Frank J. How they dress on the job: clues to the informal organization. *Personnel,* 34(3), 1957, 35–41.
30. Katz, E. and Lazarsfeld, P. *Personal Influence: The Part Played by People in the Flow of Mass Communications.* Glencoe, Ill.: The Free Press, 1955, 400p.
31. Kittles, Emma L. *The Importance of Clothing as a Status Symbol Among College Students.* Ph.D. Thesis, Ohio State Univer., 1961.
32. Kroeber, A. L. On the principle of order in civilization as exemplified by changes in fashion. *Amer. Anthrop.* 21 New Series, 1919, 235–263.
33. Langer, L. *The Importance of Wearing Clothes.* New York: Hastings House, Publishers, 1959, 334p.
34. Laver, J. *Taste and Fashion.* New York: Dodd, Mead & Co., 1938, 271p.
35. Linton, R. *The Study of Man.* New York: Appleton-Century-Crofts, 1936, 503p.
36. Mead, G. H. *Mind, Self and Society.* Chicago: University of Chicago Press, 1934, 400p.
37. Meyersohn, R. and Katz, E. Notes on a natural history of fads. *Am. J. of Soc.* 62, 1957, 594–601.
38. Miller, Sylvia. Old English laws regulating dress. *J. of Home Ec.* 20(2), 1928, 89–94.
39. Parsons, F. A. *The Psychology of Dress.* Garden City, N.Y.: Doubleday & Company, Inc., 1923, 358p.

40. Parsons, T. An analytical approach to the theory of social stratification. *Am. J. Soc.* 45(6), 1940, 841–862.
41. Patrick, G. T. W. The psychology of crazes. *Pop. Sci. Mon.* 57, 1900, 285–294.
42. Richardson, Jane and Kroeber, A. L. Three centuries of women's dress fashions, a quantitative analysis. *Anthrop. Records.* 5(2), 1940, 111–154.
43. Rosencranz, M. L. Clothing symbolism. *J. of Home Ec.* 54(1), 1962, 18–22.
44. Rosencranz, M. L. Sociological aspects of clothing studied. *J. of Home Ec.* 42, 1950, 206.
45. Ruttenber, E. M. *The American Male; His Fashions and Foibles.* New York: Fairchild Publications, Inc., 1948, 353p.
46. Steiner, R. I. and Weiss, J. Veblen revised in the light of counter-snobbery. *J. of Aesth. and Art Crit.* 9, 1951, 263–268.
47. Stephenson, R. M. Comments on relationship between research and theory. *Am. Soc. Rev.* 14, 1949, 313–314.
48. Sybers, Ruth and Roach, M. E. Clothing and human behavior. *J. of Home Ec.* 54(3), 1962, 184–187.
49. Treece, Anna J. *An Interpretation of Clothing Behavior Based on Social-Psychological Theory.* Ph.D. Thesis, Ohio State Univer. 1959.
50. Vener, A. *Stratification Aspects of Clothing Importance.* M.S. Thesis, Michigan State College, 1953.
51. Wertenbaker, T. J. *The First Americans, 1607–1690.* New York: The Macmillan Company, 1927, 358p.
52. Winakor, G. *Time Lag Between Fashion and Accepted Fashion.* M.S. Thesis, Drexel Inst., 1954.
53. Young, Agnes Brooks. *Recurring Cycles of Fashion 1760–1937.* New York: Harper & Row, Publishers, 1937, 214p.
54. Young, K. *Social Psychology.* New York: Appleton-Century-Crofts, 1935, 680p.

Chapter 4

Clothing and the Wearer
His Personality and Self-concept

We have only to look at differences in choice of clothes and in attitudes toward them to realize that pressures from society are not the only forces which influence clothing and behavior toward clothing. Just as groups differ from one another so do individuals vary within a group in their thinking regarding clothing.

Clothes are an intimate part of ourselves. A slighting remark about an individual's clothing may be taken as a personal insult, for it not only reflects on the person's appearance but also on his taste and personal preferences. William James, an early psychologist, put it:

> The old saying that the human person is composed of three parts—soul, body, and clothes—is more than a joke. We so appropriate our clothes and identify ourselves with them that there are few of us who, if asked to choose between having a beautiful body clad in raiment perpetually shabby and unclean, and having an ugly and blemished form always spotlessly attired, would not hesitate a moment before making a decisive reply [18:292].

We are as unique and individualistic in the way we dress as in our finger prints. If two women wear identical dresses to a social function they are embarrassed and yet show their individuality by their choice of accessories and by subtle differences such as the tightness of a belt. This obvious individuality in the selection and wearing of clothes and in grooming has led us to look for relationships between choice of clothing and other more fundamental individual differences.

We consider that clothes are an expression of the self but just what do we mean by *self* in this connection? Psychologists have used many terms such as *self, ego, personality,* and *self-concept,* but, unfortunately, there are no definitions of these terms which are accepted by all or are used consistently by all. In our discussions we will distinguish between the self as doer and knower and the self-concept. The self as doer and knower behaves in characteristic ways in adjusting to his environment. In describing these characteristic ways of reacting we will use the term personality. The self-concept is the individual's perception of his own characteristics, his abilities or his failings, his appearance, and the total organization of characteristics which he perceives as distinguishing him as an individual.

Self-concept

The phenomenal self or self as perceived by the individual was important theoretically in the early days of psychology. It occupied a prominent place in the psychology of William James. The perceived self he termed the *me* and he distinguished between the *material me,* the *social me* and the *spiritual me.* James is still quoted today in almost any discussion of self or self-concept, and his chapters on the self contain not only the most vivid writing but also some of the clearest thinking we have on this topic.

As behaviorism came into vogue and experimental psychologists were concerned with problems such as learning which could be brought into the laboratory, the self was dropped almost entirely from the psychologist's vocabulary. Freud was the notable exception, but, because his theories were so foreign to their way of thinking, the experimental psychologists tended to reject everything in his system.

In recent years with the emergence of the field of social psychology we again find that the self has a prominent place in psychological, or, at least social-psychological theories, especially in the role theory of social psychology. However, experimental work has not as yet caught up with theory and we still find relatively little research on problems related to the self.

SOMATIC SELF

To organize our discussion of this complex topic, we will differentiate between various aspects of the self-concept. The first of these we will call the *somatic self.* By this term we will mean the self as body or the physical characteristics of the self which are perceived.

Clothing plays a very important part in one's concept of the somatic self. The limits of the body seem to be extended or contracted by the clothing. Most of us have noted that if the clothing is padded or extended we feel that the body itself is larger in that dimension or if the clothing is snug we feel smaller. Flügel (14) has pointed out how clothing can extend the perceived limits of the body, and as early as 1897 Lotze gave examples of this, such as, feeling the body extend to the end of the cane.

Compton (9) found that mental patients with weak body-image boundaries preferred clothing fabrics of more saturated colors and strong figure-ground contrasts which would tend to help define body limits. Unfortunately, there is no direct measure for the perceived body limits. In this study the body-image boundary was measured indirectly by the Rorschach test.

The perceived appearance or relative attractiveness of the somatic-self is obviously even more dependent upon the clothing of the individual than are the limits of the body. Most of the studies on the perceived appearance of the self have dealt with feelings of satisfaction or dissatisfaction with one's appearance. Kitamura (19) reports on this sort of study with adolescent boys. He found that interest in appearance and feelings of dissatisfaction increased with age during adolescence.

Ryan (27) related (1) the individual's concept of his appearance and the group's concept of it; (2) the individual's concept of his appearance and his estimate of the group's concept; and (3) the individual's estimate of the group concept and the actual group concept. The hypotheses were that those who over- or underrated themselves as compared with the group ratings and with their estimate of the group ratings would differ in interest in clothing, personality factors, and in social participation from those who were accurate with their estimates of the group rating. However, nearly one-half of the girls rated themselves and estimated the group rating the same as the group rated them. The remainder who over- or underrated themselves as compared with the group did not differ on the various factors listed in the hypotheses from those who rated themselves the same as the group. These results may have been due to the fact that the sample was fairly homogeneous and that there were few poorly dressed individuals in the sample. The technique of rating the self, the others in a small group, and estimating the groups rating of the self, however, might prove valuable in further studies of the self-concept.

SOCIAL-SELF

Under social-self we will classify two general types of self-concept—the *sort-of-person-I-am* and the self as a *member* of a group. Probably the most common reference we make to ourselves is as this or that sort-of-person. The concept a person has of himself possessing certain characteristics is an important determiner of his behavior or of the roles which he assumes. Certainly it is going to play an important part in his choice of clothing. The woman who thinks of herself as a *femme fatale* will choose quite different clothes from the woman who considers herself an efficient business woman. The relationship does not end here, however. The way in which a person dresses is also going to influence his self-concept. The woman who is wearing a business suit is not likely to perceive herself as a *femme fatale* while she is wearing the suit, but at other times and in other clothes she may see herself as attractive to the opposite sex.

In addition to the class of social-self concepts which deal with the sort-of-person-I-am, we also have another large group of self-concepts that are related to belongingness or membership in groups, classes, or divisions. The membership may be in an organized group such as a sorority, a larger group such as the Presbyterian church or the Democratic party; it may be unorganized such as housewife, career woman, college-educated, or white collar worker; it may be a group the individual has chosen to join such as the country club or the League of Women Voters, or a group into which the individual was born, such as female, white, and a citizen of the United States. In many of these, like the sort-of-person-I-am, the self as member is aided and strengthened by clothing. The nun, because of her habit, is continually reminded of the fact that she belongs to a certain order and that as a member of the order certain things are expected of her, while as a professor I tend to choose suits which I consider appropriate, and wearing a suit reminds me of the role I have assumed. We will discuss influence of the self-concept on the role in more detail in the following chapter when we deal with the effects of clothing on behavior.

The self-concepts vary according to the situation. Obviously at any one given time I am not going to be aware of all possible parts of the somatic and social selves but only the aspects which are relevant to the situation. At one time one aspect of the self is perceived and at another time another aspect.

Each of the types of self-concepts are composed of characteristics which vary in consistency and in importance or centrality. One day, dressed in certain clothing and groomed in a particular way I may perceive myself as being very chic and fashionable and at another time I may see myself as being old-fogyish, while I might always be consistent in thinking of myself as being neat about my clothes. The perceived importance or basicness of traits may also vary. Combs and Snygg (8) have termed the characteristics of the perceived self which vary from time to time and which are not as important or as central to the personality the *phenomenal self* while the characteristics which are consistent as central perception of the self they term *self-concept*. Although recognizing that perceived characteristics vary in permanency and centrality we have not used these distinct terms. In the first place we do not believe that there is a clear-cut line between the two. Rather perceptions of both consistency and fundamentality vary along continuums. Furthermore, these continua may be independent of each other. For example, I might nearly always consider myself neat in my appearance but at the same time consider this as a trivial aspect of my total personality.

We should also make clear that the self-concept may or may not agree with the person as seen by other people or measured by some independent means. I may, for example, consider myself as very friendly and yet others may consider me very reserved.

In summarizing the relations of clothing to self-concept we might point out that, theoretically at least, clothing plays a relatively important part in establishing the self-concept and conversely the self-concept is important in determining our choice of clothing. For each of the types of self-concept we can give examples which illustrate the importance of clothing. There is very little research evidence, however, which indicates the relative importance of clothing or gives us situations under which clothing affects the self-concept or how it affects it.

We can formulate some hypotheses. For example, we might expect clothing to be of greater influence on the more trivial and less consistent aspects of the self (Comb's and Snygg's phenomenal self) than on the more permanent and central characteristics. Symonds (35) has suggested that a common way of enhancing self-esteem is to identify and copy the clothing of an admired person. Another hypothesis might be that the less favorable the over-all self-concept the greater the interest in clothes and the felt need for clothes.

Personality

In an earlier chapter (Chapter 1) we discussed the way in which the perception of personality characteristics was influenced by the clothing and grooming of the perceived person. In this chapter we are concerned with the *wearer* and whether his clothing choices or clothing behavior are related to the particular kind of person he is or to specific personality characteristics.

Many popular articles and some textbooks have assumed that there are very specific relationships between the type of personality and the colors and lines which each type will choose. They have gone one step further and assumed that body build and physical coloring are correlated with personality types and that each type does or should wear certain colors and lines. What evidence do we have which supports or contradicts these theories? What evidence do we have that there is any relationship between clothing choices and the personality or between clothing and any specific personality characteristics?

Before we attempt to answer the questions we should understand what we mean by personality. First of all we will rule out the popular conception of personality as referring to an individual's superficial attractiveness. In this sense personality is considered as something which individuals possess in quantity. We hear people describing someone as having "loads of personality" or as having "very little personality." Personality as defined by the psychologist and as we wish to use it here is much more than this superficial aspect of manners.

Personality, as we will use the term, is a description of an individual's typical behavior or the roles which he most frequently assumes. We will follow the definition of Allport who says "Personality is the dynamic organization within the individual of those psychophysical systems that determine his unique adjustments to his environment [2:48]." Each individual behaves in characteristic ways or assumes characteristic roles and it is the characteristic behavior which constitutes his personality.

In describing these systems of unique adjustment in the individual we will use the term *trait*. A trait is one mode of adjustment of the individual. Any personality is described by the use of a large number of these trait names. A trait is not something which is possessed completely or not at all, but rather may be regarded as something which is possessed to a certain degree. Thus, one person may adjust to relevant situations with a certain amount of aggressiveness while another may meet situations with less or more aggression than the first individual. Most of the adjectives ordinarily used in describing any person may be considered as traits as long as they describe consistent modes of his adjustment. Thus, in describing the personality of an individual we would use as many or as few trait names as necessary to describe his characteristic adjustments and each trait might be typical of the person to a certain degree.

This definition of the term is very different from the "type" theories of personality which, as mentioned earlier, frequently have been used for giving assumed relationships between clothing and personality. The number of types vary from one theory to another. One theory often used in relating clothing to personality divides everyone into two types—the Yin and the Yang. This is conceived as a scale much as the masculine–feminine scale with an undetermined number of gradations between the extremes. Other theories have used a larger number of classifications but instead of varying along one scale the classifications are like pigeon holes and each person is assigned to his particular pigeon hole. Thus, we may have people divided into three types such as the ingénue, the garçonne, and the dramatic or perhaps into five or six types. These theories are all similar in that they make the assumption that all people fit into the given number of classifications and that there is a correlation between the physical build and coloring of the individual, a group of personality traits, and the clothing which is "right" for his particular "type." The difficulties with this approach are obvious if you attempt to classify your own friends using any of these systems. The type-theories generally are unacceptable because they oversimplify the description of personality. They assume that an individual, either has or does not have a given trait rather than allowing for a continuum between two extremes; they assume that if an individual has one trait he also has all of the related ones; and they also assume correlations between physical coloring and build which have not been confirmed by research.

It is disappointing to many that we cannot give specific "rules" for expressing personality. It would be very convenient to be able to know you were "dressed right" if you followed a specific formula. Not only does the average individual wish to find some relations between body and intelligence and temperament but scientists themselves have hoped to find positive relationships. Many of the studies which have shown negative results were undertaken in the hope of finding significant relationships. As Paterson has said:

> Man's search for an intimate connection between inner function and outer structure seems merely to reflect his universal tendency to think in terms of positive, rather than negative, relationships. The history of science itself shows there has been far keener interest in establishing a new relationship than in discovering the absence of a relation previously assumed to exist. Many there are who insist upon the scientific value of positive findings and deny, or at least disparage, the issue of negative results. With this in mind, the writer is quite prepared to see his audience somewhat crestfallen and disillusioned at the trend toward negative evidence manifest throughout our discussion of the relation between physical and mental development [15:168–169].

The only positive results in this sort of study have been those of Sheldon (30) who, basing his work on Kretchmer's theory, measured a group of 200 men and subjected them to a temperament analysis in which they were rated on 60 traits of temperament. There was, in the case of these men, a positive correlation between three classifications of body build and three clusters of traits which were classified. Thus the endomorph (softness and roundness predominating) was usually a viscerotonic (relaxation, love of comfort, need for affection and approval, pleasure in eating, amiability, and tolerance); the mesomorph (bone and muscle predominating) was usually the somatotonic (assertiveness in posture and movement, energetic activity, love of power and risk, physical courage, directness of manner, noisiness and need of action when troubled); and finally the ectomorph (linearity and fragility predominating) was usually the cerebrotonic (restraint and tightness in posture and movement, love of privacy, emotional restraint, unpredictability of attitude, poor sleep habits, and need of solitude when troubled). There has been criticism of these studies in that there are too few cases and that the men who were expecting

to find a positive relationship were the ones who were making the classifications. Also it has been pointed out that there would naturally be a relationship
in some of these instances. For example, the man who enjoys eating and is
relaxed would be expected to be fat while the man who loves physical activity
would naturally be more muscular. Sheldon has not attempted to say whether
the body build determines the temperament or whether the temperament determines the body build. Whether future research will show that not even
this much is true or will show that there are more significant positive relationships is impossible to say. The results so far, however, are far from the specific
relationships between physical characteristics and personality which the type
theories assume.

These studies have not dealt with clothing and it might be argued that
relationships between clothing and personality would be more probable than
relationships between personality and physical characteristics since the individual does choose his own clothing and does not choose his physical appearance. On the other hand, when we were discussing the perception of personality characteristics we found that judges were unable to identify correctly by
more than chance the personality characteristics from the observation of the
person. If there were positive relationships between specific colors or lines and
personality traits, they surely would have been learned and we would be able
to judge correctly. Therefore, we cannot expect to find many clear-cut positive
relationships between specific attributes of clothing and personality characteristics. This does not mean, however, that there are none and we may find
other sorts of relationships between various personality characteristics and
clothing interest, attitudes, or behavior.

One theory, which we mentioned earlier (see Introduction), assumes a
positive relationship between interest in clothing or the emphasis placed upon
clothing and certain aspects of personality. Specifically the theory postulates
that the individual who is unsure of himself or has low self-esteem, especially
in the social situation, will place more emphasis on the importance of clothes
than will the individual who is self-assured socially. We have some research
evidence which contributes to this point.

Stepat (34) investigated concern about clothing and appearance in relation
to certain aspects of personality. A check list of 102 items was developed to
measure the concern in areas of clothing and appearance. The items were divided into three areas and six categories. The areas were: (1) personal and
social aspects, (2) judgment or feelings of ability to make satisfactory decisions, and (3) skills and information. The categories were: selection, wardrobe planning, relation of clothing to mental health, finance, shopping practices
and grooming and care of clothing. Personality was measured by one of three
tests. Two of these were tests designed to measure social and emotional ad-

justment.[1] The third (Mooney Problem Check List) gives lists of problems in a number of areas such as health, finance, and social activities, and a high number of problems checked in any given area suggests maladjustment in that area. The sample in this study consisted of college freshmen, all from one institution. The girls who checked the fewest number of problems in clothing and grooming tended to have high scores on the personality adjustment scales or to check the fewest problems in other areas. In short, the girls who had more clothing problems seemed to have less satisfactory social and emotional adjustment. There was also evidence in this study that those who had the fewest clothing problems have a broader range of interests, activities and experiences. The significant relationships were between total scores on the clothing problem check list and personality factors rather than those involving clothing problems in a specific area or category. This study does lend support to the theory that those who are less secure have a greater need and hence place greater importance on clothing, but it is merely suggestive. The clothing problem check list may have reflected difficulty in every area. The crucial test would come if we could solve the clothing problems and find if improvement in the areas of social and personality adjustment then followed.

In a clinical study Machover asked her subjects to draw a human figure. They were given no other instructions (22). These drawings were used as a projective technique to see if this simple procedure could be used in the place of more complicated projective techniques. As a small part of her conclusions she found that:

> . . . study of drawings in coordination with clinical histories reveals a small, but significant proportion of individuals who consistently over-clothe the figures they draw with a great deal of conviction and energy spilled into the drawing task. For purposes of convenience, those who overclothe the figure may be referred to as clothes-narcissists. Although both of these groups share in common infantile and egocentric emotionality and more than an average degree of sexual maladjustment, they do offer interesting contrasts in their drawings, and correspondingly in their personalities. . . . The clothes narcissist is superficially quite sociable and extraverted. The sociability is, however, more motivated by a strong appetite for social approval and dominance than by genuine object interest. Drawings of self-sex done by females of the clothes-narcissist types are characterized by overattention to cosmetic features, adornment, and glamour. In general, these individuals veer toward a psychopathic type of adjustment. The body-narcissist, with his

---

[1] The tests were the Washburn Social Adjustment Inventory which is composed of six objective-type subtests of social and emotional adjustment: happiness, alienation, sympathy, purpose, impulse-judgment, control; and the Minnesota Personality Scale. This is designed to measure five aspects of personality: morale, social adjustment, family relations, emotionality and economic conservatism.

display of muscle power, accords more with the schizoid, self-absorbed, and introverted type of personality. He is preoccupied with his body processes, often to the point of engaging in long and strenuous periods of body development for its own sake. Sexually he probably restricts himself largely to auto-erotic stimulations. He derives no genuine satisfaction in social intercourse, preferring his own fantasy ruminations [22:77].

This study suggests possible lines of research but should not be taken as valid and reliable evidence that Machover's conclusions hold true. In the first place the criteria which are used to diagnose the personality differences are not given. In the second place the number of cases upon which her conclusions are based is not given. Finally, there is no indication of how consistent the findings are.

In a study by Ryan (27) a possible technique for relating interest in clothing to personality adjustment was investigated. Five college women who had a very low interest in clothing were given the Rorschach personality test and compared with five who indicated great interest in clothing. There were obviously too few cases to show significant results. Nevertheless, assuming the validity of the Rorschach test, the results did indicate that this procedure might be a profitable one to pursue further. The results of the tests on these few cases seemed to indicate that there was no difference in the severity of the problems of adjustment but that there might be a difference in the mode of adjustment adopted by the members of the two groups. The low interest group tended to be:

1. swayed less by emotion;
2. less dependent upon the environment for stimulation, having a richer imaginative life;
3. slightly more mature in its emotional response to the environment;
4. felt less anxiety from an inadequately controlled affectivity, and was helped by a greater capacity to work out disturbance in fantasy activity.

The high interest group tended to be:

1. thrown more on the environment for its adjustment;
2. more responsive to its pressures, and showed more anxiety directed toward the environment;
3. tended to emphasize modes of adjustment more closely related to overt patterning of behavior. (The emphasis placed upon clothing is an illustration of this.)

It is suggestive that the results in these two studies are similar. Those who emphasize clothing in their drawings and those who have high interest in clothing were in both cases more sociable and more dependent on others while those who underclothed their figures and those who were uninterested in clothing were more introverted and dependent not upon others but upon fantasy for adjustment. These studies indicate that there is need for more work along this line.

A recent study by Aiken (1) uses a promising technique for finding relationships between personality and specific kinds of interest in clothing. He took statements concerning clothing behavior and clothing interest from a number of studies (Flügel, Hartmann, Silverman and Barr). These were checked as true or false by 300 students. He found thirty-three statements which grouped themselves into five clusters of items which tended to go together: decoration in dress, comfort in dress, interest in dress, conformity in dress, and economy. The new list of thirty-three statements was again presented to 160 students of the original group who were also given a personality inventory test and the Allport-Vernon-Lindzey values test.

As measured by the tests in this study, those who checked the "Decoration in dress" cluster tended to be conscientious, conventional, nonintellectual, sympathetic and social. Those checking "Comfort in dress" were self-controlled, sociable, and deferent to authority. Those with high "Interest in dress" tended to be conventional, conscientious, stereotyped in thinking, persistent, tense, suspicious and insecure. Those high in "Conformity in dress" more often were conscientious, moral, sociable, traditional, submissive. Finally those checking the "Economy" cluster were responsible, conscientious, alert, efficient, precise, controlled and intelligent. Although, these results cannot be projected beyond the population from which his sample was drawn, this study suggests another method of attacking the problem of personality as related to specific types of interest in clothes. Aiken points out that the students in the sample with which he was dealing were higher in religious values than the population as a whole. They may also have been high on certain personality traits such as conscientiousness and conformity which are found in several groupings. These traits, then, may differentiate his sample from the population as a whole rather than be characteristic of those with specific clothing interests.

RELATIONSHIP BETWEEN PERSONALITY FACTORS AND CHOICE OF CLOTHES

Several studies, especially those dealing with adolescents have shown that those who are rated high by others in appearance tend to be more sociable and outgoing than those who are rated low (for example, Silverman's study described in Chapter 13). This would be expected since we have just noted that those who are most interested in clothing or assign to it the greatest importance are more socially oriented. The studies give no indication of which is cause and which effect. It may be that those who are most interested in clothes become more sociable as a way of displaying their clothing. Whatever the cause there does seem to be a positive correlation between sociability and good appearance as rated by others.

Many would like to find relationships between personality and clothing choices more specific than just well or poorly dressed, such as the relationship between the choice of certain colors, lines or designs and specific personality traits. A number of studies have been planned to test for such relationships. Hoffman (17) compared the scores on a personality inventory, the Allport-Vernon test of values, and scores on an Art judgment test with analysis of clothing modeled by the participants and with ratings (by the interviewer) of esthetic qualities in the subject's home. She found high correlations among various esthetic factors (such as color, design, fit, fashion) but few significant relationships between any of these and personality or interest scores. She found *no* statistically significant relationships between color(s) in the ward-robe and any personality factors. She did find, as we noted in the previous chapter, that a preference for dressy clothes and for "dressing up for home entertaining" was related to the social factor in the personality test and to self-confidence. This seems to confirm the results on interest in clothing and sociability. Another result which confirmed a result mentioned earlier (see Chapter 3) was that greater interest in clothes was exhibited by those from urban areas than those from rural areas.

Bjerstedt (5) and Barrett and Eaton (4) report studies which have attempted to relate color preference to personality factors. In both of these studies the object was to relate preference for color per se rather than choice of color in clothing, but positive results in such studies would furnish hy-pothesis, at least, for relations between personality and choice of color in clothing. Bjerstedt investigated differences between the preference for warm (red–yellow) and cool (blue–green) colors. Although the studies were preliminary and only thirty subjects were used in the part of the research relating color preference to personality, he found differences which might serve as bases for further work. Individuals preferring warm colors tended to greater activation, that is shorter reaction times and quicker tempo of tapping. In addition they tended to display a higher degree of "immediate stimulus receptivity." This was shown in two major ways: they had less tendency to rework contradictory data and to have less ability to keep out distractions. Differences were small and not strong but if results are confirmed in a larger study which the author planned then they may serve as hypotheses in clothing choices as related to personality. The second study by Barrett and Eaton also investigated the preference for colors, tints or shades in relation to personality. Of the 114 subjects only 10 preferred the shades (that is, the darker colors) and so comparisons were made between those who had a definite preference for color and those who liked tints best. The subjects were given a battery of tests relating to personality differences and on the majority of the aspects measured there were no differences between those who preferred the light colors (tints) to those who preferred medium brightness (colors). However, there were some differences between the two groups.

> The group of subjects preferring colors, while differing among themselves, as a group had fewer associations to words, a higher annoyance score on the Personal Audit, a lower morale score on the Minnesota Personality Scale, took a longer time to complete Cason's Annoyance Test, tended toward greater overestimation of the number of dots on cards, scored more toward the masculine end of the Terman and Miles scales, and more often believed that their own emotions were usually or almost always recognized by the behavior, and reported fewer changes of mind on social and economic issues.
> The data of these experiments have been interpreted to mean that individuals who prefer colors respond more directly and with greater interest to the objects and objective events of the external environment while the persons who prefer tints view the external world from the point of view of subjective values and live more in their own thoughts [p. 231–232].

These studies suggest that the choice of various classifications of colors such as the warm versus cool or saturated versus unsaturated colors rather than specific hues might be related to personality differences. This agrees with the conclusions we reached when discussing the perception of personality characteristics as dependent upon color (see Chapter 1). It should be emphasized that these results are not only tentative, but that they are concerned with simple color preference in the abstract and not with the choice of colors to wear.

Compton (10) has more nearly answered our question concerning personality as related to clothing choices, analyzing color and design preferences in clothing fabrics. College women were given paired comparison choices of (1) eighteen fabrics in which six different hues were each presented in a tint, a shade (that is, dark) and a saturated color (2) fifteen choices of fabric designs; in each pair the designs were alike but varied in contrast. (3) fifteen choices of fabric in which one in each pair had a large design and the other a small design. Those who gave strong preferences in their choices were compared on some personality factors, scores on the Johnson Home Economics Interest Inventory and on their physical build and coloring. No relationships were found between their choices and their physical characteristics. Those with high sociability scores, that is those who were outgoing, sociable and forward, tended to choose either the saturated colors or the deep shades rather than tints. Those who chose the small design rather than the large design: were more often interested in the merchandising of clothing than in other home economics professions; scored higher on the good impression personality measure; that is, were more anxious to present themselves as unaffected, natural and modest; and they also tended to have high femininity scores.

The range of color preference (that is, the number of colors liked) has also been found to be related to personality. In a study of teenage girls Pearson's subjects who had the highest range of color preference tended to be well balanced emotionally, extroverted and to dominate others, while those who concentrated their preferences on the smallest range of colors tended to dislike solitude, and to seek advice often (26). This suggests another dimension in which relationships between clothing choices and personality might be investigated further.

In recent study, Ditty (12) investigated the preference for masculine versus feminine clothes of college women as related to their masculinity–femininity, sociability–individuality, and social aspirations. The scales on which she measured masculine-feminine clothing preferences were a series of pictures of: sleepwear, leisure or sportswear, slips, daytime dresses, date or dance dresses, and suits. The series of pictures for each type of garment had been ranked by judges according to femininity. Increased femininity, as measured in this study,[2] was related to the more feminine clothing choices for items of sleepwear, slips, and leisure or sportswear, (but not to choice of feminine daytime dresses, date dresses, or suits), and to greater fluctuation in clothing choices. Individuals who were high in social maturity were more consistent in their choices among the six types of clothing than were those who were classified by their test scores as socially immature. Her conclusions were that as social maturity increased, clothing became a medium of self-expression while as maturity decreased there was greater variation in clothing preferences possibly indicating that the clothing choices were related to the individual's perception of the social role rather than individual self-expression.

Summary

The concept we have of ourselves determines to a great extent the clothes which we choose. At the same time the clothing which we wear influences the way in which we perceive ourselves. In the discussion of self-concept as related to clothing we differentiated between the *somatic* self and the *social* self. The social self includes the sort-of-person-I-am and the self as a member of a group. In each of these classifications of the self-concept we can give examples from our own experience of the interdependence of self-concept and clothing, but as yet we have little research evidence to support our hypotheses.

Type theories and rules for dressing to fit the personality has been the

---

[2] The test used was the Personal Preference Scale by Maurice H. Krout and Johanna K. Tarbic as revised in 1951. This is designed to discriminate: masculinity vs. femininity, social extroversion vs. introversion, and aspirational tendencies.

most common approach to relationship between personality and clothing. We find almost no research evidence to support such theories. We do find some evidence that interest in clothing for the self is related to the type of adjustment the subject makes to his environment and also that specific types of interest may be related to specific personality traits. We also have some evidence that preference for certain broad classifications, such as dark versus light colors, saturated versus unsaturated colors, dressy versus tailored clothes, may be related to personality differences.

Bibliography

1. Aiken, Lewis R. The relationship to selected measures of personality in undergraduate women. *J. Soc. Psychol.* 59(1), 1963, 119–128.
2. Allport, G. W. *Personality; A Psychological Interpretation,* New York: Holt, Rinehart and Winston, Inc., 1937, 588p.
3. Allport, G. W. The ego in contemporary psychology. *Psychol. Rev.* 50, 1943, 451–478.
4. Barrett, Dorothy M. and Eaton, Elizabeth. Preference for color or tint and some related personality data. *J. of Personality* 15, 1947, 222–232.
5. Bjerstedt, A. Warm-cool color preferences as potential personality indicators: preliminary note. *Percept. Mot. Skills.* 10, 1960, 31–34.
6. Byers, Margaretta and Kamholz, Consuelo. *Designing Women.* New York: Simon and Schuster, Inc., 1938, 276p.
7. Combs, A. W. A phenomenological approach to adjustment theory. *J. of Abn. and Soc. Psychol.* 44, 1949, 29–35.
8. Combs, A. W. and Snygg, D. *Individual Behavior: A New Frame of Reference for Psychology.* New York: Harper & Row, Publishers, 1949, 386p.
9. Compton, Norma H. Body-image boundaries in relation to clothing fabric and design preferences of a group of hospitalized psychotic women. *J. of Home Ec.* 56, 1964, 40–44.
10. Compton, Norma H. Personal attributes of color and design preferences in clothing fabrics. *J. of Psychol.* 54 (1) 1962, 191–195.
11. Dearborn, G. The psychology of clothing. *Psychol. Rev. Monogr.* 26, 1918, 1–72.
12. Ditty, Donna D. *Social-Psychological Aspects of Clothing Preferences of College Women.* Ph.D. Thesis, Ohio State University. 1962.
13. Flaccus, L. W. Remarks on the psychology of clothes. *Pedag. Sem.* 13, 1906, 61–83.
14. Flügel, J. *The Psychology of Clothes.* London: Hogarth Press, 1930, 257p.
15. Harris, J. A., Jackson, C. M., Paterson, D. G., and Scammon, R. E. *The Measurement of Man.* Minneapolis: University of Minnesota Press, 1930.

16. Hartmann, G. W. Clothing: personal problem and social issue. *J. of Home Ec.* 41(6), 1949, 295–298.

17. Hoffman, Adeline. *Clothing Behavior Factors for a Specific Group of Women Related to Aesthetic Sensitivity and Certain Socio-Economic and Psychological Background Factors.* Ph.D. Thesis. Penna. State Univer. 1956.

18. James, W. *Principles of Psychology.* Vol. I, New York: Holt, Rinehart and Winston, Inc., 1890.

19. Kitamaura, S. On the feelings of satisfaction and dissatisfaction with one's own appearance and disposition. *Tohoku Psychologica Folia.* XII (3–4), 1951, 67–81.

20. Landis, J. T. Personality: a 1954 view. *J. of Home Ec.* 46, 1954, 459–462.

21. Laver, J. *Taste and Fashion.* New York: Dodd, Mead & Co., 1938, 271p.

22. Machover, Karen. *Personality Projection in the Drawing of the Human Figure.* Springfield, Ill.: Charles C Thomas, 1949, 181p.

23. Morton, Grace. *The Arts of Costume and Personal Appearance.* New York: John Wiley & Sons, Inc., 1943, 400p.

24. Murphy, G. *Personality: A Biosocial Approach to Origins and Structure.* New York: Harper & Row, Publishers, 1947, 999p.

25. Neiman, L. J. and Hughes, J. W. The problem of the concept of role— a re-survey of the literature. *Social Forces.* 30, 1951, 141–149.

26. Pearson, Lois Helman. Teen-agers' preference in clothes. *J. of Home Ec.* 42 (10), 1950, 801–802.

27. Ryan, Mary S. *Psychological Effects of Clothing: Part I, II, III, and IV.* Cornell Univer. Ag. Exper. Sta. Bull. 882, 898, 900 and 905, 1952–54.

28. Sarbin, T. Role theory. Chap. 6, 223–258 in Vol. I, *Handbook of Social Psychology* (Lindzey, G., Ed.). Cambridge, Mass.: Addison-Wesley Publishing Co., Inc., 1954.

29. Sheldon, W. H., Stevens, S. S. and Tucker, W. B. *The Varieties of Human Physique.* New York: Harper & Row, Publishers, 1940, 347p.

30. Sheldon, W. H. and Stevens, S. S. *The Varieties of Temperament.* New York: Harper & Row, Publishers, 1942, 520p.

31. Silverman, Sylvia S. *Clothing and Appearance, Their Psychological Implications for Teen-age Girls.* New York: Teachers College, Columbia University Contributions to Education, 912, 1945, 140p.

32. Spranger, E. *Types of Men.* Translated by Pigors, Paul, Niemeyer, 1928, 402p.

33. Stallings, Amelia. *A Study of Clothing Selection and Personal Appearance in Relation to Personality with Emphasis on Self-Acceptance.* M.S. Thesis, Southern Illinois Univer., 1957.

34. Stepat, Dorothy. *A Study of Clothing and Appearance Problems in Relation to Some Aspects of Personality and Some Cultural Patterns in a Group of College Freshman Girls.* Ph.D. Thesis, New York Univer., 1949.

35. Symonds, P. M. *The Ego and the Self.* New York: Appleton-Century-Crofts Inc., 1951, 229p.
36. Wilson, Shirley. *Selected Aspects of Clothing Behavior Associated with Success in Role Achievement and with Striving Among a Specific Group of College Women.* M.S. Thesis, Penna. State Univer., 1960.
37. Wylie, Ruth C. *The Self Concept.* Lincoln, Neb.: University of Nebraska Press, 1961, 370p.

Chapter 5

Individual Values, Interests, and Attitudes as Related to Clothing Behavior and Clothing Choices

*I*t is obvious that individuals vary as to the importance they place upon clothing, what they want it to do for them, and their reasons for choosing the clothes they do. We assume that their attitudes toward clothing are consistent with their attitudes and values in other areas. Thus, we would expect that the woman who tried to impress others by the elegance of her clothes would also want to impress others by the apparent expensiveness of her home, her car, and the clubs to which she belonged. In this chapter we shall look at some of the research evidence we have on clothing values, attitudes and interests and the way in which these are related to general values, attitudes and interests.

Values

We shall use the term *value* as a broader and more basic concept than attitudes or interests. Attitudes or interests are specific to a given topic while values are fundamental beliefs and feelings which include or direct our specific attitudes and interests. We assume an individual's basic values from his specific attitudes and interests. Thus, we may be interested in clothing design but if there is a basic value underlying the interest it might be the importance we place upon esthetics generally, and, in many facets of life, we would be interested in looking for and creating beauty. How we interpret what we see is determined by our basic values as well as the situation itself. Values, then, act as a directive or motivating force in behavior and in decision making. It can be assumed that values will operate as a directive force or motivate the individual in the field of clothing behavior and clothing choices as well as in other areas. This was suggested in the first report of the Northeast Regional Research Project in Textiles and Clothing. One of the hypotheses formulated as the result of the research project was: "Relationships between general satisfaction with a garment and specific components of satisfaction will vary with:

a. purpose for which the garment was chosen
b. differences in the wearers' motives, experiences, and values, some of which also may be expressed in other areas of living [26:60]."

Values are derived from an individual's experience, part of which is determined by the culture in which he lives. Thus certain values will be commonly held by members of a specific culture, but within each culture we also will find individual differences in the relative importance of various values. The question, then, is to determine the basic values and to discover how these relate to attitudes and interests in clothing and how they operate in determining clothing choices and clothing behavior.

Some may have a single value of such importance to them that it dominates and is the principal motivating influence in their lives. Most, however, have a number of values, some more important than others. Most of the research relating values to clothing has used the Allport-Vernon, or, more recently the Lindzey-Allport-Vernon, test based upon Spranger's six types of man. The purpose of this test is to rank the various values in order of their importance to the individual. The six basic values in this classification are:

(1) *The Theoretical.* The dominant interest of the theoretical man is the discovery of *truth.* In the pursuit of this goal he characteristically takes a "cognitive" attitude, one that looks for identities and differences; one that divests itself of judgments regarding the beauty or utility of objects, and seeks only to observe and to reason. Since the interests of the theoretical man are empirical, critical, and rational, he is necessarily an intellectualist, frequently a scientist or philosopher. His chief aim in life is to order and to systematize his knowledge.

(2) *The Economic.* The economic man is characteristically interested in what is useful. Based originally upon the satisfaction of bodily needs (self-preservation), the interest in utilities develops to embrace the practical affairs of the business world—the production, marketing, and consumption of goods, the elaboration of credit, and the accumulation

of tangible wealth. This type is thoroughly "practical" and conforms well to the prevailing stereotype of the average American business man . . . the economic man wants education to be practical, and regards unapplied knowledge as waste.

(3) *The Esthetic.* The esthetic man sees his highest value in *form* and *harmony*. Each single experience is judged from the standpoint of grace, symmetry, or fitness. He regards life as a manifold of events; each single impression is enjoyed for its own sake. He need not be a creative artist; nor need he be effete; he is esthetic if he but finds his chief interest in the artistic episodes of life.

The esthetic attitude is in a sense diametrically opposed to the theoretical; the former is concerned with the diversity, and the latter with the identities of experience. The esthetic man chooses, with Keats, to consider truth as equivalent to beauty, or else to agree with Mencken, that, "to make a thing charming is a million times more important than to make it true."

(4) *The Social.* The highest value for this type is *love* of people; whether of one or many, whether conjugal, filial, friendly, or philanthropic. The social man prizes other persons as ends, and is therefore himself kind, sympathetic, and unselfish. He is likely to find the theoretical, economic and esthetic attitudes cold and inhuman. In contrast to the political type, the social man regards love as itself the only suitable form of power, or else repudiates the entire conception of power as endangering the integrity of personality. In its purest form the social interest is selfless and tends to approach very closely to the religious attitudes.

(5) *The Political.* The political man is interested primarily in *power*. His activities are not necessarily within the narrow field of politics; but whatever his vocation, he betrays himself as a *Machtmensch*. Leaders in any field generally have high power value. Since competition and struggle play a large part in all life, many philosophers have seen power as the most universal and most fundamental of motives. There are, however, certain personalities in whom the desire for a *direct* expression of this motive is uppermost, who wish above all else for personal power, influence, and renown.

(6) *The Religious.* The highest value of the religious man may be called *unity*. He is mystical, and seeks to comprehend the cosmos as a whole, to relate himself to its embracing totality. Spranger defines the religious man as one "whose mental structure is permanently directed to the creation of the highest and absolutely satisfying value experience." Some men of this type are "immanent mystics," that is, they find in the affirmation of life and in active participation therein their religious experience. A Faust with his zest and enthusiasm sees something divine in every event. The "transcendental mystic" on the other hand seeks to unite himself with a higher reality by withdrawing from

life; he is the ascetic, and, like the holy men of India, finds the experience of unity through self-denial and meditation. In many individuals the negation and affirmation of life alternate to yield the greatest satisfaction.[1]

In the test the subject gives his preference for a series of paired-comparison statements and ranks in order of preference statements with four possible attitudes or answers. As each value is compared with every other value an equal number of times, the higher the score on a given value the greater the importance that value is assumed to have as a motivating influence for the individual.

The first research which used this test in relation to clothing was done by Newman, Nickerson and Bryer, (5) who related scores on the Allport-Vernon test of values with general "interest in clothes." The "interest in clothes" score was obtained from a questionnaire which asked questions such as the extent to which clothes affected the subjects' estimates of women, or their own personal satisfaction in wearing stylish clothes. They found no relation between men's interest in clothes and their scores on the value test. However, women who were high on economic, esthetic, or political values were also high on clothing interest, while there was a negative relation between clothing interest and scoring high on either religious or theoretic values. In this study there was also an attempt to relate specific interest in clothing to specific values by asking the respondents to rank the following:

"As far as my income allows I try to keep in style because:
(a) it creates good impression on other people. [Political]
(b) I obtain personal satisfaction from being well dressed even though no one sees me. [Esthetic]
(c) it helps me to make friends. [Social]
(d) stylish clothes show I am not poor [Economic]" (p. 267).

The authors found a low correlation between the answers checked in this question and the subjects' general values. The correlations were in the predicted direction, however, so they suggest that there is a relationship which more rigid experiments would disclose. The authors concluded that the specific interest of both sexes in their own appearance was generally consistent with their prevailing values.

The above study gave one set of specific relations between general values and attitudes toward clothing. Hartmann (10) suggested other clothing attitudes which might be related to the same classification of general values. He hypothesized the following relations:

---

[1] From G. W. Allport, P. E. Vernon, and G. Lindzey. *Study of Values. A Scale for Measuring the Dominant Interest in Personality,* rev. ed. Manual of Directions. Boston: Houghton Mifflin Company, 1960, pp. 13–14.

SPRANGER TYPE	CORRESPONDING EMPHASIS IN CLOTHING CHOICE
Theoretical	Stresses objective properties of fabrics, accurate measures.
Economic	Shrewd purchases; eliminates all "waste."
Esthetic	"If it is good-looking, nothing else matters."
Social	Conscientious; disturbed by rags vs. riches.
Political	Requires effects evoking admiration or submission from others
Religious–philosophical	Follows simplicity as ideal; original Quakerism.

These relations have never been investigated.

Lapitsky (15) hypothesized still other relations between general values and clothing values. In this instance the results were put to experimental test. For general values Lapitsky used the same general classification but dropped the theoretical and religious values because she believed these would not be related to interest in clothing. A second social value was added. The social value as described by Spranger and measured by the Allport-Vernon test stressed the philanthropic nature of the social value. Lapitsky hypothesized that in addition to this there was a value which stressed the need to be accepted and approved by others. Individuals in whom this value was dominant did not desire power over others and so would not place the political value first but they did want to have a feeling of belonging to the group. This value she hypothesized would be especially important to clothing attitudes and values. She formulated the following:

CLOTHING VALUES

Esthetic: The desire for, appreciation of, or concern with beauty in clothing.

Economic: The desire for comfort in clothing and for the conservation of time, energy, and money in relation to clothing usage or selection.

Political: The desire for obtaining prestige, distinction, leadership, or influence through clothing usage.

Social I: The expression of regard for fellow beings through clothing behavior.

Social II: The desire for obtaining social approval through clothing usage with conformity playing a prominent role.

She proposed, and the results of her study confirmed, the following hypotheses: (1) "the esthetic and economic clothing values will have more dominant positions in the value configuration of adult women than any of the other clothing values investigated," and (2) "positive relations will exist between clothing values and parallel general values [p. 78]." The importance of this study lies not only in the specific results obtained but also in the development of a device for measuring clothing values which already has proved useful in other studies and should be used in further experiments. It is only through repeated use of such tests with wide varieties of respondents that their validity and usefulness are established for general use. As they are used with many people in many different circumstances norms will be developed which will increase their worth as a research tool.

The Lapitsky clothing test was used in a study by Altpeter (3) in an investigation of relations between clothing values and certain aspects of consumer behavior. She found from a group of young married women that those who were rated above average on esthetic value enjoyed shopping, preferred to shop alone, searched until they found clothes they considered beautiful and unusual, and had a high interest in clothing. An above-average score on the economic value was related to buying traditional and comfortable styles, shopping primarily at local department stores, examining seams before buying and having little interest in shopping for clothes. Thus, this study together with Lapitsky's has shown us that our general basic values are consistent with values in the clothing area and that these in turn are consistent with at least some attitudes concerning clothing and behavior in the selection and use of clothing.

In a larger study Creekmore (6) related specific clothing behaviors to specific value orientations and specific needs. We have already described this study in some detail in the chapter on motivation (see p. 48–49). Creekmore used the Allport-Vernon-Lindzey test of values and compared the results with a clothing-interest inventory and a test of needs. She found that some clothing behaviors related to specific values more often than others. She hypothesized that the following relationships would be found between values and clothing behaviors and each of these was *partially confirmed* by her findings.

Clothing behavior	*Value rated high*
Management of clothing	Economic
Experimentation in clothing	Exploratory
Status symbol	Political
Appearance	Esthetic
Conformity	Social
Fashion	Political
Modesty	Religious

She also hypothesized the following relationships, but the data indicated that these hypotheses should be *rejected,* that is, there seemed to be no relationship between the specific clothing behavior and the value as predicted.

Clothing behavior	Value
Altruistic use of clothing	Social
Symbolic meaning interest	Religious
Theoretical	Theoretical
Clothing construction	Exploratory, sensory, economic, or esthetic

It should be kept in mind that her results for these latter hypotheses showed no positive relationships by *the measures* which she used or for her population. Her hypotheses may still be found to hold true with the use of other means of measuring clothing behavior or values. They might also hold for other populations.

In an earlier study Hoffman (11) found that those who scored high on the social-value scale of Allport and Vernon showed greater preference for dressy clothes and for dressing up for home entertainment and there was a positive relationship between suitability of wardrobe and high economic value. She found no positive relations, however, between esthetic values and factors in the respondents' wardrobe. There was a high positive relation between high political-value scores and the design quality of the wardrobe, the esthetic level of the home, and self-confidence in clothing.

Another attempt to develop a test of clothing values parallel to some of the values measured by the Allport-Vernon test was made by Finlayson (7). She related the scores on the Allport-Vernon test for the social, economic, and esthetic values to the relative importance of six components of satisfaction with sweaters: (1) becomingness, (2) beauty, (3) comfort, (4) likely to be admired by friends, (5) ease of care, (6) good buy. The relative importance of components of satisfaction was measured by two methods. The first consisted of a series of paired comparison statements such as: Would you rather have a sweater that is:

(1) Beautiful or becoming on you?
(2) Likely to be admired by friends or comfortable?
(3) Good buy (low cost and long wearing) or beautiful?

Each of the six components of satisfaction was paired with each other one. The interviewee was also asked to arrange the movable sections of a pie graph which were labeled with the six components. Her results showed that there was "a strong tendency for a general value to be operative in the selection of certain components that will bring satisfaction in clothing" [p.35]. The results of the preferential ranking of the six components by the two methods showed a perfect correlation when the mean ratings were compared. While there was some variation in individual cases, over 70 percent rated the same component as their first choice by the two instruments. In cases where there were differences the adjustable pie graph seemed, on further questioning, to give the most valid results. It was also less time consuming, therefore these results would indicate that the adjustable pie graph might be a better tool than a series of paired comparison statements for obtaining the relative importance of components of satisfaction with clothing.

Although there is still much research to be done, the evidence so far suggests that our general values are reflected in clothing values and that these in turn are related to specific clothing attitudes, interests, choices and to behavior in the selection and use of clothing.

Attitudes toward Clothing

We have already observed that attitudes concerning the relative importance of clothing are related to basic values. Those who have high religious and theoretic interests are inclined to put little emphasis upon clothes while those high in economic, political or esthetic values assign greater importance to clothes. In an earlier section (see p. 64–68) we also found that attitudes towards the importance of clothing vary with the socioeconomic status or occupation of the subject. In general, the white-collar worker or a member of the upper middle-economic group thinks that clothing is of greater importance while those of the upper-upper and the lower socioeconomic categories consider clothing less important. A number of studies (for example, Stout and Latzke (20)) have also shown that the importance placed upon clothing varies with the size of the subject's home town. Those from larger cities consider clothes more important than do those from small towns.

Variations may occur, however, not only in the attitude concerning the relative importance of clothing but also in the reasons which people feel make clothing important or not important. Alexander (2) listed the following reasons given by a large number of subjects for wanting to be well dressed.

I Physical Appearance:
    a. Minimize physical imperfections.
    b. Enhance physical attributes.
    This category includes all items which refer to clothes making the individuals' appearance more attractive physically.

II Expression of Personality (attempt to communicate):
    This category is concerned with items which deal with clothing as representative of the social aspects of self. Included are general statements which say something about the value of clothing in expressing individuality or personality.

III Impression (evokes a favorable judgment from others):
    a. To attract attention (same and/or opposite sex).
    b. To evoke initiating behavior of others (from attitudes favorable to friendship, hiring for a job, etc.).

This category includes items which indicate the importance of clothing in making an impression on someone else. If the respondent just mentioned making a good impression or attracting attention, subheading a. is used. If, however, the respondent goes farther and mentions effect or behavior desired or produced by someone else as a result, subheading b. is used.

IV Acceptance (belongingness, keeping friends, conforming):
The items included in the acceptance category have a definite in-group feeling. That is, a concern for the closer relationship involved in belonging and being accepted as an associate.

V Status (symbolic effect):
   a. Indicator of position and responsibility (e.g., I am a member of this group, therefore I must dress as people expect a person of my position to dress.)
   b. Associative effect-links position to the person (e.g., I want to be *like* a person in a certain position therefore I will dress like persons in this position.)
   This category is reserved for statements which give clothing importance as an indicator of a certain job or position in society. In the status category, the desire for audience approval is, essentially, subordinate to the desire to have people recognize—and respect—the job or position represented. Serving as an example for others is included in this category as it does have the connotation of position or authority.

VI Personal Satisfaction:
   a. Feeling of well-being and self-confidence.
   b. Physical comfort.
   This category includes items having to do with the respondent's feelings about himself. References to self-confidence and being able to devote oneself fully to the activity at hand when feeling self-assured are included here. The physical comfort subheading is to be used only when the respondent is quite specific that this is meant. For example, "makes me feel good" would be placed under the subheading a. if it appeared alone with no other explanatory words.

VII Negative (no importance):
   The negative category includes all responses which indicate that there is little or no importance attached to feeling well-dressed [p. 10–14].

For both men and women at various age levels the two reasons most frequently mentioned for desiring to be well-dressed were (1) it gives a feeling of self-confidence and well being and (2) it creates a favorable impression on others. Nevertheless there were differences between age groups and between the sexes in the frequency of certain reasons. Men, especially high school boys, more often than girls or women said that it was important to dress well because of the impression made upon others. High school girls and boys both more often mentioned acceptance by the group. As we shall see when we discuss implications of clothing for adolescents, this is consistent with their need to conform to the group. Self-confidence or a feeling of well-being was given relatively more often by both college girls and adult women, but was seldom mentioned by adult men. Women often said that feeling well-dressed gave a boost to their morale while men almost never mentioned this. Adult men were almost alone in saying that clothing was important as an indication of status. This study indicates not only some of the most commonly held attitudes towards the reasons for the importance of clothing but also shows how these attitudes vary with the age and sex of the respondent. Unfortunately the wording of the questions was not identical for all groups and until we have further evidence we cannot assume that the differences between the groups are valid differences. Furthermore the adults and college women were all from relatively high socioeconomic groups. The men were either sales clerks or professors and the women informants were their wives. The high school respondents were selected in that they were in high school rather than dropouts, but otherwise were from random distribution in social classes.

Form and Stone (8) found that not only the relative importance but the meaning of clothing varied with the occupational group. White-collar workers appraised clothing in terms of its potential for favorably impressing others at work. Clothes, they thought, were a symbol which they could use to influence others, while manual workers were often unaware that others might judge them by clothing. White-collar workers likewise were more tolerant of people who "spend lots of time, money and effort on their clothes and personal appearance" (p. 14) than were the manual workers. Similarly, when the respondents were asked reasons for rejecting inappropriate work clothes the manual workers felt that inappropriate clothing should be rejected because it might interfere with work performance, comfort, or safety on the job. The white-collar worker gave reasons related to the expectations of reference groups, (such as employees, clientele, customers or the public) or because inappropriate clothes were not in good taste.

We have discussed some general attitudes toward clothing—its importance and reasons for its importance. Other more specific attitudes, such as the factors necessary for a satisfactory garment, will be discussed in following chapters.

Interest in Clothes

Interest is a "liking" for a class of things or a field of study as opposed to indifference or dislike. It includes a readiness to be concerned with the class of things or field. The greater the interest the individual has in something, the more attention he will give to that subject and the more he will perceive things which relate to that interest. Thus, when we say that an individual has an interest in clothes we infer that he likes clothes and is observant of clothes. By measuring the extent of this interest we may be able to answer many questions concerning clothing motivation and clothing behavior such as: Does the socially well-adjusted individual generally have great or little interest in clothes? Does interest in clothes vary with age, with socioeconomic status or education? Is the individual with high interest in clothing apt to be better dressed? Does she spend more time, effort and relatively more money on clothes? What factors lead to greater or less interest in clothes? Does the individual with high interest have a better chance of success in the merchandizing of clothes, the designing of clothes or the teaching of clothing?

MEASUREMENT OF GENERAL INTERESTS

The measurement of various kinds of interest in a systematic way dates from about 1920. Since that time measurement of interests has played a prominent part in individual psychology and has been used extensively in vocational counseling, in guidance work, and by personnel departments in industry.

The early work in measuring interests was largely concerned with sampling a large number of possible interests to see which occupation would be most acceptable to an individual. A test of this sort might contain a large variety of occupations from which the individual was to indicate those occupations which he felt he would like and those he thought he would dislike. The disadvantages of such a method of measurement is that some chance factor such as a great respect or fondness for an individual in a certain occupation might color an individual's attitude toward that occupation. The results also "depend upon the ways in which the questions are phrased, for some questions concerning vocational interest are so put as to elicit information concerning vocational choice, some to ascertain vocation preferences, and some to evoke vocational fantasies. The degree of realism represented by the expression of interest varies with the type of question asked" [23:377].

Other attempts at measuring interest included lists of activities for choice such as "skilled handwork," "broad planning," "attention to detail." The difficulty with this type of test is that it is so broad it is difficult for the individual to answer accurately. A person may like to "pay attention to detail" in one area and not in another.

The more recent developments of interest measurement can be illustrated by a discussion of Strong's (22) "Vocational Interest Inventory" and the research which has been carried out with it. The 420 items in this inventory are classified into 8 parts: (1) occupations, (2) amusements, (3) school subjects, (4) activities, (5) peculiarities of people, (6) order of preference of activities, (7) comparison of interest between two items, and (8) rating of present abilities and characteristics.

The aim has been to take a sample of all kinds of interests and aversions and to find which groups or patterns of interests differentiate different occupational groups. The scoring of the tests is developed by giving the inventory to large numbers of persons in various occupations. If the majority in occupation "A" show preferences for a certain number of items as contrasted to individuals not in that occupation, then a weighted scoring key can be made up for interest in that occupation. A scoring key can be made up for each occupation which has a unique pattern of interests shown by those in that occupation. One of the difficulties of these inventory studies is that the individual taking the test often checks the items which he thinks will give the best impression rather than the ones in which he is really interested. Present-day techniques attempt to avoid this shortcoming by including a very large number of items of such varied sorts that it is difficult for the subject to decide how to mark them to give the best impression. This flaw in the inventory method must, however, be kept in mind.

The inventory test discovers the patterns of interest common to a particular group but does not tell us anything about the depth of interest nor the kind of interest. We can say that the individual has interests in common with professionals in a particular field, but it tells us nothing about the individual who is interested in a particular area as a hobby. For example, we could find that an individual has the same interests as a musician but we would not find out his degree of interest in listening to or playing music for his own enjoyment. The items of the inventory are answered by checking "like," "indifferent" or "dislike." In some cases five instead of three categories are given, but in all cases it is the individual's own judgment of whether he "likes," "likes very much" or is "indifferent" to an object, occupation or whatever item he is checking. In another type of item the respondent is asked to rank several statements in order of preference.

Another type of test which has been used to measure interest is often termed the objective type of test. As opposed to the subjective judgments in the inventories, this type of test is an objective test of information, memory, or amount of activity in a certain area. The assumption underlying objective tests is that if an individual is interested in a certain area then this interest will be manifested in his activity, in the information he has acquired, or in his memory for items pertaining to that area. Very little work has been done using the amount of activity as indication of interest because of the obvious inaccuracies which would distort the results. For instance, one might be very much interested in sailing but his work might keep him in an inland city and he might lack the means to travel to indulge this interest, while another might live near the water and, although not interested in sailing, spend considerable time in this activity because his friends enjoyed it and he wanted to spend time with his friends.

Attempts have been made to measure interest by the use of memory tests. Cattell (4) used pictures to represent various interests. A number of large sheets of paper, each containing 15 of these pictures, would be shown one at a time to an individual for a short period. His recall of specific pictures was used as an indication of interest in that field as opposed to the fields for which the representative picture was not recalled. The results of this test agreed with the estimation of the subject's interest based on observation of his daily life. The difficulties in selecting the pictures, however, are great; they should be equally attention-compelling as to color and uniqueness. For example, if some of the pictures were in color and others in black and white, there would be a tendency to recall the colored pictures regardless of interest. The pictures should have a common form of reproduction; should not be bizarre and thus attract curiosity. Also, they should be selected so that the subject does not feel it would "look better" for him to remember one and not another. Furthermore, it must be made certain that each test picture represents only one interest and not several.

The third type of objective test of interest is the information test. The assumption underlying this test is that if an individual is interested in any area he will acquire information concerning that area. Thus it is assumed that a person who is interested in sports will at least read about them in the daily paper even if he cannot afford the time to engage in them himself or if he cannot attend all of the sports events. From his reading he will know the names of prominent people in sports, and the rules and terms used in the various games. In an objective test of this sort there is at least the possibility of obtaining a measure of depth or the degree of interest in any one field if you are willing to assume the person with the greatest fund of information on the topic is the one who has the greatest interest. With this sort of measure of depth of interest, it would be necessary to control in some way intelligence level and ability to recall or recognize the kind of items which are being used.

This discussion of the measurements of interest in all fields has been included for a number of reasons. First, measurement of interest in clothing is basic to many research problems concerned with the psychological aspects of clothing. Second, the term *interest in clothing* has been used loosely and if we are to make significant progress in research in this area we must define our terms so that we know exactly what we are measuring. Third, various techniques are applicable to different meanings of the term *interest* and we need to know which technique is best for our problem.

INTEREST IN CLOTHING

An inventory type of test which was developed for various occupational fields in Home Economics is the Johnson Home Economics Interest Inventory (12). This test can be scored for interest in (1) clothing merchandising, (2) designing and (3) textile testing. It was designed to show a girl whether her interests are more like those of a group professionally employed in one of these areas than in others. The number of cases used in establishing the norms for the textile and clothing occupations was small, however, and recent tests of validity have not been published. While its purpose is to guide the counselor in suggesting occupations for the student, it is still more of a research tool than a validated test. It is not designed to measure depth of interest nor is it supposed to measure interest in the selection and wearing of attractive clothes.

The first thing we should note, then, concerning "interest in clothes" is that there is more than one type of interest, and that we will need different research tools to measure each type. The Johnson test is intended to measure interest in certain specified occupations related to clothing. In this book we are concerned with relating clothing interest to clothing choices and to the individual's clothing values and attitudes. Therefore, we are primarily concerned with the individual's interest in his *own* clothes and to the extent of his concern in dressing attractively and appropriately and not to his professional interests.

Rosencranz (17) developed a test which was designed to measure the depth of interest in clothes for oneself. The test is of the objective type, and is primarily in the form of a series of check lists. Two of the questions were of the information type. In one the subject is to pick from a list of 20 names all those she recognized as designers of clothing. Ten of the names are designers and the remaining ten are familiar names in other fields. She found a high relationship between the score on this question and the score on the questionnaire as a whole, therefore, it seems to be a good question. There is the possibility, however, of obtaining a very good score on this type of question with little interest in clothing. Many of the names can be easily eliminated as not being designers because they are known in other connections. In answering this particular question, for example, I obtained a perfect score although I knew only 6 out of the 10 designers. By chance the names other than the clothing designers were all sufficiently familiar to me so that I knew they were *not* designers. This illustrates one of the difficulties of this type of question. If names of those who are not designers are not names of actual persons, then an individual might obtain a high score by checking familiar sounding names, whereas if names of actual people are used then there is the chance of the subject's answering on the basis of these rather than on the names of the designers. The second information type of question listed brand and designers' names and the subject was to check whether the name was associated with fabrics, shoes, hats, suits, or dresses. This type of information question does not present the same difficulties as the question discussed above, but it does have disadvantages because each brand or designer is associated with a definite price range. Rosencranz attempted to overcome this difficulty by including a wide variety of price ranges.

The remaining questions on Rosencranz's interest test were all of the activity type. The questions were constructed so as to indicate the time, money, energy and thought devoted to clothing. Some sample questions are: How often have you read passages in books or read newspaper accounts of social events largely because they contained vivid or accurate descriptions of costume? How often do you help your girl or women friends select clothing? How often do you glance over or read fashion ads in the newspaper? If you won $100 on a radio program tomorrow how much of it would you spend for your own clothing? If you had been doing housework all day how often would you change clothes to have your evening meal? All of these questions had a list following them for checking. The list usually consisted of five possible answers such as "almost always, most of the time, sometimes, seldom, practically never."

A few other questions were more indirectly based upon activity. They were questions based on the size of the wardrobe. While these might seem to be dependent upon economic level, Rosencranz states that statistical tests showed that the relationship between the test and income was not significant. The test was administered to women representing various socioeconomic levels, married and single, with urban and rural backgrounds and of various ages.

As a check on the validity of the questionnaire, three of the highest and lowest scoring persons were interviewed. This is, of course, a very small number to be used for validation and is a weakness of this study. The weighting of the various questions to obtain the total score might also be questioned. The exact weighting of some of the items is not given. It appears possible that some questions with more parts received a greater weighting than shorter questions. In spite of these criticisms it is a good beginning in an area which had not been investigated. It should be improved, norms established, and validity tested so that it could serve as a valuable research tool. Rosencranz found that the younger women were more interested in clothes than the older women; women under twenty-five tended to have a higher score than those over thirty. There was likewise a significant variation among the various income groups. Those who had the smallest incomes tended to be the least interested in clothing. In addition she found that those coming from urban areas had significantly higher interest scores than those from rural areas. Other factors which correlated to a lesser degree with the interest scores were: education, marital status and children, membership in organizations.

Two of the questions and a modification of a third question from Rosencranz's questionnaire were used in a later study by Ryan (19) when interest in clothing was one factor to be correlated with several other items. The questions were: (1) How often do you glance over or read fashion ads in the newspaper? Almost always, most of the time, sometimes, seldom, practically never? (2) If you had been away on a month's vacation and hadn't done any reading at all, and if you were waiting in a doctor's office with these new magazines in front of you, which would you pick up first? *Saturday Evening Post, Life, Ladies Home Journal, Charm, Vogue?* The third question was a modification of Rosencranz's question, "How often do you discuss style changes with your friends?" It was worded: "Are clothes an interesting topic of conversation? Always, often, sometimes, never?"

The questionnaire which included these questions was given to over 1000 college girls. The interest score developed from these questions was validated by an interview with a random sample of 100 girls who answered the questionnaire. In the interview the girls were asked to estimate their own interest in clothing as compared to the other girls in the University by rating themselves on a 10-point scale. The interviewer also noted her estimate of the individual's interest after the interview. There was a very close and significant relationship between the girls' estimate, the interviewer's estimate, and the scores as obtained from the three interest questions. The subjects in the study, however, were a much more homogeneous group in regard to education, age and socioeconomic background than those studied by Rosencranz. The same questionnaire was also given to boys and girls in a rural and an urban high school. The high school girls had significantly higher interest scores than the college girls. Thus, the trend found in the Rosencranz study was found to continue to the high school level. Ryan did not find significant differences within either the college or the high school groups due to age or class, but the ages within either group are so close that differences might not be evident. This study further corroborated the study by Rosencranz on the differences in interest in clothing between the rural and the urban individuals. The college and high school girls from the city were more interested in clothes than the girls from rural areas.

Katz and Lazarsfeld (13) in their study of fashion leadership asked three questions which were designed to serve as an "index of fashion interest." Whether this is the same sort of interest which Rosencranz was measuring or not we do not know, but from the questions we can assume that the two are similar. The three questions used to derive the index of fashion interest were: (1) "Do you feel it is very important, moderately important or not important at all to be in style?; (2) Have you recently changed anything about your hairdo, type of clothing, cosmetics, make-up or any other change to something more fashionable?; (3) How many new dresses have you bought or made since the beginning of last summer? (twelve months earlier)." This test has not been used, as far as I know, except in this study and we have no evidence of its validity. Katz and Lazarsfeld found that there is a strong relationship between fashion interest as measured by this test and fashion leadership. They also found that a woman's age and marital status are associated with the degree of her interest in fashion. Interest in fashion is at its peak among young single women (80 percent were scored as having high interest); it decreases by one third among married women under 45; and falls sharply among married women over 45 (only 34 percent were scored as having high interest in fashion). The scores on this test were also highly correlated with social status; the proportion having a high-interest score increased with each step up in status. There was also a positive relationship between interest in fashion and a score on gregariousness, although the correlation was not as high as it was for position in the life cycle.

Vener (24), as we have seen earlier (see p. 65–66), investigated the relationship between personal estimates of clothing importance and social status, social (occupational) mobility and social participation. The estimates of clothing importance in his study can be considered an indirect measure of clothing interest. His data indicated that there was a low but positive relationship between upward mobility and personal estimates of clothing importance. The relationship between social status and the importance which subjects attributed to clothing was positive up to a point. Those in the medium high status groups had the greatest proportion of persons who had received high clothing-importance scores, while clothing seemed to decrease in importance for those in the highest status categories. In general, he also found high social participation related to high personal estimates of clothing importance. This confirms results from both the Rosencranz and Ryan studies. Rosencranz found that those who belonged to the most organizations had greater interest in clothing and Ryan's results showed membership in a sorority to be related to interest in clothes. We do not know which is the causal factor here. It may be that the girls who have the greatest interest spend more time and money on clothes and are therefore more attractive and are asked to join more organizations. On the other hand it may be that the person who is more socially oriented has more interest in anything which is related to people, and that clothing is one of these interests.

A second, and more extensive, study by Rosencranz (18), while not directly concerned with interest, nevertheless contributes to our knowledge in this field. As we have seen earlier (see p. 23), Rosencranz used a modified TAT, that is, she asked her subjects to tell stories about certain pictures, in order to obtain a "clothing awareness" score. Clothing awareness can be considered, indirectly at least, a measure of clothing interest. It is comparable to the use of memory tests or information tests (see p. 109–110) as indicators of interest in a subject. The assumption is made that there is greater awareness of clothing because of greater interest in clothing. In this study, Rosencranz found clothing awareness to be greater for those of high socioeconomic status, higher educational level, higher verbal intelligence, and belonging to more social organizations. This confirms her findings and those of Ryan on interest and those of Vener on personal estimates of clothing importance. However, she did not find differences due to age nor to rural versus urban background.

DEVELOPMENT OF INTEREST IN CLOTHES

Ryan interviewed college girls chosen because of their very high or very low interest scores or answers to specific questions on their questionnaire. The girls were asked what factors they thought had contributed to their interest or lack of interest in clothing. The most important factor, the girls thought was their families' attitudes toward clothing and the second most important reason was whether or not they had been allowed to choose their own clothes. (See Tables 5 and 6).

Reasons	NUMBER OF TIMES GIVEN
Mother and family interested earlier	25
Allowed to choose own clothes	21
Training (school) or work in dress shop	15
Interest in feminine things	12
Interest in color and design	7
Friends' interest	6
Felt unattractive, tried to compensate	3

table 5 Factors that increase interest in clothing.

Reasons	NUMBER OF TIMES GIVEN
Mother or family—little interest	22
Not allowed to choose own	10
Very little money for clothes	10
Friends and community not interested	10
Disdain for trivial—clothes trivial	6
Tomboy, not interested in feminine things	4

table 6 Factors that decrease interest in clothing.

It should be noted here that these were the opinions of the girls as to the reason for their interest or lack of interest in clothing. They may not have been aware of reasons equally or more important. Also these were given in response to an open-end question and therefore the frequency cannot be used as a true measure of relative importance. A girl might have given one answer and feeling she had answered the question adequately fail to mention other reasons. This can then only be used as suggesting the reasons which in the opinions of the girls seemed to influence their degree of interest or lack of interest in clothes.

Conclusion
~~Summary~~

We have seen that individuals vary in their interest in clothing, their attitudes toward clothing and the values which they assign to clothing. These differences are related to the individual's general values which are expressed in other areas of living.

Attitudes towards the importance of clothing and interest in clothing for oneself vary with: socioeconomic background, occupational mobility, age, education, and size of home town. Interest in clothing seems to reach a peak during late adolescence and to decrease with increasing age. Interest increases with increase in socioeconomic position up to the highest socioeconomic group where interest in clothing is lower. Most studies have found that those coming from urban areas have a greater interest in clothing than do those from rural backgrounds.

Bibliography

1. Allport, G. W., Vernon, P. E., and Lindzey, G. *A Study of Values: a Scale for Measuring the Dominant Interests in Personality,* rev. ed. Boston: Houghton Mifflin Company, 1960.
2. Alexander, Olive Ness. *A Pilot Investigation of the Motives Underlying the Desire to Feel Well-Dressed at Various Age Levels.* M.S. Thesis, Cornell Univer. 1961.
3. Altpeter, Barbara K. *An Investigation of Consumer Behavior in Clothing Purchases as Related to Clothing Values.* M.S. Thesis, Cornell Univer. 1963.
4. Cattell, R. B. The measurement of interest. *Character and Personality.* 4, 1935, 147–169.
5. Cantril, H., and Allport, G. W. Recent applications of study of values. *J. of Abnorm. and Soc. Psychol.* 28, 1933, 259–273.
6. Creekmore, Anna Mary. *Clothing Behaviors and Their Relation to General Values and to the Striving for Basic Needs.* Ph.D. Thesis, Penna. State Univer., 1963.

7. Finlayson, B. *An Investigation of Consumer Motivation in the Selection of Sweaters as Related to General Personal Values.* M.S. Thesis, Cornell Univer., 1959.

8. Form, W. H. and Stone, G. P. *The Social Significance of Clothing in Occupational Life.* Michigan State College Ag. Exper. Station Bulletin No. 247, Je 1955.

9. Fryer, D. *The Measurement of Interests.* New York: Holt, Rinehart and Winston, Inc., 1931, 448p.

10. Hartmann, G. W. Clothing: personal problem and social issue. *J. of Home Ec.* 41(6), 1949, 295–298.

11. Hoffman, Adeline M. *Clothing Behavioral Factors for a Specific Group of Women Related to Aesthetic Sensitivity and Certain Socio-Economic and Psychological Background Factors.* Ph.D. Thesis, Pennsylvania State Univer., 1956.

12. Johnson, Hildegarde. *Johnson Home Economics Interest Inventory.* Iowa State College Press, 1955.

13. Katz, E. and Lazarsfeld, P. *Personal Influence.* New York: Free Press of Glencoe, Inc., 1955, 400p.

14. Kohlmann, Eleanore L. Personal values, what are they? *J. of Home Ec.* 54(10), 1962, 819–822.

15. Lapitsky, Mary. *Clothing Values and Their Relation to General Values and to Social Security and Insecurity.* Ph.D. Thesis, Penna. State Univer., 1961.

16. Parker, J. F., Jr. and Hackman, R. C. The relationship between attitude toward the army and acceptance accorded Q.M. items of issue. *J. of Appl. Psychol.* 40, 1956, 329–332.

17. Rosencranz, Mary Lou. A study of women's interest in clothing. *J. of Home Ec.* 41(8), 1949, 460–462.

18. Rosencranz, Mary Lou. Clothing symbolism. *J. of Home Ec.* 54, 1962, 18–22.

19. Ryan, Mary S. *Psychological Effects of Clothing Part I: Survey of the Opinions of College Girls.* Cornell Univer. Ag. Exper. Station Bulletin No. 882, Sept. 1952. *Part II: Comparison of College Students with High School Students.* No. 898, 1953 and Part III: *Report of Interviews with College Women.* No. 900, 1953.

20. Stout, Dorothy and Latzke, A. Values college women consider in clothing selection. *J. of Home Ec.* 50(1), 1958, 43–44.

21. Stone, G. P. and Form, W. H. *The Local Community Clothing Market: A Study of the Social and Social Psychological Contexts of Shopping.* Michigan State Univer. Ag. Exper. Sta. Bull. No. 262, Nov. 1957.

22. Strong, E. K. *Vocational Interests of Men and Women.* Stanford, Calif.: Stanford University Press, 1943, 746p.

23. Super, D. E. *Appraising Vocational Fitness.* New York: Harper & Row, Publishers, 1949, Chap. 16, 17 and 18.

24. Vener, A. M. *Stratification Aspects of Clothing Importance.* M.S. Thesis, Mich. State College, 1953.

25. Vernon, P. E. and Allport, G. W. A test for personal values. *J. of Abnor. and Soc. Psychol.* 26, 1931, 231–248.
26. Whitlock, Mary (ch.), Ayres, Ruth and Ryan, Mary S. *Consumer Satisfaction With Women's Blouses Part I: Field Study in Four Communities in the Northeast.* Ag. Exper. Station, University of Rhode Island Bulletin No. 349, Northeast Regional Bulletin No. 34, Je, 1959.

Chapter 6

Clothing Practices
and the Effects of Clothing
on the Individual

*A*s a basis for studying the effects of clothing upon the individual we need to know the normal practices regarding clothing,—how clothing is acquired, the number of garments of various types in an average wardrobe for a given group, when and where different types of clothing are worn, and when and why garments are discarded. Furthermore, we need to know how all of these vary with age, the socioeconomic background, location, and with individual values and interests. With this information we can then determine how individuals vary from the norm and how different factors affect that norm. Unfortunately our knowledge of these basic facts is very limited. From various sources we can glean bits of information which help us to form a general picture, but it is far from complete.

Clothing Practices

WARDROBE SIZE AND COST

From marketing and production data we can determine the number of garments of particular kinds which are produced and sold. Studies of financial management indicate the amount and proportion of the family income spent for clothing and how this varies with the total income and the age of family members. Studies of economic consumption supply us with information on the numbers and types of garments owned by some specific age, economic, and geographic groups.

All of these are based upon research in economics and since our main concern in this book is with the psychological aspects of clothing we will not consider them in detail, nevertheless we should recognize that such studies give us the norms which should be used as a basis for studies concerning the effects of clothing on the individual. We should also recognize the variables which influence the norms. Although the data are scattered, we find from various studies that certain factors are related to the size of the wardrobe or to the amount spent on clothing.

Income. As would be predicted, most of the data indicate that as income rises the absolute and relative amount spent for clothing rises up to a certain point. At the higher-income levels the amount in dollars spent on clothing may still increase but the relative amount decreases.

Age. One of the most important variables in the size of the wardrobe or the amount spent on clothing is the age of the individual. Numerous studies have shown that between the ages of sixteen and twenty-five, or the students in high school and the years immediately following high school, the largest amount of money is spent on clothing, and wardrobes are largest. In adult groups the younger men and women spend more on clothes and own more clothing than do older adults. Klitzke (27) for example, found this true in her study of clothing inventories of farm families. At the lower end of the age scale the elementary school children have smaller and less expensive wardrobes than do the younger adults. Infants and adults over sixty-five have the smallest wardrobes and their clothing costs the least.

Sex. In general the expenditures for clothing of wives tend to be below those for husbands (and girls below that of boys) among the low-income families, but this is reversed for the middle-income groups where more money is spent on the women's and girls' clothes than on men's and boys'. The results here are not clear cut, however. The difficulty of equating women's and men's wardrobes has been one of the obstacles in research. Another factor which makes the comparison difficult is that more women's clothes are made at home and the method for assigning equivalent prices has varied from study to study.

Rural vs. urban. Individuals living in an urban area, or born in one, tend to have larger wardrobes and spend more on clothing than do those from a rural area. People living in a suburban or rural area but working, shopping, and finding recreation in an urban area are similar to urban groups.

The differences between the urban and the rural groups are greater for some garments than for others. Stone and Form (41) found, for example, that urban women owned relatively more suits and formal gowns, and owned fur coats significantly more often than rural women, while the difference between the two groups was not significant for housedresses, good dresses and cloth coats.

The difference in clothing inventories between farm men and urban men was greater than that for women. Urban men owned more suits, jackets, separate trousers, dress and sport shirts than did farm men. The farm men owned more work shirts than the urban men. When the subjects in this study were asked about an ideal wardrobe, again there were differences between the urban and the rural populations. The urban women mentioned more items, especially suits, in the ideal wardrobe. Rural women placed greater stress on basic items such as slips and undergarments. Farmers included more functional items such as overalls in their ideal wardrobes.

Occupation. As would be expected white-collar workers spend more on clothing and have larger wardrobes than manual workers even when income is held constant. Women working outside of the home have larger wardrobes and spend more on clothing than do wives who are not employed outside the home.

Social participation. Dorothy Dickins pointed out the dependency of social participation upon the size of the wardrobe (11). She has emphasized that in establishing minimum clothing standards, clothes which merely provide warmth and decency are not adequate. Since clothing serves a social function primarily, her argument has been that minimum clothing standards are not useful unless they meet minimum standards for social participation of the individual. For the sample which she was using (white farm families of Mississippi) the church was the center of social activity, therefore she used the minimum wardrobe of those who participated in church activities as the minimum standard wardrobe which would be adequate for the needs of individuals in that region. Other studies (for example, the Stone and Form study mentioned above) have shown that in higher-income brackets as well as in the lowest there is a positive correlation between the size of the wardrobe and the amount of social participation. We do not know which is cause and which effect. It may be that with a larger wardrobe the individual wishes to go out more to show it off or it may be that the individual who participates in more organizations or groups feels the need of more clothing items.

Other variables related to size and cost of wardrobe. Stone and Form (41) confirmed hypotheses concerning a variety of social factors and their effect on the number of clothing items owned. They found that social class, the individual's self-rating of class membership, education, and magazine readership, as well as social participation and urban background, were positively related to the total size of the wardrobe and to the number of garments owned by type of garment. In this study the number of garments was not actually counted but was reported as the interviewee remembered them, a method which usually gives a lower number than counting. Social class was measured by the Warner Index which included occupation, source of income, house type, and dwelling area. Self-rating of class membership was determined by asking the respondents whether they belonged to the upper, middle, working or lower class. Magazine readership groups were those who reported reading none or one type of magazine, two types, or three or more types.

GENERAL METHODS OF ACQUIRING GARMENTS

Limited and sketchy as our data are on the size and cost of wardrobes for various groups, they are even more limited and scattered concerning information on the use of clothing and clothing practices. A few studies have given us information on the method of acquiring garments. The United States Department of Agriculture study of family clothing supplies (43) gives us the most complete data on this point. The proportion of the total clothing acquired during a single year from supplemental sources such as gifts, handed down, made-over, or homemade were relatively insignificant. "However, for some items of clothing for men and women and for an appreciable number of items of clothing for children these sources are important [No. 5, p. I]." Men received one fourth or more of their shirts (sport and dress), sweaters, pajamas, and certain accessories such as gloves, scarfs, and ties as gifts. Women received one fourth or more of their lingerie, accessories, blouses, skirts, and housedresses as gifts. Estimating the price value of the gift clothing as related to the total value of the clothing acquired during the year, about one tenth of the total clothing value was acquired as gifts by husbands and wives, one fifth for boys and one quarter for girls. The number who received made-over clothing was insignificant for all groups, but over one third of both boys and girls received one or more handed-down garments during the year. One fifth of the girls' snowsuits, suits, separate jackets, and separate skirts and boys' ski-pants, suits and bathrobes were handed-down garments.

In a more recent study by the textiles and clothing research group of the Northeast (37), 28 percent of men's favorite and 38 percent of their least-liked shirts had been received as gifts. Women received nearly half of their slips (48 percent of their favorite and 46 percent of least-liked), but fewer (13 percent of favorite and 15 percent of least-liked) casual street dresses as gifts. These results show us that although gift and other supplementary sources of garments may not account for a very large proportion of the total wardrobe it varies with the type of garment and for some garments, at least, the source is an important factor which must be taken into account. It is especially important in studies dealing with satisfaction since the later study showed that some types of garments received as gifts tended to be less satisfactory than those chosen by the wearer for himself.

The length of time different types of garments last or are kept in the wardrobe is another factor which may be important as basic data. We have almost no information on this point. Hall (18) found that for ninety-two urban low-income families the average life of a woman's coat was 7.8 years, a man's topcoat 16.1 years and his shirts 4.25 years. We need this type of information on other garments and for various age and income groups. Such information is especially valuable for those who are attempting to teach or help others in wardrobe selection and planning.

Behavior Toward Clothing and Use of Clothing

PATTERNS OF USE

Information on the frequency with which certain types of garments are worn is needed for a complete understanding of the psychological aspects of clothing behavior as well as basic information concerning the wardrobe. Ryan (36) obtained a partial answer to this question on one garment only—women's blouses. In her study, women were interviewed concerning all of the blouses they owned. The total number of blouses upon which data were obtained was 2227 (a mean of 8.4 for each of the 265 respondents who owned them). The interviewees reported 61 percent of the blouses were worn frequently, 35 percent seldom worn and 4 percent never worn. A classification of reasons which were given for frequent wearing of a particular blouse showed that 558 reasons were practical (for example, "easy to care for" and "goes with several things"), 362 were reasons classed as esthetic ("like the looks," "like color," etc.) and 267 were reasons connected with comfort ("cool in summer," "fits well," "easy to get on and off"—or a specific aspect was mentioned as being comfortable). The newer blouses and the blouses chosen by the wearer tended to be worn more frequently than older blouses and those received as gifts. This confirms the findings of Lynn who investigated the reasons for frequent or infrequent wearing of adolescents' school clothes. (See Chapter 13.) As garments hung in a closet and seldom or never worn constitute an economic waste which should be avoidable, this is an important area for research.

A Northeast regional study (51) gives us more specific information on the patterns of wear for a single garment over a short period. The garment is again women's blouses. The interviewers in this project had observed the purchases of the blouses and interviewed the purchasers three to six weeks later. Within that period 96 percent of the women had worn the blouse. Some had worn it only once or twice, others had worn it 3 or 4, 5 or 6 or over 9 times with the percentages approximately the same for each classification. At a second interview approximately ten to twelve weeks after the first interview 32 percent had worn the blouse 1–9 times, 29 percent 10–19 times, 20 percent 20–29 times and 16 percent had worn it over 30 times. The majority of the respondents owned from 1 to 10 similar blouses and reported that they wore their new blouses about as often as their others which were suitable for the same kind of occasion.

OTHER CLOTHING PRACTICES

We have more information concerning consumer behavior in the selection and purchase of garments than on any other aspect of clothing behavior. We will, however, discuss consumer behavior in the section of this book dealing with various consumer problems. (See Part Two.)

Concerning other clothing behavior we have just scattered bits of information. For example the Northeast Regional Clothing Projects (37 and 51) have supplied us with data on the way certain specific garments (men's shirts, women's blouses, slips, and casual street dresses) are cared for. These studies also give us some information on the relative number of women who remember and who follow the directions for care on garment labels.

In discussing clothing practices, it would be helpful if we could give the types of clothing worn for various activities and the way in which this varies for different age, socioeconomic, and geographic groups and how it varies with education or with urban, rural, or suburban backgrounds. Unfortunately we do not have information to fill out this picture; the most complete we have is on the adolescent (see Chapter 13).

Effects of Clothing on Behavior

It can be accepted without a doubt that clothes, at least for some people on some occasions, affect the mood and behavior of the wearer. An individual may feel gay and peppy in a bright new outfit, less efficient in shoes which hurt the feet, or self-conscious in an inappropriate costume. Countless articles have been written on the effects of clothing. The designer of ski clothes says that the right clothes help to improve skiing, the child psychologist says that self-help clothes develop independence, the welfare worker stresses the importance of clothing in helping to combat delinquency, even the cartoonist pokes fun at the effect of a new hat on a woman's morale. The problems for research in this field are to find what these effects are, under what conditions and whom they affect, how long the effects last, and what factors in clothing affect the wearer in various ways.

We will divide our discussion into three main subtopics: (1) the effects of feeling well or poorly dressed, (2) the effects of physical comfort of clothing, and (3) the effects of specific types of clothing or of specific colors, lines, textures or styles.

PSYCHOLOGICAL EFFECTS OF FEELING WELL OR
POORLY DRESSED

It has long been recognized that feeling well or poorly dressed may influence not only our emotions but even our actual behavior. In 1918 Dearborn said:

Without much thought, the following at least may be suggested as social movements greatly or slightly, as the case may be, determined by one's raiment, and others there are aplenty.

1. How much one "goes out," both into the street, and
2. into society in general, how many "calls" one makes;
3. The time of day or night at which one goes out when living in town, for several reasons.
4. Where one goes, that is, the sort of place to which one goes, both in town and in the country.
5. How much company one invites to his home, and,
6. To some extent, the nature of that company.
7. How much one attends church, disgusting Easter parades, etc.
8. How much one attends the theater, and the nature of the entertainment so designated, whether it be a dark movie among often unfashionably or ill-dressed people, or the grand opera with its brilliant promenade and conspicuous visiting.
9. Clothes frequently help people to get "jobs," and to hold them, but (see below)
10. Clothes help others to miss positions and lose them.
11. The amount of exercise one takes and its variety. . . .
12. How much one sits and where and how one sits. . . .
13. How much one eats and drinks is determined to some extent by the clothing.
14. How much checking-balance one may keep at the bank determines behavior to a noteworthy degree.
15. One's personal beauty (in the case of the beautiful sex) [10:29].

In 1926, Grace Morton wrote that:

Clothes help to make us self-confident, self-respecting, jolly, free, or they make us self-conscious, shy, sensitive, restrained. They determine how much we go into society, the places we go to, the exercise we take. They help us to get jobs and to hold them, to miss them and to lose them [30:585].

Both of these authors suggest that participation or no participation in social events is influenced by the felt adequacy of the wardrobe. This point was confirmed by Dickins (11). She found that the majority of people do not participate in social events without clothing comparable to that of the other members of the group. The degree to which this is true apparently varies with the age of the subject. Silverman found that, within the high school group she studied, there was a marked tendency for older girls to forgo social events because they did not have what they considered adequate or appropriate clothes for the occasion (no percentage at age twelve—31 percent at age eighteen). Ryan (35) reports that the high school girls in her sample were more likely than the college to have refused invitations because they thought they did not have an appropriate costume. Ryan's results may have been due to differences in economic level since the college group would be biased in the direction of high income. Nevertheless, the age pattern for clothing affecting social participation follows the same age pattern as that of interest in clothing.

This seems to be another bit of evidence confirming the theory stated earlier (see Introduction) that interest in clothing and the felt need for clothing varies inversely with the general feeling of adequacy or self-confidence in the social situation. That is, the more secure the individual feels in the social situation the less importance he attaches to clothing and the less it will affect him. We would predict from this theory that the adolescent, because he is at the period in life when he feels the least sure of himself would have the greatest interest in clothes and also would be the most apt to have clothing affect his social participation. This prediction seems to be confirmed by the results obtained in the above studies.

We have been discussing the effects of clothing on the actual presence or absence of the subject from a social event. Perhaps a greater effect may be evident in the way in which the subject participates. The individual who feels well-dressed may participate more actively, that is, join in the activity to a greater extent, speak at a meeting or in class, or assume some form of leadership. The individuals in Ryan's study who felt well-dressed reported that they were more relaxed, less conscious of themselves, and their clothing. They tended to be "peppier," talk more and enter into the activity at hand, while, when they believed themselves to be poorly dressed, they felt self-conscious, ill at ease, conspicuous and tended to be quieter and keep away from the center of the group.

The implications of the part clothing plays in both actual physical participation and the degree of active participation on school drop-outs and students' accomplishments in school are obvious. In Middletown: A Study in Contemporary American Culture, (28) we find the following:

> One mother whose son dropped out of school said, "We couldn't dress him like we'd ought to and he felt out of it"; and another "The two boys and the oldest girl all quit because they hated Central High School. They all loved the Junior High School down here, but up there they're so snobbish. If you don't dress right you haven't any friends."

Several authors have suggested that feeling well-dressed affects the efficiency of work. Dearborn (10) asked a group to write on relationships between success and clothing. Over half said that consciousness of good appearance frees the individual from fear of criticism. Hurlock (22) asked directly: "Does your dress affect your efficiency, i.e., can you do better work if you feel that you are well dressed?" While this question suggests that a positive answer is expected, nevertheless the fact that 88 percent answered in the affirmative leads us to suppose that feeling well-dressed is a factor in efficiency of work. In Ryan's study many students said that the most important reason for being well-dressed was that it allowed the individual to concentrate on other things, which would imply greater efficiency in work.

The most obvious consequence of feeling well-dressed, at least for the majority of the women, is the boost it gives to morale. This has long been a joke for cartoonists, but there is some truth in this joke. Alexander (1) found that "feelings of personal satisfaction and well being" summed up the reasons given most frequently by high school girls, college girls, and adult women for the importance of being well-dressed.

Ninety-five percent of those who answered Hurlock's (22) questionnaire said that dress did affect their happiness, and 97 percent said that feelings of

"Are you sure it looks like something no sober-minded schoolteacher would wear?

Side Glances BY GALBRAITH.
© 1960 NEWSPAPER
ENTERPRISE ASSOCIATION

© 1960 by NEA, Inc. T.M. Reg. U.S. Pat. Off.   10-17

self-confidence increased by being well and appropriately dressed. Although these questions were worded in such a way that the positive answer might have been suggested, nevertheless the results are so overwhelmingly on the affirmative side that we can assume that in general the results would be confirmed in more adequately controlled research.

Silverman, working with young adolescents, found that 79 percent of the girls answering her questionnaire said that:

> ... clothes were a necessary concomitant to happiness, though there was a difference in how outstanding the clothes had to be in order to contribute to this feeling. For 30 percent they had to be above average, and for 49 percent average clothes were sufficient. Hence, the majority of the girls could not be happy if their clothes did not measure up to at least the standards of their group.
>
> Other personal aspects of clothes and appearance were their relationship to feelings of ease and self-confidence. The differences in these responses with age were slight. Sixty-two percent of the group indicated that consciousness of their clothes resulted in their feeling ill at ease. While 51 percent said the feeling of self-consciousness was not sufficient to make a marked difference to them, 11 percent of the group said they became so preoccupied with their clothes and their feelings of self-consciousness about them that they could not enjoy the event in which they were taking part. Here the girls were presumably referring to their negative feelings about their clothes—that their clothes were inappropriate, ill-fitting, or unbecoming. The results indicate either that for the proportion of girls mentioned (11 percent) their clothes were actually inferior, or that these girls were unusually sensitive to any defects in their appearance, possibly projecting other feelings of inferiority onto their clothes. On the positive side, 76 percent of the group said that knowing she had a good appearance gave a girl a considerable amount of self-confidence. The answers to both these questions indicate that clothing and appearance have a direct effect on the girls' moods or on their immediate emotional reactions [39:53].

Not only does feeling well-dressed lift the spirits of normal women, it is also found to be effective in helping the morale of the mentally ill. Thompson (45) reports that fashion therapy in the treatment of the mentally ill in California state hospitals has been very successful. She gives examples of patients whose start on the road to recovery has been through help in dress selection and grooming. Baker reports (3) the same conclusion for the patients at the Larned State (Kansas) Hospital. Improvement and attention to the clothing of the patients contributed to morale, the sense of self-worth, and the patients' over-all outlook on life, and helped to prepare the patient for return to his social community.

EFFECTS OF CLOTHING ON PHYSICAL COMFORT

Many of the physiological effects of clothing upon the body have been measured. As early as 1929, the United States Department of Agriculture published a bibliography of 1184 references on the relation of clothing to health (33). In recent years the Quartermaster Research and Engineering Command and others have measured the physiological effects of various clothing in extremes of temperature and humidity. Under hot, normal or cold temperatures they have measured variations in skin temperature, electrical conductivity of the skin, the perspiration rate, heart rate, and so on of the body clothed in garments varying in design and in fiber content.

We have no objective measure of comfort comparable to the physiological measures. Attempts have been made to correlate subjective judgments of comfort with the physiological measures in the hopes that the physiological measurements might serve also as a measure of comfort. Unfortunately the judgments of comfort have been inconsistent with the physiological indices (see 2). One of the difficulties in obtaining a comfort scale is that the body rapidly adapts to different temperatures and humidities so that judgments of comfort are constantly changing.

The fact that comfort cannot be measured objectively does not mean, however, that it is not extremely important. The Northeast Regional Textile and Clothing study (51) found that comfort was the most important component for over-all satisfaction with blouses, and a more recent study (37) confirmed this for men's shirts. These studies were concerned with all aspects of comfort, fit and texture as well as characteristics related to temperature.

We know that a shoe that pinches the foot, a too-tight girdle, a scratchy sweater or a slipping shoulder strap not only makes the wearer uncomfortable, but also may make her feel cross, be less efficient, or reluctant to tackle a difficult task. If we could determine the extent to which these findings are true it might be of great practical importance. At first thought, it would seem relatively simple to ask individuals to perform certain measurable tasks with comfortable clothing and again with uncomfortable clothing, and to compare the two conditions. The difficulty with an experimental design of this sort is that there is no control of effort or motivation. Even though a subject may feel fatigued or uncomfortable because of a too-restricting garment, and normally would perform less well, in the test situation the subject may simply exert more effort and so do as well as he would when comfortable. The same difficulties in controlling effort have been found in attempts to measure fatigue and stress. Even under extremely fatiguing conditions and at times when the individual is under such great stress that his condition is obvious to the most casual observer, his performance in various psychological tests or set tasks may be as high as under normal conditions.

One way to overcome this difficulty would be to have the subject unaware that he was taking a test or performing a measured task under the two situations. Using this technique a preliminary experiment was undertaken at Cornell University. Nine subjects were each fitted to two pairs of shoes. One pair was supposed to fit perfectly and the second to be too tight for comfort. The test situation was presented so that the subjects thought they were taking part in several experiments, one on the comfort of shoes, and the others completely unrelated to the shoe experiment. The general plan was to (1) pretest the subject, (2) have her wear the shoes for three hours. During this time she was on her feet for 25 minutes and sitting five minutes out of each half hour. (3) An after test. The same procedure was carried out one day with comfortable shoes and another day with uncomfortable ones. The differences in the two days were then calculated. To control the effect of practice, half of the girls wore comfortable shoes and half wore uncomfortable shoes on the first test day. Even if the results of this preliminary experiment had shown that the subjects made a different score on the tests in the two different situations, the results could only be considered suggestive. Many more subjects or many more observations on the same subjects would need to be made before the results could be considered significant. The results on these nine subjects, however, were not consistent enough to encourage further work along this line. One of the difficulties was that the shoes were not equally uncomfortable to the subjects and there was no objective way of determining the correctness of fit.

More techniques need to be developed before we can discover the psychological effects of clothing comfort. Any new techniques used in work on fatigue should be watched as they may offer suggestions for this type of experimentation. When such techniques are found, much valuable information can be gathered. Dearborn said:

> Purely, of course, as a rough judgment, I believe that the discomforts of people of relatively free efficiency that come from ill-fitting clothes, in various ways, detract very considerably from their practical efficiency. As I look back over my work hours and see how very many of them were disturbed, not to say spoiled, by various kinds of discomforts of ill-fitting clothes, of one kind or another, I judge that on the average, fully 10 percent of inefficiency may come from the lack of proper, that is, primarily, comfortable, clothing [10:68].

If, for example, it is found that efficiency is sufficiently hampered by poorly fitted or designed shoes, employers might find it worthwhile to supply shoes of proper design and fit for their employees.

Although the field is too specialized for this work, the student should be aware of the studies of functional clothing. The Quartermaster Research and Engineering Command and industry have both done considerable work on the design of clothing for specific jobs such as the design of gloves or mittens which permit the finger dexterity needed for certain jobs. There have also been studies on garments such as helmets which effect the safety of the men on the job. Even the color coding of helmets for construction workers contributes to their safety [see p. 15].

Some beginning has also been made on clothing designs for handicapped individuals. The United States Department of Agriculture, for example, has worked on clothing needs of physically handicapped homemakers (see, for example, Scott[1]) and there have been a few master's theses on clothing for young girls with specific handicaps. There is a whole field of study to be done here which should be made available to the handicapped and to clothing producers.

INFLUENCE OF SPECIFIC TYPES OF CLOTHING OR SPECIFIC COLORS, LINES OR TEXTURES ON MOOD AND BEHAVIOR

In the preceding chapter we discussed the effect of clothing upon the self-concept. The role we play at any given moment is inextricably connected with our self-concept. A person who perceives himself as a certain sort of person acts in a way that seems appropriate to him. The role is the organization of habitual responses and attitudes of an individual to a class of situations, and clothing makes an important contribution to the ease with which a person is able to play various roles appropriate to his self-concept and to the situation. Murphy has said:

> It is likely, indeed, that the psychology of clothing has too often been conceived in terms of a simple narcissistic delight in one's appearance; clothing is largely a means of making real the role that is to be played in life. Flowing gowns make the role of gracious hostess easier, partly through the kinesthetic smoothing of activity, partly through the sheer associations given in social convention. Corduroy pants make the girl who is ready for hiking or boating a rougher and readier participant in the activity, more likely to tussle with her masculine counterpart—
> "it's natural to fight when you're wearing the pants" [31:495].

Coutu (9) distinguishes between *role playing* and *role taking*. Role playing is the "socially prescribed way of behaving in particular situations for any person occupying a given social position or status" [p. 180]. Role taking is the process by which a person pretends to himself that he is another person. Role taking is one of the techniques used by the clinical psychologist to help the individual understand or be sympathetic to another individual. By pretending to be that other person he comes to understand the problems and the behavior of that person. Actors on the stage or in a movie are, of course, our

---

[1] C. L. Scott, Clothing needs of physically handicapped homemakers. *J. of Home Ec.* 51 (8), 1959, 709–713.

best known example of role taking. For the amateur at least, appropriate costuming does make the taking of a role easier. If you have taken part in amateur theatricals or even played such games as charades or been to a masquerade party you will recognize that it is easier to act the part of a given character if you are costumed for the part or at least use some element of the costume.

In much the same way clothing seems to help us in role *playing*. It may determine the role we play and help or hinder us in playing that role. When, after the assassination of President Kennedy, his body was lying in state in the Capitol, the waiting crowd outside became so great that it broke through the ranks of police. A group of sailors stepped out from the crowd, offered their services, and helped to restore the crowd's orderly approach. It is unlikely that they would have done so, or that they would have been effective, if they had not been in uniform. They were living up to their roles as United States servicemen, also they probably recognized that the crowd would respect and obey them because of their uniforms.

The effect of clothing on the playing of a role came forcefully to my attention recently when I was asked to lecture on clothing and personality to two sections of a course. To start the discussion I asked the classes to describe the kind of person they perceived me to be. It was the first time I had seen or talked to either group so their impressions were based entirely on my appearance. For the first section I wore a tailored suit. The girls in reply said they thought I was businesslike and efficient. I then went on with my lecture. The next day, when I met the second section, I was wearing a navy silk dress with a small woven pink design. The girls that day described me as matronly, sweet and motherly. (On both occasions they were tactful enough to give only favorable comments.) I again went on with the lecture using the same notes that I had used the day before. Later, looking back on the two days, I realized that my performance had been completely different on the two occasions. The first day, wearing the suit and knowing that the class members thought I was businesslike and efficient I presented the material in a crisp, concise manner. On the second day, clad in the silk dress and knowing that the class thought I was motherly, my presentation was slower, my voice softer, and I smiled a great deal more. This was not deliberate on my part and at the time I was giving the lectures I was not conscious of a difference. (Unfortunately, I do not know which class remembered best the points I was trying to make.) In this case I had immediate verbal reports of the groups' reaction to my appearance. In most instances we would not have such reports, nevertheless, there undoubtedly would have been some difference without their comments. We play certain roles because we think others are perceiving us in a given way.

The above example brings out another important point concerning the playing of roles. We play not one but many roles. The role we play depends upon our self-concepts, the situation, and the people with whom we are inter-acting. James has given us the oft-quoted statement "a man has as many social selves as there are individuals who recognize him" [23:294]. This might also be paraphrased "a man plays as many roles as he has different types of costume."

In addition to the distinction between role taking and role playing we should also distinguish between the *social or cultural* role and the *personal* role. The incident of the servicemen at the Capitol following President Kennedy's death is an example of a *cultural* role being played. Here we are concerned primarily with the personal role. An individual might feel well and appropriately dressed for a given situation but the line, color, or texture of the garment might affect the role she assumes and so her mood or actions. For example, a college girl at a dance might wear either a bouffant pink organdy or a clinging black velvet dress. She would feel appropriately and well dressed in either but in the first she might play the role of a sweet young girl and in the second a sophisticated woman.

Specific items of clothing may be symbolic of certain roles or types of people. When an adolescent, a fur neck piece symbolized to me the height of luxury and sophistication. When I finally was given one I took on various mannerisms which I thought were appropriate to such elegance. In the first quarter of this century silk shirts, because they were worn by men of wealth and leisure, symbolized wealth and gentility to the laboring class who could not afford them. When, therefore, it became possible for a laboring man to buy and to wear a silk shirt he felt he should act the part of a gentleman. It has been suggested (4) that the silk shirt influenced labor-management re-lationships and made the strikes of that day less bloody than they had previ-ously been. Only roughnecks threw bricks, and if a man was wearing a silk shirt then he was not a roughneck and therefore he did not throw bricks.

Although we can think of many examples of the fact that clothing does influence at least the ease with which a personal role is assumed, we have almost no research evidence[2] that points either to the degree of the importance of clothing in assuming a role or to the way in which it influences. As Treece (46) points out, the social-psychological theories which seem to explain cloth-ing choices and the effects of clothing most adequately are those in which the self-concept and role play a dominant part. It is to be hoped, therefore, that we will see research undertaken using this theoretical framework.

The color, line, texture or weight of fabric in garments may also have an effect on the mood of the wearer. This effect is less specific than those we have been discussing but is perhaps more common. One of the questions which

---

[2] A report of a project in this area reached the author too late to be included here. See Wass, B. M. and Eicher, J. B. Clothing as related to role behavior of teenage girls *Quart. Bull.* Mich. Ag. Exper. Sta. Vol. 47(2) Nov. 1964, 206–213.

G. Stanley Hall (14) asked in his questionnaire was: "Do materials of your dress affect your feeling?" Among the answers obtained from this question were observations that heavy clothing gave a depressing effect, softness in clothing made women feel dainty, happier, graceful or gentle; stiff material made them feel formal, awkward or self-conscious. Other examples were obtained from an investigation by Flaccus (14). "A broad hat makes me feel jolly," "If my hat is flat on my forehead, I feel depressed," "If I have a fancy hat on, I am in a coquettish mood," and "I feel brighter in a hat that rolls away from my face."

Ryan (35) obtained more examples of this sort from a questionnaire. The question dealt with the influence of color, texture, or type of costume upon mood. The subjects were asked first simply whether or not these did influence their mood. In the first group of 1072 college girls, 641 said that their mood was influenced by these factors, and 330 said they were not. Those who answered in the affirmative were asked to give examples. The answers were then classified in two ways. First, all moods induced or influenced by clothing were listed. The classification obtained from the girls' answers contained the following categories:

1. gay, perky, happy, extroverted
2. sophisticated, ladylike, regal, older, refined
3. confident, at-ease, poised, serene
4. efficient, businesslike
5. quiet, serious, subdued, solemn
6. inconspicuous, uninterested, dull
7. uneasy, strained, self-conscious, out-of-place
8. depressed, sad, tired
9. feminine, graceful, dreamy
10. sexy, daring, glamorous, mysterious

Second, a classification was made from the clothing area. This second list was classified as to color, texture, line (full versus straight skirts), and type (formal, casual, tailored, or peasant).

Gaiety as induced by clothes was reported more often than any other mood. Bright colors were mentioned by 77 as contributing to a gay mood, and 50 mentioned red specifically as contributing in this way. Others recorded light or pastel colors. Full skirts, taffetas, and, in a few cases, dressy dresses also were mentioned. Dressy clothes, dark clothes, and black were mentioned as contributing toward feeling sophisticated, or ladylike. Confidence, poise, serenity, and a feeling of ease were given as the mood produced by slacks, tailored clothes, old or informal clothes, wools or rough textures, bright colors, dark colors, or blue by different girls. Dull, dark and unsaturated colors were most frequently mentioned as responsible for feelings of depression and sadness. A variety of features made the students feel feminine, dreamy, or graceful. Among those given as examples were: simple lines, fussy detail, full skirts, dressy dresses, soft textures, taffetas, and pastel colors. Textures were usually responsible for sexy, or glamorous feelings. Several girls, for example, said that satin or velvet made them feel "sexy"; another "that taffeta, satins, and other rich fabrics give me a glamorous feeling." The examples given by the respondents show that color was reported as influencing mood more frequently than any other feature of dress. While many agreed on which colors induced a certain mood, the same colors were always given by someone else as creating an entirely different mood. For example, some girls gave bright colors as creating a strained, uneasy, or self-conscious mood. On the other hand, no one said that bright colors made them feel sad or depressed, dull or uninteresting. The nature of the question was such that a large number agreeing on any one example would be highly improbable. If a large number of individuals were asked specific questions we could determine the relative number of people in which a specific feature tended to induce a specific mood. The open-end question was used here, however, because we know so little about this aspect of dress that it was feared some effects might be overlooked in designing a checklist. With the examples now collected such a specific question could be asked.

We have no research capable of giving us any indication as to how widespread any of these effects are; whether some of them are simply individual reactions or whether they are common to the majority of people; how dependent these are upon the cultural background of individuals.

If the influences of colors upon moods is dependent upon past experience and the association between a mood and color has been built up over a period of time, we would expect that some reactions would be individualistic, some be true in small cultural groups and others true for larger cultural groups. In a given culture certain associations may be made by all of the individuals in that culture. For example, in the world in which the college girls in Ryan's sample grew up, the young usually wear the brilliant colors, while older people are likely to wear blacks and subdued colors, likewise on holidays and for celebrations, bright colors are used as decorations, in fact we speak of the bright colors, especially those at the red end of the spectrum as "gay colors" therefore this association is common to nearly everyone within that large cultural group.

Although the studies thus far have merely been an extension of casual observation, they offer a basis upon which research could be carried out.

TEMPORARY VS. PERMANENT EFFECTS OF CLOTHING
UPON THE WEARER

Thus far, we have discussed the temporary effects of clothing upon the wearer, that is, while an individual is wearing a specific garment. Although the majority of effects undoubtedly are of this sort, the possibility of permanent effects should at least be considered even though we have no research data on this point.

If an individual were forced to wear ragged clothes or those which embarrassed him, or conversely, if he owned clothes he thought were superior to those of the others in his cultural group, it is entirely possible that either might have a permanent effect upon his personality or his self-concept. Although we can hypothesize about a number of ways in which clothing might permanently affect the individual, it will be a long time before we have anything more valid or reliable than casual observation as a basis for theorizing. If we tried to compare a large number of people who thought they had inadequate clothing over certain years with a second group who had adequate clothes, as to their social participation, personality factors, or any other variable we would still not have an answer to our problem. It would be next to impossible to find groups which varied on the adequacy of their clothing that did not also vary in economic level, which in turn would indicate differences in housing, nutrition, education of parents, and so on. Any differences between the two groups might be attributable to any one or several of these variables. We may hypothesize certain permanent effects, however. An individual who has not participated in social events because of a felt inadequacy in clothing over a long period of time would not be expected to participate even if he obtained adequate clothes. The habit of participating would not have developed and the individual would feel shy and uneasy at social events. The self-concept, too, would be formulated over a period of time and a change in the adequacy or in type of clothing might not automatically change his self-concept.

Bibliography

1. Alexander, Olive. *A Pilot Investigation of the Motives Underlying the Desire to Feel Well-dressed at Various Age Levels.* M. S. Thesis, Cornell Univer., 1961.
2. Andreen, J. H., Gibson, J. W., and Wetmore, O. C. Fabric evaluations based on physiological measurements of comfort, *Tex. Res. J.* 23, 1953, 11–22.
3. Baker, Hazel. The psychology of clothing as a treatment aid, *Mental Hyg.* 39, 1955, 94–98.
4. Belding, H. S. The beneficent influence of the workman's silk shirt, *Literary Digest,* May 15, 1920, 62, 65.
5. Belding, H. S. Clothing for cold weather, *J. of Home Ec.* 43, 1951, 200–203.
6. Birren, F. *Color Psychology and Color Therapy,* New York: McGraw-Hill Book Co., Inc., 1950, 284p.

7. Bowie, Alice and Dickens, Dorothy. *Clothing Supplies of Socially Participating White Farm Families of Mississippi.* State College, Miss.: Miss. Agr. Exp. Sta., Tech Bull. 30, 1942.

8. Coleman, Jettie. *Selective Factors Which Influenced the Purchasing of Clothing by Groups of Housewives and Professional Women,* M. S. Thesis: Prairie View Ag. & Mech. College, Prairie View, Texas, 1950.

9. Coutu, W. Role-playing vs. role-taking: an appeal for clarification, *Amer. Soc. Rev.* 16, 1951, 180–187.

10. Dearborn, G. The psychology of clothing, *Psychol. Rev. Monog.,* 26(1), 1918, 1–72.

11. Dickins, Dorothy. Social participation as a criterion for determining scientific minimum standards in clothing, *Rural Soc.* 9, 1944, 341–349.

12. Dickins, Dorothy, and Bowie, Alice. *A Guide to Planning Clothes for the Mississippi Farm Family,* State College, Miss.: Miss. Ag. Exper. Sta. 372, 1942.

13. Fitzsimmons, Cleo and Perkins, Nellie L. Some Illinois clothing consumption patterns, *J. of Home Ec.,* 39(8), 1947, 495–497.

14. Flaccus, L. W., Remarks on the psychology of clothes, *Ped. Sem.,* 13, 1906, 61–83.

15. Gates, Ruth. *Clothing Behavior Associated with Types of Mobility and with Extrinsic-Reward Orientation Among a Specified Group of Nonemployed Wives.* Ph.D. Thesis, Penna. State Univer., 1960.

16. Gilbert, T. F. Experiments in Morale. *J. of Soc. Psychol.* 43, 1956, 299–308.

17. Habberstad, Bea A. Unpublished Study at Cornell University, Ithaca, New York.

18. Hall, Katharine. *A Study of Some of the Factors that Contribute to Satisfactions and Dissatisfactions in the Clothing of 92 Low-income Families.* PhD. Thesis, Penna. State Univer., 1955.

19. Hoffman, Adeline. College clothing expenditures, *J. of Home Ec.* 52(8), 1960, 665–666.

20. How buying habits change, *Bus. W.,* Nov 22, 1952, 111–112.

21. Horning, Priscilla. *Observed Activity of Women Shopping for Blouses,* M.S. Thesis, Cornell University, 1961.

22. Hurlock, E. B. Motivation in Fashion, *Archives of Psychology* No. 111. 1929.

23. James, W. *Principles of Psychology,* New York: Henry Holt and Co., 1890.

24. Kelly, J. B. Heat, cold, and clothing, *Scientific Amer.* 194(2), 1956, 109–116.

25. King, B. *A Study of the Role of Clothing in Family Relationships in 25 Selected Families.* M.A. Thesis, Mich. State College, 1949.

26. Kittles, Emma. *The Importance of Clothing as a Status Symbol Among College Students.* Ph.D. Thesis. Ohio State Univer., 1961.

27. Klitzke, Dorothy. *Clothing Inventories of Outerwear of 103 New York Farm Families.* Cornell Univ. Ag. Exper. Sta. Bull. 892, 1953.

28. Lynd, R. S. and Lynd, H. M. *Middletown: A Study in Contemporary American Culture,* New York: Harcourt, Brace & World, Inc., 1929, 555p.

29. Lynn, Mary Jean. *Inventories of 86 Freshman Girls' School Wardrobes to Determine Factors Relating to the Popularity of School Clothing.* M.S. Thesis, Cornell Univer., 1952.

30. Morton, Grace M. Psychology of dress, *J. of Home Ec.,* 18(10), 1926, 584–586.

31. Murphy, Gardner. *Personality: A Biosocial Approach to Origins and Structure,* New York: Harper & Row, Publishers, 1947, 999p.

32. Newburgh, L. H. (ed.). *Physiology of Heat Regulation and the Science of Clothing,* Philadelphia: W. B. Saunders Co., 1949, 457p.

33. O'Brien, Ruth, Peterson, E. C., and Worner, R. K. Bibliography on the Relation of Clothing to Health, *U.S. Dept. of Ag. Misc. Pub.,* 62, 1929, 146 p.

34. Pressey, S. L. Influence of color upon mental and motor efficiency, *Am. J. Psychol.* 1921, 32, 326–356.

35. Ryan, Mary S. *Psychological Effects of Clothing:* Parts I and II, Cornell Univer. Ag. Exper. Sta. Bull. 882 and 898, 1952–53.

36. Ryan, Mary S. A Study of Factors in the Selection and Care of Blouses which Relate to Consumer Satisfaction, *J. of Home Ec.,* 46, 1954, 149–154.

37. Ryan, M. (ch.) Ayres, R., Carpenter, V., Densmore, B., Swanson, C. and Whitlock, M. *Consumer Satisfaction with Men's Shirts and with Women's Slips and Casual Street Dresses. Part I: Field Study in Four Communities in the North-east.* Cornell Univer. Agr. Exp. Sta. Bull. 984, 1963.

38. Saul, Ezra V., and Jaffe, Jack. The Effects of Clothing on Gross Motor Performance, *U.S.A.Q.M. Res. and Engineer Center.* Natick, Mass. 1955, project reference; 7-95-20-003B.

39. Silverman, Sylvia S. *Clothing and Appearance, Their Psychological Implications for Teen-age Girls.* New York: Teachers' College, Columbia Univer. Contributions to Ed. No. 912, 1945, 140p.

40. Smith, Madorah. A study of the causes of feeling of inferiority, *J. of Psychol.* 5, 1935, 315–332.

41. Stone, G. and Form, W. *Clothing Inventories and Preferences Among Rural and Urban Families.* East Lansing, Mich.: Tech. Bull. 246, Mich. State College Ag. Exper. Station, 1955.

42. Stone, G., Form, W. H., & Strahan, Hazel B. The Social Climate of Decision in Shopping for Clothes. *J. of Home Ec.,* 46, 1954, 86–88.

43. Studies of Family Clothing Supplies, Preliminary reports 1—5 U.S. Dept. of Ag., Bureau of Human Nutrition and Home Economics, 1950–1951.

44. Thompson, H. M. & Jelks, V. F. Clothing practices among low-income families. *J. of Home Ec.,* 33(2), 1941, 78–81.

45. Thompson, Thelma. Fashion Therapy. *J. of Home Ec.,* 54(10), 1962, 835–836.

46. Treece, Anna J. *An Interpretation of Clothing Behavior Based on Social-psychological Theory.* Ph.D. Thesis, Ohio State Univer., 1959.
47. Vaupel, Virginia M., *The Expressed Prestige Interest in the Use of Clothing as Related to the Remembered Felt Deprivations in Youth for a Specified Group of Women.* M.S. Thesis, Penna. State Univer., 1957.
48. Van Konynenburg, Kathleen. *A Study of Selected Clothing Practices of Cornell Junior Women.* M.S. Thesis, Cornell Univer., 1961.
49. Webb, W. M., *The Heritage of Dress.* London: E. G. Richards, 1908, 393p.
50. Weiner, J. S. Biological Assessment of Clothing for Tropical Service. *Brit. Med. Bull.,* 5, 1947, 20–24.
51. Whitlock, Mary (ch.), Ayres, R., and Ryan, M. S. *Consumer Satisfaction with Women's Blouses. Part I: Field Study in Four Communities in the Northeast.* Univer. Rhode Island Agr. Exp. Sta. Bull. 349, Northeast Reg. Bull. 34, June 1959.
52. Wilson, Shirley. *Selected Aspects of Clothing Behavior Associated With Success in Role Achievement and with Striving Among a Specified Group of College Women.* M.S. Thesis, Penna. State Univer., 1960.
53. Zimmerman, Carle C. *Consumption and Standards of Living.* Princeton, N.J.: D. Van Nostrand Co., Inc., 1936, 602p.

Part Two

Social-Psychological Aspects
of the Individual as a
Consumer of Textiles
and Clothing

W E turn now to the individual as consumer. Let us examine his shopping behavior, why he selects particular garments and his satisfaction with the garments he has purchased. His general motivation, the part society plays in his choice of clothing, his personality, self-concept, interests, values and attitudes which we have discussed in Part One are all important factors governing his choice of specific items of clothing.

It is advantageous, here, to focus on specific problems related to the purchase of clothing items, because one of the most important tasks confronting home economists at the present time is to aid individuals in making decisions leading to satisfactory purchases. The wide variety of goods in our affluent society makes it difficult for the consumer to make those decisions which will give him the greatest satisfaction. It is equally difficult for the producer to know what factors are most important to the consumer. This is especially true in the field of clothing. New fibers and new finishes, giving fabrics properties which have never been available before, or new combinations of old properties, new methods of dyeing giving greater variety in colors, and new and more rapid methods of production all lead to an almost endless variety from which to choose.

Before the consumer can be helped by the educator or before the producers put the most satisfactory garments on the market, we need to know what factors the consumer values most. What does he want in clothes? Why does he choose one garment rather than another or like one better than another? How and why were certain garments purchased? What attributes of garments have and have not given satisfaction in use and what were the reasons for satisfaction or dissatisfaction? With this information we should be able to predict what will be satisfactory in the future, and consequently do a better job of helping consumers make beneficial choices.

With the material in Part One as a background, we can now concentrate on the factors related to the purchase of specific garments and to their interrelationship, keeping in mind the basic material already discussed in our consideration of specific problems.

Studies by economists of consumption are also valuable aids in evaluating the material we will be discussing in this section. Such studies give us the norms with which to work and point to areas in which social-psychological research is most needed. We will also find that there is much relevant material from studies in marketing, although these have been initiated from the point of view of business and industry. Researchers in marketing have found that to answer questions about what items will or will not sell, they need to know a great deal about the consumer—what he wants and what he does at the point of purchase under varying conditions. Therefore, even though our interest is in the consumer rather than in selling a product, the research findings from marketing are often useful in understanding the consumer.

In this section we will attempt to pull together the social-psychological theories and research findings which contribute to our understanding of the consumer of clothing items. Thus, initially we will be concerned with consumer motivation and why the individual chooses specific garments. We will also discuss his behavior at the point of purchase and factors which enter into his decision to purchase or not to purchase, what information he has obtained, where he has obtained it, and what additional information he desires. Finally, we will be concerned with his satisfaction with garments in his wardrobe. The assumption we will make here is that by measuring the degree of satisfaction with garments and relating this to factors in their selection, we can predict what elements will lead to greater satisfaction in future purchases.

Bibliography

1. Brew, Margaret. A home economist looks at marketing. *J. of Marketing.* XIV(1), 1949, 72–76.
2. Canoyer, Helen G. *The American Consumer: A Critical Appraisal.* Proceedings 4th Annual Institute, Sponsored by the New York State College of Home Economics at Cornell Univer.
3. Canoyer, Helen G. Home economics in marketing research. *J. of Home Ec.* 50(6), 1958, 419–420.
4. Warning, Margaret. Future explorations in home economics: clothing. *J. of Home Ec.* 52(8), 1960, 646–651.

Chapter 7

Consumer Motivation

*T*he knowledge of why consumers have made particular choices is basic to consumer education. Also it should help us to predict what will be purchased the next time. Even the most cursory glance at the clothing industry indicates that companies can make fortunes or become bankrupt depending on the accuracy or inaccuracy of their predictions of consumers' choices of clothing. The need for information which might help to predict consumer choices or help the consumer to make wise choices has led to a great deal of research and speculation in the field of motivation relating to the purchase of clothing. Unfortunately, however, it has not led to an easy answer or even to agreement on how the problem should be attacked.

Theoretical Considerations

As discussed in Chapter 2, on motivation in general, some authors consider that the reasons for choosing a particular garment would be obtained if we could find out why we choose certain types of clothing or even why we dress at all. This may be true; but, on the other hand, these approaches may give us only a partial answer or no answer at all. When we are concerned with why we dress or why we decide to buy a new garment, it is equivalent to the psychologist's view of motivation as an explanation of why we undertake a task. That is, the psychologist, when he studies motivation, is usually concerned with such problems as why the rat will cross an electric grid, or, why the human being will undertake a job. Many psychologists, as we have seen, expect to answer this question in terms of basic needs. The questions the psychologist is asking are comparable to why we dress or set out to buy a new garment—not to why we choose this particular one. The same term—*motivation*—has unfortunately also been used to discuss the problem of why we choose one garment instead of another, although this may be an entirely different kind of problem.

Copeland (15) distinguishes between these two uses of the term motivation. He calls the motives governing the consumer to purchase a certain general kind of article the "primary motives" and those directing the consumers' expenditure to one particular article the "selective motives." In this chapter, we shall be considering the "selective motives" or why we like or choose a given garment. Although many of the primary motives, or factors which we have discussed when considering motivation in general, undoubtedly influence the choice of a particular garment, before we design experiments, we should be clear on just what our problem is, how we are defining the term *motivation* and the kind of data needed to answer our particular question. Even if we focus our attention on the reasons why we choose a particular garment, there has been little agreement on the methodology or even on what is acceptable as an adequate answer to this question. If we simply ask the consumer why he likes a particular garment, or why he chose it, the answers are so varied that they create a meaningless array. One individual might say she chose a dress because she "needed a dress for the PTA meeting," another that she "liked the color," it was "a bargain," it was "becoming," she "saw it in the window and liked it," or "I had a nylon jersey before and wanted another."

There have been two basic approaches to getting around this dilemma. One group believes that, in order to find an adequate answer, we need to dig deeply and get at the "real" underlying motives. This has been called *motivational research,* or *MR,* and has become what we might call a fad in marketing studies. It has been hailed by some as an entirely new approach to explanations of consumer behavior, and its proponents have implied that it is *only* through MR that we will obtain the true answers to why people buy what they do. Although MR is based upon the psychoanalytic concept that our real motives are buried in the unconscious and uses the same techniques as the psychoanalysts, the psychoanalytical theories themselves have been largely ignored. From psychoanalysis the motivation researchers have borrowed the use of extensive or "depth" interviews and various modifications of projective techniques. Each technique has its advocates. Dichter (16), for example, has found that depth interviews have given him the best results. Smith (47) reports focused group interviewing to be a productive technique, while others, such as Cheskin (10), considered the indirect technique to be far superior. The indirect or projective techniques have included: (1) *Modifications of the TAT (Thematic Apperception Test)*. In this type of test the subject is shown a picture and asked to tell a story about it. One type of variation is cartoonlike pictures with the "balloons" above the characters empty; the subject is to supply what the figures in the cartoon are saying or thinking. Another type of variation is to show the individual a product or picture of a product, and to ask what type of person would use that product and to tell all he can about the individual. (2) *Word association tests*. The subject in such a test is given one word and asked to respond with the first word that comes to him. (3) *Sentence completion tests.* (4) *Role playing*. In this last technique, the respondent is asked to pretend that he is another person in a specific situation and to act out what he would do. The theory is that he will reveal his own motivation without realizing that he is doing so.

Not all of these techniques have actually been used in investigating motives in the selection of clothing, but because of the personal nature of clothing, this is a field which might be considered especially appropriate for these methods. All of them have merit in that they try to elicit motives which the subject does not verbalize, and they tend to minimize the effect of rationalization, that is, the tendency for people to justify or excuse their choices on reasonable and socially "approved" grounds. On the other hand, these techniques are time-consuming and are dependent on the interpretation of the researcher. Because of the individual characteristic of each interview or response to the projective test, conditions cannot be controlled, the sample is necessarily small and the data do not lend themselves to quantitative treatment. Therefore, the reliability of the results cannot be ascertained. Also, in spite of the fact that they are considered by their advocates to give the "real" motives, the validity of the data cannot be checked. Their chief value lies in suggesting the possible range and variety of motives which may be operating at any given time. MR has emphasized the complexity and intangibility of the field, and, although this type of research is costly, it is productive of new ideas and is valuable in the planning stage of research in that it yields a wealth of material for the formulation of hypotheses.

The second approach to marketing research has been through statistical studies. These have included preference studies in which the respondent has been asked to say which fiber, color, or other attribute of a garment he likes best; research in which respondents have been asked to rank attributes or factors in order of preference or rate each on a scale as to degree of liking or satisfaction; and projects in which the respondents have been given a list of attributes or factors and asked to check those they consider when buying or those they consider important. In any of these methods the data can be numbered to be treated quantitatively, without subjective interpretation by the researcher. Also, it is usually possible to use a larger sample than with the MR studies. The assumption is made that if we know what people prefer at one point, we can predict what they will want at another time, and that if we get answers to what people want, we can infer *why* they want it. The principal advantages of these methods are that they can be treated quantitatively and the reliability and the validity determined. One of the disadvantages is that the experimenter may have overlooked important aspects in devising his questions and, therefore, may not have information on vital points.

The most important difference in the two types of methods, however, is that they yield different kinds of information. Starch (48) has suggested this difference by listing three levels of subjective awareness:

1. S knows the why and is willing to tell,
2. S is aware of the why but not willing to tell,
3. S is not aware, the reason is complex and hidden so that S cannot tell why.

He points out that survey methods will yield answers in the first category, not in the second and third and that it is here that motivational research is most useful. Whenever we undertake research we need to know, then, which type of information will be the most useful to us. Perhaps one of the reasons why we have not progressed further in answering questions concerning motivation in the selection of clothing is confusion over the meaning of the word *motivation* and an understanding of just what information we want or need. A theoretical framework should make clear where the various sorts of information contribute to our understanding of the entire problem. Therefore, our first task is to develop such a framework and to see where the scattered information we have fits and where we have gaps in our knowledge.

A THEORY OF CONSUMER MOTIVATION AND SATISFACTION

We will define consumer motivation in clothing as the reason an individual chooses to buy one garment instead of another. First of all, we will make the assumption that he wants to buy a particular garment because, for some reason, he likes that one better than others. This liking is an affective reaction to a garment. Therefore, our first problem is to get some measure of his degree of liking and disliking and an explanation of why he likes to that degree. Thus far, consumer motivation and consumer satisfaction are alike. In both instances the individual can express in some way his relative liking or disliking of a garment. Our concern is with finding out both the degree of liking and the explanation for the liking, so that we can predict what he will want in the future or what will best satisfy him later. As we shall see, many of the same techniques have been used in motivational research and in research on consumer satisfaction.

Consumer motivation and consumer satisfaction differ in the point at which the reasons for liking or disliking the garment are determined. In consumer motivation we are working at the time of purchase, while in consumer satisfaction the respondent is considering the experience of a garment as compared with his experience with other garments of that type.

The first point in our theory, then, is that in consumer motivation as well as in consumer satisfaction, we are trying to determine why a garment is liked or disliked. It is in deciding what information will adequately answer the "why" that we find authorities differing. Some consider that we can get an adequate answer by finding preferred qualities, while others think that it is necessary to get at basic values and personality factors of the individual consumer. Our position is that both sorts of information are necessary for a complete understanding, but that to solve immediate problems it is necessary to decide the type of information needed. To see the total picture we should discuss the various types of information comprising it.

Strata of Explanation. At the *first stratum* are the attributes of the garment itself—factors which are completely independent of the respondent, and can be measured objectively, such as color, fiber, weave, price, style, shape of collar, and so on. These characteristics are easily verbalized and are often given in response to the question "why do you like this garment?" Respondents are really listing *what* they like about the garment. At this point, we can find out not only what the respondent likes but his preference within each attribute. That is, we can find which color or fiber he prefers, or his ranking of a series of colors or fibers in order of preference. We will review some of these studies later; they are probably the most numerous of those dealing with consumer motivation. The data from these can be treated statistically and the methods for obtaining them are relatively clear-cut and simple to design. The greatest disadvantage is that this kind of data is insufficient by itself for the majority of problems. For example, if we find that a given fiber is preferred for women's blouses we have no way of predicting whether or not it will still be preferred if a new fiber comes on the market, or whether it will be preferred for dresses or other garments unless we know something about why it was preferred.

The *second stratum* of explanation is concerned with the properties of the individual attributes or the components of satisfaction. Examples of responses are: ease of care, durability, appearance, performance during use (wrinkling, holding shape, and so on), adaptability to various occasions or to other garments. These properties as well as the attributes can usually be measured in the laboratory or the respondent's judgment of the properties be determined. If asked why he likes a particular attribute such as fiber, the respondent usually has a reason at this second stratum.

One of the greatest criticisms of the research in the area of consumer motivation and consumer satisfaction is that these two strata have not been differentiated. Thus, we often have studies in which we find a table listing the reasons for liking a particular garment and the percentage of respondents giving a particular reason. For example, we may find 20 percent saying they like the fiber, 30 percent the color, 10 percent the ease of care, 15 percent the appearance, and others. If we are interested in finding out how many are influenced by the ease of care, we are in a quandary as to whether to take just the 10 percent or whether to add to it the 20 percent who said they liked the fiber. How many of those who liked the fiber did so because it was easy to care for? Or from the other side, if we are interested in how many are concerned with the fiber of the garment, should we add to those who mentioned this point any who mentioned durability or ease of care or perhaps some of those who listed appearance? In other words, unless we decide at which stratum we want information before we begin any research and design our method accordingly, our data may be meaningless. For this stratum also we can obtain data by survey techniques and the findings can be treated statistically. The affective reaction is the importance the consumer places upon this property in relation to other properties and the comparison of garments on basis of a given property. Thus we can find either by questioning or by statistical means: (1) the degree of ease of care, or durability, and so on, a consumer attributes to one garment in relation to others; and (2) whether the consumer considers ease of care more or less important to over-all satisfaction than, say, durability. We will discuss methods of determining the relative importance of various components in greater detail when we discuss measuring satisfaction with garments (see Chapter 9).

A possible *third stratum* of explanation of motivation in the selection of clothing is found in the relationship between the interests and values in clothing and the general interests and values of the individual. Responses in this area are usually more difficult to verbalize. For example, the individual who is anxious to impress people and especially desirous of his group's approval may be interested in clothing mainly because of the impression it will make on others. Another person may be interested in practical considerations, in durability as related to price. Hartmann, as we have seen (Chapter 4), has suggested that Spranger's personality types could be expressed in clothing choices. In the discussion of attitudes and values (Chapter 5), we mentioned a number of studies which related values to consumer choices. For some problems survey methods can be used, while for others indirect or clinical methods are necessary.

The ultimate explanations of why the individual has interests and values which lead to consumer choices is the *fourth* and last *stratum* and the one at which the most theorizing takes place. The theories discussed under general motivation in clothing attempt explanations at this level. No research indicates that any one theory of motivation is adequate while others are inadequate; however, more adequate theories could be formulated at this level, with increased knowledge and understanding at the other strata. Furthermore, many problems in the area of motivation in clothing selection can be solved adequately at the other strata where research is less difficult and costly. For example, both the clothing manufacturer and the teacher in consumer education might be content with the information that the majority of women prefer wool sweaters rather than sweaters of man-made fibers (stratum one) because of the warmth (stratum two). They would know then that if a man-made fiber warmer than wool were developed, it would be preferred. For the immediate problem neither the manufacturer nor the consumer–educator would need an explanation beyond this point; it would make no difference to their work or teaching whether it was ultimately due to an instinct for self-preservation or whether they liked the warmth because it was like the warmth of a mother's womb. However, it might be extremely important for either of them to know something concerning the patterns of components at either of the first two strata. For example, they would need to know how important the warmth of the sweater was in relation to ease of care, appearance, and so on, and how much of one could be sacrificed to other components without changing motivation.

You may have noticed that as we have been discussing various strata, certain factors such as fit, becomingness, and comfort have not been mentioned. This is not because they are unimportant, but they differ somewhat from the levels we have been describing. Fit is a specific attribute which, in some respects, is comparable to our first stratum, but it differs because it is dependent upon the wearer. A garment fits or does not fit the particular wearer. Comfort and becomingness are similarly comparable to the second stratum, but they likewise are related to the physical person. Both comfort and becomingness are dependent on certain attributes (fiber, style, color) but are also dependent on fit. For many problems, fit can be grouped with attributes at the first stratum of explanation, and becomingness and comfort with properties or components of satisfaction on the second stratum, but the differences should be kept in mind and for certain problems these factors should be treated separately.

Minimum levels of liking for or satisfaction with garment characteristics. The next point in our theoretical framework is that there is a certain minimum level for each component of satisfaction (second stratum) that must be attained for the garment to be considered satisfactory or acceptable. For example, a garment no matter how beautiful or becoming would not ordinarily be acceptable if the consumer expected that it would last for only two wearings; or a garment acceptable as to durability, ease of care, and comfort might be rejected by the consumer if it only came in a color which he felt was extremely unbecoming. For some of the components such as ease of care and durability the minimum levels acceptable to various groups could be determined and these related to laboratory tests. A garment that meets the individual's bare minimum requirements would theoretically be acceptable, but would not be highly satisfactory. Whether or not it would be purchased by the consumer would be dependent upon the felt need. A consumer who thought he must have a garment for a specific occasion or who thought he needed to replace a worn-out garment might purchase one which met the minimum levels on all components, if none he considered better were available; but, if he felt no great need, would reject such a garment.

For the garment to be highly satisfactory or highly desired, we would hypothesize that it would have one or several components higher than the minimum level. We would also hypothesize that possessing one component to an extreme degree might compensate for another or others at the minimum level. Thus, a garment which just meets the minimum requirements for durability, ease of care, and beauty might be purchased and prove very satisfactory if it happened to be extremely comfortable.

The minimum levels of liking for, or satisfaction with, each of the garment properties or attributes would vary with the interests and values of the consumer (stratum three). For example, the person who is interested in esthetical aspects of objects and puts a high value on beauty would be expected to require higher minimum levels of beauty in garments than would those without this special interest. For him, a garment which was extremely beautiful would be considered highly satisfactory even though it met only the minimum levels of satisfaction for other properties. In other words, not only do minimum levels of satisfaction for each component vary with the interests and values of the consumer, but the patterns of relationship between the components also vary.

The patterns of components and the minimum levels of satisfaction with each garment attribute, or property, would also vary with the purpose for which the garment was intended. A consumer would presumably demand a higher minimum level of durability in bluejeans than in an evening dress, for example.

Summary. In summary the theoretical framework for reviewing research in consumer motivation and satisfaction is the following:

Consumer satisfaction, motivation, and preferences are similar in many respects. In general, the distinction between consumer motivation and consumer satisfaction is a temporal one. We speak of consumer motivation when we are considering the purchase of a garment; satisfaction is measured after the garment has been in the possession of the consumer. In both cases, the concept of various strata of explanation and the measurement of the relative importance of factors at one of these strata is equally applicable.

General satisfaction with a garment can be evaluated by the individual, but this over-all satisfaction is made up of various strata of explanation. At the most specific and impersonal level we have such garment attributes as color, fiber, or cut. The term *preference* is concerned with measurement at this first or most specific stratum. The specific or objective attributes of garments in preference studies can be related to either consumer motivation or consumer satisfaction. At the second stratum, we are concerned with components of satisfaction with garments or perceived properties. Examples are: ease of care, durability, and appearance. At the third stratum relationships between factors in the first two strata and the interests and values of the individual are investigated. Finally, the fourth or last stratum is concerned with the ultimate explanations of behavior. "Motivational Research" seeks explanations at the last two strata and proponents of this approach consider that it is only through this means that we can predict consumer behavior.

It is our contention that the stratum of explanation at which we work should depend on the problem we are trying to solve and the use which is going to be made of the results. For a complete understanding of consumer motivation, we need information at all strata and relationships between the various strata.

We hypothesize that, at the more objective and specific strata, there are certain minimum levels for each attribute or component below which a garment is rejected. There are also levels below which a garment would never be rated as highly desirable. A high degree of satisfaction or desirability on one attribute or component may compensate for minimum levels on other components. The minimum levels for each individual will be related to the purpose for which the garment was purchased and to the interests and values of the individual.

Research on the Selection of Specific Items of Clothing

PREFERENCES

In discussing consumer motivation, it has been indicated that at the first stratum of explanation we are concerned with the attributes of garments. In both marketing and consumer education, two basic assumptions have been made when using the results of such studies. The first assumption is that the attribute being studied, such as color, *is* important in the selection of the garment. The second assumption is that if we can find the preferred attribute, for example, the favorite color, we can predict the consumer will purchase, or be most satisfied with, a garment which has the preferred attribute. This type of research is relatively clear-cut, easy to understand; and there is a long history of such experimental work using accepted techniques.

Therefore, it is not surprising that a large proportion of the experimental work in marketing has been the study of preferences.

In studies on preferences, the subject is comparing the pleasantness of one object or attribute of the object with that of another. Much of the experimentation, especially the earlier work, has been known as *experimental esthetics*. It was initiated by Gustav Fechner in the 1870s when experimental psychology was in its infancy. Fechner conceived the idea that, if a large number of people indicated preferences, individual differences would be canceled out and esthetic norms for the group would be determined, and from this, underlying principles or rules of art could be determined.

A number of methods of obtaining preferences of the group were developed.[1] Among these are:

(1) *Naming* of preferred item or quality. Here the subject is asked to name his favorite color or style or whatever is being measured.

(2) *Choice.* In this method the subject merely states which of a number of stimuli he likes the best or the least. Using this method, it is possible to discover only the one stimulus which is considered best or worst by the group, and it is impossible to obtain a progression from best to worst and therefore, to derive any principles.

(3) *Order of Merit.* In recent years, this is generally called the *ranking* method. With this method the subject is given a number of stimuli which he is to arrange in order of preference. By assigning weights to the various positions on the scale, it is possible to obtain a scale of preference for the group.

(4) *Rating.* A scale for the rating of the various stimuli is set up in advance, and may have any desired number of steps. For example, it may be merely 3 steps such as "like, neutral, and dislike" or it may have 5 or 7 steps. By using weights it is also possible to obtain numerical scores, but the statistical procedure is complicated by the fact that individuals differ in the way in which they interpret such a scale. Some individuals tend to use only the center part of the scale, others to use the entire scale, and still others tend to use either the upper or lower parts of the scale to a greater extent.

(5) *Paired Comparisons.* The stimuli are presented to the subject in pairs and the individual is asked to say which of the two stimuli he prefers. Each stimulus is presented with every other stimulus in a given series, and from the data a preference scale is obtained.

In all of these methods the stimuli are kept identical except for the one variable being studied. Thus, if the problem is to find color preferences, squares of paper of identical size and texture might be used and shown on a neutral background. If the problem is to find the preferred proportions

---

[1] For discussion of methods in experimental esthetics, see Woodworth, R. S. *Experimental Psychology.* New York: Holt, Rinehart and Winston, Inc., 1938. (Chap. 16, pp. 368–392).

for a rectangle, the rectangles are identical in every respect except for the dimensions.

Color preferences. There have been many studies on color preferences—color preferences of men versus women, of children versus adults, of people from one cultural or geographic group versus people of another cultural or geographic group. Many of the older experiments did not describe the stimuli accurately as to hue, brightness or saturation, and were poorly controlled in other aspects. Therefore, results were often contradictory and confusing. In fact, in 1925, after extensive controlled studies, Allesch (2) said that the more refined and careful the work, the more the subjects disagreed and the more the individual subject was apt to contradict himself. More recently, however, Guilford (22) and Eysenck (18), using well-controlled situations and rigorous statistical treatment of the results, have found that there is some system in color preferences. Yet, even if color preferences can be determined for groups under the special controlled situation in the laboratory, it may be impractical to apply the results to the field of clothing. In clothing we have not only the variables of different tints and chromas, but also the texture of the material and the lines and form of the garment. Furthermore, the color is usually combined with one or more other colors, and the combinations, as well as the relative amounts of each color, influence the final result. In addition to these variables, the color(s) will vary in becomingness to the individuals who wear them.

A study of color preferences in dresses was made by Philip (44). This was mainly a study in methodology and the results are tentative. The test material consisted of five sets of colored fashion plates and each set of plates contained one dress of each of five colors—green, blue, red, black, and brown. He used pictures cut from the current issues of *Vogue* Magazine to insure equal emphasis on fashion. All of the pictures were approximately the same size and all were of afternoon dresses, but they did vary in line, form, and trimming. The sets were presented in random order to the subjects who ranked the pictures in order of preference. The subjects were 19 college men and 9 college women. The results for the men were statistically reliable and showed that this method might be a productive one. "With the caution that this investigation has been carried out with few subjects, and that factors other than color such as style and pattern were not controlled, there are indications that the men place considerable emphasis on color in their rankings, blue being the favorite color and black the next . . ." [p. 113]. The women seemed to base their preferences on other factors, and color was subordinate in their preferences; green and blue, however, tended to be chosen more often than other colors.

Pearson (41) obtained adolescents' preference for dress colors by a different method. In a questionnaire, she asked 125 high school girls to check the preferred colors from a list. Twenty-one different colors were listed and of these the first preference was for light blue and the second for pink. The method of naming colors and asking for preference has been a common one. It has the obvious disadvantage of not revealing the saturation or tint nor the exact hue of the color which the subject has in mind. Two subjects may both give blue as a favorite color but be referring to quite different hues.

Preferences for line and design. Experiments have been conducted using simple geometric forms, or finding the point at which a line should be placed to give a pleasing balance in a line drawing. These, however, have been on extremely simple forms and, therefore, have little application to the esthetics of clothing. Lundholm (32) found that when he asked his subjects to draw a beautiful line, the lines themselves varied greatly, but when they were asked to describe what they had done, there were similarities. The subjects said that a beautiful line was one that had gradual, smooth curves, and that it should have symmetry and continuity. These are often terms used by designers in describing dresses and could be used as hypotheses in preference studies.

In a carefully controlled study, Jacobson (26) attempted to investigate the basic factors underlying beauty in costume by measuring preferences of large groups for certain dress designs. In the preliminary studies the esthetic factors of balance, rhythm, proportion, and emphasis seemed to be criteria upon which preferences were made. These, consequently, were the variables with which she worked. Her stimuli in each series consisted of historical costume plates. Historical, rather than contemporary costumes, were used so that the influence of fashion and of personal experience with the design or aspects of the design would be minimized as far as possible. Texture, color, and other variables were eliminated by the use of outline drawings. A given design was used as the standard, and experimental variations were made in the balance and proportion. For example, a given design might be kept identical in all variations except for the size of a cuff, or the length of a jacket. Thus, a given series consisted of a design and of variations of this design. The method of paired comparisons was used, and each variation of a design was shown with every other variation. Her subjects consisted of 33 experts in art and design, 162 nonexperts, and 24 trained in psychological laboratory techniques. The results showed that when beauty is reduced to a few factors, there is the greatest agreement. There was high agreement between the experts and the nonexperts, as well as within the two groups. The factors of proportion, balance, rhythm, and emphasis were found to be operative in the judgment of beauty in costume design as in other art forms. Perhaps the greatest contribution this study has made is in demonstrating that the methods used in studying perception and in experimental esthetics are also applicable to the study of beauty in costume.

Consumer preferences. Studies of consumer preferences for specific attributes comprise a major part of the research on consumer motivation. The most complete studies of this kind in the area of clothing have been done under the auspices of the United States Department of Agriculture. The first study had to do with women's preferences for various textile products (51). Data were collected by the interview method, and the study covered not only women's clothing but also household textiles. The sample was designed to be representative of all women in the United States and consisted of 1782 respondents. Both checklist questions and open-ended questions were used to obtain preferences in fiber for a number of types of garments and household textiles. The results of this study showed that cotton was the most favored fiber in 1946 when the interviewing took place. With many new fibers on the market in recent years, this picture may have changed, but other results of the study still may reflect consumer motivation as adequately as when the study was made. For example, the women were shown a list of eight characteristics and asked to choose three out of the list that they considered most important for each of four kinds of garments and one household fabric. For three of the garment categories—summer street dresses, one-piece winter street dresses, and short-sleeved blouses—the appearance of the garment was considered important by the largest number of respondents. For house dresses, the laundering qualities and for curtains, the durability were checked most frequently.

A later study of consumers' preferences for fabric characteristics (14) was designed to study consumer motivation and satisfaction, at what we have termed the second stratum. Women were asked to rank a list of fabric characteristics in order of their importance. The most important fabric characteristic for the women in this sample was the ability to hold shape, wrinkle resistance was next in importance, and color-fastness third. When the women were asked to name the characteristics which influenced the choice of the last dress bought, the most frequent answers were attributes of garments (stratum one) such as weave, color, feel on skin; and the characteristics which they had ranked previously as important were seldom mentioned. To find the reason for this discrepancy, a subsample was revisited. Color fastness, shrink resistance and ability to hold shape were the characteristics which repondents considered standardized by the manufacturer. In other words, these characteristics are considered to be adequately provided by the manufacturer and, therefore, the consumers did not feel the need to consider them at the time of the purchase. This brings out an important point. In terms of our concept of minimum levels, we can say that most garments on the market are above the minimum levels for these factors. There are doubtless other, less important, factors which also are found at an adequate or above minimum level in most garments. Future studies in marketing or consumer motivation should be designed to determine whether or not the important garment characteristics are being met at an adequate level and standardized so that they do not enter into purchase decisions.

This important study also determined preferences for various attributes such as color, sheerness, and weave. Navy and black were preferred for winter dresses, and pastel blue or other pastels for summer dresses. Twill or plain weave was favored for winter street dresses, plain or satin weave for summer street dresses and satin weave for special occasions. These attributes were related to the fabric characteristics ranked in the other parts of the study. This research is a good example of a design in which the strata we hypothesized have been kept separate, and relationships between the strata established. A USDA study concerning men's preferences among selected clothing items (36) was similar to the study of women's preferences for the textile products. The sample and the types of questions were similar. The parts of the study having to do with preferences were again mostly concerned with fiber and weave. The men were asked whether or not they owned particular items of clothing, the fibers they preferred for each type of item and their beliefs as to the advantages and disadvantages of each fiber. Those who preferred cotton said they did so primarily because they thought cotton was comfortable to wear. Comfort was most often given as the reason for preferring wool in winter socks, winter underwear and robes, and also for preferring rayon for summer sport shirts, extra summer trousers, socks, and pajamas.

A more recent extension of this last study (37) shows that cotton is still the most popular fabric for most items in men's wardrobes, and its outstanding virtue for most men is that "it's cool." In other words, comfort is still the most important factor for men. In certain items—slacks, summer suits and sport coats—wool was listed as the preferred fabric, and the reason given most frequently was its wearing quality.

The studies cited above have been the survey type of research in which a large sample is questioned about their preferences. Another kind of study uses methods which the psychologists have employed in perceptual studies and called *psychophysical methods*. The United States Testing Company has been using such methods (which they call *psychometrics*) to test the acceptability of various fabrics before they have been manufactured for the market. For this type of test they have used a selected sample of individuals and brought them into the laboratory, where all extraneous influences are removed. They use a smaller sample of individuals than would be used in a survey form of study, and these subjects are tested more intensively. By methods of paired comparisons or ranking, the subjects indicate preferences for various fabrics or garments on a number of variables such as color, drape, or hand. In such research, it is assumed that chance variables are either controlled in the laboratory or cancelled out by the number of trials given each subject. If there is not wide variation among subjects, it is assumed that there would not be wide variation with larger samples. This kind of research is especially adaptable to certain factors such as the hand of fabric and is useful in product development when manufacturers wish to predict the acceptability of a new fabric. When the problem is to find the relative importance of various characteristics for a given population, these methods are not appropriate.

Factors affecting preferences. A number of studies have been made on the factors influencing preferences. Although the majority of these used relatively simple stimuli, we can assume that they may affect the preferences in the same way, if the stimuli are more complex as in the case of clothing.

Washburn and Powelson (49) found that suggestion might influence preference. They asked their subjects to rate colors on a seven-point scale from extremely pleasant to extremely unpleasant. Verbal suggestions either as to pleasantness or unpleasantness were given to those colors which were placed in the middle of the scale, with half of the subjects receiving suggestions in one direction and the other half in the other direction. The suggestion was a favorable or unfavorable adjective pronounced by the experimenter as the color was shown. When retested, 25 out of 35 subjects made judgments in the direction in which the suggestion was made. This implies that we might prefer a dress, because it was praised rather than because of an actual liking for any one attribute, or that a given attribute might be preferred because of former praise. Suggestion may be less direct than this but still operative. One individual, for example, might be very much impressed by expensiveness of clothing and, when comparing two garments with visible price tags, might be influenced to choose the more expensive dress as the more beautiful. The same sort of suggestion might be given by making known the name of the designer, the knowledge of the store at which it was purchased, or the fact that it was advertised in a certain magazine.

Hunt (24), in a study on color preferences, found that the results were in part a function of the number of stimuli and the number of categories used. The variability of the responses was greater the larger the number of stimuli and the higher the number of categories in which judgments were made. We might expect, then, that the variability of responses would be greater for clothing than they would be for simple colors, because the stimuli are more complicated. Hunt also found that the variability decreased as the number of times the stimuli were presented increased, showing that there was learning in preferences as well as in other tasks.

Another factor that may affect preference is the subject's experience with the objects being judged. Pepper (42) found that disliked colors tended to gain in attractiveness and preferred colors tended to lose attractiveness, as the subject saw them frequently. His subjects were first given a preference test for colors, then, for a period of a year, the subjects were exposed to the colors for one hour each week with a preference test every fourth week. The colors which in the first test were most preferred tended to diminish in attractiveness, and those which were least preferred in the first test tended to gain in attractiveness. This may be the same phenomenon which we observe taking place when a radically new fashion is introduced. At first people dislike the new trend and say that they are not going to follow it, but as it grows in popularity in the group it grows in popularity for the individual, and he not only accepts the new fashion but finds it beautiful.

Although the expert may be more consistent in his own judgments because of increased experience, a study by Gordon (21) has shown that the experts may agree less with each other in their preferences than do the nonexperts. Gordon used two series of 25 pictures of oriental rugs, which the subjects were asked to arrange in order of beauty. Several weeks later, part of the group arranged the same series again. "Experts" were usually not like the group as a whole, and there was in addition a low correlation among the "experts." The hypothesis to explain this might be that, the "experts" knew more variables on which to judge oriental rugs than did the nonexperts. Not only would consistency decrease with an increase in complexity of the problem, but, also, one expert might have been judging on one variable while another was judging on a different variable. If all were asked to judge along one specific dimension, the agreement might be greater because of either or both of these reasons.

Studies on attractiveness and repulsiveness of the human face (43) have shown that people tend to judge average features as most attractive and the farther away from the average a feature is the less attractive it appears. In clothing designs, also, even though the designer strives for uniqueness and distinctiveness, the extremely different is considered repulsive. This is evident from comments on high fashion each year as they are pictured in newspapers and magazines. Those deviating greatly from what we are accustomed to are perceived as ugly and are ridiculed. The limits beyond which a design cannot venture and still remain attractive probably varies from group to group. That is, within certain groups the deviation from the average or accepted must be very small while in other groups the variation could be much greater. Many interesting research problems could be carried out on how far a given form can go from the average or standard and still be accepted as attractive by the individual or the group, and the factors which influence the acceptance or rejection of variations from the norm.

Evaluation of Various Methods of Studying Consumer Motivation

Cheskin and Ward (11) have pointed out that any research that asks direct questions concerning preferences may be subject to error. Individuals may indicate their liking for one object, while, if they are given a choice, actually choose another object. These authors give as an example a study in which the subjects were asked to rank 6 kerchiefs as to beauty. Then a contest was conducted in which the same women were offered a kerchief as a prize. Only 10 percent chose the same kerchief in the two situations. This experiment is quoted often by those interested in *Motivational Research* as illustrating the point that preference studies are not adequate for market research, and that in order to be able to predict consumer demands we need to know the "why's." This may be true. On the other hand, it may be that the assumption underlying many preference studies that the consumer will purchase the preferred item is at fault. Perhaps in this case the women believed that their first choice was most beautiful but they did not select it as a prize because it would not look well with their other clothes. A question on which kerchiefs they would choose might have given results which could have been used in predicting. Further research is needed to indicate, if and when, preference studies are adequate for predicting consumer purchases or consumer satisfaction.

Nybroten (40) discusses some of the difficulties in consumer preference studies. He states that if one asks a subject about a particular commodity he may say that he "likes" it but you do not know the degree of liking, and different subjects may mean different things by "like." The best way to measure preferences, he feels, is by giving an individual the choice of two or more alternatives, that is, by using the psychophysical methods such as those used by the United States Testing Company. Nybroten also suggests, however, that prices might be fixed to the choices so that the individual would have to indicate how much more he would be willing to pay for the preferred article. This method would theoretically give a scale and would indicate the relative distances on the preference scale for the various objects being compared. In practice, however, this technique has many difficulties. In the first place money itself has a variety of meanings and values for different individuals. To one, a dollar more may indicate a great difference in the acceptability of a given article, and, to another, it may mean little. This is true even within the same income groups. Furthermore, the price someone is accustomed to pay for an article influences the amount he is willing to pay. For example, the individual who usually pays $5.00 for an article will be less willing to pay $1.00 more for that article than the individual who usually pays $10.00, and yet neither does the percentage of increase give a more accurate picture.

In spite of many criticisms of preference studies, if the limitations are recognized and the various factors which influence preferences are controlled or varied systematically, we may gain much from the use of such studies. The first step in knowing why a person chooses a given item of clothing is to know *what* he chooses or what garment attributes he prefers. Preference studies are usually designed to investigate the preferences within a single attribute such as color or fiber, but, they may also be used to determine the relative importance of various attributes.

To predict consumer behavior in the future, or to understand the data from the preference studies at the first stratum, we need additional information on the perceived properties of garments. We have called this the second stratum. Problems at this level include determining the relative ease of care, wrinkle resistance, or durability of garments or comparing the relative importance of these factors for the consumer. These characteristics can then be related to the specific attributes of the garment in stratum 1. For the majority of practical problems, information on these two levels is sufficient, but for a complete understanding of consumer motivation, we need to relate information from these levels to the values and interests of the consumers and to the basic motivating factors.

Almost no research has been carried out thus far on the third and fourth strata in the purchase of clothing, but indirect techniques which would be useful in such problems have been used in other areas of psychology of clothing and have proved useful. We hope, therefore, that research directed at investigating relationships between specific values or interests and preferences for specific attributes or perceived properties of garments will be undertaken. We will see, when we discuss satisfaction, that some beginnings have been made in this direction.

Bibliography

1. *A Bibliography of Theory and Research Techniques in the Field of Human Motivation.* An Advertising Research Foundation Publication, 1956, 105p.
2. Allesch, G. J. von. Die Aesthetische Erscheinungsweise der Farben, *Psychol. Forsch.* 6, 1925, 1–91, 215–281.
3. Allport, G. W. The trend in motivational theory. *Amer. J. of Orthopsychiatry.* 23, 1953, 107–119.
4. Bauer, R. Sigmund Freud, Supersalesman. *Contemporary Psychol.* 3(10), 1958, 292–294.
5. Bayton, J. A. Consumer preference research in the department of agriculture. *Agr. Ec. Res.* 2, 1950, 105–112.
6. Bilkey, W. J. The vector hypothesis of consumer behavior. *J. of Mktg.* 16, 1951, 137–151.
7. Britt, S. H. The strategy of consumer motivation. *J. of Mktg.* 14, 1950, 666–674.
8. Brown, L. O. What motivational research is and how it works: Its advantages and shortcomings. *Advertising Age.* 26(30), 1955, 65–69.
9. Bruner, A. W. U.S. testing unit to determine fabric appeal via psychometrics. *Women's Wear Daily.* 74, 1952 (Oct. 14), 29.
10. Cheskin, L. *How to Predict What People Will Buy.* New York: Liveright Publishing Corp., 1957, 233p.
11. Cheskin, L. and Ward, L. B. Indirect approach to market reactions. *Harvard Bus. Rev.* 26, 1948, 572–580.
12. Clark, L. H. (Ed.). *Consumer Behavior.* Vol. I, New York: New York University Press, 1954, 128p.
13. Coleman, Jettie L. *Selective Factors Which Influence the Purchasing of Clothing by Groups of Housewives and Professional Women.* M.S. Thesis, Prairie View Agr. and Mech. College, Prairie View, Texas, 1950.

14. *Consumers' Concepts of Fabric.* U.S. Department of Agriculture, Marketing Research Report No. 338, July 1959.
15. Copeland, M. T. Consumers' buying motives. *Harvard Bus. Rev.* 2(2), 1924, 139–153.
16. Dichter, E. *Handbook of Consumer Motivations.* New York: McGraw-Hill Book Co., Inc., 1964, 480p.
17. Dichter, E. These are the real reasons why people buy goods. *Advertising and Selling.* July 1948, 33–34.
18. Eysenck, H. J. A critical and experimental study of color preferences. *Amer. J. of Psychol.* 54, 1941, 383–394.
19. Ferber, R. and Wales, H. G. (Eds.). *Motivation and Market Behavior.* Homewood, Ill.: Richard D. Irwin, Inc., 1958, 429p.
20. Finlayson, B. B. *An Investigation of Consumer Motivation in the Selection of Sweaters as Related to General Personal Values.* M.S. Thesis, Cornell Univer. 1959.
21. Gordon, K. Study of aesthetic judgments. *J. of Exper. Psychol.* 6, 1923, 36–43.
22. Guilford, J. P. There is system in color preferences. *J. of Optical Soc. Am.* 30, 1940, 455.
23. Haire, M. Projective techniques in market research. *J. of Mktg.* 14, 1950, 649–656.
24. Hunt, W. A. Variability in the affective judgment. *Amer. J. of Psychol.* 51, 1938, 507–513.
25. Jacobson, Wilhelmina E. An experimental investigation of the basic aesthetic factors in costume design. *Psychol. Monog.* 45(1), 1933, 147–184.
26. Jacobson, Wilhelmina E. Human motives underlying fashion changes. *Practical Home Ec.* 14, 1936, 230–231.
27. Katona, G. Attitude change: instability of response and acquisition of experience. *Psychol. Monog.* 72(10), 1958, 1–38.
28. Katona, G. The predictive value of data on consumer attitudes. *Consumer Behavior.* Vol. II (Clark, Lincoln, Ed.), 66–77.
29. Katona, G. Key to consumer apparel color choices sought in test. *Women's Wear Daily.* 1953, 1, 33.
30. Lazarsfeld, P. F. The art of asking why in marketing research. *The Nat'l Mktg. Rev.* 1(1), 1935, 26–38.
31. Leonhard, D. *Consumer Research with Projective Techniques.* Shenandoah, Iowa: Ajax Corporation, 1955, 143p.
32. Lundholm, Helge. The affective tone of lines, experimental research. *Psychol. Rev.* 28, 1921, 43–60.
33. Luther, W. F. What consumers want in fabrics. *Modern Tex.* 33(9), 1952, 79 and 112.
34. Martineau, P. *Motivation in Advertising.* New York: McGraw-Hill, Book Co., Inc., 1947, 210p.
35. McGregor, D. "Motives" as a tool of market research. *Harvard Bus. Rev.* 19, 1940, 42–51.

36. *Men's Preferences among Selected Clothing Items.* Misc. Pub. 706, U.S. Dept. Ag. 1949.
37. *Men's Preferences for Cotton, Wool, and Other Fibers in Selected Clothing Items.* U.S. Dept. of Ag., Marketing Research Report No. 244, 1958.
38. Newman, J. W. *Motivation Research and Marketing Management.* Boston: Harvard University Graduate School of Business Administration, 1957, Part I, 3–66.
39. Nolan, Francena and Levine, D. What women expect in clothes and fabrics. *Agr. Marketing.* Aug. 1959, 12.
40. Nybroten, N. Rate of commodity disappearance and consumer preference. *J. of Farm Ec.* 31, 1949, 346–350.
41. Pearson, L. H. Teen-agers' preferences in clothes. *J. of Home Ec.* 42, 1950, 801–802.
42. Pepper, S. C. Changes of appreciation of color combinations. *Psychol. Rev.* 26, 1919, 389–396.
43. Perrin, F. A. C. Physical attractiveness and repulsiveness. *J. of Exper. Psychol.* (4), 1921, 203–217.
44. Philip, B. R. A method for investigating color preferences in fashions. *J. of Appl. Psychol.* 29, 1945, 108–114.
45. Ryan, T. A. Drives, tasks, and the initiation of behavior. *Amer. J. of Psychol.* 71, 1958, 74–93.
46. Schreier, F. T. and Wood, A. J. Motivation analysis in market research. *The J. of Mktg.* 13, 1948, 172–182.
47. Smith, G. *Motivation Research in Advertising and Marketing.* New York: McGraw-Hill Book Co. Inc., 1954, 242p.
48. Starch, D. What is new about motivation research. *Printers' Ink.* 252(7), 1955, 58–61.
49. Washburn, M. F. and Powelson, I. The effect of verbal suggestion on judgments of the affective value of colors. *Amer. J. of Psychol.* 24, 1913, 267–269.
50. Wolf, H. A. (Ed.) *Motivation Research: A New Aid to Understanding Your Market.* Boston: Motivation Research Associates, 1955, 80p.
51. *Women's Preferences Among Selected Textile Products.* Misc. Pub. No. 641, U.S. Dept. of Agr., 1947.

Chapter 8

Consumer Behavior

*T*here are two general methods of studying consumer behavior. One is from the point of view of economics or marketing. Such studies are concerned with consumption, and the factors influencing consumption. The focus is either on the product and the factors which make one product take a larger or smaller share of the family's total expenditures, or it is on the total disposable income and the relative amounts spent for different types of goods and services.

The second general method of approaching the topic of consumer behavior is from the viewpoint of the consumer. Home economists, with their focus on family and individual welfare, are interested in shopping and buying habits, decision making, and factors which influence purchases. Psychologists are also interested in consumer behavior from this standpoint. We shall, in this chapter, analyze this method of approach, but we must recognize that the first approach offers us a basic framework for understanding the total problem. It is especially important in giving us perspective when we are dealing with a limited aspect of the entire problem—in this case consumer behavior in the purchase of clothing.

The rural sociologists have given us a theory which promises to be helpful in formulating hypotheses concerning consumer behavior. Beal and Rogers (2) used it as a basis for studying consumer acceptance of new fibers. In this theory, the act of adopting a new product is not considered a simple unit act but rather a complex series of acts occurring over a period of time. The process is broken down for convenience into five stages: (1) Awareness stage. The individual is exposed to the new idea or product and is aware of its existence but knows nothing about it. (2) Information stage. The individual is motivated or interested in the product and gets more information about it. (3) Application stage. The individual is interested in whether the product would be satisfactory for him. He weighs the relative advantages and disadvantages of this product over others for his personal use. (4) Trial stage. The individual is interested in actually trying out the new product. (5) Adoption stage. The individual decides whether the product is satisfactory for his particular needs and, if so, decides to make continued use of the product. The next problem is to find the sources of information available to, and used by, the consumer at each of these stages. The authors in this particular study were interested in the adoption of nylon, Orlon, and Dacron fabrics. The informational sources were classified into: (1) Mass media—radio, television, magazines, and newspapers. (2) Agencies—extension service, high school home economics. (3) Informal—relatives, neighbors, friends. (4) Commercial—sales personnel, displays, written material. (5) Self—own experimentation and information. They found that mass media were most important at the awareness stage; informal sources were especially important at the information and application stages; and commercial sources most important at the trial stage. This study is especially interesting in that it gives us a theoretical framework for future studies. As others use the classifications adopted here we will be able to compare the results of one study with those of another, and find how the various media used at different stages vary with the age, the socioeconomic status, education, size of home town, type of product, and so on. This is far superior to the small scattered studies which we have at present.

The study of adoption of certain brands, as well as fibers, could use this approach and, it might also be used for garments with little variation in style such as men's shirts or work clothing, underwear, stockings and socks which are purchased repeatedly. On the other hand, many clothing purchases are unique in that there is little or no expectation that the same style of garment will be purchased again. For research with these garments, a modification of the approach could be used. The classification of informational sources would be the same for all. The classification of the total process, however, would need to be revised. The first stage, comparable to awareness, might be the recognition of need or desire for a new garment for a specific purpose. The second stage, as in the adoption process, would be the information stage in which the individual is comparing styles, fabrics, and so on, to decide what to look for in making a selection. The first and second stages in this process we have discussed under the topic of motivation—the awareness of a need for a new garment has been discussed under the general topic of motivation and the desired attributes of garments and perceived properties of the attributes in the previous chapter on consumer motivation. The third stage might be the actual shopping and the fourth stage the final selection. As with the adoption process, one of the first problems in the shopping and selection phases is to find the sources of information most important at each stage.

Consumer Practices

Let us turn now to see what information we have on the actual purchase of garments and how this varies from group to group. As Jacobi (23) has noted, *by the time the consumer is ready to purchase he has already done a certain amount of narrowing so that his choice is already limited.* In the first place, the consumer either plans to shop in his own town or neighborhood or to go to another city. Stedman (41) analyzed the data from questionnaires sent to 34 towns in New York State varying in population from 4000 to 45,000. He found that 44 percent often shop away from their home town, 49 percent seldom shopped away from their home town, and 7 percent never did. This, as we would expect, varied greatly with the size of the town. The chief classification of merchandise which was purchased outside of the home town was clothing and the reason mainly was a search for a wider variety. Comish (15) in a study in Oregon found similar results. Those shopping in another city for women's wear varied from 34 percent in one city to 86 percent in another, and, again, the reason given for going to another city was the better assortment of goods in the second city.

The place where people will go to shop is expressed by Converse (16) in a "law of retail gravitation." This law states that two competing towns will attract trade from intermediate towns in direct proportion to the population of the two towns and inversely as the squares of the distances from these towns to intermediate towns. He finds that consumers will travel farther for fashion goods, such as clothing, than for foods, drugs, bulk goods or service goods, and that women will travel farther than men for clothing items. Finally, those with higher income will shop at a greater distance than those of low income and more of those with low income make purchases by mail.

Stone and Form (42) note that women reared in rural areas and small cities shopped locally more often than did women reared in large cities. They also found that the socioeconomic status of the shopper was a factor in where she shopped—again the women from higher socioeconomic groups were more likely to go outside the local shopping area.

We also have marketing studies which indicate the importance of such factors as public transportation, the ease of parking, store arrangements and appearance on where the consumer shops. Whatever the reason, the radius within which a consumer shops limits the choice of goods available to him. The narrowing process, however, is not only limited by the town(s) which the consumer considers his shopping area, but also by the stores which he favors. For example, I remarked to friends the other day that there was not a dress in Ithaca of a certain type. Actually I had looked in only four stores— the stores in which I regularly shop. In any shopping area, we soon recognize that there are retail stores which carry merchandise that is beyond our means or which we consider cheap and unacceptable. There may also be stores which we have learned do not carry the correct size for us, just "never" have any- thing we like, or have sales personnel whom we dislike. The habits and values of the individual also determine the number of shops from which he will make his choice. Some individuals regularly shop around to try to find the most satisfactory garment, while others tend to go to one store and choose what they think is best from that store's assortment. A Northeast Regional research study (46) found that only a little over a third of their sample of 380 women had shopped around before making a particular blouse purchase. The per- centage was higher in the largest city (Providence, Rhode Island) than in the smaller communities. When the reasons for choosing the particular store were compared for the various cities, it was found that in Providence only 14 percent of the respondents went to a given store bcause it was their habit to shop there, while in the other three cities from 33 to 43 percent went to a particular store for this reason. In a later study (40) in which the garments under consideration were men's shirts and women's slips and dresses, there were statistically significant differences on this point for various garments. Approximately 31 percent generally purchased shirts at a specific store and 25 percent went to many stores. A slightly higher proportion of women (33 percent) purchased slips and still more purchased dresses (37 percent) at a particular store, while 20 and 21 percent went to many stores. This is sur- prising in view of the common belief that women shop around more than men.

Stone and Form (42) asked women in their study whether when shopping for clothes they did other shopping too, or, whether they usually shopped just for clothes on one trip. The outstanding finding from this question was the relationship between the answer and the socioeconomic status of the shopper. "The 'higher' the social status of the Vansburg women, the more specialized was her shopping; the 'lower' her social status, the more likely she was to include other activities in that shopping" (p. 18). From the lower socioeconomic groups, approximately half of the respondents combined shop- ping for clothes with marketing for groceries. Women from the middle socio- economic groups spent less time shopping for clothes than did women in the higher and lower-status groups. Younger women tended to shop during the afternoons in the latter part of the week, whereas older women preferred to shop in the mornings in the early part of the week. Those in upper-status groups also preferred shopping on mornings of the earlier days of the week. Stedman (41) did not analyze his data according to the age or socioeconomic grouping of the shoppers, but found that 57 to 62 percent of those from New York State cities shopped in the afternoon.

A great deal has been written about impulse versus planned buying, but our information on this point is still lacking in validity. In a study by the New York University School of Retailing (1) of 1707 who were interviewed as they left stores, 50.9 percent had made a purchase and of these 65.7 percent said it was a planned purchase rather than impulse buying. When asked why they did not buy, the most frequent reason was that they couldn't find what they wanted, and only 1.9 percent said that they wanted to shop around. When the figures are broken down by type of merchandise, we find somewhat less impulse buying in clothing than in other areas.

In the blouse study by the Northeast Regional textiles and clothing research group (46), 60 percent had planned to buy a blouse and 39 percent reported that they had not planned to purchase a blouse on that day. Mueller (37) reported that, of 361 purchasers of men's sport shirts, 63 percent had planned to buy on that day and 30 percent had visited stores other than the one in which they made the purchase.

Stone and Form (42) asked Vansburg women:

> "When you shop for clothes do you know exactly what you want, do you have a general idea, or are you not quite sure?" Interestingly enough, there was a slight tendency for those who liked to shop for clothes to be somewhat less certain of what they were going to buy than those who disliked shopping . . . . Generally, the younger, high school educated, Class III (middle socioeconomic group), upward aspiring, cosmopolite-oriented women reported they knew exactly what they wanted when they shopped for clothing. The older, either college educated or only grade school educated, Class I or Class V (high socioeconomic or low socioeconomic group), nonaspiring, locality-oriented Vansburg women were uncertain of what they wanted. It could well be that the purchases of the latter group may be more exposed to social and social-psychological forces at work in the shopping situation (p. 17).

We mentioned earlier that much of the data on impulse versus planned buying is not completely valid. This is primarily due to the definition of these terms and what we mean by impulse buying. For example, some of the women in the blouse study who said that they had not planned to buy a blouse on that particular day may not have been true impulse buyers. While they had not actually planned to buy a blouse on that day, they may have decided earlier that they needed blouses for particular outfits and, when they saw what they wanted, they took the opportunity to purchase one. Recently, I accompanied my daughter looking for a dress. As she passed the glove counter, she noticed yellow gloves which she had been hunting for all season. This was not impulse buying as the term is usually used and yet she had not planned to buy gloves when she went on the shopping trip.

Mueller (10) has attempted to attack this problem by constructing indices for five dimensions of deliberation: (1) extent of circumspectness, (2) extent of information-seeking activity, (3) choosing with respect to price, (4) choosing with regard to brand, and (5) number of features considered (other than price or brand). The five indices were combined to obtain a comprehensive measure of deliberation. She used this measure in comparing the difference between purchase decisions involving durable goods and men's sport shirts. As would be expected, the sport shirt purchase was less frequently planned than the other and there was much less information-seeking prior to it. "On the other hand, there was less brand consciousness; hence consumers tended to choose more freely among a number of brands. There was no evidence that less attention was paid to price in the selection of a sport shirt than in the selection of major household goods, or that wants were less specific with regard to sport shirts." (p. 53). With more research of this type data on impulse buying versus planned buying will be more valid and hence more valuable to us.

Buying Activities at the Point of Purchase

The study by Stone and Form (42) which has been mentioned earlier in this chapter gives us our most complete data on practices in shopping for clothing items. That the shopping trip for clothing is considered a special situation was shown by the fact that over 90 percent of the women interviewed reported that they changed their clothes before they went shopping for clothing. The women were asked the kind of outfit they usually wore for such shopping. Approximately 30 percent said they wore "dressup clothes," 40 percent that they wore a "semi-casual dress," such as a street dress or skirt and blouse, and 30 percent that they wore a "casual dress" such as a housedress, cotton dress or sweater and slacks. The amount of dressing up depended to some extent, on the age of the respondent and her socioeconomic status. None of the women between 30 and 39 reported wearing "casual dress" for clothes shopping. In general, the higher the social status the more likely the respondent would be "dressed up" for shopping. Also, if she belonged to several organizations, she was more likely to dress up than if she did not belong. When asked whether they thought the way they dressed made any difference in the way they were treated by salesclerks, 70 percent replied in the affirmative. As would be expected, those who dressed up for shopping were more apt to give an affirmative reply. Also, those who shopped away from the local shopping area were more apt to say that their clothing was important, while others who shopped locally more often said their clothing was unimportant in the shopping situation.

More than three-fourths of the women reported they enjoyed shopping for clothes. Those who most often said they enjoyed shopping were from rural or small towns, were relatively young, with two or three small children, were well educated, frequent magazine readers, and were those whose husbands had moved either up or down the occupational ladder. "Women in the middle-status range spent less time shopping for clothes than women in the higher- and lower-status levels" (p. 4).

Shopping alone or with others was related to the age of the respondent. The young homemaker more often tended to shop alone while women in their forties more frequently shopped with others. About 30 percent of those who had shopping companions were accompanied by their husbands, about one-fourth by friends and about the same proportion were accompanied by younger family members, such as a daughter or daughter-in-law. The younger married women tended to be accompanied by their husbands and the older married women by their daughters or daughters-in-law.

Some customers, Stone and Form found, have the image of the salesclerk as a person, and others as an agent. This influences whether or not the customer asks the clerk for advice or even listens to her advice. Almost half of the informants reported that they included the salesclerk in their purchasing decisions; almost one-fourth excluded the clerk; and about a third were undecided. More than 60 percent of those who included the clerk viewed her as a person, while 80 percent who excluded the clerk from their purchasing decisions looked upon her as an agent.

In another study (46) from a sample of 380 women from four cities about one-fourth of the women were shopping with a companion. Fourteen percent asked the advice of her companion and 15 percent were observed to ask advice of the clerk. Despite the fact that only 15 percent of the respondents were observed asking advice of clerks, when questioned during a later interview, half reported that they usually took the advice of someone else when buying blouses, and the majority of these said that it was the clerk's advice. There seemed to be two very distinct groups of customers: (1) those who asked for, and took, the clerk's advice and later reported that they did so because they thought the clerk had special knowledge which would be helpful. These customers trusted the clerk and had great respect for her knowledge. (2) Customers who refused and did not want advice from the clerk. They reported they "knew what they wanted" and did not trust the clerk's opinion. They thought the clerk would say anything to make a sale. Very few people seemed to have opinions between these extremes. Those who asked for and took the clerk's advice in this study may have considered the clerk as a person while those who refused advice may have considered the sales person merely an agent. The clerk may be viewed as either person or agent depending upon the situation, the garment being purchased, the type of store, as well as the customer and the clerk.

In the Northeast Regional study (46), the women were actually observed as they purchased a blouse and their behavior recorded on a check sheet. Only 38 percent of the customers were observed to examine the fit or becomingness of the blouses in any way even including holding up the blouse to themselves (see Table 7). The percentages varied with the price of the blouse and the type of store.

Observed Activity	PERCENTAGE OF RESPONDENTS
	(n = 380)
Customer mentioned seeing advertisement	1
Customer mentioned seeing display	9
Customer mentioned previous experiences	3
Shopping with companion	26
Asked advice of companion	14
Asked advice of clerk	15
Examined construction of blouse	6
Looked at labels	7
Tried on in fitting room	21
Tried on over dress	6
Held up to self	11

table 7 Percentage of respondents observed having various activities in store. Data: Northeast Regional Bull. 34 Je., 1959 p. 26.

Customers were more apt to try on the more expensive blouses and those purchased in a specialty shop. They were least likely to try on the blouse if they bought it in a department store.

Although only 7 percent were observed to look at labels, nearly 40 percent reported later that they remembered removable tags on their blouses and, almost two-thirds of these reported that the tags had held useful information. It is obvious that we need new techniques for obtaining information on the extent to which labels are used. If the observational data are valid then the women, when they were interviewed, were either answering questions as they thought they should be answered rather than truthfully, or else they only read the labels after they had purchased the blouse and taken it home.

Horning (22) compared those who had purchased a blouse with those who looked at blouses but did not make a purchase. The data which she used was obtained from the store observations in one of the cities in the Northeast

Regional research. Those who purchased blouses were more frequently shopping with a companion and asked either the companion's or the clerk's advice, or both, more frequently. (see Table 8)

Activity	DID BUY *169*	DID NOT BUY *137*
	Percent	
Tried on in fitting room	12	12
Tried on over dress, held up	18	9
Looked at labels	6	5
Examined construction	5	5
Shopping with companion	27	17
Asked advice of companion	14	9
Asked advice of clerk	15	8
Mentioned seeing display	7	9
Mentioned advertisement	1	1
Mentioned previous experience with blouse	2	1

table 8   Percentage distribution of shopping activity by purchase. From Priscilla Horning, *Observed Activity of Woman Shopping for Blouses.* M.S. Thesis, Cornell Univer., 1961.

In contrast to the low percentage of women in the Northeast Regional study who were observed to look at labels, 80 percent of the 992 women interviewed by Drake and Grimes (17) said that they looked or asked for a label on dresses, at least sometimes. Fifty-three percent said they made a practice of always or usually looking for labels. Women with higher income and educational levels and those in the age groups 30–39 and 40–49 more often looked for labels than those in other groups. Those who reported that they sought label information when purchasing also reported using the information, especially the instructions on care. The authors also checked the kinds of information on dresses in stock and found that "less than one-third of the dresses examined had most of the information women looked for, such as whether to dry clean or wash, washing instructions, fiber name and percentage of fiber (note: this study was published in 1958 before the Fiber Identification Act was law), ironing temperature, finish, shrinking and color-fastness. Labels on dresses costing under $20 supplied much more of this information than those costing $20 or more" [p. 5]. Since women with higher incomes were looking for labels more than those of lower income this last finding would indicate that their desires were not being met as well as those of lower income groups.

We have discussed the process of narrowing the choice of garments by limiting the shopping areas and the stores considered within a given area. The narrowing process continues, however, in the store itself: the first element, obviously, is size. In a store with open racks, we first hunt out the correct size and do not consider those on other racks. The price may be another factor which limits our choice. Price has already entered into the narrowing process to some extent in our choice of stores, but it also may be a factor which further limits our choice within the store. The type of garment, or the occasion for which we want the article of clothing, will further limit our choice. Finally, personal preferences or prejudices limit the choice still further. Looking through a group of dresses we may immediately discard some from consideration because we "never wear red," "round necklines are not becoming," or we "don't want a sleeveless dress." Often then our choice is narrowed to four or five garments or perhaps even less. Jacobi (23) says that this is the "critical attribute phase." If those garments from which we are making our final choice are alike in price, style, and fabric but differ in color, then color becomes the critical attribute. Because the consumer is basing a choice on this deciding factor, it may be the attribute mentioned when questioned later. Thus, a woman may have narrowed the price by the stores she considered and the racks within the stores, then, from the rack she chose the dress with the color and fabric she preferred. When asked later about why she chose that particular dress she may list color and fabric, but forget to mention price, since it was almost automatically limited during the process.

In the Northeast Regional study of blouses (46) mentioned earlier, the observers noted what the customer asked the clerk, or what she mentioned, about the blouses she was considering. Those who purchased a blouse and were interviewed later spoke of color more often than any factor other than size. The fiber, style, sleeve, and whether or not it would be suitable or go with other garments were mentioned by over a quarter of the respondents. These are attributes which Jacobi would term *critical*. Shrinkage, colorfastness, and finishes were almost never mentioned by the customers. Horning (22), in comparing the data for the 169 who bought a blouse and 137 who were at the blouse department but did not buy one, found that the customers who did not buy a blouse asked about color, style, fiber and fabric, and decorative detail significantly more often than did those who bought a blouse. Presumably they were not satisfied with the assortment of factors available to them.

The results of both the Northeast Regional research and those of Horning suggest that women were generally more interested in the appearance of the blouse than in its performance in use and care. Drake and Grimes found, also, that appearance was given as the reason for selecting a dress more often than any other attribute. Mueller found the same results when studying factors considered in the selection of men's sport shirts—characteristics related to appearance were mentioned relatively frequently, while those relating to durability or performance were seldom considered.

Summary

The home economist interested in consumer problems needs to know not only why the consumer selects a certain garment, but also how he makes his selection.

It is clear that the consumer does not have unlimited choice of all items on the market. He limits his choice by the cities or villages in which he shops; by the stores he considers; by the sections of the store (s) he visits; and finally, he limits his choice to certain garments because of personal preference or prejudice. These limitations vary with the socioeconomic group, the age, the size of the home town, and various other factors in the local community.

One of the important problems in consumer behavior is to determine the sources of information used by the consumer at each stage of the decision-making process. Mass media are important at the awareness stage. Informal sources appear to be the most important for information at the point of selection. This has been shown by research which has investigated relationships between shopping companions and the consumer and between the clerk and the customer. When the customer asks advice of either the clerk or the shopping companion, she is more likely to purchase a garment than when she does not seek such advice.

The sources of information used by the consumer should be investigated in relation to impulse versus planned buying; however, we have no valid research in this area as yet.

Observation at the point of sale has given us data not only on the source of information but also on the type of information desired. Questions at the point of sale for women's blouses showed greater concern for factors related to appearance than to factors related to performance in use and care.

Bibliography

1. ———. Ask your customers! A survey of customers in the Fourteenth Street shopping district, New York City. *J. of Retailing.* 27–28, 1951–52, 123–132.
2. Beal, G. M. and Rogers, E. M. Informational sources in the adoption process of new fabrics. *J. of Home Ec.* 49(8), 1957, 630–634.
3. Bilkey, W. A psychological approach to consumer behavior analysis. *J. of Marketing.* 18(1), 1953, 18–25.
4. Bilkey, W. J. Psychic tensions and purchasing behavior. *J. of Soc. Psychol.* 41, 1955, 247–257.

5. Blankertz, D. F. Motivation and rationalization in retail buying. *Public Opinion Quart.* 13(4), 1949–50, 659–668.
6. Brightman, H. W. Growth of consumer influence in the retail field. *J. of Home Ec.* 29, 1937, 505–511.
7. Brown, G. H. Measuring consumer attitudes towards products. *J. of Marketing.* 14, 1950, 691–698.
8. Campbell, Persia. *The Consumer Interest: A Study in Consumer Economics.* New York: Harper & Row, Publishers, 1949, 660 p.
9. Campbell, Persia. The reality of satisfying abundance. *J. of Home Ec.* 49(8), 1957, 623–626.
10. Clark, L. H. (Ed.) *Consumer Behavior, Vol. I, The Dynamics of Consumer Reaction.* New York: New York University Press, 1955, 128p.
11. Clark, L. H. (Ed.) *Consumer Behavior, Vol. II, The Life Cycle and Consumer Behavior.* New York: New York University Press, 1955, 125p.
12. Clark, L. H. (Ed.) *Consumer Behavior, Research on Consumer Reactions.* New York: Harper & Row, Publishers, 1958, 469p.
13. Clover, V. T. Relative importance of impulse buying in retail stores. *J. of Marketing.* 15, 1950, 66–69.
14. Coles, J. V. *Consumer Demand in Missouri for Selected Articles of Clothing.* Mo. Agr. Exper. Research Bull. 300, 1939.
15. Comish, N. H. Where do they buy and why? *Dun's Review and Modern Industry.* 63, Apr. 1954, 51–52, 81–82.
16. Converse, P. D. Factors determining retail shopping preferences. *Dun's Review.* 55, Aug. 1947, 21–23, 62–72.
17. Drake, Phyllis and Grimes, Mary Anna. Use of label information on ready-made dresses. *Texas Agr. Progress.* IV(2), 1958, 4–6.
18. Family buying decisions: who makes them, who influences them? *Printers' Ink.* 264, Sept. 19, 1958, 21–29.
19. Fitzsimmons, Cleo. *Consumer Buying.* New York: John Wiley & Sons, Inc., 1961, 539p.
20. Fitzsimmons, C. and Perkins, N. L. Some Illinois clothing consumption patterns. *J. of Home Ec.* 39, 1947, 495–497.
21. Hoffman, Adeline. *Clothing Behavioral Factors for Specific Groups of Women Related to Aesthetic Sensitivity and Certain Socio-economic and Psychological Background Factors.* Ph.D. Thesis, Penna. State Univer., 1956.
22. Horning, Priscilla. *Observed Activity of Women Shopping for Blouses.* M.S. Thesis, Cornell Univer., 1961.
23. Jacobi, J. E., and Walters, G. Dress-buying behavior of consumers. *J. of Marketing.* 23(2), 1958, 168–172.
24. How buying habits change. *Business Week.* Nov. 22, 1952, 110–118.
25. Jonassen, C. T. *The Shopping Center Versus Downtown.* Columbus, Ohio: Bureau of Business Research, Ohio State Univer., 1955, 170p.
26. Katona, G. *The Powerful Consumer, Psychological Studies of the American Economy.* New York: McGraw-Hill, Book Co., 1960, 276p.

27. Katona, G., and Mueller, Eva. *Consumer Attitudes and Demand.* 1950–1952, Survey Research Center Institute for Social Research, Ann Arbor: Univer. of Mich., 1953, 119p.

28. Klitzke, Dorothy. Clothing owned by New York farm families. *J. of Home Ec.* 43, 1951, 716–718.

29. Labarthe, J. Your money's worth in clothing and textiles. *J. of Home Ec.* 46(9), 1954, 640–644.

30. Laird, D. How the consumer estimates quality by subconscious sensory impressions. *J. of Applied Psychol.* 16, 1932, 241–246.

31. Latzke, A. C. and Windhorst, M. M. What college women spend on clothes. *J. of Home Ec.* 35, 1943, 555–559.

32. Leibenstein, H., Bandwagon, snob and Veblen: effects in the theory of consumers' demand. *The Quart. J. of Ec.* 64, 1950, 183–207.

33. Mack, Ruth. *Factors Influencing Consumption: An Experimental Analysis of Shoe Buying.* Tech paper 10, Nat. Bureau of Ec. Research Inc., 1954, 123p.

34. Meiklejohn, Helen E. Dresses—the impact of fashion on a business. *Price and Price Policies* (Hamilton, Walton, Ed.). New York: McGraw-Hill Book Co., 1938, 299–393.

35. Monroe, D. Problems in analyzing clothing data from consumer purchases study. *J. of Home Ec.* 31, 1939, 571.

36. Morgan, James N. *Consumer Economics.* Englewood Cliffs, N.J.: Prentice-Hall, Inc., 1955, 440p.

37. Mueller, Eva. Effects of consumer attitudes on purchases. *Amer. Ec. Rev.* XLVII, 1957, 946–965.

38. Nybroten, N. Rate of commodity disappearance and consumer preference. *J. of Farm Ec.* 31, May 1949, 346–350.

39. Phelps, E. L., Petzel, F. E., Loring, A. S., and Nielson, E. A. A study of certain factors related to consumers' choices in the purchase of "silk" street dresses and silk yard goods. *J. of Home Ec.* 31(6), 1939, 393–398.

40. Ryan, M., Ayres, R., Carpenter, V., Densmore, B., Swanson, C., and Whitlock, M. *Consumer Satisfaction with Men's Shirts and with Women's Slips and Casual Street Dresses.* Part I. Field Study in four communities in the Northeast, Cornell Univer. Agr. Exper. Sta. Bull. 984, 1963.

41. Stedman, G. H. Determining attitudes and habits of retail shoppers. *J. of Retailing.* 27, 1951, 133–142.

42. Stone, G. P., and Form, W. H. *The Local Community Clothing Market: A Study of the Social and Social Psychological Contexts of Shopping.* Tech. Bull. 262, Mich. State Univer. Agr. Exper. Sta., Nov. 1957.

43. Stone, G. P., Form, W. H., and Strahan, Hazel B. The social climate of decision in shopping for clothes. *J. of Home Ec.* 46, 1954, 86–88.

44. Van Syckle, Calla. *Practices Followed by Consumers in Buying "Large-Expenditure" Items of Clothing, Furniture and Equipment.* Tech. Bull. 224, Mich. State College, Agr. Exper. Sta., 1951.

45. When a woman shops, what's on her mind? *Printers' Ink.* 254, January 20, 1956, 25–27, 68–71.

46. Whitlock, M., Ayres, R., and Ryan, M. *Consumer Satisfaction with Women's Blouses.* Part I: Field Study in four communities in the northeast, Northeast Reg. Bull. 34, Agr. Exper. Sta. University of Rhode Island, Kingston, R. I., Je, 1959.

47. Wines, Mary Elizabeth. *Consumer Behavior in Buying Slips.* M.S. Thesis, Cornell Univer., 1947.

48. Wolgast, E. H. Do husbands or wives make the purchasing decisions? *J. of Marketing.* 23, 1958, 151–158.

49. Women buy a lot, but not everything. *Business Week.* Jan. 7, 1950, 30–34.

Chapter 9

Consumer Satisfaction
in the Use and Care of Clothing

We as home economists are concerned with the psychological and social aspects of clothing primarily because such knowledge enables us to help consumers obtain greater satisfaction with clothing. Therefore, all that we have studied thus far has been included with this purpose in mind. We can have a better understanding of what will be satisfactory to the consumer if we know: why people choose the clothes they do; how society influences them in their selection; the relationships between personal values, interests, attitudes, self-concepts and personality factors; and the effect of clothing on individuals. One reason that home economists have studied consumer motivation and consumer behavior is: they have hoped that by finding the kinds of behavior which have led to the purchase of satisfactory items of clothing, they can better advise others on what to do, and what not to do, when shopping for clothing.

Consumer satisfaction is likewise important to those in the clothing business—both in the manufacturing and marketing of clothing. Manufacturers, wholesalers, and retailers assume that the consumer will look for, and buy, garments having features which have proved satisfactory in the past, and avoid garments with characteristics which have proven unsatisfactory. Some of the uncertainties of the apparel market will be eliminated for the businessman, he hopes, if he has knowledge of what the consumer has considered satisfactory or unsatisfactory.

General Satisfaction

The first basic requirement in any investigation of satisfaction with apparel items is to have a valid and reliable measure of over-all satisfaction. Fortunately for research, respondents are able to rate the general over-all satisfaction of a garment. This seems remarkable when we know that: we expect more of an expensive garment than an inexpensive one; the purpose for which a garment was purchased influences satisfaction; garments vary on a number of properties and they may be satisfactory on one but unsatisfactory on another; and further, that the importance of various properties varies from individual to individual, probably with the values of the individual. Before making any judgment on the degree of satisfaction, it would seem necessary, then, to take all of these into account, and to give weights to various factors in proportion to their importance. Deliberately going through each of these steps and verbalizing would, we know, be a complex process which would be difficult for the respondent to perform. This, apparently, is not necessary, since the respondent is able to give almost immediately a judgment of satisfaction or to rate a garment as to its degree of satisfaction. When asked to give a rating or judgment, the respondent very likely simply says to himself: "I've worn this garment a lot and always liked it, therefore, I'll give it a good rating" or "I've never liked that garment so I'll rate it low." There is, furthermore, some evidence that these ratings are reliable and valid measurements. Reliability has been demonstrated in several studies in which respondents have been asked to rate the same garment on over-all satisfaction at different times (for example, that Northeast Regional Research project [24]). In an effort to test the validity of such ratings, 49 women were observed unknowingly each work day for seven weeks. A record was kept to determine the blouses worn most frequently and least often. Later the subjects were asked to rate these blouses. Then they were told that they had been observed, and asked to give reasons for the frequent or infrequent wearing of the blouses. The mean ratings on general satisfaction of all respondents for the blouses worn most frequently was 2.35 and for those worn only once was 4.00, when one was the highest level on the rating scale and nine the lowest, or least satisfactory. The difference in average rating between those most frequently worn and those worn once was highly significant, giving evidence that the ratings are a valid measure (24:85).

Components and Attributes of Satisfaction

Unfortunately, the rating on general satisfaction with a garment does not give us all of the information needed for predicting what will prove satisfactory in future purchases. Since the respondent does not go through the entire process for us in communicating his satisfaction, it is left to the experimenter to force consideration of all the variables which might have influenced judgment. In other words, we need to know what specific features have made the garment satisfactory or unsatisfactory. One commonly used method is simply to ask the respondent what makes it satisfactory or unsatisfactory or to furnish him with checklists of features to be marked. A technique used by the Northeast Regional group was to compare the favorite with the least-liked garment of a specific type. Another, more exact, method (also used in this study) is to ask the respondent to rate, or evaluate by some other means, various characteristics of the garment as well as over-all satisfaction. As discussed under Consumer Motivation (see Chapter 7), this is most meaningful if we focus attention on one stratum of explanation at a time; that is, we may either concentrate on the specific attributes of garments which lead to satisfaction, or on the components of perceived properties of these attributes.

The first task in research concerned with determining the relative importance of various attributes or properties of garments is to develop an exhaustive list of the characteristics on a given stratum. The Northeast Regional Research projects (13 and 24) on men's shirts and women's blouses, slips and casual street dresses have concentrated on the components of satisfaction at the second stratum, that is, the perceived properties of the garment such as comfort or ease of care. In these studies, open-end questions served as a check on the variety of components which might lead to satisfaction. Components listed by respondents were:

appearance or becomingness
comfort
durability
ease-of-care
ease in putting on and taking off
performance in use over time (shrinkage, fading, pilling, etc.)
performance while wearing (stays neat, doesn't cling, stays in place, etc.)
suitability to occasion or versatility for many occasions.

Swanson (20), studying the components of satisfaction for sweaters with college women, differentiated between physical and psychological comfort ("feel good in it" or "wearing it lifts my morale"). The psychological comfort, as she used the term, may be simply another wording for general or over-all satisfaction. Further investigation is needed to determine whether it is a distinct component of over-all satisfaction or synonymous with general satisfaction. In either case, it points to the necessity of specifying physical comfort when this component is being investigated. Swanson also had the additional component—"Friends Approval." Fodor (2) found that for adolescent girls it was important to have blouses similar to those of their friends. This component is more difficult than the others to investigate, but it is likely to be found important, especially for adolescents.

Shannon (15) used a basic classification with sub-classifications which is similar in some respects to the two strata we have mentioned. Her classification of factors contributing to satisfaction with fabrics is:

1. Sensory satisfaction
     appearance
     color
     design
     texture
2. Suitability
3. Satisfaction in use
4. Fabric reaction in use
     maintenance of original condition
     long lasting
     ease of care
     ease of construction
5. Price
6. Prestige
7. Fashion

In the Northeast Regional studies (13 and 24) ratings on the various components of satisfaction were compared with ratings on general satisfaction with garments to determine the relative importance of the various components. The assumption is that when the rating on a given component correlates with the rating on general satisfaction it indicates that this component is important to satisfaction with the garment. For all of the garments studied, comfort and appearance, or becomingness, were found to be extremely important while durability and ease of care were relatively less important. Comfort was first in importance for blouses and shirts and second for slips and dresses, while appearance was first in slips and dresses. Appearance was second in importance for shirts and becomingness second for blouses.

The attributes, or physical characteristics of garments, such as fiber, weave, color, or cut which are conceived as contributing to these components, or per-ceived properties, have been investigated in a number of studies. One method has been to ask the respondent "what makes it comfortable (uncomfortable, beautiful, and so on)." By this method the Northeast Regional research found that the attributes most closely related to comfort of all garments were both fit and fiber or fabric. For dresses, color was most closely related to appearance; for slips, the decorative detail; and for shirts, the shape of the collar. Fiber was the attribute most often thought o be responsible for ease of care and durability of garments. Relationships between the components and attributes, or between factors on the various strata, are complex. In relating attributes to the components of satisfaction in sweaters for college women,

Swanson (20) found that color was mentioned by over half of the respondents as related to becomingness, fulfillment of purpose for which purchased, beauty, and friends' approval. One-fourth or more also saw color as related to ease of care, good buy, and psychological comfort. Thus, the color of sweaters seemed to serve many components of satisfaction. Style likewise was related to many components. Fit was mentioned by the majority of respondents in respect to becomingness and physical comfort. The only components which a majority of the group saw as related to fiber were ease of care and beauty. It is evident from the results thus far that one attribute can contribute to one or several components and that each component is dependent on a varying number of attributes. Presumably the relationship between attributes and components would be somewhat similar for different garments, but certain relationships would be found for some types of garments and not for others.

In addition to those studies which have attempted to investigate all of the components of satisfaction with garments, there have been additional studies which have focused upon one component or attribute. For example, there have been several studies on consumer's attitudes toward "wash-and-wear" garments. Research sponsored by du Pont de Nemours and Co. (8) noted that the major reason for satisfaction with "wash and wear" clothes was that they required less ironing, and, the most disliked household task was ironing. Also, 79 percent of the respondents said that "wash-and-wear" garments were cheaper to maintain.

The Consumer Interest Committee of the American Home Economics Association gave consumers an opportunity to list characteristics which they considered essential, important, or desirable for high-, medium-, and low-priced garments (19). The list of characteristics desired in housedresses was classified into four attributes: style, fabric, cut, and dress details. The dress fasteners seemed to be the factor of greatest concern to the woman providing the list. Apparently, these women had had buttons lost, buttonholes ripped, or other difficulties with fasteners, in the housedresses they had worn and washed.

Warden (22) used an interesting technique to measure the degree of satisfaction with the wardrobe as a whole. She asked college women about the replacements they would make if their wardrobes were destroyed. She asked, first of all, whether or not they would replace their clothing with the same kind, quality, and quantity of garments if they were given the same replacement value as their present wardrobe. She asked the same questions if they were given one and one-half the replacement value and also if they were given only half the replacement value. She found that, given the replacement value, 58 percent would have replaced their present wardrobe with the same kind, quality, and quantity of garments. When they were imagining an increase over the replacement value, 64 percent would have used at least part of the increase to improve the quantity of clothes and 31 percent would have used at least part of the increase to improve the quality. When they considered that the replacement value would be cut in half, 76 percent said that they would keep the same kind and quality but would decrease the quantity. It is interesting to note that the students seemed to have settled on a standard of quality with which they were satisfied and that any differences in amount to be spent would have been reflected in the number of garments rather than their quality. This same technique might also be adaptable to the study of specific components of satisfaction with clothing items or the attributes of specific types of garments, which lead to satisfaction. For example, the question might be worded to ask if they were replacing a certain garment would they look for another garment that was like this one in comfort (ease of care, and so forth) or whether some other factor would be more important.

Hall (3) asked her respondents whether or not they were happy with the kinds of clothing they owned and wore for various types of occasions— such as, for work or dress. She then asked them to tell what changes they would make, if any, in the kind of clothes the various family members owned and wore for various occasions. The majority of women were reluctant to call garments unsatisfactory and yet when asked to list complaints many gave specific factors which they disliked. These complaints generally fell within the first stratum or attributes of garments, and more were expressed about clothing for dress than clothing for work or leisure wear. Items relating to the cut of the garment, the fasteners or the amount of ironing needed were frequent complaints. Using another technique to study satisfactions, Hall asked each respondent about her favorite blouse and the reasons why it was a favorite. Of the 71 women who answered this question, 25 said they liked it because it was easy to do up, 15 liked the style and 13 mentioned the comfort. These same women were asked what influenced them to buy the blouse; 16 mentioned style, 11 color and 8 just said they liked it. Other answers were scattered over a variety of reasons.

Other investigators have attempted to study relative satisfaction by looking at the opposite end of the continuum and finding factors which have made garments unsatisfactory. Labarthe (6) has done this by studying articles returned to the store. He has stressed that good consumership is recognition of those causes of dissatisfaction with garments which are the fault of the consumer, that is, mistakes in selecting inappropriate items or mistakes in care, and, those that are the fault of the merchandise itself. The reasons for dissatisfaction obtained by using this method usually are concerned with specific attributes (stratum one), that is, fiber, seams, and so on, and these specific complaints are then taken to the laboratory to determine whether or not the merchandise was at fault. He finds that even when the merchandise is at fault, only a small percentage of the garments on the market with this fault are returned.

In answer to a survey questionnaire, Monday (9) reported that almost a third of the complaints concerning clothing items were due to color change, 29 percent to dimensional change and 17 percent to poor quality of fabric or poor construction.

Another method for obtaining more information on satisfaction and dissatisfaction is to ask respondents about garments as they are ready for disposal. This would include garments which have been both satisfactory and unsatisfactory. Wilson[1] attempted to use this method. One of her problems was to find the most effective method of contacting people who had garments they considered ready for disposal. A combination of an advertisement and a newspaper article was superior to trying to contact by telephone or mail. The latter methods were extremely time-consuming for research personnel, since only a small percentage of those contacted had items they considered ready for disposal. However, when people had such items, they were willing not only to be interviewed concerning them, but, to give or lend the garments for further study in the laboratory. Sixty-five individuals were interviewed in this pilot study and a total of 153 garments were discussed with the respondents and examined more closely in the laboratory. Only 10 percent of the garments were considered "worn out," 44 percent were not worn out but were ready for disposal and 44 percent were not worn out but were relegated to different types of use than that for which they were originally purchased (that is, a garment purchased for work was now used for dirty jobs around the home). The most frequently mentioned reasons for disposing of garments, or using them for different types of occasions from those for which they were purchased, were reasons relating to fabric. According to the laboratory analyses: 82 percent of the garments had some kind of fabric failure—usually "worn thin," "holes," or "frayed" in the sleeve or pocket areas of the garments; 61 percent had some kind of construction failure, usually "seam failure due to broken stitching" occurring in the underarm, lining, and waistband areas, and of a type that could very easily be repaired; 69 percent were classified as having some kind of color change. The color change was often not great but was frequently from stains or spotting. This type of study offers opportunities to combine data from the laboratory with opinions of the wearers on factors which have proven satisfactory or unsatisfactory. The field part of such a study could well include desirable properties (stratum two) as well as specific attributes (stratum one).

A method with even greater potential is the inventory study which in-

---

[1] Shirley Wilson, *A pilot study of textile product performance of garments as related to use-life and to satisfaction.* Unpublished study done at Cornell University.

cludes all of the garments of a specific type owned by the respondents with information on their satisfaction and the amount worn. Streufert (17) made some preliminary studies on possible techniques for such a study. She classified garments as active, inactive, or discarded. The schedule and methodology which she developed might well be used in future studies.

Lynn (7) obtained inventories of college freshmen girls' school wardrobes with data on whether they wore each garment "much, little, or not at all" and, if it wasn't worn much, why it was not. The most frequent reasons for not wearing specific garments were: (1) poor fit; (2) poor buying habits (for example, doesn't match other things in my wardrobe); (3) care (for instance, too hard to iron); and (4) the garment was saved for special occasions or seasons. Since the completion of this study we have had most of the work on measuring satisfaction. With advances in theory and techniques we could now obtain more informative data on the reasons for wearing garments frequently or infrequently.

Minimum Levels

We noted earlier (see Chapter 7) that the concept of minimum levels of desirability or satisfaction is especially important in understanding either motivation or satisfaction. It is not sufficient to know that comfort or appearance is the most important component. We know that for a garment to be satisfactory it must not only be high in the most important component, but that also it must reach at least a certain minimum level on all of the other components, if the garment is to be considered satisfactory. If minimum levels of satisfaction on each of the components could be established for various types of garments, they could be related to laboratory tests and allow us to set up meaningful standards for garment production comparable to food and drug standards. Unfortunately, research in this area is extremely complex and we have made only the first tentative steps toward obtaining the data needed for establishing these minimum levels. The Northeast regional project (13), for example, found that 75 of those who rated shirts, slips or dresses as "extremely satisfactory" also rated them "extremely satisfactory" on comfort and "above average" on the other components.

> Before making definitive statements concerning minimum levels of satisfaction for specific components in relation to general satisfaction, however, consideration must be given to the garments rated low on general satisfaction. Possibly most garments, unsatisfactory as well as satisfactory, were rated high on the specific component. For example, most of the "extremely satisfactory" slips were rated high on durability but, before it can be concluded that a high rating on durability is necessary for extreme satisfaction, knowledge is needed about the durability rating on slips considered to be unsatisfactory [p.37].

In this study the results showed that:

Only in respect to comfort were the "extremely satisfactory" garments rated 1 (high) by 75 percent or more of the respondents and the "unsatisfactory" garments rated above average by 25 percent or less. Since the results were not dependent on the fact that most garments were comfortable, the rating for a minimum level of satisfaction was established at 1. Similarly the rating for a minimum level of satisfaction for appearance was 1.5 for shirts and 2 for slips and casual street dresses. [A 5 point scale was used in which 1 = extremely satisfactory to 5 = extremely unsatisfactory.]

The findings of this study confirm the hypothesis that high general satisfaction with a garment requires minimum levels of satisfaction for specific components such as comfort and appearance. The results also indicate that the minimum levels of satisfaction for specific components, necessary for the high general satisfaction, vary with the type of garment [p.37].

The next step in research should be to combine field and laboratory studies to determine the attributes of garments which would correspond to the specific ratings.

Summary

The measurement of consumer satisfaction with garments and the determination of factors which lead to satisfaction are extremely important if we are to advise consumers on future purchases or produce and market clothing which gives the greatest satisfaction. This can best be done, if in our research we distinguish between the physical attributes of the garment (stratum one) and the perceived properties of these attributes or the components of satisfaction with garments (stratum two), as we did for motivation.

We especially need research which relates the degree of satisfaction to tests in the textile laboratory. If we are able to determine such relationships, we can set minimum standards for certain properties which will give minimum levels of satisfaction for various components necessary for over-all satisfaction. For the two components—comfort and appearance—which research thus far has shown to be most important for general satisfaction with garments, this would be impossible. Both of these components are subjective and personal. However, it would be most helpful to consumer and producer alike, if we could establish minimum standards in fibers, fabrics, and garments which would be correlated with minimum satisfaction on other components of satisfaction with garments. This would be possible for such components as durability, ease of care, performance during use (for example, wrinkling) and performance over time (for instance, fading).

If consumers knew that minimum levels on these factors were guaranteed, they could eliminate these elements from consideration in their decisions concerning garment selection. Research in this area is still in its infancy and new techniques need to be developed, but a start has been made on determining minimum levels of satisfaction and in relating field and laboratory studies by the textile and clothing research group from the Northeast region.

Bibliography

1. Barlow, F. D. Economic effects of Wash and Wear cotton. *Agr. Marketing.* 1959, 3.
2. Fodor, Wilda Story. *Relative Importance of Components of Satisfaction for Girls' Blouses and Slips to Eighth and Eleventh Grade Girls and Their Mothers.* M.S. Thesis, Cornell Univer., 1963.
3. Hall, Katherine. *A Study of Some of the Factors that Contribute to Satisfactions and Dissatisfactions in the Clothing of 92 Urban Low-income Families.* Ph.D. Thesis, Penna. State Univer., 1955.
4. Jebe, E., Beveridge, Elizabeth, Hawkes, G. R., Potgieter, Fannie, and Roberson, Opal. How to study consumer satisfaction with children's clothing made of different textile fibers. *J. of Home Ec.* 50(3), 1958, 213–18.
5. Labarthe, J. Your money's worth in clothing and textiles. *J. of Home Ec.* 46(9), 1954, 640–644.
6. Labarthe, J. Ten thousand and one customer complaints. *Tex. Research J.* XXIV(4), 1954, 328–342.
7. Lynn, Mary Jean. *Inventories of 86 Freshman Girls' School Wardrobes to Determine Factors Relating to the Popularity of School Clothing.* M.S. Thesis, Cornell Univer., 1952.
8. Market Research Section, Textile Fibers Dept., E. I. du Pont de Nemours and Co. *Consumer's Views of "Wash and Wear."* MMR 58–18–A. 1958.
9. Monday, Dazel. *A Study of Consumer Dissatisfactions with Textile Products.* Ph.D. thesis, University of Missouri, 1953.
10. Petzel, Florence. Fifty years of research in textiles. *J. of Home Ec.* 51(8), 1959, 701–704.
11. Phillips, Velma. College students study their own buying habits. *J. of Home Ec.* 46(9), 1954, 665–666.
12. Randle, Texanita and Rosencranz, Mary Lou. What about disposable clothing and textiles? *J. of Home Ec.* 54(1), 1962, 856–857.
13. Ryan, M., Ayers, R., Carpenter, V., Densmore, B., Swanson, C., and Whitlock, M. *Consumer Satisfaction with Men's Shirts and with Women's Slips and Casual Street Dresses,* Part I, Field Study in four Communities in the Northeast, Cornell Univer. Agr. Exper. Sta. Bull. 984, 1963.

14. Ryan, Mary S. A study of factors in the selection and care of blouses which relate to consumer satisfaction. *J. of Home Ec.* 46(3), 1954, 149–154.
15. Shannon, L. E. *Consumer Satisfaction with Cotton Fabrics in Relation to Selected Physical Characteristics.* Ph.D. thesis, Florida State Univer., 1961.
16. Stein, Alice Powers. *Some Clothing Problems of "Underprivileged" Children.* M.S. thesis, Cornell Univer., 1955.
17. Streufert, Hildegarde. *Technique for the Enumeration of Active, Inactive, and Discarded Clothing.* M.S. thesis, Iowa State Univer., 1957.
18. Strong, E. K., Jr. Satisfactions and interests. *Amer. Psychol.* 13, 1958, 449–456.
19. Sundquist, Alice and Whitlock, Mary. The consumer speaks about house dresses. *J. of Home Ec.* 38, 1946, 562–568.
20. Swanson, Charlotte La Tour. *Interrelationships Among Factors Related to Satisfaction in Sweaters.* M.S. thesis, Cornell Univer., 1959.
21. Thompson, Henrietta and Jelks, Vivian. Clothing practices among low-income families. *J. of Home Ec.* 32, 1941, 78–81.
22. Warden, Jessie. *Some Factors Affecting the Satisfactions and Dissatisfactions with Clothing of Women Students in the College of Education and the College of Liberal Arts.* Ph.D. thesis, Penna. State Univer., 1955.
23. Warning, Margaret. Future explorations in home economics: clothing. *J. of Home Ec.* 52(8), 1960, 646–651.
24. Whitlock, M., Ayres, R., and Ryan, M. *Consumer Satisfaction with Women's Blouses.* Part I: Field Study in Four Communities in the Northeast. Northeast Reg. Bull. 34, Agr. Exper. Sta., Univer. of Rhode Island, Kingston, R.I., June, 1959.

Part Three

Social-Psychological Aspects
of Clothing Related to
the Age of the Wearer

CLOTHING is an extremely important part of the child's or adolescent's world. Listen to any group of adults reminiscing about the years when they were children or adolescents and you will find that many of their most vivid memories concern clothing. They may recall the great joy or pride in receiving or wearing a much loved garment, or perhaps, more often their memories will be of the embarrassment caused by an inappropriate garment or by something happening to their clothing. As examples of such reminiscences illustrating the importance of clothing in the child's or adolescent's world, let me give examples from three generations in my own family. My mother's earliest memory is of going calling with her mother when she was about four years old. At that period (c. 1880) the princess-coat style dress was in vogue. My mother wore such a dress which was buttoned down the front. The hostess thought it was a coat and started to unbutton it. Mother was so horrified and embarrassed that she could not speak. The women present—all friends of her mother—thought it was amusing and probably immediately forgot it, but, to the child, it was such a traumatic experience that she never forgot it.

For my part I remember vividly the time I sneaked into Sunday school so that no one, especially my mother who was Sunday school superintendent, would see the big tear in the front of my "Sunday" dress. We children always left church at the end of the junior sermon and were supposed to stay with a leader until time for Sunday school. On this particular Sunday, several of us skipped out and climbed a cliff in back of the church. In doing so, I tore my dress. I was convinced that everyone would see it and

190

know that I had been a bad girl, and that my mother might even scold me or ask about it in front of everyone. Never since has any task taken the courage that it did to go into the Sunday school room on that day.

I have not asked my adolescent daughter for reminiscences because I remember very clearly one episode in which the importance of clothing to her was graphically illustrated. When she was in seventh grade, we had purchased a new dress which she planned to wear to a class dance. Before the occasion she, apparently, had described it, and, I'm afraid, bragged about it to her classmates. Before the party, she wore it to a restaurant for dinner and spilled something on it. I was not home at the time and, as neither she nor her father knew how to get the spot out, she had to change to an old dress. She came home from the party in tears because "no one liked her," "no one danced with her unless they had to," and she had to walk home alone. Nothing would comfort her. Every instance we could give of her popularity at other times was simply an exception to the rule. Every person we named who liked her she was sure really didn't like her but just "*had to be nice*" to her for some reason or other. A few weeks later she went to the next dance of the same group. This time she wore the new dress. We waited anxiously for her to come home, wondering if our bias had blinded us to the fact that she really was a social outcast. She returned literally hoarse from yelling and laughing. When we asked if she had had a good time, she was amazed at our ever considering any other possibility. It had been "wonderful"; she had had plenty of partners to dance with; everyone liked her dress; she had come home with a crowd; and on and on. The difference in the two occasions probably was not due to the others' reactions to her clothes, but to her own behavior. On the first occasion, she doubtless was on the defensive or glum because she had bragged about it and then not worn the dress. On the second occasion, she was confident and was her usual happy self. Extreme as this case seems, it is a true story of a girl who is ordinarily less, rather than more, concerned with clothes than the average girl her age.

These are stories about just three individuals in one family. I have chosen the women in the family as examples, but I might equally well have chosen the men and boys for such insights. These anecdotes do not, of course, give proof of the relative importance of clothing to the child nor do they give us any accurate information on the how's and why's. They can indicate by their prevalence, however, that this is probably a fertile field for investigation. Such incidents, moreover, may give us hypotheses to be tested in research and in addition point dramatically to the difference between the child's world and the adult's world.

What are simply amusing incidents or trivial occurrences to the adult are extremely important or embarrassing to the child or adolescent. These differences between the adults' attitudes and the childrens' attitudes towards clothing are not limited to individual instances. Almost every decade and every locality seems to have a garment or garments which causes friction between parents and their children because of different points of view.

Those who were in school just before World War I are usually very vehement about long underwear. In talking with a group of this age, one gets the impression that all of them were forced to wear long underwear when "nobody else" had to wear it. (Perhaps all of those who were allowed to go without it died the early deaths their mothers predicted.) Individuals who are younger recall their conflicts over snowsuit pants—one friend reports that she wore them out of the house as required but took them off as soon as she rounded the corner and was out of her mother's sight. Others report conflicts over knickers versus long pants, long stockings versus knee-length socks, straight versus full skirts, rubbers, the amount of eye make-up, leather jackets, duck-tail haircuts, and so forth. A Pakistani student describes the differences between her contemporaries and their parents over what is proper and modest for a Pakistani girl. She feels that the differences are greater in her culture than in our own. This may be true, or it may be that she has experienced the one and only observed the other as an adult.

Conflicts are perhaps inevitable in a world such as ours in which adults make the decisions concerning the clothing of their children. The *history of children's clothing reflects,* not the activities and attitudes of children in the various ages and cultures, but rather *the attitude of parents toward children.* In some cultures such as in Pakistan, small babies are dressed in gold and weighted down with jewelry as show pieces or possessions to be exhibited. Until the Middle Ages in our Western culture, the child was simply ignored or considered a miniature adult. As soon as the baby was out of swaddling clothes, he was dressed in clothing similar in style and colors to that worn by adults. Rousseau is credited by Young (17:28) for bringing a new status for children in which they were respected as individuals differing from adults; growing and needing to have greater freedom of movement. Whether the credit belongs to Rousseau or whether he was simply following the ideas of the times, beginning in the later part of the eighteenth century, children, or at least boys from the aristocratic class, had clothing which set them apart from adults. This differentiation between clothing for the child and the adult came later for girls and for children whose parents were peasants.

In the early twentieth century, a sharp distinction was made between children's and adult's clothing. The boy wore short pants or knickers until he was considered a man and graduated into long trousers; a girl had short dresses and wore her hair hanging down her back or in braids until she was considered old enough to dress as an adult with long dresses and her hair done up. During this period, children were recognized as individuals with abilities and needs different from adults, and this recognition was reflected in clothing. No note was taken of a period between childhood and adulthood, however; and it was not until the 1920s and 1930s that we began to think of adolescence as a period distinct from both childhood and adulthood. Now, in the second half of the twentieth century, we differentiate between many periods—infancy, the toddler age, preschool, school, preadolescent and adolescent—but as we have continued to be aware of more and more distinct age groupings, the clothing differentiations seem to have broken down and the same type of clothing may be worn by many if not all groups.

In our culture the attitude of society toward the sex of the child is an interesting study. In the nineteenth and early twentieth century, all very young children were regarded apparently as either sexless or as feminine dolls. Babies were clothed in long flowing dresses. Little boys and girls alike wore dresses and had long hair from the time they began to crawl until they were old enough to go to school. The age at which a boy's clothing became different from a girl's has gradually been pushed down during the twentieth century, so that at present the boy from the first week is dressed in boy's clothes and his hair is always kept short. The differentiation between the clothing of the sexes for small children is again breaking down, but now the girl is dressed in the T-shirts and overalls formerly reserved for little boys.

In recent years we have become very smug because we recognize, as we think other times and cultures have not, that children are individuals and that they should be treated as such. We believe that they need freedom from restricting clothing in order to develop motor skills; we frown upon the mother who bundles her child too much or who buys a too large snowsuit so that it will last the child longer; we look for self-help features which will train our children to be independent; we congratulate ourselves because we have developed textiles and clothing designs which are easy to care for so that the child does not need to be constantly reminded to be careful of his clothing. All of these changes are probably improvements, but do we really have reason to feel smug? Do we dress the child in clothing which would contribute the most to his development? Are we even aware of the factors in clothing which are most important to children? While we cannot answer all of these questions at this time, we should give them careful consideration.

Child psychologists have contributed very little specific knowledge in this area. Of the many textbooks in child development and child psychology, only a very few even list "clothing" or "dress" or "appearance" in the index. Perhaps they have considered the topic trivial, but, as we can observe any time we watch children, it may not be trivial to the child.

Textbooks about children's clothing do give some lip service to psychological implications of clothing. They usually emphasize the importance of clothing to children, and often go on to say that neat, comfortable, attractive, appropriate, and becoming clothing contributes to the child's well-being and self-confidence. The assumption is made that attractiveness, becomingness, and so on are the same for the child as for the adult, and that the same values which are important to the adult are also important to the child. It is further assumed that the same values are important throughout childhood. Stress is laid upon clothes as a factor in character building and the effects of clothing upon the behavior of the children. The rowdiness of the naughty child is attributed, at least at times, to the child's cowboy outfit or to old and unkept clothing. We are warned that the child who is too elaborately dressed may become conceited. The well-dressed child is expected to be the well-behaved child. None of the authors assert that clothing can always explain behavior nor that it is a magic panacea for all children's misbehavior. They do imply, however, that it is possible to make such generalizations as: the well-dressed child will be better behaved than the poorly dressed child, and the child who learns to dress himself early advances more rapidly in other areas as well.

Are these implications correct? Are they correct at some ages or for some groups and not for others? What do we mean by attractive and becoming clothing? Is it the child's standards, the parents' standards, or the author's standards which we are using? What aspects of clothing, if any, are important to the child? Do they affect his mood and behavior? Can they be used to train him in other areas? How do they affect his development? What are his preferences? How do all of these vary with the age of the child? In the following chapters we shall examine what evidence we have on each of these questions and try to evaluate that evidence by examining the methods used. In certain areas we will have no research data, and can only point to the need for research, or from our general knowledge of child psychology formulate hypotheses for investigation. Even though we do not have all of the answers, it is time to pull together what research there is and our knowledge of children and of clothing, organizing the information so that we can see both where we are and where we need to advance.

One weakness in the generalizations which have been made thus far, is that children of all ages have been lumped together; it has been assumed that what is true of children of one age is also true of those of all ages. For example, certain authors have stressed the child's need to conform or the child's desire for bright colors in clothing. Most of the needs, attitudes, and preferences of children change rapidly from one age to another throughout the growing years. Why, then, should we expect their needs and preferences in clothing to remain constant? We will attempt to overcome this difficulty by discussing various age groups separately. However, the divisions into age groups in this book are still very general. As our knowledge in this area increases, it will be possible to pinpoint more exactly at what stages of development various attitudes, needs, and preferences are prevalent.

Before we discuss the results of research for any one age group, we need to have some background in the types of research methods which have been used or are appropriate at various age levels.

Research in which children are the subjects is, in many ways, more difficult than research with adults. In the first place we have the problem of verbalization. Even after children are old enough to talk, their vocabulary is limited and they are unable to express the nuances of meaning which we expect with adults. It is also much more difficult to control motivation with children. For example, in experiments on ease of dressing, the child may become distracted or lose interest and simply not attempt to finish the dressing process; while adults, in general, will complete to the best of their ability any task given to them in an experimental situation. A further difficulty encountered with children is their short span of attention. Consequently, any experiment dealing with them, whatever the type, needs to be of short duration. Research projects in child development or child psychology can be divided into three basic categories: (1) descriptive, case study or observation, (2) tests and measurements and (3) experimental.

The earliest work in child psychology was usually in the first category of descriptive studies. It was usually in the form of diaries or *biographies* of individual children. These were day-by-day accounts of an individual child's behavior. Child psychologists now feel that they have outgrown this method and they try to use better controlled conditions and if possible a large number of subjects so that the results are applicable more generally. The biographies of individual children, nevertheless, may be considered a first step. They serve to form hypotheses for later work. If we had records of a number of children's reactions to and comments concerning clothes, and their preferences at various ages, they would be helpful in formulating specific problems. For example, the records of several individual children might show that at the age of six or on entering school they all were anxious to have their clothing conform to the styles of other children in their group. We then might investigate whether or not this is generally the age at which it is important for children to conform to the group in clothing, and the influence of school upon the child's desire to conform. Without biographies to suggest that six might be the age at which to look for the first desire to conform, a great deal of initial groundwork of interviewing parents or teachers, or observing children might be needed.

The case study, or clinical method, is a more sophisticated extension of the biographical method. In the clinical approach, case histories often deal with the defective, retarded, or abnormal child as contrasted with the average or "normal" child. Various tests, such as the projective tests, may be used as an integral part of the case study. The observations are made by a trained and disinterested observer and therefore should be more reliable and valid than biographies kept by some member of the child's family. Nevertheless, the case study usually is still uncontrolled, impossible to replicate, subject to the biases of the clinician, and the children being studied generally deviate in some way from the average child.

The *controlled observation* method is a refinement of the biographical method, which has been used frequently in recent years. In this method the environment is not rigidly controlled. Often the observations are made in a nursery school where the children are engaged in their usual activities. The observer watches and records the actions or remarks of one or more children. In order not to influence the child's behavior, the observer is often behind a one-way screen. For the results of such observations to be reliable, the observer should undergo a period of training so that he knows exactly what he is looking for and records the same activity in the same category each time. By having more than one observer record the activity of a given child, the reports can be compared to determine if the observers are interpreting the activities in the same way, that is, if the results are reliable. This appears on the surface to be a simple method which would yield useful data. But, unless the task for the observers is made extremely simple, it is very difficult to obtain reliable results. Children are so active that two observers seldom agree on what a given child has done.

The observational or descriptive methods have been valuable in that they have yielded some general understanding of children—their activities and abilities at different age levels. They also serve to develop hypotheses for further research. They are necessarily limited, however, to what the child does and can not answer why he does it.

The second basic category of types of research includes *tests, measurements, and survey methods.*

The questionnaire or interview method has been used to obtain data from the parents or from the children themselves. The chief advantage of this type of method is that a large number of people can be reached in a relatively short time and the data are relatively simple to analyze. The major disadvantage is the difficulty of wording a questionnaire or interview which will be understood by children and which they will answer truthfully. Children often give whatever answer they think the adult wants to hear and are unconcerned with the truth of their reply. Questionnaires or interviews with parents will yield parent's opinions of children's attitudes, but these may not reflect accurately the children's attitudes.

Testing is another method frequently used in child psychology today. Intelligence tests were the first employed. Tests of manual dexterity and mechanical aptitude have also been developed and standardized for various age groups. A difficulty often encountered in using tests on young children is in gaining the cooperation of the children. Goodenough (7) has listed suggestions for obtaining their cooperation in the test situation, but even with precautions, this difficulty is often insurmountable. In using any test, the results are meaningless unless norms have been established for the given age group used. The validity and reliability of the test not only in general, but for the given age group should be known, if the study is to be adequate.

In recent years projective tests have received a great deal of emphasis. Such tests are used as a means of diagnosing the individual's total personality. The theory behind projective tests is that, due to differences in experience and endowment, each individual will perceive and react to objects or events differently, and the way in which he reacts gives a clue, if properly interpreted, to the personality of the individual. The Rorschach test is probably the best known of the projective techniques. It consists of a series of inkblots. The individual being tested tells what he sees in each of these nonsense figures. This test has been frequently used with children. Ford (5) and Ames *et al* (1) have established norms by describing characteristic responses at different age levels.

Some other projective techniques which have been used are the interpretation of children's drawings and the observation by a trained observer of children in doll play. The danger involved with all projective tech-

197

niques is that an untrained individual may feel qualified to interpret the results or to devise a new technique or modification of an established one. In spite of all that has been written concerning the Rorschach test, an individual would not be qualified to give and interpret the test without extensive training. Erroneous interpretation of projective tests would not only make research results inaccurate but might do harm to the individuals tested if the results were given out. One of the drawbacks of these tests is that to the uninitiated they seem simple to interpret. Before the results of any such test are used to correlate with other data, the validity and reliability of the test on a given age group should be determined.

The third category of method used in child study is termed the *experimental method*. In this case the environment is rigidly controlled and one variable in the environment is systematically changed and any variation in the child's response is correlated with it. For example, the young infant might be brought into the experimental situation at the same time each day and everything in the environment kept the same except the temperature. A device for recording the infant's activity might show that the amount of activity varied with the temperature of the room. This type of study is more exact in some ways than are other methods. It allows for the testing of hypotheses by manipulation of the variables. As we will see later, some of the research on learning to dress as related to types of fastenings or style of garment has used the experimental method. An experimental design adaptable to many problems in the area of childrens' clothing is that of setting up two groups: an experimental and a control group. In such an experiment the two groups of children would be alike in age, abilities, and background. They would be treated alike except for one variable, in this case something concerning clothing. The two groups would then be tested or compared in some measurable way and any differences between the groups would be assumed to be dependent on the variable. However, the experimental method has the disadvantage of being useful only under limited conditions. Usually the activities of the child are so diverse and complicated that the move into the experimental situation makes the situation very artificial and a great deal of the behavior that normally takes place is lost.

There are some variations in methodology which cut across several classifications. One of these is the cross-sectional versus the longitudinal approach. In either the descriptive or the testing types of research it is possible to describe or measure in some way either a number of children at certain ages or to follow specific children over a long period of time testing them at various ages. This latter method gives a truer picture of the progressive stages of development. Unfortunately, it is also necessary to wait for the children to pass the manifold stages of development, so that the research project must take many years to complete.

Another variation in methodology which is applicable, theoretically at least, to experimental methods as well as descriptive and testing procedures is the cross-cultural approach. In such research children are observed or tested in a wide spectrum of cultures. The assumption underlying cross-cultural studies is that the variable which is being investigated can be examined while all other variables cancel each other out. For example, the problem may be to determine the effect of restricting the movements of a baby on the age at which a child learns to walk, or on the muscular skills at a particular age. It would be best, of course, if this problem could be undertaken by the experimental method within one culture, but very likely it would be impossible to carry out such an experiment; parents in our culture would not allow their babies to be bound so that they could not move their arms or legs; and in cultures which usually bind the baby tightly or strap it to the mother's back, parents would be equally unwilling to change their customs. In such a problem the cross-cultural approach might be possible. If enough cultures similar in climate, nutrition, means of child care, and so on could be found, in some of which the children are habitually bound, and some in which children are not bound then such a comparison could be made. In cross-cultural studies it is usually too expensive and time consuming to undertake one such study at a time. Therefore, the practice has been to collect data on a very large number of variables at one time and later to analyze it for information on such specific problems. Thus far very little data of this sort have been analyzed, if collected, with clothing as a variable, but we hope that many cross-cultural studies in this area will be completed in the future.

Studies on the psychology of clothing as related to children have made use of the methods described here and all of them could be used for work in this area. As yet, however, most of the material on the psychology of clothing as related to children is usually the result of casual observation or memory of the particular writer's own childhood reactions to clothing rather than being founded upon research findings. Everyone, even a child psychologist, seems to think that he is an expert and that having experienced clothing as a child and adult or having watched and worked with children, he can give an adequate answer to any question concerning clothing for the child. We must be careful, however, to separate opinions from research findings and to examine critically the methodology of the research before coming to conclusions.

199

Bibliography

1. Ames, L. B., Learned, J., Metraux, R. W., and Walker, R. N. *Child Rorschach Responses: Developmental Trends from Two to Ten Years.* New York: Harper & Row, Publishers, 1952, 310p.
2. Aries, Phillippe. *Centuries of Childhood, a Social History of Family Life.* New York: Alfred A. Knopf, Inc., 1962, 437p.
3. Barker, R. G., Kounin, J. S., and Wright, H. F. *Child Behavior and Development.* New York: McGraw-Hill Book Co., Inc., 1943, 1–15, 485–490.
4. Diaz, Winnifred Elizabeth. *Instruments for Determining Characteristics of School Clothing Important to Ninth Grade Girls and Their Mothers.* M.S. Thesis, Iowa State Univer., 1959.
5. Ford, Mary. *The Application of the Rorschach Test to Young Children.* Univer. Minn. Inst. Child Development and Welfare Mono. No. 23, 1946, 114p.
6. Gardner, D. B., Hawkes, G., and Pease, D. Development and use of research method in child development. *J. of Home Ec.* 50(3), 1948, 201–206.
7. Goodenough, F. *Mental Testing.* New York: Holt, Rinehart and Winston, Inc., 1949, 609p.
8. Jebe, E., Beveridge, Elizabeth, Hawkes, G. R., Potgeiter, Fannie, and Roberson, Opal. How to study consumer satisfaction with children's clothing made of different textile fibers. *J. of Home Ec.* 50(3), 1958, 213–218.
9. Jones, Mary Cove and Burks, Barbara S. Personality development in childhood: A survey of problems, methods and experimental findings. *Monogr. of Soc. for Res. in Child Devel.* 1(4), 1936, 205p.
10. Koshuk, R. P. Social influences affecting the behavior of young children. *Monogr. of Soc. for Res. in Child Devel.* 6(2), 1941, 71p.
11. Lerner, E. and Murphy, L. B. Methods for the study of personality in young children. *Monogr. of Soc. for Res. in Child Devel.* 6(4), 1941, 289p.
12. Mussen, P. H. and Conger, J. J. *Child Development and Personality.* New York: Harper & Row, Publishers, 1956, Chap. I, 14–23.
13. Pahopin, Jo. *An Exploratory Study of Techniques for Determining Consumer Preferences in Children's Wear.* Ph.D. thesis, Ohio State Univer., 1958.
14. Ritchie, O. and Koller, M. *Sociology of Childhood.* New York: Appleton-Century-Crofts, 1964, 323p.
15. Tate, Mildred T., and Glisson, Oris. *Family Clothing.* New York: John Wiley & Sons, Inc., 1961, 394p.
16. Thompson, Henrietta, and Rea, Lucille. *Clothing for Children.* New York: John Wiley & Sons, Inc., 1949, 406p.
17. Young, Florence E. *Clothing the Child.* New York: McGraw-Hill Book Co., Inc., 1938, 253p.

Chapter 10

Infants
and
Preschool Children

*T*he very young baby does not recognize objects or people. His awareness of life consists largely of consciousness of himself, particularly of his physical self. The infant's world is limited to those things which impinge directly on his sense organs. While the infant's eyes function and he is able to follow a moving light, he does not perceive visual objects as such. His visual world is composed of a meaningless mass or as James so aptly expressed it, the baby's world is "one great, blooming, buzzing confusion" [15:488]. Although we have evidence (for example, see 7 and 29) that the infant discriminates between lights of varying hues, there is no evidence to suggest that he reacts differently to different hues. Therefore, even color, the most obvious diversification in the appearance of clothes, is probably not perceived by the infant.

The Infant

THE INFANT'S WORLD AND IMPLICATIONS FOR CLOTHING

The sense of touch functions almost perfectly from birth. Sensitivity to pain develops after the first few days, and there is reaction to cutaneous irritation usually by the end of the first week. The baby withdraws the part of the body being irritated or is generally restless and cries. Furthermore, his skin is more tender than that of the older child and is more easily chafed. Therefore, we can assume that the baby will be more comfortable and will cry less if his clothes are soft and pliable. The soft knitted fabrics which have been popular in recent years are especially good for this reason. Not only should the fabric be soft to give the greatest comfort but there should be no rough, unfinished seams or fastenings which irritate the skin. When we consider the dresses stiff with starch which babies used to wear, we are not surprised that grandmothers often comment that babies are "better" now than they used to be.

The baby's skin is also sensitive to temperature changes, as is shown by his crying or refusing to take milk or water if it is too cold or hot. There have been reports of infants shivering within a few hours after birth. The baby gives more pronounced reactions to stimuli which are colder than his body than he does to warmer ones. There is no exact way of determining whether or not the baby is dressed to give the most comfortable temperature. The appearance of the baby's skin, whether or not he is perspiring and the adult's own perception of temperature are the only guides we have in determining the amount of clothing necessary for comfortable temperature. Mothers often err by keeping the infant too warm because they fail to take into account the amount the baby is exercising. Studies on adults have shown the great range in clothing needed for the resting body as compared to the active body. The baby when he is awake is continually kicking and waving so that he raises his body temperature and needs less when awake than the more inactive adult. Because the baby is so small and his movements short we overlook the extent to which his body is involved.

In several studies infants have been placed in a controlled environment, such as a Skinner crib,[1] and one aspect of the environment varied while measuring the amount of movement or the amount of crying. This type of research has given us some information concerning the effect of clothing versus no clothing, but not the effect of one kind as opposed to another kind of clothing. Irwin (14) found that infants were less active when clothed than when unclothed, and Halverson (9) found that the strength of the gripping reflex was greater in the nude situation than in the clothed situation. In both studies the infants cried more in the nude situation than when they were clothed. The greater strength and activity of the baby when nude may be the result of greater muscle activity because of crying, or because of restlessness due to discomfort which in turn is caused, as Halverson suggests, by changes in his skin temperature. This explanation seems logical when we examine the results of a study by Pratt (23). Pratt found that there is both greater activity and also a greater amount of crying when the infant is wet than when he is dry. There is also the possibility that the results of these studies may be due to a change from the usual conditions. That is, the baby who is usually clothed is un-

---

[1] This is an infant crib, enclosed in glass, and designed so that the temperature and humidity can be controlled.

comfortable and cries when he is nude, while a baby who is usually nude would cry when clothed. The same experiments should be repeated on both babies who are accustomed to wearing clothing and babies who have been living in controlled temperature situations and have always been nude.

It is difficult to determine what these studies mean in terms of what is "best" for the baby. Certainly the infant who is clothed and dry cries less and we can assume is more comfortable. But the nude or wet child not only cries more but is generally more active and has greater muscle tonus so may thus become stronger. These studies give the immediate results, but no indication as to whether or not there are any lasting effects.]

The same problem confronts us when we discuss clothing which hampers a child's movements. Most writers on clothing for infants have warned against clothing which is hampering. Watson (35) years ago pointed out that restricting an infant's movements elicits rage. The infant's dislike of having his arms or legs restricted is often demonstrated when he is being dressed or undressed. In our culture we have assumed that it is best not to restrict the child's movements. In other cultures and at other periods in our culture the baby's limbs have been restricted. In some cases it has been long and heavy garments, in others tight wrapping and in still others the way in which the baby is carried (for instance, in a cradleboard on the mother's back). While our position of allowing freedom of movement seems logical, it must be pointed out that it has not been proven that hampering clothing or wrapping either delays or effects qualitatively the later development of the child. As we suggested in the last chapter, cross-cultural studies comparing children whose limbs are and are not confined might answer this question. In the studies we have, there have been too few cultural groups to eliminate the effects of other possible variables. For example, Smith *et al.* (27) found that the children of Hawaii on the average walk somewhat earlier than those from Iowa, which might be due to the fact that they had worn fewer clothes. On the other hand, the results might be due to the difference in climate, the amount of sun they receive, or to different methods in caring for children. Furthermore, the results of this study did not show whether the children who learned to walk first retained their superiority in this respect for any length of time.

The Toddler

We will use the term toddler to designate the child from about six months to two and a half years.

The toddler's world has greatly expanded from that of the infant. He recognizes people and objects. His gain in muscular skill is enormous. During this brief period he learns to sit, stand, creep, walk, run, and climb. He is able to get about to investigate and to explore. He recognizes members of his family and others whom he sees regularly. The number of objects he sees and recognizes is greatly enlarged because he has been mobile so that he can feel, see, and taste them. He learns to imitate and to speak and respond to others.

His own physical comfort is still the dominate interest in his world and his attitude toward clothing is dependent upon this. The toddler very often actively dislikes clothing of any sort. He considers it a nuisance and wishes to discard it if possible. Like the baby, he hates to be dressed and undressed; he fights against having garments put on and runs away from them if he can. At this age his muscular development is not great enough to dress himself, but he is able to take some garments off, and he often does so at the first opportunity.

The first prerequisite for clothes from the point of view of the very young child, then, is that they be as few in number as possible and that they do not restrict his movements. The more comfortable the clothing and the less it interferes with his activity the better it is from his point of view. This is particularly true of shoes. The child learning to walk and run uses his toes to help him balance. Stiff soles prevent his using these muscles and make it harder for him to walk and run.

It is at this age also that the child is trained to go to the toilet and is shifting from diaper to training pants. Because training pants are less bulky and cumbersome than diapers the privilege of wearing them is often an incentive to learn to use the bathroom. To aid in this training process training pants should be loose enough so that the child can pull them down easily and quickly by himself.

The appearance of his clothing is still of little concern to the toddler. The older age groups are concerned with the appearance of clothing for social reasons. They value clothes which will gain for them the approval of others. In most instances the baby or very young child *does* have the obvious approval of everyone around him and so this need for clothing is not experienced.

The Preschool Child and His Clothes

Although the space of time between a child's second birthday and his sixth seems to us relatively short, it is a period in which great changes take place in the child. He develops from an almost helpless baby who is just learning to walk and talk into a relatively independent school boy. The importance of clothing for the youngster has also changed drastically. As an infant or toddler he was either unaware of his clothes or they were a nuisance to him, but when he is a three or four year old clothing may be a wonderful means of getting adults to notice him. Clothes may make him look "like Daddy," his favorite hero, or a "big boy." He can demonstrate how "big" he is, by his ability to dress or undress himself. He even becomes so socially sophisticated that he notices the clothing of others.

PHYSICAL AND MOTOR DEVELOPMENT OF THE PRESCHOOL
CHILD AND IMPLICATIONS FOR CLOTHING

Between the ages of two and six the child not only makes great advances in height and weight but the body proportions also change (for illustration of these changing proportions see 32:146–147). During this period the head growth is slow while the limb growth is rapid. Thus, while caps and hats which fitted the child at two to three years may still fit him when he is five- or six-years old he may have outgrown three or four snowsuits.

At the same time he is loosing his baby fat; as a consequence, the child now has a waist line and is much more successful at keeping up pants or skirts with elastic tops. Likewise while it was necessary for the preschool child to wear overalls or straps over his shoulders, by the time he is ready for first grade the boy usually can wear "regular" pants, while girls can wear skirts with petticoats instead of being limited to dresses or jumpers and full-length slips. By the end of this period his proportions are much more nearly those of the adult.

Between two and six the child also makes great strides in how he can use his body. He makes tremendous progress in control of both the large and the small muscles. At two, the normal child is able to walk, but he tends to bump into things and his balance is precarious so that he has many falls. At three he is not only steadier but he can climb stairs and ride a tricycle, while at four he can climb, run, jump, roller skate, ride a scooter and even play ball.

"Be sure and notice his shoes. He just learned to tie them."

COURTESY *Better Homes & Gardens* MAGAZINE. MARCH 1965.

As these are all new activities he enjoys doing them repeatedly. The child in the age range two to six is more active than he will be at any later period in his life. We hear of the football player who attempted to follow a preschool child in all of his activities and was soon completely worn out. Even watching a lively nursery-school child for a period is exhausting for the average adult.

As was the case with the infant and toddler, there are no studies on how hampering of the child's movements affects later physiological or psychological development nor do we have studies on the factors which hamper movement. Watching active children will indicate some of the difficulties which would be encountered in trying to measure activity under varying conditions. Furthermore, parents would be unwilling to consent to have their children's activity restricted over a period of time. Even cross-cultural studies would not be of help since after the child is of walking age there are no cultures in which the child's movements are deliberately restricted. We make the assumption that the active preschool child should be exercising his muscles and acquiring new muscular skills and that therefore his clothing should be designed and chosen with this in mind.

Nursery school teachers and clothing specialists as well as mothers have observed and written about some of the factors which seem to hamper the child's movements. The most frequent of these is bulkiness caused either by too large or too much clothing. Many mothers purchase snowsuits which are large for the child hoping that they will last for more than one season. The result is that the too-long pants are bulky and make running difficult. The child, as a consequence, fights against wearing the snowsuit.

Lifting the arm may be restricted by too-tight armholes, too-tight sleeves, by too short, or too tight a waist line, or by straps which fall over the shoulders. Likewise pants which are too tight in the legs or through the crotch may hamper leg movement. The new stretch fabrics may be the answer to many of these problems.

Learning to dress. We have noted the preschool child's progress in the control of the large muscles. There is likewise tremendous progress in the control of small muscles such as those of the hand. It is during this period that the child learns to dress himself. Dressing and undressing are complicated processes, and skill in this area is difficult to measure accurately. Some garments are more difficult to manage than others; some parts of the body are more difficult to reach than others; some children are more highly motivated than others.

By dividing the dressing process into units, Key and her co-workers (17) were able to measure the progress of children in learning to dress and to determine which units were most difficult for the child to master. They first classified the garments as to the part of the body covered ("torso," "leg," and so on) and then each type was divided into units of accomplishment (for example, "one arm in hole," "arms in two holes," "garment adjusted"). The child's total score for dressing was the percentage of units which he finished correctly. As would be expected, the authors found that chronological age is the most potent factor in ability to dress, although there were large individual differences especially among the younger children. The child between one and a half years and two years can master 12 to 63 percent of the dressing units and takes from 15 to 25 minutes to get dressed. The two-and-a-half-year to four-and-a-half-year-old child can accomplish a higher percent of the units but may take longer (5 to 45 minutes) because of less help. The four-and-a-half to five-year-old child takes just 5 to 15 minutes and is able to master all of the dressing units.

In learning to dress we see a marked sex difference. Girls, because they have better fine motor coordination than boys at this age, learn to dress themselves earlier and do so more efficiently. Key *et al.* (17) in the study mentioned above confirmed this fact. Wagoner and Armstrong (34) have shown that girls were faster than boys in learning to button and unbutton garments.

Wagoner and Armstrong also found that age in learning to button and unbutton garments is not correlated with intelligence tests but does correlate positively with scores on performance tests. Their sample consisted of thirty nursery school children who were given the Stanford-Binet intelligence test, the Merrill Palmer Performance tests, the Goodenough Drawing Test and also a buttoning situation. For the buttoning test, jackets were made up with three one-inch buttons on the front or with similar buttons on the back. The children were timed for both buttoning and unbuttoning a jacket with front opening and one with back opening. The correlation was highest between the buttoning score and a test in which the task was to assemble a nest of cubes. In a second part of the experiment each child had two series of jackets with three in each series. All of the jackets had three buttons in the front and three on each side. The three jackets in each series differed in the types of button holes (horizontal, vertical, and loop) while the jackets in the two series differed in size of buttons. There were correlation of +.77 and +.75 between the Merrill Palmer performance test scores and time scores for buttoning and unbuttoning the front buttons on the jacket, but only +.095 and +.154 between the Stanford-Binet Intelligence test scores and the time scores on buttoning and unbuttoning.

These authors found that the buttoning ability was also related to some personality traits of the child. The children were rated by two nursery-school teachers and one of the experimenters on the following traits:

1. Self-dependence and self-reliance
2. Perseverance and completion of tasks
3. Interest and care in detail.

All three of these traits correlated very highly (+.82 to +.90) with the buttoning score.

Gesell (8) points out that there seems to be no relationship between dependency in dressing and emotional dependence. The emotionally dependent child is not as a rule especially dependent on the mother for help in dressing. On the other hand, if too much in the way of independence in dressing is expected of the poorly coordinated child, then his adjustment to school may be disturbed.

From observations in the Yale laboratory, Gessell and his colleagues have formulated a developmental sequence which gives us an index of what to expect of the normal child in dressing at various age levels:

DRESSING

15 months—1. Cooperates in dressing by extending arm or leg.
18 months—1. Can take off mittens, hat and socks.
            2. Can unzip zippers.
            3. Tries to put on shoes.
24 months—1. Can remove shoes if laces are untied.
            2. Helps in getting dressesd—finds large arm-holes and thrusts his arms into them.
            3. Helps pull up or push down panties.
            4. Washes hands and dries them but does neither very well.
36 months—1. Greater interest and ability in undressing. May need some assistance with shirts and sweaters.
            2. Is able to unbutton all front and side buttons by pushing buttons through buttonholes.
            3. In dressing does not know back from front. Apt to put pants on backwards, has difficulty in turning socks to get heels in back. Puts shoes on but may put them on wrong feet.
            4. Intent on lacing shoes, but usually laces them incorrectly.
            5. Washes and dries hands.
            6. Brushes teeth with supervision.
48 months—1. Is able to dress and undress himself with little assistance.
            2. Distinguishes between front and back of clothes and puts them on correctly.
            3. Washes and dries hands and face.
            4. Brushes his teeth.
60 months—1. Undresses and dresses with care.
            2. May be able to tie shoe laces (usually at 6 years).[2]

---

[2] A. Gesell *The First Five Years of Life, a Guide to the Study of the Pre-School Child.* New York: Harper & Row, Publishers, 1940, p. 248.

The factors in garments which make them easy or difficult for the child to put on have been investigated. Key *et al.* (17), in the study cited earlier, found that some units or processes were much easier for the child to learn than others. For example, the easiest units for the child are putting the arms or legs into a hole or pulling up a garment. The more difficult units are those requiring adjustment of the garment or involve coordination and orientation in space such as getting the heel of the sock placed correctly.

Garments which are supposedly easy for the child to put on and take off by himself have been called *self-help* clothes and have been promoted by the home economist for many years. Features considered necessary for clothing to be termed *self-help* include:

Large armholes

Back and front either easy to tell apart or alike

Front opening

Fasteners easy to manipulate, that is, no small fasteners.

Much of the discussion about self-help clothing was done before zippers were commonly used. Fasteners were usually buttons, and to satisfy the self-help requisite needed to be large. Large buttons often seemed out of proportion on small garments and were not esthetically acceptable to the mothers. Boettke and Zook (3) demonstrated that it was possible to design clohing which had self-help feaures, allowed for growth, were comfortable and still were acceptable in design.

In recent years the invention of new fastenings and the use of many stretch knit fabrics, which need no fasteners, have eliminated the need to put emphasis upon some of the self-help features.[3] In addition, children's clothes have become greatly simplified and they wear fewer garments. The child of today can, therefore, dress and undress himself at a much younger age than could a child when clothes were more complicated and more garments were worn. Gesell (8:248) has pointed out that this may make us expect too much from the young child. Dressing is still dependent on motor coordination and the child can only master the skills in dressing as he develops appropriate muscle coordination.

We should not finish a section on learning to dress without some reference to the speed, or rather the lack of speed, with which this process is usually accomplished. Dawdling is normal and, unfortunately for the mother, very common, especially with the four-, five-, and six-year-old child. By this time the novelty of dressing himself was worn off so that it is no longer a game. It is still not automatic, however, and he can't do it rapidly while thinking of something else. Therefore, the child is apt to put on one garment then stop

---

[3] The new fastenings may also have their disadvantages. M. L. Rosencranz points out that fastenings like Velco are so easy to undo or pull open that the child seldom has his coat fastened. If he tries to fasten it by himself, he has difficulty in putting the two sides of the garment together evenly.

to play or watch someone else, and needs to be reminded again and again before the entire dressing process is completed. Herein, lies one of the major difficulties in conducting research in this area. It is very difficult to control the child's motivation or the effort he is expending in attempting to dress. If he accomplishes the task we are studying we know he is able to do it, but, if he doesn't accomplish it, it may be because he is unable to do so; something else is more interesting for him at the moment; or he is just not in the mood.

Independence in dressing as soon as the child has developed sufficient motor control has value beyond the obvious advantages to nursery school or kindergarten teacher and mother. There is evidence that independence in one area carries over to independence in another. If the child is trained by progressing from easy tasks to harder ones with praise for success, it leads to more mature and independent work on another task (for research evidence on this point see 16). Dressing, which is a daily task, has gradations of difficulty naturally incorporated within the total task. Therefore, it may be a very natural and convenient way for the mother to teach the child to acquire greater independence in general.

THE PRESCHOOL CHILD'S WORLD AND IMPLICATIONS FOR CLOTHING

The world of the preschool child is widening, and he is beginning to be aware of others. Until the age of two his contacts have been mainly with his family. At three or four, while his social contacts are mainly with his family, he begins to have contacts with other children either in nursery school or in the neighborhood. However, he is still very self-absorbed and he usually plays alone, even when other children are present. While he is learning that other children have mothers and fathers and that they feel as separate entities, he still assumes that others see the world as he does. He has no real sympathy or empathy with other children. If another child is hurt and cries he may run over to him and attempt to comfort him as he has seen adults do, but a few minutes later he may hurt another child.

Not only is he very self-centered, but he wants to be the center of attention for all those around him. At the same time he is becoming aware of the fact that he may not be the focus of attention, but that it is possible for him to make others notice him. He soon learns that one of the easiest ways to attract attention to himself is through his clothes. This is not surprising when we consider adult behavior toward children. Parents, other relatives, nursery school teachers, Sunday school teachers, and adults friends all make comments, many times extravagant comments, about new clothing or special garments. When we first meet a small child and greet him, we commonly remark about something the child is wearing. This is understandable since there are so few avenues of communication between preschool children and adults. Such topics as weather, politics, the world series, common friends, good books, popular with adults, are obviously inappropriate. The adult tends, therefore, to comment either on a toy, if the child is playing with one, or on some aspect of his clothing. The child thus learns very soon that clothing, especially if it is new, will command attention. Bright colors, and decoration also bring attention from adults and so take on added value. A child learns, also that if he does not immediately get attention he can soon obtain it by calling attention to his clothes. We all have heard children say to an adult or to a group, "See my new mittens" (or dress or hat). This never fails to bring favorable comments and attention from the adult and, therefore, satisfaction to the child.

CLOTHING AND THE CONCEPT OF SELF IN THE CHILD

Hurlock says (13:302) :

> The reason the child's clothing has such a pronounced affect on his behavior is that he identifies himself with his clothes and looks upon them as part of himself. This tendency is even more pronounced in children than in adults because the child lacks the consciousness of self as an individual that the adult possesses.

The child from infancy has been learning the limits of his body and by three or four years knows the various parts of the body and what articles of clothing belong to them. He knows that other people have the same parts and is able to point to various features on himself, another person, a doll, or a picture. He knows that people vary in size and are "big" or babies. He is also learning at this age that there are two sexes and to which sex he belongs. Clothes help him to identify the sex of others and his own. By having garments "like Dady's" or "like Mommy's" the child learns that he is going to become a man or woman. Clothes help him to learn to play the appropriate sex role. By wearing clothing like his father's, for example, the child tends to try to act like his father and so learns what behavior is and is not appropriate for a man.

Vener and Weese (33) conducted an interesting study on the preschool child's perception of adult sex-linked cultural objects. The children were asked to remove articles from a suitcase one at a time and to indicate whether the article belonged to "Mom" or "Dad" or both. Included among the objects were wearing apparel and small tool items suggestive of household tasks. The results showed that "both the preschool boys and girls of this highly purposive middle-class sample population are more accurate in their perception of the cultural objects associated with the mother role" [p. 53]. As the authors point out the capacity to recognize the appropriate appearance and task objects for a sex cannot be assumed to be the same as recognition of their own sex-role identity.

To see how important a factor clothing is in teaching the child about the various roles he will play we have only to watch him in his play. Very often the child "dresses up" or puts on at least one adult garment in a game of "let's pretend." A pair of high heels enables a little girl to pretend she is a mother, a cowboy neckerchief helps the boy to pretend he is the current television hero.

The mistake many adults make is in underestimating the child's imagination. They buy the child elaborate cowboy outfits, nurses' costumes, spaceman suits, and so on, while often just a simple garment or piece of cloth would suffice. One woman, who was more observant than many mothers, saved a good deal of money by finding out just what a cowboy suit meant to her son. He wanted a suit to play "cowboys" with his playmates. The neighbor's child had a cowboy suit which cost over $20.00—more than this woman could afford. By listening, observing, and questioning, she found that to her son a "cowboy suit" consisted of: bluejeans, an embroidered shirt, a neckerchief, and, of course, holster and gun. The boy already had the bluejeans and the gun and holster so for $.15 she purchased a cowboy neckerchief, and for $1.19 a plain red cotton-flannel shirt. On the shirt she put "embroidery" which was really no more than basting stitches. The complete outfit had cost very little, yet it satisfied her son as completely as the elaborate costume. The child may very well not perceive the difference between the elaborate and expensive costume and the makeshift. He certainly has not as yet had enough experience in judging quality and expensiveness to know that one is "better" than the other. In fact a simple "dress-up" item such as long skirt or high-heeled shoes or length of material is often preferred by the child because it can be different things on different days.

Girls are more fortunate than boys in the matter of dressing up. They can wear hats, high heels, carry bags, gloves, furs; they can drape a length of material or pin up a long skirt. Boys, on the other hand, cannot wear their father's pants or coat and still be mobile and the only obvious diffeernce in shoes for the boy and the man is their size. The question then might be asked, do girls find it easier to assume their sex role because they have had more practice pretending to be mothers? And if so, do girls pretend to be mothers more than boys pretend to be fathers because of the ease of dressing up or because they spend more time with their mothers than boys do with their fathers? These are problems for future research.

WHAT THE CHILD LIKES OR PREFERS IN HIS CLOTHING

Habberstad[4], in a pilot study, instructed nursery school observers to record everything that the children mentioned about clothing. Her sample was small. Furthermore, it may be easier for the child to verbalize concerning some aspects of clothing than it is others, and so number of times mentioned may

---

[4] Unpublished study done at Cornell University.

not be a valid means of measuring the importance of various aspects of clothing for the child. Nevertheless, such a count of the number of times the children mentioned various aspects of clothing can give us some ideas of what is important to the child. The aspects mentioned in order of frequency were: newness, decoration, similarity to or unlike garments of another person, color, prettiness, need for help in dress.

Newness we have already discussed as an important attribute to the child because it calls attention to himself. Self-help clothing has also been discussed. The following paragraphs bear on some of the other aspects mentioned.

Color. Children of preschool age are sensitive to color and especially enjoy saturated colors. Red is usually the first choice of the younger child. Hunt (10) found that primary colors and the more saturated colors, except violet, were preferred over others by both sexes at all ages of three through ten. In color combinations the preschool child prefers a combination of his two favorite colors whether or not they blend or harmonize.

The importance of color for the preschool child has been demonstrated by Brian and Goodenough (5). Their data indicate that between the ages of three and six color appears to be accorded greater relative significance than at any other age. The subjects in this experiment were shown a standard and two other objects and asked which of the two was like the standard. One of the objects was the same shape as the standard but differed in color. The second was the same color but differed in shape. Before the age of two and a half and increasingly after the age of six children tended to match on form rather than color. Between the ages of two and a half and five, however, a higher percentage of subjects matched on color rather than form.

Perhaps one explanation for the importance of color for this age group is that it is at this period that children are first learning color names. Parents and other adults repeatedly ask them to name the color of various objects. The child may for this reason think that color is of great importance to adults, or it may give them a "set" to respond in terms of color rather than another attribute.

Texture. Texture is another attribute of garments which is very important to young children. At this age they are learning about the world around them and one of the ways they learn is through touching and feeling. They love to let soft mud squeeze between their toes or fingers. It is common to see a child stroking the fur on a coat. Hunt (10) found that fur was the most preferred texture of all children between three and ten but that it decreased in popularity with increasing age of the children. Velvet is another soft texture which apparently appeals to most youngsters of this age. Perhaps one of the reasons for the popularity of stuffed toy animals is their soft texture.

Burton (6) also investigated preschool children's preferences for texture.

Eighty-nine subjects were asked, by the method of paired comparisons, about their preferences for garments which differed in texture. Insofar as possible, the color, size, and style of the garments in each pair were alike. In one series comparisons were made between preferences when the subjects were allowed to both see and feel the garments and when they were allowed to feel but could not see the garments. Both boys and girls preferred Orlon fleece over wool coating both with and without vision. They preferred knit to terry towels when they used the tactile sense alone but the terry when they could both see and feel. Mothers agreed with the children in most instances. They differed in that they preferred the bulky knit sweater and cotton underpants while the girls preferred the fine knit sweater and the nylon underpants.

Decorative detail. The preschool child loves decorative detail, especially if it is tiny. He likes to find a little animal, person, or object in a print, button, or pin. Children are alert in observing such details not only in their own clothing but in that of others. In fact, it is often a tiny decorative detail that will make a child choose one garment over another. Hurlock tells us that "children are very much like primitive peoples in their attitudes toward clothing. Decorative features are important to them. The more ornaments the costume has the better the child will probably like it" [13:311]. The child has little of what the adult calls "good taste." He is so fond of ornaments that, if so allowed, he wants to put on all he owns at one time. A little girl bedecked like a Christmas tree is completely pleased with her appearance and, what's more, will be envied and admired by others in her age group.

Comfort. For the infant and toddler we found that comfort was the most important aspect of clothing. For the preschool child the comfort of the clothing is just one of several important aspects. This, however, does not mean that comfort itself is any less important for the preschool child than it was for the infant. Reid (26) goes so far as to say that no child is ever irritable if he is comfortable. The most common source of discomfort for the preschool-age child is found in his clothing. The three main varieties of discomfort with clothing are:

1. Temperature. The clothing may make the youngster too hot or too cold.
2. Restriction. Clothing which is too tight may cause discomfort as well as restricting bodily movements.
3. Irritating texture. The material may be scratchy or otherwise irritate the child's sensitive skin.

At times the child will indicate, either verbally or by pulling at the offending part, that a garment or a part of a garment is causing discomfort. Many times, however, the child does not say what is bothering him. He may not be aware of the cause himself or be unable to verbalize about the discomfort or cause of the discomfort. For example, when my daughter was this age she disliked overalls or dungarees. She insisted on a skirt for play as well as for dress occasions. Questioning never brought out any reason except that she wanted to wear a skirt and did not want to wear pants. We concluded that she was very feminine and wanted the prettiness of dresses rather than over-alls. It was only after several months that a remark to her grandmother made us realize that a pair of dungarees which she had worn two or three times had a seam on the inside of the leg which was stiff and irritated the skin. She had generalized the discomfort of this garment to all pants, but could not, or for some reason did not want to, tell us the reason.

Effect of associations or familiarity on the child's liking for garments. Either the familiarity of the garment or the fact that it has become associated with certain objects or events in the child's earlier experience may influence his liking or disliking a garment. Clothes having pleasant association tend to become preferred while those retaining unpleasant associations tend to be dis-liked. For example, Mary remembers that as a little girl she had a dress which she particularly disliked. When her mother urged her to wear it she cried and refused. When questioned about the reason she replied that she was al-ways spanked when she wore that dress. The family recalled that she actually had been spanked a number of times when she wore that dress. In this case the unpleasantness became associated with that particular dress. In other cases it might have become associated with the color or some other aspect of the dress. In the same way pleasant experiences may become attached to a garment and a child may learn to love it because it is one she wears to parties where she has a good time, or, when she has worn it she has been the center of attention.

Often children associate home, comfort, or security with a given garment and are attached to it for that reason. We laugh at Linus and his blanket in the comics, and have known of children who are unhappy if their favorite blanket, toy, or garment is taken from them. In a certain measure, the same thing is true of most children. Every child derives sense of security from old and familiar garments. It may not be the identical garment each time but the fact that it is familiar may help in a new situation. A child going alone to kindergarten or to a friend's home for the first time may find it easier if he wears an old jacket or sweater.

Preschool children often seem to feel insecure if they are told to discard a familiar type of garment. Every nursery school teacher has had children who refuse to give up mittens, caps, or coats when the weather turns warm. Mothers tell us of youngsters who will suffer in the heat rather than give up the familiar overalls for the more comfortable shorts.

ASPECTS OF CLOTHING WHICH DO NOT INTEREST
THE PRESCHOOL CHILD

Although the list of attributes which are important to the preschool child seems long there are some aspects of clothing which seem important to the adult but not to the preschool child.

Becomingness. The child has no concept of becomingness and so is not in the least interested in this aspect usually stressed by mothers.

Appropriateness. The child has not yet learned what is appropriate for his age, for the time of the day, the season, or the occasion. If a little girl's favorite dress is her party dress she may beg to put it on every day. By the end of the preschool period the child usually does distinguish between party and play garments but still may not make other distinctions.

Durability, ease of care, price. The child, of course, has no interest in the price of the garment, how long it will last and how easy it is to wash and iron.

Conformity. Unlike the older child, the preschool child is usually not interested in whether or not his clothing conforms to the type that other children are wearing. He doesn't yet belong, or wish to belong, to a peer group and so is not interested in factors which make him conform to the group.

Size of wardrobe. The adolescent or the adult is interested in having a variety and large number of clothes, but the preschool child is completely indifferent on this score. He would be most happy if he could wear his favorite outfit every day.

Source of garment. The older child may rebel at wearing handed-down clothing, but the preschool child does not object to hand-me-downs if he likes the garment itself. In fact, he may be proud and pleased to wear something which belonged to an older child because it shows how "big" he is getting.

Cleanliness and neatness. Last but certainly not least, the preschool child is not at all concerned with the cleanliness of his clothes or his person. Splashing through puddles, making mud pies, smearing finger paints (or any substitute), exploring and handling anything new are far more important to him than any traces left on the clothes. The child who is overly concerned with cleanliness is not the normal child and often has difficulty adjusting to the group. The mother who shows very great concern over the cleanliness of her child or his clothes is in a way restricting his freedom and making him anxious and watchful.

IMPORTANT VALUES TO THE MOTHER

We have reviewed what the child wants in clothing. These are not always what the child's mother wants and looks for in buying his clothes. One study by Blake *et al.,* (2) listed the factors considered important by 100 mothers in one city. These, in order of importance, were:

1. Durability
2. Price
3. Fit
4. Comfort to wearer
5. Ease of laundering

   6. Color
   7. Child's attitude toward garment
   8. Beauty
   9. Other

These values certainly are not the same as the child's values. The mother obviously would need to consider such aspects as price, durability, and ease of care which have no importance to the child, but many of the factors which are important to the child are either not considered or are considered under "child's attitude toward garment," and this is far down on the list of attributes important to her. This would seem to indicate that there is need for education in this area. Perhaps the mother places little emphasis upon the child's values because she is unaware of them.

Effect of Clothing upon the Preschool Child

Sweeping statements have been made about the effect of clothing on the mood and behavior of the child. It has been said that a child who is better dressed is better behaved, that a child who is dressed like a cowboy is louder than he is when dressed in ordinary clothes. Statements have also been made about the effect of color on the child. Red is said to make the child excitable, while a soft cool color has a quieting influence. These and similar statements are usually based upon casual observations of children and we do not know how reliable and valid such statements are for children in general. The difficulties encountered in doing anything more than making uncontrolled observations of preschool children are so great that it is not surprising that we have no experimental evidence on these points. The number of variables that it would be necessary to control are staggering just to consider. Therefore, at the present time we must use the observations which have been made as hypotheses, but keep in mind that we are basing our statements upon uncontrolled observations and not upon research evidence.

Our hypothesis related to the statements made above is that clothing might have a temporary effect on the behavior of the child, but not a lasting effect. That is, we would predict that a child who was dressed in his best clothes and whose mother stressed that they were "best" would be better behaved for a short period, but by the end of the hour the child would have forgotten his clothes and would be acting as he would in old clothes. Likewise the child who is dressed in a cowboy outfit might be very noisy while playing cowboys for a brief time, but he might soon change to another activity and be no more noisy than usual. We would also hypothesize that dressing the child in clothing which is "better" in the sense of more appropriate, neat, of better quality, or more esthetically pleasing in design would have no effect upon him.

We have already mentioned several other effects of clothing on the child. Uncomfortable clothing may make a child irritable. We would expect this effect to last as long as the child was wearing the garment. Clothes which hamper the movements of the child lessen the amount of his activity and also may make him irritable. Clothing which encourages independence in dressing may not only hasten independence in this area but carry over to other areas as well. Finally, we have also already discussed the sense of security which the preschool child may gain from a familiar and loved garment.

Summary

Infant. (Birth to six months.) The infant's world is limited to those things which directly impinge upon his sense organs, therefore, the texture of his garments and whether or not they keep him at a comfortable temperature are the most important considerations in clothing. Studies have shown that the baby has greater muscle tension and also cries more when nude than when clothed.

Toddler. (Six months to two and a half years.) The toddler dislikes the restriction of clothes and being dressed or undressed. He prefers the freedom of nudity. Watching that clothing does not restrict movement is the most important factor in clothing for the child while he is learning to sit, stand, crawl, run, and climb.

Preschool child. (Two and a half to six.) The child at this age is learning to dress. Studies have shown that learning independence in one area fosters independence in other areas, so clothing that is easy to put on and take off may be beneficial beyond the particular skill of dressing.

The preschool child wants to be the center of attention. Since he has learned that adults will remark about new clothing, he likes any new garment. He wants comfortable clothing which allows for his very active life; he prefers bright primary colors, especially red; he likes soft textures; he admires decorations, especially tiny ones; he likes something which, for him at least, is "like" his father's or mother's clothing or the hero of the moment; and finally, he likes old familiar garments, especially when he is put into a new situation where he feels insecure.

He is not interested in becomingness, appropriateness, durability, price, variety or a large wardrobe, conformity in dress or cleanliness.

Bibliography

1. Baldwin, Alfred. *Behavior and Development in Childhood.* New York: Holt, Rinehart and Winston, Inc., 1955, 619p.
2. Blake, Evelyn, Glisson, Oris, and Tate, Mildred. A study of the preschool child's clothing in 100 families of Radford, Virginia. *J. of Home Ec.* 45, 1953, 179–186.

3. Boettke, E. M., and Zook, M. W. Dress designs with self-help features for the preschool child. *J. of Home Ec.* 48, 1956, 643–646.
4. Breckenridge, M. E., and Lee, Vincent E. *Child Development.* Philadelphia: W. B. Saunders, Co., 1960, 648p.
5. Brian, C. R. and Goodenough, F. L. The relative potency of color and form perception at various ages. *J. of Exper. Psychol.* 12, 1929, 197–213.
6. Burton, Mary C. *Texture Preferences of a Selected Group of Pre-School Children and Their Mothers.* M.S. Thesis, Iowa State Univer., 1961.
7. Chase, W. P. Color vision in infants. *J. of Exper. Psychol.* 20, 1937, 203–222.
8. Gesell, Arnold. *The First Five Years of Life.* New York: Harper & Row, Publishers, 1940, 393p.
9. Halverson, H. M. The differential effects of nudity and clothing on muscular tonus in infancy. *Pedagol. Sem. and J. of Genetic Psychol.* 61, 1942, 55–67.
10. Hunt, L. A. A developmental study of factors related to children's clothing preferences. *Soc. for Res. in Child Devel. Monog.* 24(1), 1959, 3–47.
11. Hurlock, E. B. *Modern Ways with Babies.* Philadelphia: J. B. Lippincott Co., 1937, 347p.
12. Hurlock, E. B. *Child Development.* New York: McGraw-Hill Book Co., Inc., 1950, 669p.
13. Hurlock, E. B. *Modern Ways with Children.* New York: McGraw-Hill Book Co., Inc., 1943, 393p.
14. Irwin, O. C., and Weiss, L. A. The effect of clothing on the general and vocal activity of the newborn infant. in *Studies in Infant Behavior.* by O. C. Irwin, L. A. Weiss, and E. M. Stubbs, *University of Iowa Studies,* 9, 1934, 151–162.
15. James, William. *The Principles of Psychology.* Vol. I, New York: Henry Holt and Co., 1890, 689p.
16. Keister, M. E. and Updegraff, R. A. A study of children's reactions to failure and an experimental attempt to modify them. *Child Devel.* 8, 1937, 241–248.
17. Key, C. B., White, M. R., Honzik, M. P., Heiney, A. B., and Erwin, D. The process of learning to dress among nursery-school children. *Genetic Psychol. Monog.* 18, 1936, 67–164.
18. Koshuk, R. P. Social influences affecting the behavior of young children. *Soc. Res. in Child Devel. Monog.* 6(2), 1941, 71p.
19. Langford, Louise M. *Guidance of the Young Child.* New York: John Wiley & Sons, Inc., 1960, 349p.
20. Murphy, L. B. *Social Behavior and Child Personality.* New York: Columbia University Press, 1937, 344p.
21. Mussen, Paul Henry and Conger, John J. *Child Development and Personality.* New York: Harper & Row, Publishers, 1956, 569p.
22. Myers, G. C. *Building Personality in Children.* New York: Greenberg Publishers, 1931, 360p.

23. Pratt, Karl C. Note on the relation of temperature and humidity to the activity of young infants. *Pedagol. Sem. and J. of Genetic Psychol.* 38, 1930, 480–484.
24. Rea, Lucille. Clothing and child development. *J. of Home Ec.* 42, 1950, 717–718.
25. Read, Katherine. Clothes help build personality. *J. of Home Ec.* 42, 1950, 348–350.
26. Reid, Edith Lockridge. Why children are cross. *Hygeia.* 3, 1925, 384–386.
27. Smith, M. E., Lecker, G., Dunlap, J. W., and Cureton, E. E. The effects of race, sex, and environment on the age at which children walk. *J. of Genetic Psychol.* 38, 1930, 489–498.
28. Staples, Ruth. Color vision and color preferences in infancy and childhood. *Psychol. Bull.* 28, 1931, 297–308.
29. Staples, Ruth. The responses of infants to color. *J. of Exper. Psychol.* 15, 1932, 119–141.
30. Tate, Mildred T., and Glisson, Oris. *Family Clothing.* New York: John Wiley & Sons, Inc., 1961, 412p.
31. Thompson, H. M., and Rea, L. E. *Clothing for Children.* New York: John Wiley & Sons, Inc., 1949, 406p.
32. Vincent, Elizabeth Lee. *Human Psychological Development.* New York: The Ronald Press Company, 1961, 522p.
33. Vener, Arthur M. and Weese, Audray. The preschool child's perceptions of adult sex-linked cultural objects. *J. of Home Ec.* 57, 1965, 49–54.
34. Wagoner, L. C. and Armstrong, E. M. The motor control of children as involved in the dressing process. *Pedagol. Sem. and J. Genetic Psychol.* 35, 1928, 84–97.
35. Watson, J. B. What the nursery has to say about instincts. *J. of Genetic Psychol.* 32, 1925, 293–327.

Chapter 11

Elementary School Children

The jump in size, abilities, and interests from the preschool to the school-age child is not so great as the one found between infancy and preschool age. Nevertheless, there are very important differences between children of these age groups, and some have implications for clothing.

One of the greatest differences is in the social development of the child. The preschool child has little interest in his peer group. His social contacts are mainly with his family. The elementary school child, on the other hand, attains a certain degree of independence from his family; he is in the "gang age"; he plays as a member of a team in organized sports; he joins scouts or other formal organizations. Elementary school children bunch together in informal cliques as gangs; they congregate into groups which work or play together for specific purposes, or they may be part of a peer group which spends most waking hours together.

Although they are becoming socialized, children of elementary school age have not as yet developed much sympathy or empathy for other individuals. They are often very cruel in teasing one another. The gang or group jeers at the outsider, and frequently, unfamiliar clothing is the object of their derision.

The child of school age is not quite as active as the preschool child and is able to sit still for a longer period, yet he has more skill in using his muscles and is extremely interested in sports.

Increased Motor Skills and Implications for Clothing

As we have said, the school child is greatly interested in sports. One of the chief means of obtaining prestige at this age is through skill in a sport; the most popular children and group leaders are often those who excel at games, and their heroes are those who are prominent in the sports world or who have accomplished some great physical feat. Since the child who has greater muscular skill in games is looked up to by his peers, his self-confidence in general is increased, and he is apt to be the leader of his group in other areas as well as sports. This interest in sports is not limited to boys, for girls in the elementary school are often "tom boys" and their interests are likewise centered around sports.

Baseball caps, football outfits, or other clothing which identifies the school child with a particular sport or with a team are especially coveted. From the opposite position, the most hated clothes are those hindering his muscular skills. The child will object to wearing any garment which slows his running, catching, jumping rope, or interferes with his pitching arm. The ruggedness of the school child's clothing is important for the same reasons as clothing which allows freedom of movement. At this age, as any parent knows, clothing must be able to "take it." The child wants and needs to be able to climb, explore, run, jump, tackle, slide into base, and so on, without worrying about injuring his clothing.

SKILL IN DRESSING AND CARE OF CLOTHES

We think of the child as learning to dress himself before he is old enough to go to school, but there remain skills in dressing which are usually learned after the child has reached school age.

Gesell and Ilg (10 and 11) have given an indication of what to expect, at the various age levels of school-age children, in dressing and care of clothes. Their "growth gradients" in this respect are:

6 years—1. Can dress self except for tying shoe laces and buttoning very difficult buttons. If they do tie shoe laces, tie them too loosely.
2. May need some help and is unwilling to accept this help, Mother needs to be nearby to give some assistance.
3. Dawdling.
4. Boys brush hair; girls need to have hair combed.
5. Careless about clothes even though they may be clothes conscious.
6. Drop clothes off as they remove them, or fling them about.
7. Not responsible for keeping clothes clean and tidy, except for a few girls.

8. Mother needs to select clothes, and may need to lay them out.

9. Accessories are frequently lost.

7 years—1. Many can dress without any help if clothes are selected for them. Others dawdle, lack interest, and need help. May dawdle till he gets ready to dress, then actually dress quickly.

2. Variable in appearance. Some girls like to look neat; children often neater than at eight; some boys like to look sloppy.

3. Still careless about clothes; drop them as they remove them; do not report tears. A few put away clothes after removing them; hang up pajamas.

4. Can tie shoe laces but does not like to bother.

5. Slow and distractible about dressing. May suddenly speed up and finish.

8 years—1. Can dress without assistance. Can choose what dress or suit to wear and may be able to select out-of-door clothing suitable to the weather.

2. Girls with braids still have hair combed.

3. Some children (mostly girls) can take good care of clothes, hanging them up, or piling on a chair on removal. Some take full responsibility: select clothes, hang them up, put dirty garments in hamper, report on tears or buttons. Many are completely careless. Clothes may be dirty and torn, and not tucked in.

4. May hang up clothes at night, but not hang up outdoor clothes in daytime.

5. No longer allows mother to lay out clothes, and may insist on selecting wearing apparel himself.

6. Can and do keep shoe laces tied without reminder.

9 years—1. Does complete job of dressing.

2. Boys and girls are interested in doing their own hair, but majority do not do it completely until ten years of age, and then only if it is uncomplicated.

3. Is careless about clothes, and apt to throw them around. Not concerned about how clean they are. Fairly good at reporting tears and holes. [10:267–268]

10 years—Buying Clothes: Mother and child shop together. Mother decides but consults child.

Daily Selection: Most select own, mother checks, some battles over what is suitable.

Hate idea of wearing new clothes or dressing up.

Little concern over appearance.

Care of Clothes: Extremely careless—just drop down. Doesn't notice or care if clothes are dirty or messed— don't report tears.

10 years—Grooming: Dislikes bathing, needs to be reminded to wash before meals. Mother shampoos hair.

11 years—Buying Clothes: Child exercises more say. Girl nearly always accompanies mother—boy more often lets mother buy.

Daily Selection: About half decide and half still ask what to wear.

Definite ideas about what they will or will not wear, and may refuse those they do not like. May still prefer old clothes or wear poor combinations of color.

Care: Still very poor.

11 years—Grooming: Less fuss over bath. Care of nails and teeth improved but still needs to be reminded. Hair: mother washes. Boys often refuse to comb, but girls beginning to be interested [11:315–316, 318–319].

Taylor *et al.* (41) have made studies of the expenditure of energy in dressing and undressing as compared with quiet play, standing and drawing, singing, washing wiping dishes, carpentry, sewing, and cycling. They found that dressing and undressing require more energy than any activity except cycling.

This demonstrates that there is definitely a problem in designing clothing which are easy to put on and take off for the school child as well as for the preschool child. We commonly forget to include or to look for self-help features for the child of school age. Often, a school girl's dress will have small buttons down the back or a sash which ties in the back. Miller (28) found that girls resent the dependence which such fastenings force upon them. The girl, although able to dress herself except for some of the buttons or the sash, must ask her mother to complete these bits of dressing. The mother does not object, since it takes her only a very brief time to do it, and she is often unaware that the child finds it humiliating to ask for help in dressing.

The problem of designing and choosing clothes which are easy for the child to put on and take off are even greater for the physically handicapped child. Because such children are already different from the rest of their age group, it is especially important for them to have clothing which does not also set them apart. At the same time they need clothing which allows for braces or the use of crutches. "His clothing should be functional to encourage independence in dressing and to give him confidence in doing for himself" [3:8].

Clothing Behavior and Practices

SOURCES OF CLOTHING

Numerous studies such as Huepenbacker, USDA, Warning, Terasawa have shown that today most of the clothing for the school child is purchased readymade, and a negligible amount made at home.

Usually the garments are purchased new, but gifts and hand-me-downs also account for fairly high percentages. It is difficult to compare the prevalence of hand-me-downs, as found in various studies, because the questions asked vary in each study. Table 9 summarizes the findings on hand-me-downs from a number of studies. In each case, the information was obtained on each garment at the time the garments were being inventoried. In the other studies, either the mother was asked about clothing in general, or where indicated, about a certain type of garment.

Author	Time Interval	Age of Child	Sex	Garments	Results
1. USDA (1.) (7)	year prior to interview	6–13	F	dressy dresses, skirts, jackets	Most often obtained clothing— 10, 12, 10% handed down from friend
					5, 6, 5% handed down from sister
			M	sport shirts, slacks, jackets	8, 5, 7% handed down from relative or friend
					7, 3, 6% handed down from brother
2. USDA (2.) (8)	one year	2–13	both	all	33.3% of children received one or more handed down garments during previous year
3. Huepenbacker (17)	———	9 & 10	M	slacks, shirts	60, 58% "sometimes got" hand-me-downs
4. Terasawa (42)	———	4th grade	F	all	27 out of 48 said used hand-me-downs generally
5. Rosencranz (37)	———	10–12	F	all	40% of all girls had hand-me-downs in wardrobe
6. Warning (46)	———	7, 8, 9	F	all	80% upper-middle class wore hand-me-downs 72% lower-middle class wore hand-me-downs 93% upper-lower class wore hand-me-downs

table 9 Results of research studies dealing with hand-me-down garments.

We have less information on clothing received as gifts. The USDA study on Mothers' Opinions of Fibers in Children's Clothes (31) states that 3 to 9 percent of the garments studied were most often received as gifts. The earlier USDA study on clothing inventories (7) found that nearly all of the children received one or more articles of clothing during the year as a gift from someone outside the immediate family.

There is relatively little data on the number of various types of garments owned by this age group. The Minneapolis-St. Paul study by the United States Department of Agriculture in 1953 showed that the average inventories were quite large, especially for some items, but that they were smaller than the inventories of the teen-age group. The types of clothing found in the largest amounts among the school-age children were light-weight jackets, separate trousers, club uniforms or costumes for the boys, and raincoats, ski pants, and play and swim suits for the girls. The average number of garments owned, grouped according to usage, are given below: (see Table 10)

Item	Boys
Outercoats, jackets and snowsuits	4.2
Shirts and sweaters	17.9
Hats and Caps	2.6
Shoes and boots	3.0
Socks	11.5
Pajamas, night shirts and bathrobe	4.1
	Girls
Outercoats, jackets and snowsuits	4.3
Dresses and suits	9.8
Blouses and sweaters	10.2
Skirts and slacks	5.6
Shoes and boots	3.5
Hosiery	14.0
Pajamas, nightgowns and robes	5.4

(7:6)

table 10   Grouped items: average number of garments owned by boys and by girls aged 6–11.

These numbers would in all probability, be much higher at the present time. Five years after this study was made, Hall (12) obtained inventories of children from a group of *low* income families. Although the number of families in this group who had children in the six- to nine-year range was too small (36) to make valid comparisons, it is interesting to note that she found either approximately the same number or more items owned by children from low-income families as the earlier study had for all income groups. For example, the USDA study found that girls six to eleven owned an average of 7.8 cotton dresses, while Hall found girls six to nine owned 14.7 cotton dresses. Items for the boys, such as top coats, suits, sport coats, slacks, were approximately the same, while dress shirts were owned in fewer numbers by the low-income group (1.3) than the Minneapolis–St. Paul group (2.2). In spite of the relatively high number of garments owned by the low-income group studied by Hall, most of the mothers thought that their sons and daughters had an insufficient number of clothes. Perhaps some of the garments listed were badly worn, ill-fitting or otherwise unusable. Most of the school boys in this group, however, felt that they did have a sufficient number of clothes.

The boys in this study wore jeans, T-shirts and sport shirts for school and for play, and only dressed up in slacks and a dress shirt for Sunday school and church. The girls of six to nine typically wore cotton dresses for school or jumpers with blouses. Some wore separate skirts and blouses. The elementary-school-age children, in general, owned fewer items of clothing than the teen-aged children, and girls usually owned more items than boys.

Whether children's garments are first outgrown or worn-out and how this varies with the garment type or with the age or sex of the child is still not established except for individual cases. Phillips (35) found that boys of ten and eleven wear out shoes before they outgrow them. The shoes usually lasted from 4 to 6 months for 47 percent and from seven to nine months for 35 percent of her group.

PRACTICES IN PURCHASE OF CHILDREN'S CLOTHES

In most cases it is the mother who shops for clothing, but often the child, especially if a daughter, accompanies her and helps in making the decision. Boys accompany mothers more frequently when slacks rather than shirts are being purchased primarily because slacks have to fit accurately (17).

Mothers reported in the USDA study (7) that 58 percent of the girls had "quite a bit to say" about the kinds of clothes chosen for them, and only 13 percent had practically no say about clothing selection. Boys had somewhat less to say about their clothing than girls, 43 percent had quite a bit to say, according to their mothers, and 23 percent had practically nothing to say about the clothing selected for them.

Rosencranz (37) and Warning (46) both found that the part girls played in the selection of their clothing was partially determined by family income. In the Rosencranz study, mothers in the lower-income brackets more often selected their daughter's clothes alone. Mother and daughter selected the daughter's clothes together in families of white-collar workers, or high-income families. Warning also found that the girls in the upper-middle class were more apt to help in the selection of clothing than those in the lower-middle. However, the girls in the upper-lower class had the greatest freedom of choice in clothing selection; that is, they more often made the final decision and they also began to participate in the selection earlier than those in the other socioeconomic groups.

While boys are less likely to participate in the selection of their clothing than are girls, they apparently would like to do so. All but 8 of the 96 boys in Huepenbacker's study (17) said they would like to have a part in the selection of their clothing. Half of the mothers knew that their sons liked to select their own clothing and half were unaware of the desire. Even though boys desire to participate in the selection, we might find that in the actual situation when a boy is asked if he wishes to shop for clothing, a baseball game, a scout meeting, or something that the gang is doing at the moment might be more important to him.

Income, as might be expected, also influences the types of stores in which children's clothing is purchased (Rosencranz and Warning). Those with higher income choose more often by brand name and can recall brand names of dresses purchased for a daughter; they tend to examine the construction more often and to have the daughter try on each dress for becomingness. Although these habits vary with income, some of the differences may be due to the mother's education, which in turn is likely to be related to income.

PRACTICES IN DAILY SELECTION OF CLOTHING

Studies at Iowa State University (39) have shown that children are capable of making the decision on what outfit to wear on a given day. Boys were more likely to choose an outfit because of the color, while girls were more likely to give comfort or the appearance, other than the color, as a reason for choosing a particular outfit. This sex difference may be a reflection of different values, or it may be that the girl's clothes showed greater variation than did the boys. For example, the girls could choose between a dress and a skirt and blouse, while the boys always had trousers and a shirt.

Miller (29) found that the majority of the girls in her sample of eight- to twelve-year-olds did select their own outfits each day with the percentage greater for the twelve-year-olds than the eight-year-olds. Gesell (see outline p. 223) says that the mother selects and lays out the clothing for the six-year-old; some eight-year-olds select their own; and most ten- and eleven-year-olds select their own clothing for the day, with the mother usually checking their choice.

PRACTICES IN CARE OF CLOTHING

We have seen that the child of school age is notably lacking in interest in cleanliness and neatness and is relatively disinterested in clothing itself as long as it is acceptable to the gang and comfortable. Therefore, it is not surprising that the lack of care of his clothing is the despair of his parents. Gesell (see p. 223) notes that the child usually drops his clothing as he removes it and fails to report needed repairs.

Warning reports that girls in the lower-middle socioeconomic group take more part in the care of clothes than do those in the upper-middle or upper-lower groups. They also begin to take responsibility for the care of their clothing at an earlier age than do those from the other socioeconomic groups. This same group changes their clothes after school more frequently. The reasons for changing after school also varied with the socioeconomic group. The lower-middle socioeconomic group reported that they changed after school to save on the laundry, while in the upper-lower economic group the girls changed after school to save on the garments.

Attitudes Toward Clothing and Components of Satisfaction and Dissatisfaction

CHARACTERISTICS OF CLOTHING LEADING TO SATISFACTION

As the child enters the gang age, it is, of course, important to him to be accepted by the gang. He fears rejection by his peers. Therefore, his clothing, first of all, must be acceptable to them. There must be nothing about it which will cause him to be teased. The preschool child wants attention; if he cannot have favorable attention, he would prefer unfavorable attention rather than none. The school age child, on the other hand, would rather not have attention than have it unfavorable; the fear of being laughed at is one of his greatest fears.

The most important requisite of clothing, then, for the school child, is that it is sufficiently similar to other members of the group so that he is acceptable in this respect and is not ridiculed. Phrases such as "but all of the others have . . . ," or "nobody else has to wear . . ." are very familiar to every mother. The desire of the child to dress as other members of the group dress is stressed by almost every writer who deals with children's clothes. It is a factor which is often remarked upon by teachers and it has been a problem for most parents. Because this desire to win the approval of his peer group is so strong in the child, it may cancel other desires. For instance, although a girl would prefer a dress which she could manage herself to one on which she needed help, she might choose the one more difficult to manage because that was the kind worn by the rest of the group. This suggests one method by which the various wants of the children could be investigated. A number of variables might be studied and the strength of the various wants determined by which "want" cancels out others.

Although much has been written about the child's desire to conform to the group, we have only vague notions about the age when it appears and the period during which it means the most to children. Some writers have implied that this desire is prevalent all during childhood; others have suggested that it gradually increases up to the adolescent years. Some have suggested that it begins when the child enters school and still others place it when the child reaches nine or ten. Thus far, we have only scattered observations by parents or teachers. For example, in the case of my son it was noticed when he was six. He refused to wear overalls with straps or pants with suspenders because "only the babies wear things over their shoulders to hold up pants; all of the boys in my room wear pants with belts." This, however, is only one case, he may have been conscious of what the others were wearing later or earlier than the majority of children.

Other isolated reports are open to the same criticism. Asking adults to give the age at which it was important to them to have clothes which were acceptable to the group is probably even less valid. They may either have forgotten when or how important it was to them, or, having been ridiculed, it was such a traumatic experience that it colors the memory of all their childhood. From the scattered observations we have, it seems probable that the first appearance of the need to conform only appears in the negative sense. The child is anxious to avoid anything which might make him teased or ridiculed. He does not want straps over his shoulders, snowsuit pants or anything which might make the other children tease him. But, as long as he is not ridiculed, he has little interest in the appearance of his clothes.

The first evidence of wishing to conform in the positive sense is the desire to have a uniform or other symbol of belonging to a particular group or organization, such as a Brownie or Cub-scout uniform or a "little league" baseball cap or sweat shirt. The child thinks in concrete rather than abstract terms. It is much easier for him to attribute acceptance or rejection to something tangible such as possession of the uniform or symbol of the group, than it is to attribute it to something intangible such as sportsmanship or friendliness.

It is often because hand-me-down clothing is not just what the gang is wearing that it is rejected by the school-age child. The pro's and con's of hand-me-down clothing have been argued perhaps more than any other aspect of children's clothing. Many adults state that they were made miserable as a child because they had to wear handed-down clothing; others, however, report that they also had to wear handed-down garments but that they loved them. We have no data to tell us which is the most common attitude nor what the reasons are for the two contrasting opinions about handed-down clothing. From our knowledge of children and from reports of adults, we can formulate certain hypotheses concerning the reasons for different attitudes. For example, it may make a great deal of difference who the person is who originally owned the garment. The child who has to wear what the older sister wore last year may be very unhappy, while the child who has to wear what was worn by an older cousin or aunt who is adored and looked up to may not only be happy but thrilled with wearing handed-down clothing. The attitude of the mother and the way she treats the problem may also make a difference. If the child is allowed to wear the garments as a privilege, she may enjoy it, while if it is treated as though it were unfortunate but necessary, it may be quite different. Likewise, if the garments are given to the child as they come, whether or not they need alteration, the child may be much less happy than if they are made over or the decorations are changed or in some way fixed for that particular child so that the child has a feeling that they are now his own. The specific developmental age of the child may also be an important factor. If, as we have suggested, the younger school child simply wishes to avoid ridicule, perhaps at that stage in his development he will be willing to wear any clothing which does not elicit teasing from his peers. As he grows older and the need to conform becomes more positive, he may reject any garments which differ from the type his peers are wearing at the moment. These are all hypotheses and, while they are logical from our knowledge of children and would seem to be true from reported instances, we have no reliable and valid evidence at the present time to support them.

Two attempts have been made to find children's attitudes towards clothing, in general, but both of these were made before techniques were as well defined as they are now. The first was done in 1905 when Rusling (38) asked 1700 children between eight and thirteen to answer a number of questions. The questions asked were: "(1) Do you often tear, soil, or lose your clothes, hat, shoes or anything you wear? (2) How do you feel when you do it? (3) Why? (4) What particular thing that you wear would you most dislike to tear, soil, or lose? (5) Why?" She found that recklessness decreases from eight to twelve for boys and increases at thirteen and, for girls, recklessness was less at ten to eleven than at thirteen. She did not, however, have any way of measuring the validity of her answers, and the fact that the children answered that they were more reckless at thirteen may be due to the fact that they were more conscious of the fact that they had damaged their clothing, whereas at earlier ages, they may not have noticed the damage. Rusling thinks that her results show that accidents to children's clothing are not due to natural depravity, since so many children report that they feel sad at their loss. She also says that boys are as vain as girls about their clothing. She found that boys worry most about hats and girls are more attached to mittens and coats. This study is interesting because it attempts to obtain information on children's attitudes towards clothing from inquiry about those they damage or lose, rather than by direcly asking for preferences. This method might show attitudes which would not be found by the more direct method.

The second attempt to measure children's opinions also asked children to write paragraphs in answer to several questions. Macaulay (26) asked 305 boys and girls between the ages of 6 and 15 to answer the following questions:

1. What sort of clothes do you like best to wear to a party? Say why you like them.
2. What sort of clothes do you like best to wear for everyday? Say why you like them.
3. Are there any clothes that you dislike, and would do without if you could? Say why you dislike them.

Macaulay found that with increasing age there was a decrease in the desire for bright colors. Before the age of nine, the children did not seem to be conscious of design, of appropriateness, or of fashion, but from nine on there seemed to be a growing sense of design, and the children twelve years and older considered both fashion and suitability. From thirteen to fifteen years, they wish to emphasize the good points in their physical appearance by clothing. Before the age of ten, children prefer the ornate and they like garments which will attract attention to themselves; but between ten and twelve years they begin to want the simpler designs and more subdued colors. They want simple durable garments at this age which will withstand rough treatment. The boys ten to twelve said that for everyday wear they wanted "any old thing." There was a small percentage of children of the older groups who mentioned very unsuitable clothes in answering the second question, such as satin or velvet, ruffles, extravagant jewelry, or trains. These were usually children who were mentally retarded. Some were from very poor homes, who were leading a phantasy life, and thought that such clothes were always worn by the very wealthy. In answering the last question, the children showed a dislike for tight, restricting garments and for rough textured or heavy clothing.

More recently, Hall (12) noted that the children from the low-income families she studied, in general, were in their mothers' opinions, satisfied with their clothing. The mothers reported that boys hated to dress up and refused to wear slacks. "One mother told of her son's coming home at lunch and taking his only pair of jeans that she had washed that morning off the clothes line and putting them on. He had been teased too much at school about his slacks. [12:115]" None of the girls were said to dislike dressing up, but a large percentage of the girls six to nine were reported to like "nothing special" when the question was concerned with characteristics of clothes which gave the greatest satisfaction.

Several recent studies have investigated the school child's preferences in clothing. Miller (29) found that the amount of decoration was of primary importance to the eight-year old child, and Terasawa (42) determined that it was still most important for the fourth-grade child. These studies indicated that with increasing age the value placed on decorative detail declined and color became more important.

Hunt (18), in a more extensive study, obtained data on some of the specific preferences of children. She found that at age five to six, red was usually preferred in clothes, and that at age nine to ten, green was generally preferred with orange and violet always the least-liked colors. All children from 3 to 10 preferred the saturated colors and those of light or medium brightness over the darker more subdued colors. Solid colors and geometric designs were preferred to checks and stripes by all ages, but checks increased with popularity as age increased. In style, the school-age boys tended to prefer play clothes and girls party clothes. The soft textures, such as fur, were still the most liked.

A feature sometimes overlooked in designing or selecting clothes for the school child is number and size of pockets. Children are collectors. Empty the pockets of a school-age boy and it is very evident that he needs many and large pockets to house all his treasures. Girls of this age also enjoy collecting and need pockets to carry their finds.

Comfort is important to children of school age as it is to all age groups. When 28 children in a pilot study were interviewed about features they liked about clothing, 11 gave color as a reason and 8 gave comfort. However, when it came to the dislikes, 19 children mentioned uncomfortable. This was almost half of the total number of dislikes expressed.

Pahopin (34) compared several methods of measuring boys' preferences in clothing as to their reliability and validity. Using data obtained as a part of a North Central regional research project in textiles and clothing, she compared the following methods.

A. Mock store. The mother was presented with a set of jeans from which she was asked to make a selection.
B. Same as A. but she was asked probe questions concerning her preferences for specific features.
C. Probe questions plus both verbal and nonverbal materials. As questions were asked about preference for a given feature, garments were shown which varied on that feature.
D. Probe questions concerning the mother's satisfaction or dissatisfaction with a garment which had been worn and cared for in the home.

All of the methods yielded data on preferences for various features and reasons for the preferences and buying habits related to the purchase of jeans. When each of these was compared with the observed purchase of jeans, it was found that Method C.—probe questions plus both verbal and nonverbal materials—was the most valid method, and Method A.—the mock store without questioning—was the least valid method of studying this type of problem.

ASPECTS OF CLOTHING UNIMPORTANT TO
THE SCHOOL CHILD

As with the preschool child, we can find almost as much about children by the things they do not care about in clothes as by their desires.

First of all the child is not interested in cleanliness or neatness. The boy of school age is not only disinterested in cleanliness but fights against it. As we have said, he is interested in what his gang will accept, but does not care about fashion in general. While he is becoming more aware of appropriateness, he is still not much interested in what is appropriate for the occasion.

Large numbers of garments which will make variety in the wardrobe are also usually unimportant to the school child. He is ordinarily happy with few changes if they are outfits acceptable to his group.

Furthermore, the school child is not yet aware of the concept of becomingness, and it is, therefore, unimportant to him. For example, I remember vividly the arguments with my mother over the way I should comb my hair when I was in the fourth grade. I wanted to wear it one way because "all the other girls did," while my mother insisted it was not becoming that way. This was unimportant to me and I finally had my way, but pictures taken at that time show how right my mother was!

COMPARISON OF MOTHERS' AND CHILDREN'S ATTITUDES AND PREFERENCES

Clothing has traditionally been considered an area of conflict between mothers and their sons or daughters. There are obvious differences of opinion in the area of cleanliness, but recent studies have shown that there are fewer differences between mothers and children in the selection of clothing than had been assumed. Terasawa (42) found general agreement between mothers' choice of garment characteristics and her fourth-grade daughter's choice. Mothers and their nine- or ten-year-old sons also agreed on first choices when given a selection of slacks and shirts in a study conducted by Huepenbacker (17). They differed, however, in the order in which they ranked the remaining shirts and slacks. In general, the boys were less critical than their mothers. Hunt (18), Terasawa (42), and Miller (28) have noted that mother and child agreement tends to increase with the age of the child.

Some fundamental differences between mothers and fourth-grade daughters in clothing values were shown by a study conducted by Miller (28). In her study, the mothers placed most emphasis on becomingness, and comfort was considered second in importance, with "like friends" and "self-help" features very low. The daughters, on the other hand, thought the beauty of the garment itself more important than its becomingness, and both "self-help" features and "like friends" were relatively more important for the daughters than the mothers.

Effects of Clothing on the Child

We have already mentioned that the physical aspects of clothing may affect the child. That is, if the clothes are so constructed or the fit is such that his clothes hamper his activity, he may not become as skilled in games or sports; and skill in these activities is one of the principal ways in which he is respected by his group and one of the ways in which he gains self-confidence.

There are, however, other ways in which clothing or behavior in relation to clothing may affect the child. Young (49:68) emphasizes the point that children may develop self-consciousness and feelings of inferiority from having to wear clothes considered different by the other children in his group.

Some authors report that it is not only the child who is dressed like the others in the group but also the child who is attractively dressed who is said to have advantages over the child who is less attractively dressed. Hurlock (19:512) states that "a well-dressed child is more self-confident, better mannered, and less rowdy than a poorly dressed one." Nash (33) writes that children in the Vineland Training School were noticeably better behaved when well dressed. As was pointed out in the chapter on preschool children, this may be an observable effect which is temporary and soon wears off.

Hardy (13) demonstrated that the effects of attractive clothes may not only be on the child's own behavior but on the behavior of the group toward the child. She obtained a measure of social recognition by asking the children to list those whom they preferred to be with in various situations. The children were ranked as to the number of times they were chosen and the top 20 percent were compared with the bottom 20 percent. These were related to ratings made by the teachers. Two-thirds of the socially successful (top 20 percent) were described as having an attractive appearance while less than one-fifth of the unpopular (low 20 percent) were so described. No child called ugly was chosen as the one whom they most desired to be. It was also found that those with better health, better posture and those who were mentally alert were more popular. Since these latter variables would probably be correlated with attractiveness, the results may be misleading. It may be that health or mental alertness is really the factor which makes for popularity and attractiveness is incidental to these. Even though the cause may be something else, it is the more attractive child and the one who conforms who is more often chosen as the popular child.

Austin and Thompson (2) also used the sociometric technique of asking children to name their best friends. In addition they asked the children to tell why they preferred an individual. They repeated the test in two weeks and in instances where the best friend had changed, they endeavored to find the reasons. They found that physical appearance was given by 4.1 percent of the group as to why they had chosen another individual as a best friend. Although this percentage does not seem to be high enough to be significant, it must be remembered that children were volunteering their reasons, and that in many cases appearance might have been one factor if not the most important reason. On the other hand, some children may have given appearance simply because it is a concrete factor easy to verbalize.

A different method was used by Tuddenham (44) to get at this problem. He used the "guess who" test in which the children were given descriptive phrases and asked to fill in the name of the child who best seemed to fit that description. He found that, in all of the grades, there was a fairly stable association of popularity with attractiveness. That is, the same names given as fitting a description of popular were given for the description of attractive. With the girls of the fifth grade, "tidy" was also associated with popularity, but this was not the case for the girls in the lower grades nor for the boys in any grade. Cannon and Staples, (5) on the other hand, using sociometric tests found no significant relationships between appearance and social acceptance at the elementary school age.

A small study in which just 28 students, their mothers, and their teachers were interviewed indicated that teachers thought that girls were more socially outgoing and more self-confident when they were well-dressed, but that it made no difference to aggressiveness, independence, cooperativeness, obedience, or studiousness. Mothers' answers indicated that being appropriately dressed had no effect on either the rowdyness, or the manners of the child and that the child did not realize that the amount of activity should be regulated by clothing. Mothers did feel that attractive clothing made the child more willing to perform before a group.

In looking at the other side of the picture, various writers have pointed out the dangers in laying too much stress on clothing and in the parents making too many sacrifices in order to dress their children attractively. Young, (49) for example, points out that children who are overdressed have a tendency to become snobbish and affected; they may gain too much self-confidence and feel that they are superior to others simply because their clothes possess certain qualities. This naturally would lead to unpopularity and a more difficult social adjustment. Also those who are dressed beyond their parents' means may come to expect continued sacrifices from them in all ways, according to Myers (32). Although these seem logical conclusions and we assume that the person who is most likable is the one who is well dressed and yet thinks least of his attire, there has been, as far as I know, no actual research on this problem of overdressing the child.

Summary

The elementary-school-aged child is in the "gang" age. Acceptance by this peer group is very important to him and he fears ridicule. Usually his greatest interest is in muscular skills, and his hero is an athlete. He is not particularly interested in clothes during this period apart from their contribution to his activities.

Hurlock has summarized the clothing wants of the child as follows:

1. The child wants his clothes to conform to the style of the group. Any deviation that is great enough to be noticed or ridiculed by other children is the source of much distress to the child and may readily lead to feelings of inferiority which will cause the child to withdraw from the group.

2. The child wants his clothes to be admired and envied by other This gives him a feeling of importance, especially when other children copy the model he has set.
3. The child wants his clothing to be easy to manipulate. He becomes impatient if dressing is too long and laborious a task and he is embarrassed if he must ask for help in putting on or taking off a garment.
4. The child wants his clothes to be comfortable. Many adolescents or adults will sacrifice comfort to style, but this is not true of children. They are interested only in clothes that offer them the freedom they need for the strenuous lives they lead.
5. The child wants clothes that are durable. Healthy, active boys and girls are not interested in clothes which cannot stand the wear and tear of active lives. A dainty, fragile garment is all right for an adolescent or an adult, but the typical American child of today is not interested in it if it means sacrificing fun when he wears it [19:512].

If we review the wants of the school child in clothing together with the aspects in which he is not interested, we realize that it is guarding against undesirable features rather than supplying positive features that is important. Generally speaking, the school child, especially the boy, ignores clothing unless it is uncomfortable, interferes with his activity, or causes him to be teased. In these cases he is unhappy and wants something to be done about it. In a positive sense the school child wants clothing that is acceptable to the group and in some instances, as in uniforms, definitely marks him as one of a particular group.

The elementary school child is still developing skills in dressing, and these should be considered when designing or selecting clothing for this age group. Children are capable of making decisions on what outfit to wear on a given day, and the majority of girls help in the selection of their clothes. Boys are less likely to participate in selection, although they report that they would like to do so.

Various psychometric measures have shown that there is a positive correlation between the popularity of school children and their appearance.

Bibliography

1. Ackerley, Lois A., and Thompson, Ouida. Persistent problems in family life from the elementary school child's point of view. *J. of Home Ec.* 33(8), 1941, 564–565.
2. Austin, M. C., and Thompson, G. G. Children's friendships: a study of the bases on which children select and reject their best friends. *J. of Ed. Psychol.* 39(2), 1948, 101–116.

3. Bare, C., Boettke, E., and Waggoner, N. *Self-help Clothing for Handicapped Children.* Nat. Soc. for Crippled Children and Adults, 1962.

4. Breckenridge, M. E., and Vincent, E. Lee. *Child Development.* Philadelphia: Saunders Publishers, 1960, 648p.

5. Cannon, K. L., Staples, R., and Carlson, I. Personal appearance as a factor in social acceptance. *J. of Home Ec.* 44, 1952, 710–713.

6. Chittenden, Gertrude, Murphy, M. N., Hamilton, A., Forrest, P. E., and Patterson, M. Developmental tasks: how we can help. *J. of Home Ec.* 45(8), 1953, 579–583.

7. *Family Clothing—Inventories by Age.* Minneapolis-St. Paul, 1949, U.S. Dept. of Agr., Bureau of Human Nutrition and Home Ec., Studies of family clothing supplies, Prelim. Report No. 3, 1951.

8. *Family Clothing—Gift, Home-made, Handed-down.* Minneapolis-St. Paul, 1948–49, U.S. Dept. of Agr., Bureau of Human Nutrition and Home Ec., Studies of family clothing supplies, Prelim. Report No. 5, 1951.

9. Garth, T. R. A color preference scale for one thousand white school children. *J. of Exper. Psychol.* 7, 1924, 233–241.

10. Gesell, Arnold and Ilg, Frances L. *The Child from 5 to 10.* New York: Harper & Row, Publishers, 1946, 475p.

11. Gesell, Arnold and Ilg, Frances L. *Youth: The Years from 10 to 16.* New York: Harper & Row, Publishers, 1956, 542p.

12. Hall, Katherine. *A Study of Some Factors that Contribute to Satisfaction and Dissatisfaction in the Clothing of Ninety-two Low Income Families.* Ph.D. Thesis, Penn. State Univer., 1955, pp. 112–129, 147–156.

13. Hardy, M. C. Social recognition at the elementary school age. *J. of Soc. Psychol.* 8, 1937, 365–384.

14. Hardy, Mamie Lou, Huepenbacker, Agatha, and Warning, Margaret. Who chooses children's clothes? *Iowa Farm Science.* 12(1), 1957, 621–622.

15. Harnall, Sophia. Personal appearance is important—very. *Childhood Interests.* 13(2), 1935, 78–83.

16. Hawkes, Glen R. and Stevens, Kathryn. Children can choose if you let them. *Iowa Farm Science.* 10(8), 1956, 181–183.

17. Huepenbacker, Agatha Louise. *Factors that Influence Mothers and Sons in the Selection of Boy's Slacks and Shirts.* M.S. Thesis, Iowa State College, 1956.

18. Hunt, Lucille. A developmental study of factors related to children's clothing preferences. *Society for Research in Child Development Monographs.* 24(1), 1959, 3–47.

19. Hurlock, Elizabeth. *Child Development.* 2nd ed. New York: McGraw-Hill Book Co., Inc., 1956, 597p.

20. Hurlock, Elizabeth. What children want in clothes. *Hygeia.* 26, 1948, 596–597.

21. Hurlock, Elizabeth. What hand-me-downs mean to your child. *Today's Health.* 29, 1951, 68.

22. Hurlock, Elizabeth. *The Modern Ways with Children.* New York: McGraw-Hill Book Co., Inc., 1943. (Chap. 14)
23. Jebe, Emil, Beveridge, Elizabeth, Hawkes, Glenn R., Potgieter, Fannie, and Roberson, Opal. How to study consumer satisfaction with children's clothing made of different textile fibers. *J. of Home Ec.* 50(3), 1958, 213–218.
24. Katz, S. E. and Breed, F. S. The color preferences of children. *J. of Applied Psychol.* 6, 1922, 255–266.
25. Kodlin, Dankward and Thompson, Donovan J. An appraisal of the longitudinal approach to studies of growth and development. *Society for Research in Child Development Monographs.* 23(1), 1958, 47p.
26. Macaulay, E. Some notes on the attitude of children to dress. *Brit. J. of Med. Psychol.* 9, 1929, 150–158.
27. Michaels, G. M. Color preferences according to age. *Amer. J. of Psychol.* 35, 1924, 79–87.
28. Miller, Martha Showalter and Ryan, Mary S. Mothers and daughters select school dresses. *J. of Home Ec.* 52(6), 1960, 455–456.
29. Miller, Nancy Marie. *The Attitudes Toward Their Clothing of a Selected Group of Eight to Twelve Year Old Girls.* M.S. Thesis, Oregon State College, 1957.
30. Moeller, Fay and Tingley, K. A. *Girls from 9 to 13—Their Clothing Abilities.* Extension Bull., Storrs, Conn.: Univer. of Conn., 1952.
31. *Mothers' Opinions of Fibers in Children's Clothes.* U.S. Dept. of Agr. Market Research Report 429 and Supplementary Report, Sept. 1960.
32. Myers, G. C. *Building Personality in Children.* New York: Greenberg Publishers, 1931. (Chap. 2)
33. Nash, A. M. The effect of clothing upon the minds of children. *The Training School Bull.* 7, 1910, 216–219.
34. Pahopin, Jo. S. *An Exploratory Study of Techniques for Determining Consumer Preferences in Children's Wear.* Ph.D. Thesis, Ohio State Univer., 1958.
35. Philips, A. C. *Consumers' Preferences and Satisfaction in the Selection, Purchase and Utilization of Shoes for Boys Age 10 and 11 Years.* M.S. Thesis, Ohio State Univer., 1961.
36. Pintner, R. and Lev, J. Worries of school children. *J. of Genetic Psychol.* 56, 1940, 67–76.
37. Rosencranz, Mary Lou. *Relevance of Occupation and Income to Mothers' Selection of Clothing for Daughters.* Mich. State Agr. Exper. Sta. Tech. Bull. 268, August 1958.
38. Rusling, Lillian. Children's attitudes toward clothes. *Pedagol. Sem. and J. of Genetic Psychol.* 12, 1905, 525.
39. Stevens, Billye K. *Criteria Children Use in Daily Selection of School Clothes.* M.S. Thesis, Iowa State College, 1955.
40. Taylor, C. M., Pye, O. F., and Cladwell, A. B. The energy expenditure of 9 to 11 year old boys and girls: (1) standing drawing and (2) dressing and undressing. *J. of Nutrition.* 36, 1948, 123–131.

41. Taylor, C. M., Pye, O. F., Schafer, M., and Wing, S. The energy expenditure of boys and girls 9 to 11 years of age: (1) washing and wiping dishes, (2) boys engaged in carpentry, (3) girls sewing. *J. of Nutrition.* 44, 1951, 295–303.
42. Terasawa, Hawko. *Relationship Between Selected Factors of Fourth Grade Girls' Clothing Preferences, Their Mothers' Clothing Preferences, and the Girls' Wardrobes.* M.S. Thesis, Penna. State Univer., 1956.
43. Thompson, H. M., and Rea, L. E. *Clothing for Children.* New York: John Wiley & Sons, Inc., 1949, 406p.
44. Tuddenham, R. D. Studies in reputation III—correlates of popularity among elementary school children. *J. of Ed. Psychol.* 42, 1951, 257–276.
45. Vincent, Elizabeth Lee. *Human Psychological Development.* New York: The Ronald Press Company, 1961, 522p.
46. Warning, Margaret C. *The Implications of Social Class for Clothing Behavior: The Acquisition and Use of Apparel for Girls 7, 8, and 9 Years of Age in 3 Social Classes in Des Moines, Iowa.* Ph.D. Thesis, Mich. State Univer., 1957.
47. Why school clothes are important. *Practical Home Ec.* 31(2), 1952, 19, 50.
48. Witty, Paul and Kopel, David. The dreams and wishes of elementary school children. *J. of Ed. Psychol.* 30, 1939, 199–205.
49. Young, F. E. *Clothing the Child.* New York: McGraw-Hill Book Co., Inc., 1938, 253p.

Chapter 12

Early Adolescents

(Ages Twelve to Fifteen)

*I*n recent years there has been a great deal of discussion about the pre-adolescent group. It is fashionable to speak of preteens and teenagers rather than to use the single term *adolescents*. This means that we have come to recognize a developmental period between that of childhood and adolescence. Just as earlier in the century, we seemed to discover that there was a period in the life span in which the individual was neither a child nor an adult, so, now we recognize also a period between childhood and adolescence. It is during early adolescence that we find vast physical and emotional changes taking place. There is rapid acceleration in growth; the body is changing and taking on adult characteristics.

We will define the early adolescent period as approximately the same as the junior-high-school age, that is, from about twelve to fifteen years. We should recognize, however, that this varies with the individual and is partially dependent upon sex. Girls usually reach preadolescence about a year earlier than boys, so that girls from eleven to fourteen are typically preadolescents while boys are at the same stage of development usually between twelve and fifteen.

An understanding of this developmental period is especially important to those in the area of clothing. Keeping a rapidly changing body in clothes that fit is a large problem in itself. In addition to this, the preadolescent is keenly interested in clothes and grooming. He is breaking away from the family and is more dependent upon the peer group. Along with this he feels a great need to conform to the dress of the peer group.

Manufacturers and retailers of clothing were among the first to recognize this group and, subsequently, its importance in the clothing market. We therefore find fashions designed especially for the subteen or the preteen.

The early adolescent age is most obviously characterized by a spurt in growth. During the elementary-school years the child was steadily growing, but at a relatively slow rate. During early adolescence he very suddenly accelerates in growth, and within a period of two or three years achieves most of his adult height. Although mothers have been very much aware of this phenomenal growth in their own children, it was not generally realized how suddenly this rapid growth takes place for the majority of individuals. In the usual cross-sectional studies of growth, this sudden spurt is hidden. In such studies large numbers of individuals are measured and the mean for each chronological age obtained. Since individuals differ in the exact age at which this spurt in growth takes place, the acceleration of one individual is cancelled out by those who are growing at a different rate. To illustrate, let us look at the very much simplified figures in Table 11.

Child	Height at 11 years	Height at 12 years	Growth Between 11 and 12	Height at 13 years	Growth Between 12 and 13	Height at 14 years	Growth Between 13 and 14
John	5 ft	5 ft	0	5 ft	0	5 ft 2 in	2 in
Mary	5 ft	5 ft 2 in	2 in	5 ft 2 in	0	5 ft 2 in	0
Charles	5 ft	5 ft	0	5 ft 2 in	2 in	5 ft 4 in	2 in
Ruth	5 ft	5 ft 2 in	2 in	5 ft 4 in	2 in	5 ft 4 in	0
Average	5 ft	5 ft 1 in	1 in	5 ft 2 in	1 in	5 ft 3 in	1 in

table 11

Notice if the heights are averaged for the various ages, then there is a gradual increase of one inch in each year. When we look at the individual children, however, we see that either they did not gain any in height or gained two inches. John did not reach rapid acceleration in growth until between his thirteenth and fourteenth year, while Ruth had finished her rapid growth by that year.

In order to meet this difficulty, there have been studies based on data obtained by measuring the same individuals over a span of time. These are called longitudinal-growth studies and in them the change in rate of growth is evident. As Shuttleworth says, the results show that: "the adolescent spurt turns out to be a preadolescent phenomenon which reaches its climax not at any one age but as early as age ten or as late as age fourteen. Further, the accelerating phase for all dimensions is concentrated within a period of two or three years rather than distributed over four or five" [34:189]. As the accelerated period is usually at least a year earlier for girls than for boys, girls are often taller and heavier than boys during early adolescence.

In addition to rapid growth, the entire organism is involved in extensive changes. Primary and secondary sex characteristics are developed; girls reach the menarche during this period; for both boys and girls the body conformations change to become more adultlike; changes in physiognomy (very often the face develops unevenly with the nose prominent—a cause of embarrassment to youth); increased susceptibility to acne; changes in physiological measures such as basal metabolism, blood pressure, respiratory volume, and so on; and changes in muscular energy. The number and extent of these bodily changes naturally effect the child as a whole.

At this age emotions are more extreme for the youth; he is very sensitive and easily hurt; he is confused and uncertain of himself; he is moody, swinging from one intensity of mood to another.

Socially the child is continuing to grow away from the family. Parents are brushed aside as too old to know what is going on or are the targets of rebellion. The peer group becomes even more important than during elementary-school years, but with a new relationship. During the grade-school years the child's relationship to the peer group was more or less impersonal, but at preadolescence there are emotionally tinged friendships or crushes with a great deal of jealousy exhibited. Hero worship, such as the intense idolization of a popular singer, is another manifestation of this emotional reaction of the early adolescent. There are crushes on older members of the same sex, especially when members of one sex are thrown together continually as in a camp or preparatory school.

The girls of this age are beginning to be interested in the opposite sex. "The level between thirteen and fourteen appeared to be the breaking point between a relatively 'sexless' girlhood and subsequent sex-role identification" according to data scured by Burchinal (7:710). Usually boys in junior high school will not admit to interest in girls, but but they begin to show awareness of them by teasing, by grabbing their hats or bags, or by scuffling with them.

The differences between the elementary-school and the junior-high-school child are often emphasized by the change to a new school. The younger child often has gone to an elementary school in his neighborhood. On entering the seventh grade he often has to change to a new school, often larger, where he must make new friends and establish a place for himself.

These changes between the elementary-school child and the preadolescent are reflected in, and accompanied by, a great change in the amount of interest in clothing and by attitudes toward clothing. From a position of relative unimportance to the child, appearance and clothing become extremely important to the young adolescent.

Implications for Clothing of the Physical Changes
at Early Adolescence

When we consider the rapid acceleration in growth of the early adolescent, we realize that the most important problem is simply keeping the child clothed with garments of the proper fit. It is not unusual for parents to buy new clothing for a preadolescent only to find it too small after three months. Furthermore, the phases of acceleration and deceleration differ for different dimensions of the body. That is, the body does not grow evenly in various dimensions. The usual pattern is for the feet and hands to accelerate first. This not only makes the child look awkward, but, because he has not learned to manage the larger extremities, he often stumbles or drops objects. After the rapid growth in the hands and feet, we find the arms and legs shooting in length and, last of all, the acceleration in growth of the trunk.

One mother of four daughters suggested that adjustable clothing should be designed for this age group allowing for the change in size, just as maternity dresses allow for change in size of the pregnant woman. Such a scheme seems worth considering. Using data from the Harvard growth studies, it would be possible to determine the change to be expected in each dimension over a given length of time. Thus, if the studies showed this was needed, the garment could allow for one-inch expansion in the shoulders, and hips, two inches in width of the waistline, and three inches in length of skirt. A coat with raglan sleeves might need to allow for two inches in length of sleeves and four inches in hem. This sounds simple and practical but actually it would be costly and complicated. In the first place, for any given size there would be individuals who were at every stage of the accelerated growth period. Some would be just starting their growth, others would be in the middle and others would be decelerating in growth.

The difficulties of designing adjustable clothing for the pre-adolescent are also complicated by changes in his psychological make-up. As we have suggested, the preadolescent is very sensitive. He is worried about the impression he is making on others and whether or not he will be accepted. He is afraid of being laughed at. Therefore, he would not tolerate adjustable clothing if it looked different in any way. Any adjustable parts also would need to camouflage the fact that they were adjustable.

The fashion for separates—skirt and blouse or skirt and sweater—provides the answers in part for this age group. They automatically take care of changes in height of waist line; furthermore, the skirt of the outfit may still fit if the blouse becomes outgrown and vice versa.

Keeping the preteenager in clothes that fit is also made more difficult because of his desire for secrecy and privacy. The youth now wants to dress and undress in complete privacy. The girl may be embarrassed about the growth of her bust, and either the boy or the girl may be embarrassed to have others see the new pubic hair. Underwear may become too small because the mother only sees the child dressed and so does not automatically check the fit. The child may be hesitant about mentioning that he has outgrown underwear for fear the fit will be checked, or that it will call attention to himself and his rate of growth.

If a girl develops in the bust earlier than others in her group, she may be embarrassed about her development, and the selection of her first brassière may present a problem. She wants the fact that she is developing hidden rather than emphasized, consequently the bra should be as unseductive as possible. The answer may be a jersey bra which tends to minimize rather than emphasize the bust, but many mothers and daughters are unaware that this type exists. The girl may also be embarrassed about making such a purchase, and the mother may find it necessary to take measurements and do the shopping herself.

The preadolescent girl may also have difficulty in finding a satisfactory slip. The cotton slip with the built up shoulder has been adequate for the elementary-school child, but the preadolescent considers it "babyish." Adult slips with their narrow straps are equally inappropriate for an active twelve-year-old girl. The straps slip down over the shoulder and either break or are uncomfortable and annoying.

Clothing Practices

SIZE AND COMPOSITION OF WARDROBE

The most recent inventory figures for the preadolescent are those given by Thompson and Tucker. Their figures represent the average number of garments of various types owned by 189 eighth-grade girls (see Table 12). Also listed in the table for comparison are selected items of outerwear from the USDA, Minneapolis–St. Paul, study completed in 1948–49.

Where there are figures available in both studies, it can be seen that, with the exception of sweaters, more of each item was owned by those questioned in 1958 than by those questioned in 1948. The numbers, however, are relatively consistent and not as far apart as might be expected for this span of time. The chief difference is the increase in number of skirts and blouses. In a more recent study (33) in one city, the average number of blouses owned by eighth-grade girls was the same—eight—as the average number found by Thompson and Tucker (38) which gives support for the validity of their figures. It is obvious from these inventories, as well as from everyday observation, that the adolescent girl's uniform of skirt and blouse or skirt and sweater is also the prevalent costume for the preadolescent.

Item	Average Number Owned (from Thompson and Tucker)	Average Number Owned (from USDA study)	Percentage Owning
Heavy coat		1.2	100
Light-weight coat		1.3	82
Heavy jacket		1.2	73
Dresses (all)	6	5.7	91
Dresses: cotton	4	3.3	86
Dresses: winter	2		
Dresses: wool, rayon and mixed		2.4	
Suits		1.0	64
Skirts	7	4.8	100
Blouses	8	6.1	100
Sweaters	4	6.0	100
Shoes: all	5	3.5	100
school	2		
dress	3		

table 12 Garment type and average number owned. Data: H. M. Thompson and R. Tucker. Some clothing practices of 13-year-old girls. *J. of Home Ec.* 50, 1958, 784, and *Family Clothing Inventories by Age.* Prelim. Report No. 3, 1951, 21–24.

The USDA (14) study showed boys from twelve to fifteen years of age owning the following: (see Table 13)

Article	Average Number Owned	Percentage Owning
Overcoats	.6	56
Topcoats	.5	48
Heavy jackets	1.7	96
Light-weight jackets	.7	63
Winter suits	.8	44
Sports jackets	1.0	70
Trousers	3.7	100
Overalls, jeans	3.1	89
T-shirts	7.0	100
Sport shirt	4.9	89
Dress shirt	4.4	78
Pullover sweater	2.3	85
Sneakers	1.0	74
Street shoes	1.7	100

table 13

Undoubtedly, if we had comparable figures for boys at the present time, they would be somewhat higher, as were the girls.

SOURCE OF GARMENTS

By far the largest number of garments for both boys and girls are purchased ready-made. The figures for prevalence of hand-me-downs are difficult to interpret because the questions are worded differently. In some studies, the respondent reports whether he ever had hand-me-downs, some report the percentage that were acquired as hand-downs over a given length of time, while still others report the percentage in the wardrobe at a given time. The USDA (14) figures from 1948–49 showed that during the preceding year, over a third of the boys and girls received one or more handed-down garment during the year. Lawrence (24) found that 55 percent of the boys in her sample had hand-me-downs in their wardrobes.

Gifts are an even more important source of clothing than handed-down garments. Eighty-four percent of the boys questioned by Lawrence had received at least some item in their wardrobes as gifts, and girls are probably more likely to receive clothing as gifts than are boys. In the USDA study, one-fourth of the value of the girl's wardrobe and one-fifth of the value of the boy's wardrobe had been received as gifts.

Roach (31) found no significant relationship between social class and the utilization of used clothing, the borrowing of clothing or the use of clothing as gifts in her sample of 108 seventh-grade girls. Rosencranz (32) found the same results for girls ten to twelve. Approximately two-fifths of her group had handed-down garments in their wardrobes and one-fifth had made-over garments.

BUYING PRACTICES

Mother and daughter usually shop together for the preadolescent girl's clothes. This has been confirmed by Barnes (2), Magrabi (27), Levy (25), Morris (29), Cassidy (8), and Thompson (38). Morris and Barnes found that whether or not the mother accompanied the daughter depended upon the price of the garment. Girls might select socks and panties for themselves, but their mothers would accompany them for major purchases such as dresses or coats. Levy found that 64 percent of the preadolescents she questioned shopped with their mothers, 9 percent with both parents, 19 percent alone. Her subjects were seventh- and eighth-grade boys and girls from moderate or low-income groups. Magrabi questioned 69 twelve- and thirteen-year-old girls and their mothers on this point and found that 90 percent of both the girls and their mothers said that they shopped together. Boys of thirteen and fourteen were also usually accompanied by their mother or father when selecting clothing according to Lawrence (24). Glickman (17), however, found that 87 percent to 95 percent of the boys he questioned wanted to be allowed to pick out more of their own clothes. Rosencranz (32) found that there was a significant association between father's occupation and the persons involved in the selection of clothing for girls ten to twelve. In white-collar families the mother and daughter usually shopped together, while the mothers more often selected clothing for the daughter in families of manual workers.

Results have been contradictory concerning who makes the final decision in the purchase of garments. Some studies have indicated that the girl makes the final decision, and others that the mother makes the final decision. This is not surprising, since, in most cases, mother and daughter have usually talked it over and agreed. The way in which the question is asked or whether it is the mother or daughter answering may account for shifting percentages here. Perhaps the cleverness of the mother in making the daughter believe that she had made the decision by herself, when actually she was guided by her mother, may account for some results. Silverman (35) reports that 10 percent chose their own clothes at twelve years, but that all seek their mother's advice.

The degree of the early adolescents' independence in the purchasing of clothing likewise varies with the type of garment. As we would expect, they have less independence in the choice of major items involving greater expense. This is shown clearly in the following data from Roach's study:

Garment being chosen	Independent	Dependent
	PERCENT	
Coats	1.0	99.0
Jackets	13.6	86.4
School dresses	15.8	84.2
Dress-up dresses	5.0	95.0
Play clothes	41.5	58.5
Sweaters	14.4	85.6
Skirts	15.5	84.5
Blouses	23.8	76.2
Underclothes	18.5	81.5

table 14 Independence of choice of selected garments by seventh-grade girls. From Mary E. Roach, *The Influence of Social Class on Clothing Practices and Orientation at Early Adolescence: A Study of Clothing—Related Behavior of Seventh Grade Girls.* Ph.D. Thesis, Michigan State Univer., 1960.

She found no relation between the independence of choice and social class.
In the study by Ryan (33), eighth-grade girls were asked about the sources of ideas concerning the selection of garments. In response to an

open-end question, 90 percent volunteered that they got their ideas on what to wear from "girls at school" or "girl friends." Sales people in the stores were mentioned by 44 percent; magazines by 46 percent; and mothers by 23 percent of the girls as the source of ideas.

The factors which are considered of primary importance in the selection of garments by young adolescents have varied from one study to another. This variation has been due partly to the way in which the questions were worded and partly to the fact that different authors have been working on different strata (see Chapter 7) or on more than one strata at a time. Two authors, who inquired about attributes on the first stratum, have given color and fit as the most important factors considered in the selection of garments. Thompson (38) gives the factors in order of importance as: fit, color, style, and price. Morris (29) has the following order: color, fit, price, design, and brand. Ryan (33) primarily considered factors on the second stratum, although she included price which would be on the first stratum. The eighth-grade girls in her study were given an adjustable pie chart. Each section of the chart was labeled with a factor which they might consider in the selection of a blouse. The girls were asked to arrange the sections of the pie chart, so that the greatest space was given to the most important aspect; the factor which was next most important the next amount of space, and so on. With the pie chart, it was possible to get not only the order in which the respondent would rank each component of desirability of blouses, but also the relative importance of the components. Measurements were made in the number of degrees of the circle assigned to each component. The results are shown in Table 15.

Component	Rank	Mean Number of Degrees
Becomingness	1	76
Price	2	55
Comfort	3	52
Ease-of-care	4	48
Beauty	5	46
Like friends wear	6	41
Durability	7	39

table 15 The relative importance of various components to eighth-grade girls in the selection of blouses.

The socioeconomic level of the girl did not influence her ranking of the relative importance of the various components of satisfaction in the selection of blouses with one exception. The girls from the lower socioeconomic group more often ranked the importance of durability as higher than did girls from the higher socioeconomic groups. These results tend to lend support to the findings of Thompson and Morris. Color, which they found most important, undoubtedly is related to becomingness, and fit is probably related to both becomingness and comfort.

SOURCE OF MONEY FOR EARLY ADOLESCENT'S CLOTHING

Many writers on early adolescence have discussed the advisability of clothing allowances for this age group. There are reasons both for and against clothing allowances for preadolescents. Those in favor of allowances can point out that it is good training for the youth, and that it teaches them to make wiser decisions. They may also point out that it may be cheaper to give the youth an allowance than to pay for the garments one at a time. The preadolescent has little idea of the amount spent on clothes, and an amount less than is usually spent on his clothes appears large to him. Because of his pride in his independence, he may quite willingly manage on a clothing budget which is less than his parents have spent on his clothing in preceding years. On the other hand, those who do not favor a clothing allowance for this age group point out that the preadolescent, especially the girl, is already extremely interested in clothing and appearance and this should not be extended. Another factor that must be taken into account when considering clothing allowances is the accelerated growth rate of the adolescent. The growth rate is so varied that it is difficult to predict the number of clothes that the youth may need over a given period of time. Furthermore, when clothing is only worn for a short period before it is outgrown, there is little inducement to look for qualities which will be durable or to plan ahead.

Information about actual practices in clothing allowances is difficult to obtain and interpret since individual variations are so great. Some allowances given to adolescents by parents cover all clothing together with school, personal, and recreational expenses; others include just clothing; some that include most clothing items exclude large items such as winter coats, or exclude shoes which parents prefer to buy; some include only minor clothing items or simply accessories. Silverman (35) reports that 31 percent of twelve-year-olds in her study thought that they should have an allowance and 74 percent thought so at eighteen years. Gesell (16) mentions that by age fourteen, some preadolescents have clothing budgets.

The picture of who pays for the clothing of the young adolescent is further complicated by gifts, either of specific items in the wardrobe or of money which the adolescent spends on clothing. At this age, also, many young people are beginning to earn money. This may be earned outside of the home; it may be from a regular part-time job or the income may be sporadic as from baby-sitting jobs. Levy (25) found that 68 percent of the boys and 60 percent of the girls in her low-income group of junior-high school students earned part of the money for their clothing, and 5 percent of the boys earned all of the money for their clothes.

DAILY SELECTION

Cassidy reports that 47 percent of the children in the seventh grade of the group she studied made their own decisions on what to wear to school. Gesell (16) says that at age twelve, girls start to be responsible about changing their socks and underwear without being reminded. They also prefer to choose their own outfits for the day. At twelve they may consult their mothers, but, by the time they are fifteen they make their own decisions without any help.

PRACTICES IN THE USE OF CLOTHING

As we have seen from the inventory studies, the typical costume for school of the early adolescent girl is skirt and blouse or sweater with socks and flat-heeled shoes. For dress-up occasions on week ends, Silverman (35) reports that 24 percent of the twelve-year-olds questioned wore stockings and medium heels with some wearing high heels. On week-end dress-up occasions, almost 70 percent of the girls wore silk dresses, while 24 percent wore skirts and sweaters. Rosencranz (32) reports that almost half of the girls in her sample wore one-piece cotton dresses for school and also for Sunday. A somewhat higher percentage wore one-piece cotton dresses for Sunday. In this study the manual workers' daughters wore both cotton and taffeta dresses for more occasions than did daughters of white-collar workers. The white-collar workers' daughters in addition wore suits, skirts, blouses, sweaters and play clothes somewhat more often than did daughters of manual workers. This the author suggests probably reflects the fact that daughters of white-collar workers had more types of clothes in their wardrobes. These results were obtained from girls ten and twelve. We have no comparable data for girls over twelve.

The only information we have on how often specific garments are worn is a fragmentary bit of information from the Ryan study. The eighth-grade girls from her group reported on the frequency of wearing their most- and least-worn blouses. The results are shown in Table 16.

Frequency of Wear	Most Worn	Least Worn
More than once a week	24	0
Once per week	23	7
Once per two weeks	5	11
Less than once in two weeks	0	33
No answer	0	1
	52	52

table 16 Blouses most and least frequently worn by eighth-grade girls.

GROOMING PRACTICES

The most comprehensive study we have concerning grooming practices of girls twelve-fifteen years of age, was done nearly twenty years ago by Silverman. For daily wear the percentage of girls who used powder went from 17.2 at age twelve to 53.7 percent at age fifteen, lipstick from 3.5 to 48.2 percent, nail polish from 34.5 to 42.6 percent and cleansing cream from 10.3 to 38.9 percent. On special occasions or week-ends the percentages were somewhat higher—37.9 to 75.9 used powder, 37.9 to 81.5 lipstick, 55.2 to 74.1 nail polish, and a negligible number used eye make-up (35:37).

In 1958, Thompson and Tucker report that 95 percent of the eighth-grade girls they questioned used lipstick.

Gesell says that the average twelve-year old may fuss with her hair and wear lipstick but still be sent from the table with dirty hands. He says that twelve-year olds usually tease for cosmetics but generally are allowed to wear them only for parties. The thirteen-year old he characterizes as spending an exorbitant amount of time before a mirror fixing hair. This is true of boys as well as girls. The use of cosmetics, he says, depends upon the community, but those girls who do use it are apt to put it on too thick. The fourteen- and fifteen-year-olds usually do use cosmetics, and they use them more skillfully.

CARE OF CLOTHING

Some of the care practices which seem the simplest to the adult are among the last for the child to adopt. Hanging up clothing is one of these. Some adolescents will take time to press a wrinkled garment before wearing it and yet drop clothes on the floor or on a chair to become mussed and wrinkled. The appearance of a preadolescent's bedroom has been the despair of mothers for generations. Mothers generally expect children at the pre-adolescent age to be responsible for hanging up their own clothing, although in spite of all manner of punishments, rewards, and reminders, they seem to have little success. One method may succeed for one family and another for a different family, but none apparently succeeds with the majority. It is quite probable that it may have been a matter of time with those who feel they have succeeded, and that the young adolescent was just about to outgrow this phase naturally.

There is great variation in the amount of responsibility that the twelve- to fifteen-year old has for care of clothing. As Barnes (3) has indicated, there is an increase in responsibility for care from the seventh to the ninth grades. Gesell states that by age fifteen, most of the children are very meticulous about their clothes and often do their own washing, ironing, and mending. Levy indicates that in her group, 96 percent of the girls washed their own clothes and that 79 percent of the boys did. However, from the way the question was worded, this apparently does not reflect the usual practice of the boys and girls but simply their behavior on some occasions. Ryan found that 67 percent of the eighth graders in her sample took at least some responsibility for the care of their slips. In almost all cases in which the girls reported some part of the care of their blouses, they ironed them but did not wash them. Presumably the blouses were put in the family wash, for which the mothers were responsible. A somewhat higher percentage of girls washed their own slips. The girls from the lower-economic groups were responsible for more of the care of their garments than were girls from the higher socioeconomic groups.

SEWING

Most schools require some training in clothing at the junior-high-school level, and this often includes the construction of simple garments. Horn (20) indicates that girls 12.5-years old were comparable to those of 15.6 years in their ability to use the needle and sewing machine. However, girls 13.9 to 15.6 years rated higher than girls 12.6 to 13.9 in their ability to use shears. She found that since both ability and interest in clothing construction were high for the 12.5- to 13.9-year-old girls, simple clothing construction techniques could be taught at this age level. Roach (31) found no relationship between economic status and home sewing for this age group.

Attitudes and Interests in Clothing

It is in attitudes towards clothing and interests in clothes that we find one of the greatest changes between the elementary school child and the preadolescent. Clothing which was of relatively little interest to the grade-school child becomes extremely important to the early adolescent.

The preadolescent is much more personal in his relationships with others, and along with this, he is extremely sensitive to the opinion and the approval of others. He is very anxious to have others like and accept him and is afraid that "everyone" will notice anything that is different or wrong about his appearance. He is afraid of being laughed at or that he might make a bad impression. Just as he is more perceptive about the appearance of others, so he is aware that others will be judging him by his appearance. In Silverman's (35) study, 84 percent of the respondents said they could judge others at least to some extent from appearance.

Gesell (16) says that at thirteen, "interest in personal appearance increases and becomes quite 'narcissistic' and at fourteen, the interest becomes still more marked reaching a 'passionate' pitch in girls while the boys are anxious to 'look sharp.'" At fifteen, there is somewhat less talk and concern over clothes.

This increase in interest in clothing for the preadolescent has been confirmed both directly and indirectly by a number of studies. Crane (10) asked 174 boys and 184 girls between twelve and fifteen in New South

Wales to write an essay on "The sort of person I would like to be when I grow up." Over half of the twelve-year-old girls mentioned that they wanted good looks. More mentioned this than any other trait. A quarter of the boys also mentioned good looks and another quarter good physique. The only item that was spoken of more frequently by the boys was "possession of money"; this was stated by 30 percent. The percentage who mentioned wanting to be good looking dropped with increase in age of the children but was still remarkably high at age fifteen; it was always higher for girls than for boys.

Silverman, in her study on the psychological implications of clothing for the adolescent (35), included in her questionnaire a number of questions directed toward determining the importance of clothing and appearance. The age group which she questioned included the twelve- to fifteen-year-old group as well as the older adolescent. She found that "over 62 percent of each age group felt that they should give considerable thought and attention to clothes, while the remainder thought some attention was necessary. The fact that no girl at any age believed she need not give any attention to clothes also indicates that the girls, even at an early age, were greatly interested in their apparel [p. 52]." For 79 percent of the girls of all ages, attractive clothes were necessary for happiness. Given a large sum of money, 82 percent would spend part of it on clothing and 14 percent would spend all of it on clothes. Of the twelve-year olds in her group, 80 percent were interested in discussing the attributes of attractiveness and wanted to pay attention to their appearance in order to improve it. The younger girls were even willing to "give up movies to save money for clothes." Silverman also asked about a number of attitudes toward clothing which indirectly showed the girls' interest. For example, 95 percent thought boys were more attracted to girls who dressed well; 72 percent thought a well-dressed girl had a better chance of getting a job; 31 percent of the twelve-year olds considered appearance a factor in eligibility to clubs. Although the twelve-year-olds did not refuse invitations because of their clothing, they did indicate that the suitability of their ensembles did give them concern, and 76 percent said that "knowing she had a good appearance gave a girl a considerable amount of self-confidence" [p.53], while 62 percent indicated that consciousness of their clothes resulted in feeling ill at ease.

Eighty-five percent of the eighth- and ninth-grade girls questioned by Morris (29) said they would be happier with more and better clothes.

Several studies have investigated feelings of adequacy concerning clothing. Silverman reports that 88 percent rated themselves as average in appearance, although 24 percent of the twelve-year olds felt that they did not have enough clothes. Two-thirds of a group of junior-high-school girls, in the research conducted by Barnes (3), thought that their wearing apparel was as good as the other students'; this feeling of satisfaction with the adequacy of their wardrobes increased with the age of the respondents. Often the girls in this group owned more clothing than they thought was needed. Over half of the girls in the Morris study (29) usually felt that their wardrobes were adequate, and less than 10 percent felt they were always adequate. Also, two-thirds thought that their clothing was usually as good as their friends and classmates, and less than 10 percent thought it never was as good as their friends.

While we are discussing the preadolescent's interest in clothing, it should be kept in mind that the only aspect which is of interest to the preadolescent is *his own* clothing or wardrobe. The junior-high-school girl is not interested in color and design in the abstract. She is only interested in which colors are becoming to her, and which color combinations or designs she can wear to the best advantage. Clothing management or clothing construction are of interest to her only if she can learn ways to increase her wardrobe.

Girls aged 10.4 to 12.5 years were asked by Horn (20) to rate various topics in the clothing curriculum in order of their interest. The list was ranked in the following order: (1) grooming, (2) selection, (3) sociological aspects, (4) management, (5) construction, and (6) care. For girls 12.5 years, the order was the same except that sociological aspects and selection had reversed places. These topics may have been ordered in this way because the students felt that those at the head of the list could give them the most ideas or help on their own clothing and appearance problems.

WHAT IS IMPORTANT IN CLOTHING TO THE PREADOLESCENT

One of the primary requirements of clothing for the young adolescent is that their clothing meets the approval of the peer group. Glickman says, "above all else the boy wants his clothes to conform to the style accepted by his friends. Being different to him means being inferior" [17:36]. When boys were asked where they got their ideas of what was smartest to wear, 64 percent said "what other fellows wear" [17:21]. He also found that boys like to wear their old clothes and dislike new ones. The same basic reasons may underlie this preference; the boys know that the old ones are acceptable, but are fearful about the new. Only 5 percent of those in the Silverman study said that they were indifferent to friends' appraisal.

At this age, hand-me-downs are not as acceptable as they were in the previous age groups. Silverman notes that 45 percent at the age of twelve reject hand-me-downs. The reason for this may very likely be in the fact that the handed-down garments are not just what the group is wearing at the moment.

The relative importance of specific components of clothing vary with the way in which the question is asked, but fit and comfort are always high on the list. Lawrence (24) listed the reasons given by boys for liking clothes in order of their importance as: comfort, appropriateness to wardrobe and occasion, "it looks neat," durability and economy, color and design of material. In another study (17), boys were asked what was most important to them when they chose an article of clothing. The components and the percentage naming each component were:

fit—29
style—28
price—16
wearability—13
color—10
no answer—4

Magrabi (27) asked girls to sort criteria according to their importance as a reason for liking a garment. All the criteria which were classified under comfort, such as, "easy to fasten and stays fastened," "material feels comfortable," and so on, were placed in the two highest degrees of importance by at least half of the girls.

The mean ratings of various components of satisfaction with the most-worn and least-worn blouses and slips for the eighth-grade girls in Ryan's study are shown in table 17. If we assume that the difference between the

	Blouse			Slip		
Component	*Most worn*	*Least worn*	*LWB– MWB*	*Most worn*	*Least worn*	*LWS– MWS*
Physical comfort	1.39	2.11	.72	1.53	2.69	1.16
Good buy	1.62	2.53	.91	1.36	1.70	.34
Psychological comfort	1.71	2.28	.57	...	...	...
Durability	1.82	2.03	.21	1.97	2.09	.12
Friends would like	1.82	2.68	.86	...	...	...
Ease of care	1.97	2.47	.50	1.65	1.79	.14
Becomingness	1.97	2.76	.79	...	...	...
Beauty	1.99	2.38	.39	2.47	2.52	.05

Based on a rating scale of 1 = most comfortable and so on, to 5 = least comfortable.

table 17 Mean ratings on various components of satisfaction with blouses and slips.

rating on the most-worn and least-worn garments is a measure of the relative importance of that component, we see that "good buy" and "friends would like" are the most important components of satisfaction with blouses, and comfort is by far the most important component of satisfaction with slips.

Girls in Barnes study (3) checked reasons for *not* being happy with clothing. Fit was given most frequently (45 percent), comfort was second (32 percent), while 21 percent checked that the reason was because it was not what the other girls were wearing.

Cassidy (8) asked girls whether or not they liked the dress they were wearing on the day of the interview. Ninety-four percent indicated that they did like it, and these seventh-grade girls most frequently gave "style" (28 percent) as their reason for liking it. Design detail (22 percent) and color (14 percent) followed as next most important reasons. Style and design detail, likewise, were given frequently as reasons for liking a favorite garment.

We have little information on specific preferences on Stratum one for this age group. Macaulay (26), in a study done many years ago, asked boys and girls what sort of clothes they would like to wear at a party and for every day, and why they would like this type. The answers showed that as the child became older, he was less interested in bright colors and preferred the more subdued and pastels. From twelve years of age and on, they were losing their fondness for the ornate and wanted simpler garments. They were also beginning to be aware of becomingness and wished styles and colors which would set off their complexion, hair, eyes, and figure.

Is Clothing a Source of Conflict Between Parents and Young Adolescents?

Clothes and grooming practices generally are considered a source of conflict between parents and young adolescents. Many popular articles are written advising parents on what to do about the situation, assuming that the extent of conflict is great. A number of researchers have attempted to investigate the extent of conflict. The results are dependent, first of all, on how the problem is approached. Some researchers have assumed that there are conflicts and sought to determine the areas in which they arise. That is, research from this point of view has determined the percentage of conflicts which have to do with grooming practices, with the hour to be home at night, with table manners, with household tasks, and so on. In this type of study, clothing and grooming are usually relatively high as a source of conflict between parents and young adolescents.

A second means of approach is to investigate how frequently parents and children have conflicts when they are selecting garments, how often they have conflicts over such matters as the care of garments for each area of clothing and grooming. Naturally, results are dependent upon the area being investigated, but generally there is more agreement than disagreement. The results are also dependent upon the wording of the question and upon who are the respondents. When both parents and adolescents have been questioned, it is found that the adolescents report more conflicts than do their parents.

Let us first look at the results of research in which the first approach is taken. That is, how often are clothing and grooming the issues when there is conflict. A nation-wide survey of girls eleven to eighteen years of age made for the Girl Scouts (12) shows that in conflicts between parents and daughters, the two most frequent issues are clothing and dating hours. For girls under fourteen, clothes and make-up were the most frequent cause of conflicts. More studies using this approach have had the older adolescent as subject, and the results will be discussed in the next chapter.

More of the research projects, concerning conflicts between mothers and their young adolescent children, have used the second approach. That is, researchers have endeavored to determine the amount of conflict in specific areas.

Block (4) gave a list of fifty possible problems on which there might be conflicts between adolescents and their mothers and asked a sample of 528 junior and senior high-school students to check those that seriously disturbed them and made them unhappy. Five of the fifty problems concerned clothing and grooming. They were:

1. Insists upon nagging me regarding what I wear and how I dress.
2. Complains about how I comb my hair.
3. Fusses because I use lipstick.
4. Refuses to let me buy the clothes I like.
5. Complains about hands, neck or finger nails being dirty.

Over 75 percent of the seventh-grade girls checked the first and third statements; the third was also checked by over 75 percent of the eighth-grade girls. The ninth-grade girls checked the fourth statement, and the tenth grade checked the second statement more frequently than they did any other of the 50 problems. Her conclusions were that most conflicts between parents and their children of this age were concerned with differences in thinking regarding personal appearance, habits, manners, and so on, rather than basic issues, and that many parents were unaware that any disturbance existed.

Fodor (15) asked both mothers and daughters a series of seven questions concerning the amount of agreement between them on some of the daughters' clothing and grooming practices. The mothers and daughters agreed more than they disagreed on the questions asked (see Table 18). Both mothers and daughters said that the greatest amount of disagreement was on the question of the amount of time the daughter spends on dressing and grooming. There was no question concerning the agreement or disagree-

*"If I were wearing all the clothes my mother wanted me to
wear, I'd go right through this ice!"*

ment between mothers and daughters over the size of the daughter's wardrobe, but several mothers volunteered that this was an area in which there
was disagreement. This point should not be overlooked in future research.

In another study designed to determine the extent of conflict concerning
clothing and grooming (1), mothers and their daughters were given a list
of statements covering areas of possible disagreement. The subjects were
asked to rate each of the statements on a six-point scale of agreement–
disagreement. Social status was likewise determined. When total scores were
compared, there was no significant difference between the attitudes of mothers and daughters within social-status grouping, but when scores for special
categories of dress were considered, there were some significant differences.
In the upper status grouping, mothers and daughters differed in the fol-

Item to be checked.	Daughters (N = 94)					Mothers (N = 91)				
	always agree	usually agree	usually disagree	always disagree	equally agree and disagree	always agree	usually agree	usually disagree	always disagree	equally agree and disagree
	PERCENT									
1. On what to buy for the daughter's school clothes?	10	87	3	0	0	8	91	0	1	0
2. On the color combination the daughter wears?	40	50	9	1	0	33	60	5	1	0
3. On the amount of time the daughter spends dressing and grooming?	25	41	30	2	1	16	45	26	6	5
4. On what to buy for the daughter's dress-up clothes?	31	64	5	0	0	26	64	9	1	0
5. On the amount and color make-up the daughter uses?	42	47	11	1	0	53	37	10	0	0
6. On the kinds of accessories the daughter wears?	53	45	2	0	0	45	52	3	0	0
7. On what the daughter should wear for parties?	37	56	5	0	1	44	46	9	1	0

table 18 Amount of conflict concerning clothing and grooming practices. From Wilda S. Fodor. *Relative Importance of Components of Satisfaction for Girls' Blouses and Slips to 8th and 11th Grade Girls and Their Mothers.* M.S. Thesis, Cornell Univer., 1963.

lowing categories: formals, shoes, coats, jeans, shorts and accessories. In the middle status grouping, the categories were shoes, formals, and grooming, and in the lower status grouping, the only category in which mothers and daughters differed significantly was undergarments. These results are suggestive, but there were too few mother and daughter pairs in either the upper- or lower-status groupings to make the status variation conclusive.

As we noted when discussing shopping practices, the majority of girls shop with their mothers. Disagreements are apparently relatively infrequent and usually mother and daughter, or mother and son, decide together what to purchase. Their preferences tend to be the same, and in general, mothers and their preadolescent children agree on what is appropriate for specific occasions.

Lawrence (24) compared the mothers' and sons' reasons for liking the son's clothes and found that the ratings of various criteria were similar for both. The boys were slightly more inclined to say that there were disagreements than were the mothers. Over 90 percent of the mothers thought that they agreed, while 80 percent of the boys said they agreed on what to wear for social activities and 86 percent said they agreed on what to wear for school. Glickman (17), on the other hand, found that nearly two-thirds of the boys in fifth and tenth grades said that they usually disagreed with their parents about what they should wear. From the wording of the question, we assume that the boys and their parents disagreed on what they should wear for given occasions, and not on the initial selection of the garments.

Although parents seem to approve of their daughter's clothing (29), there does not seem to be as much agreement between mothers' and daughters' preferences as was found between mothers' and sons'. Cassidy (8) found little agreement between mothers and their daughters on the ensembles their daughters preferred. Generally, the mothers did not seem even to know their daughter's favorite colors. Although this study shows that their preferences were not the same, it did not investigate whether or not there was friction between the mothers and daughters in the selection of garments.

In assigning the related importance of various components of satisfaction with blouses on an adjustable pie chart, Ryan (33) found marked differences between mothers and their daughters. The mothers, as might be expected, gave the components ease of care and durability more importance than did their daughters. The daughters gave more importance to beauty and "like friends' " than did mothers.

Two-thirds of the girls answering Silverman's (35) questionnaire checked that they were usually in agreement with their mothers over which kinds of clothes were best suited to them; 91 percent said that their mothers favored clothes suitable to their age; 90 percent said that they should give consideration to the mother's preference, and that in selection of clothes for the daughter, there should be a compromise between the preferences of the mother and the daughter.

The selection of clothing does not seem to be a major area of conflict between parents and their children. Where there are differences, there is apparently a willingness to compromise. Nor does there seem to be disagreement between the generations concerning what is modest or socially acceptable.

In some cultures where customs are changing rapidly, as in India and Pakistan, there are grave differences between two generations about what is proper for a daughter to wear. Here, ideas of modesty are related to religious beliefs and to long-established custom. Formerly the young unmarried girl did not adorn herself with jewels or bright colors; her garments were loose so as not to reveal the contours of her body; and all parts of the body except the eyes were covered. As girls have become educated and have adopted many Western ways, they have changed the style of their dress. The modern girl still wears the sari, but her face and head are uncovered, her sleeves are often short, the neckline low and her blouse tight. The saris are bright and gay in color. The girl wants to conform to this style of dress, but her mother considers that the girl in wearing such clothing is not only improper but wicked.[1] As time goes on and modern ways become accepted by all groups and generations, such major causes of conflict should disappear.

In spite of the fact that, in our culture, there are not these major differences of opinion concerning clothing; nevertheless, there are differences as we have seen. For example, in several studies we have found that girls are often taken to task by their mothers for devoting too much time to their dress or grooming.

Results from various studies differ on the extent of agreement or disagreement between parents and their children over clothing practices. Several factors may account for discrepancies in results, especially differences obtained between responses of mothers and daughters. In the first place, there are differences in definitions and the meaning of words. The word *conflict* may mean only a major difference of opinion to one person and *any* difference to another. The young adolescent, who is extremely sensitive, may also interpret a mother's suggestion as a critical statement implying conflict. For example, the mother may comment that the blouse and skirt make a poor color combination or that the daughter's lipstick is smeared. While intended merely as helpful suggestions and not considered conflicts or differences by the mother, the daughter is hurt and resentful and takes such comment as criticism and conflict of opinion. Or, the parent may intend to tease a son about the new way in which he combs his hair, and yet the youth may be hurt and resentful. The parents, on the other hand, may become irritated because a boy or girl is

---

[1] From unpublished paper by Zahida Quraishi.

spending long periods in the bathroom trying new ways of combing hair or minutely examining each skin pore, and feel that here there is conflict, but the youth may be completely unaware of any differences of opinion. Since these are not major difficulties or differences, most mothers and perhaps somewhat less frequently daughters or sons would check "no" to any question concerning conflicts. They are, however, annoying occurrences which if repeated frequently can add to unhappy family relations.

The Effect of Clothing on Social Acceptance and Social Participation

A number of studies have investigated the relative importance of appearance and other factors upon social acceptance or rejection of young adolescents. In most instances, some form of sociometric test has been used to determine the degree of acceptance.

Cannon and Staples (9) used such tests to determine acceptability. They asked subjects to *choose a companion for various activities* and a summation of the choices given to an individual constituted that person's social-acceptance score. Appearance was measured by a series of five rating scales used by the experimenters. Results showed that there *was a significant relationship between appearance and acceptability for the junior high school girls.* All of the most popular girls from the seventh through the twelfth grades excelled or conformed to the norm in personal appearance. For the *boys* the relationship was also positive, but not as great.

Kittles (21), working with a smaller group of girls, investigated a number of sociometric and other techniques to determine the influence of clothing upon social acceptance. She used scales on social acceptance, sociometric measures of leadership and clothing leadership, rating scales for personal appearance, and a clothing-judgment rating scale. She also observed each of her subjects for four minutes at five different periods and drew sociograms showing the number of times each subject reacted with any of the others. In the small sample with which she was dealing, the rejections and choices as shown in the sociograms did not relate to appearance scores. Social acceptance and clothing judgment were related positively but there was no relationship or a slightly negative one between social acceptance and appearance. These results disagree with those of Cannon and Staples. Since Kittles had a small group (20) who were in a single class, there may have been some other factor which cancelled out any relationship between appearance and acceptance.

To determine some of the qualities or aspects of personality which children age twelve and fifteen consider desirable in each other, Tyron (39) used the *guess who* technique. Two statements which described extremes of a trait were given to the subjects, and they were asked to fill in the names of classmates who match each statement. Of the 20 traits used, two were related to appearance, one was "unkempt versus tidy" and the other "good looking versus not good looking." The twelve-year-old boys showed preference for aggressiveness, boisterousness, and unkemptness, but by the age of fifteen, the trait tidy or unkempt had become reversed and tidyness showed a positive value. Also, a clustering of good-looking with popular was evident in the fifteen-year-old subjects but not in the twelve-year-olds. For girls, on the other hand, the traits good-looking, popular, friendly, and tidy were clustered together from the age of twelve. That is, twelve-year-old girls considered good looks and tidyness desirable as well as fifteen-year-olds, while boys do not consider these traits desirable at twelve; but by the time they are fifteen, they think tidyness and good looks are desirable.

Kuhlen (23) determined the popularity of each child in a ninth grade by asking each person to give his first, second, and third choices of companions for various activities. He then compared the 25 percent who were most popular with the 25 percent who were least popular on the Mooney Problems checklist. Although in general the problems most frequently checked by the two groups were similar, the unaccepted group had more problems than the accepted group, and differences were relatively greater for some problems than for others. Unaccepted boys checked significantly more often than accepted boys that "wanting to buy my own clothes," "wearing glasses" and "selecting suitable clothes and knowing how to wear them" were problems for them. It may be that wearing glasses or not having suitable clothing was a cause of unpopularity, but, equally probable, the unpopular child attributed the cause of his unpopularity to lack of acceptable clothing rather than to some deficiency within himself.

Silverman (35) investigated the relationship between appearance and social participation in various social activities; between appearance and leadership; and between appearance and interest in various social activities. Appearance again was determined by rating scales. Teachers rated the students on six aspects of appearance. The high-appearance group participated on the average in 5.8 extracurricular activities, while the low-appearance group engaged in an average of 2.7 activities. The good-appearance group had held among them a total of thirty-five offices in the preceding three years, while those in the poor-appearance group had held only four. There was no significant relationship between appearance and age or economic level, so these factors were not influential. There was, however, a relationship between appearance and intelligence. The good-appearance group had a median IQ of 104 and the poor appearance, 95.

There seems little doubt that, in general, personal appearance and social acceptance are related for this age group. However, we are still unable to say whether the girl who has a poor appearance, is withdrawn and rejected by the group would become interested in social activities and likewise be accepted by the others if her appearance were changed. As Cannon and Staples have pointed out, "Whether a good personal appearance contributes to self-assurance with resulting social acceptability, or whether a strong social interest carries with it a desire to adopt a standard of dress and grooming which meets group approval we cannot say" [9:713]. The young adolescent, however, is apt to attribute popularity to such factors as appearance and dismiss the second possibility. It is evident that this age group clearly believes that appearance is an important factor in his acceptance.

Silverman found that 95 percent of her subjects thought that boys were more attracted to girls who dressed well. They thought a good appearance was an aid in building self-confidence, in success in getting a job, and in increasing the chances of marriage. Over half of the group which Morris (29) studied thought that clothing contributed to popularity, but there is no indication of its relative importance. Both Dixon (12) and Enty (13), on the other hand, found that girls felt that personality was more important than appearance in obtaining popularity.

We have seen that, in general, there is a relationship between appearance and social participation. It is not surprising, then, to find that nearly half of the students questioned reported that, at least at times, they have refused to go out because of clothing. See Morris (29) and Barnes (3). Over 50 percent in Barnes group also reported that if they had better clothing, it would contribute to their greater enjoyment of social events.

In summary, we can say that there is some evidence of a positive relationship between appearance and popularity. Preadolescents consider this a causal relationship, since they generally regard appearance as an important contributing factor in popularity. However, it might be hypothesized that both popularity and an attractive appearance are caused by a third factor. Another hypothesis which might be investigated is that the better known the individual, the less important are his clothes in determining popularity. For example, young adolescents in a small town who have known each other all their lives probably do not judge each other by clothing, and therefore their clothes have little influence on their popularity or feelings of acceptance.

Clothing Leadership, Fads and Fashions

We have very little reliable information on fads and fashions for this particular age group. Casual observations, however, indicate that this is the age group in which fads are most prevalent. There has been some research and discussion on fads and fashions for adolescents as a whole; we will, therefore, discuss them in the next chapter.

There is one major research study concerning clothing leadership for boys of this age group. Glickman (17) obtained a clothing-leadership index by means of sociometric questions of the "guess-who" type. In addition he obtained clothing attitudes, interests, and preferences. From the clothing preference data, he gained a "clothing conformity index" by finding the extent to which a boy agreed with other boys. In addition, he also collected personal data including the boys' participation in clubs and athletics. From the data obtained, it was possible to predict clothing leadership which, this study shows, is a specific type of leadership related, but not identical, to leadership in other areas. Those persons most likely to be looked upon as clothing leaders are those who are leaders in cooperative group activities, and who at the same time see in clothing symbols of status and acceptability. That is, they must have an interest in clothing and feel that it is an important factor in popularity. The clothing leader must also have a certain minimum degree of clothing conformity (as measured by the clothing-conformity index). A high clothing-conformity index is not by itself, however, a sufficient condition for clothing leadership. Those who have older brothers tend *not* to be clothing leaders.

There has been a good deal of discussion recently about the effects of the "wrong" type of clothing on the adolescent and relationships between certain fads in dress and delinquency. Many schools have imposed rules or codes regulating the dress of students, hoping in this way to improve behavior also. Although there may be a difference between the early and the older adolescent on the effects of clothing on behavior, the age difference has not been studied or discussed. We will, therefore, take up this topic when we discuss the older adolescent.

Bibliography

1. Angelino, Henry, Barnes, Lenorah A., and Shedd, Charles. Attitudes of mothers and adolescent daughters concerning clothing and grooming. *J. of Home Ec.* 48, 1956, 779–782.
2. Barnes, Lenorah Adams. *Difference in Attitudes of Mothers and Adolescent Daughters Concerning Clothing and Grooming.* M.S. Thesis, University of Oklahoma, 1955.
3. Barnes, Sara H. *Preferences and Practices in the Purchase, Use and Care of Clothing of 225 Junior High School Students in Zanesville, Ohio.* M.S. Thesis, Ohio State Univer., 1955.
4. Block, Virginia Lee. Conflicts of adolescents with their mothers. *J. of Abnorm. and Soc. Psychol.* 32, 1937, 193–206.
5. Breckenridge, M. E. and Vincent, E. Lee. *Child Development.* Philadelphia: W. B. Saunders Co., 1960, 648p.
6. Britton, Edward C., and Winans, J. Merritt. *Growing from Infancy to Adulthood.* New York: Appleton-Century-Crofts, Inc., 1958, p. 58–67.
7. Burchinal, Lee G. Development of girls' sex-role identification. *J. of Home Ec.* 50, 1958, 708–710.
8. Cassidy, Magdalen L. *Clothing Preferences of 150 Pre-Adolescent Girls and 50 of Their Mothers.* M.S. Thesis, Ohio State Univer., 1954.
9. Cannon, K. L., Staples, R., and Carlson, I. Personal appearance as a factor in social acceptance. *J. of Home Ec.* 44, 1952, 710–713.

10. Crane, A. R. Stereotypes of the adult held by early adolescents. *J. of Ed. Research.* 50, 1956, 227–230.
11. Diaz, Winnifred Elizabeth. *Instruments for Determining Characteristics of School Clothing Important to Ninth Grade Girls and Their Mothers.* M.S. Thesis, Iowa State Univer., 1959.
12. Dixon, Margeurite M. Adolescent girls tell about themselves. *Marriage and Family Living.* 20, 1958, 400–401.
13. Enty, J. E. *The Effect of Clothing on the Social Adjustment of the Adolescent Girl.* M.S. Thesis, Howard Univer., 1950.
14. *Family Clothing Inventories by Age.* Minneapolis-St. Paul, 1949, USDA Bureau of Human Nutrition and Home Ec., Studies of family clothing supplies, Prelim. Report No. 3, 1951.
15. Fodor, Wilda S. *Relative Importance of Components of Satisfaction for Girls' Blouses and Slips to 8th and 11th Grade Girls and Their Mothers.* M.S. Thesis, Cornell Univer., 1963.
16. Gesell, Arnold and Ilg, Frances L. *Youth: The Years from 10 to 16.* New York: Harper & Row, Publishers, 1956, 542p.
17. Glickman, Albert Seymour. *Clothing Leadership Among Boys.* Ph.D. Thesis, University of Michigan, 1952.
18. Hartung, Sara J. *Problems of the Young Teenage Girl in Buying Ready-Made Skirts and Dresses.* M.S. Thesis, Ohio State Univer., 1959.
19. Hollingsworth, Leta. *The Psychology of the Adolescent.* New York: Appleton-Century-Crofts, Inc., 1929, 227p.
20. Horn, Fern M. Developmental level related to clothing study. *J. of Home Ec.* 52, 1960, 451–452.
21. Kittles, Emma. *Experimental Use of Technique for Determining the Influence of Clothing upon Social Acceptance of Junior High School Girls.* M.S. Thesis, Ohio State Univer., 1956.
22. Kodlin, Dankward, and Thompson, Donovan J. An appraisal of the longitudinal approach to studies of growth and development. *Soc. for Research in Child Devel. Monog.* 23(1), 1958, 47p.
23. Kuhlen, R. G. Sociometric status and personal problems of adolescents, *Sociometry.* 10, 1947, 122–132.
24. Lawrence, Hazel Marilyn. *Preferences of Mothers and Sons for Clothing of Eighth-Grade Boys.* M.S. Thesis, Iowa State Univer., 1958.
25. Levy, Julia M. *Responsibilities Assumed by Some Junior High School Youth in the Purchase and Care of Their Clothes.* M.S. Thesis, Prairie View A. and M. College, 1956.
26. Macaulay, E. Some notes on the attitude of children to dress. *Brit. J. of Med. Psychol.* 9, 1929, 150–158.
27. Magrabi, Frances M. *Differences Between Parents' and Daughters' Criteria in Selection of Eighth-Grade Girl's Clothing.* M.S. Thesis, Iowa State Univer., 1958.
28. Moeller, Fay and Tingley, Katherine A. *Girls from 9 to 13—Their Clothing Abilities.* Storrs, Conn.: Extension Bull., Univer. of Connecticut, 1952.

29. Morris, Katherine. *A Study of the Clothing Preferences and Buying Practices of 788 Junior High School Students in Austin, Texas.* M.S. Thesis, University of Texas, 1958.

30. Quraishi, Zahida. *Clothing Attitudes and Problems of Children and Adolescents.* Unpublished Paper, Cornell Univer., Ithaca, New York, 1952.

31. Roach, Mary Ellen. *The Influence of Social Class on Clothing Practices and Orientation at Early Adolescence: A Study of Clothing—Related Behavior of Seventh Grade Girls.* Ph.D. Thesis, Michigan State Univer., 1960.

32. Rosencranz, Mary Lou. *Relevance of Occupation and Income to Mothers' Selection of Clothing for Daughters.* Michigan State Univer. Agr. Exper. Sta. Bull., No. 268, 1958.

33. Ryan, Mary S. *Factors Relating to Satisfaction with Adolescent Girls' Blouses and Slips: A Comparison of Mothers' and Daughters' Opinions.* Cornell Univer. Agr. Exper. Sta. Bull., 1003, May 1965.

34. Shuttleworth, F. K. Sexual maturation and the physical growth of girls aged 6 to 19. *Soc. for Research in Child Devel. Monog.* 2, 1937, 1–253.

35. Silverman, Sylvia S. *Clothing and Appearance—Their Psychological Implications for Teen-Age Girls.* New York: Bureau of Publications, Teachers College, Columbia Univer. 1945, 140p.

36. Stolz, Herbert S. How appearance affects personality. *Parent's Mag.* 17, 1942, 20–21, 34, 84.

37. Stone, C. P., and Barder, R. G. The attitudes and interests of pre-menarchael and postmenarchael girls. *J. of Genetic Psychol.* 54, 1939, 27–71.

38. Thompson, Henrietta M. and Tucker, Reba. Some clothing practices of thirteen-year-old girls. *J. of Home Ec.* 50, 1958, 783–784.

39. Tryon, C. M. Evaluation of adolescent personality by adolescents. *Soc. for Research in Child Devel. Monog.* 4, 1939, 1–83.

40. Vener, Arthur M. and Hoffer, Charles R. *Adolescent Orientations to Clothing.* Technical Bull. 270, Michigan State Univer., Agr. Exper. Sta., March 1959, 30p.

Chapter 13

Adolescents

(Ages Fifteen to Twenty)

For girls, the great acceleration in growth usually has passed its peak by middle adolescence, although some boys may still be growing very rapidly. The body continues to change and grow, however, after the rate of growth has declined. During middle adolescence, parts of the body which have not changed materially catch up with those developed earlier. For example, the youth who has been disturbed because his nose was too prominent now finds that his other features have grown so that it no longer looks out of proportion, or the former "beanpole" begins to fill out. The adolescent is taking on the appearance he will have as an adult, and is usually better looking than he was a year or two earlier. Moreover, he is learning how to manage his larger body so that he is less awkward.

The adolescent of fifteen years or over is also developing emotionally, mentally and socially, but he is still far from the poised and popular adult he would like to be (or like others to think he is). He has dropped some of his childish ways, but still retains others. For example, a high-school sophomore may run a club business meeting very efficiently and correctly, and yet a few hours later throw a tantrum over a trivial matter. Adults, not knowing whether to treat him as a child or as an adult, are inconsistent in what they expect of him. This adds to his own vacillation and makes him even more insecure and unpredictable.

The older adolescent is breaking away from the family and other adult authority. At the same time, he is still anxious for outside support, and is very sensitive and unsure of himself, therefore, he turns to his peer group for approval and acceptance. This is shown by the personal problems which adolescents acknowledge. Remmers and Radler (45) report a long list of problems checked by boys and girls from grades nine and ten in the Purdue Opinion Poll. The four problems which more than 50 percent of the group checked as being of concern to them were:

> Want people to like me more (54 percent)
> Get stage fright before group (53 percent)
> Want to gain or lose weight (52 percent)
> Want to make new friends (50 percent)

The dependence upon peer approval may also be emphasized by the situation into which he is forced. As Kuhlen puts it:

> Social consciousness is high at adolescence in contrast to adult life in part because school life forces adolescents into close contact with individuals from all sorts of backgrounds. In school, individuals with certain deficits rub shoulders with those who possess greater poise, better clothes, better family standing and more active social life—and as a result, attention is focused on such differences [32:290].

Interest in the opposite sex is increasing, and the youth worries about being attractive to the opposite sex and about anything he thinks makes a person acceptable or not acceptable.

The adolescent still thinks in concrete rather than abstract terms. It is easier for him to understand and to assign causation to something he can feel or see. Therefore, he tends to think of the reasons for social approval in terms of clothing and appearance, specific manners, or possessions rather than in the more abstract terms of friendliness, loyalty, maturity, and so on. This leads to a heightened interest in clothes and makes concern about physical appearance one of the dominating factors in his life.

Clothing Practices

As background material for research on the psychological factors involved in clothing for the adolescent, we should first know something about what the average adolescent's wardrobe contains, how much it costs, and the normal practices for the group. If an adolescent says that her wardrobe is insufficient or that "everyone" else uses make-up while she is forbidden to use it, are these statements actually true or is there some other explanation? At what age do girls start to wear high heels, stockings, or get their first formal dress? When do they take over the responsibility for the selection of their own clothes or the care of them? Do those having larger wardrobes participate more in social activities? In spite of the importance of this basic knowledge concerning inventories and typical clothing behavior, we have relatively little reliable information.

INVENTORIES

Studies of expenditure indicate that more money is spent on the teenagers' clothing than for any other group. The Bureau of Labor Statistics finds that clothing buying seems to be more sensitive to the presence of teenage daughters than to anything else.

We have only very scattered information from small and selected groups on clothing inventories for the adolescent who is still in high school. In 1956, Mayer (40) obtained inventories from 41 girls from a school serving people of middle economic level. The average wardrobe was worth approximately $395 and it held about 50 garments including 6 dresses, 2 suits, 5 coats, 12 blouses, 8 sweaters, 10 skirts, and 7 pairs of shoes.

In a study by Ryan (48:Part II) in 1953, 272 girls from a rural and a city high school were similar to Mayer's group in number of dresses and suits they owned, but had fewer blouses, sweater and skirts. Ryan's results were obtained by asking the student to supply the number of garments from memory, and thus are not so accurate as an actual count. An inventory probably would have yielded larger numbers, in almost all instances.

More recently, Dickins and Ferguson (14) secured inventories of blouses, skirts, dresses and sweaters of senior high-school students in certain schools in Mississippi. Both white and Negro students from rural and from urban areas were included in the sample. The percentage of her total population owning a given number of garments is shown in Table 19.

Type of garment	Percentage of girls owning number of garments			
	Less than 10	*10–19*	*20–29*	*30 or more*
Blouses	17	50	25	8
Skirts	10	54	29	7
Dresses	20	50	23	7
Sweaters	32	57	10	1

table 19 Average number of garments owned by white, Negro, rural and urban girls combined. From Dorothy Dickins and V. Ferguson. *Practices and Preferences of Teen-age Girls in the Selection of Blouses, Skirts, Dresses, and Sweaters.* State College, Miss.: Agr. Exper. Sta. Bull. 636, 1962, 32pp.

The number of garments decreased from the largest number owned by white urban girls, followed by white rural, then Negro urban, to Negro rural girls who owned the fewest; this is undoubtedly related to the economic level of the different groups. The differences between the white rural, white urban and Negro urban were not large, but there was a decided gap between the Negro rural girls and the other three groups.

The results in all three of these studies were obtained from adolescents attending high school, and thus should be taken as representing these schools and not the population of this age group as a whole. Those who drop out of school probably do not own as many garments as those who remain in school. Data on those who leave school might reveal inadequacies in clothing as one reason for leaving.

For the still older group of adolescents who are past high school age, we have no inventory data, as far as I know, of those who are not in college. Even for the college student, in spite of the fact that he is easily available for study, we have very few studies, either of clothing expenditures or clothing inventories.

Baumgartner (6) and Hoffman (20) investigated clothing expenditures of college students. Baumgartner asked a large random sample of students to recall the amount they had spent during the summer and early fall before their freshman year in purchasing new clothes for college. The average amount spent was $136. The amount was significantly higher for girls ($173) than for boys ($97); for those who joined a fraternity or sorority; for those whose family had a higher income or higher occupational status; for those who came from a larger home town; and it was higher for those who ascribed more importance to clothing than for those who thought clothing less important. She found that 44 percent of the men in the college of arts and sciences bought all of their clothing with their own earnings, 27 percent bought half or three-quarters and only 15 percent did not buy any of their clothing with their own earnings. Fewer of the girls (11 percent) did not earn any of the money for their clothes, but there were also fewer girls (33 percent) who earned money for all of their clothing.

Hoffman obtained actual records of clothing expenditures during the freshman and, in some cases, the sophomore year. These were expenditures made after the student reached college in contrast to the expenditures before entering which were obtained by Baumgartner. Since the Hoffman study required keeping records, the sample was limited to 75 freshmen girls and to 50 girls who kept records for two years. The annual expenditures (exclusive of gifts and clothing made at home) ranged from $35 to $800 with an average of $275. The respondents were asked to estimate the amount they thought they would spend before they started records, and 61 out of 75 underestimated their expenditures. At the beginning of the sophomore year, they were asked how much they thought they had spent on clothing during the freshman year, and their responses were no more accurate than their first estimates. It must be remembered that they were attempting to recall the amount spent over the span of a year. Recall over a shorter period, as in the case of the Baumgartner study, would be more accurate. Hoffman found no relationship between clothing expenditures and size of the family, the educational level of parents or size of the home town. This does not agree with the results of the Baumgartner study nor some of the inventory studies. Any positive relationships may have been hidden due to an unknown variable and the small sample.

The data on inventories of college students' wardrobes are even more scattered than that of clothing expenditures, and in some cases too old to be of value today. One recent study was done by Van Konynenburg (61); she obtained inventories of the clothing of junior women at Cornell University. The average number of garments owned are shown in Table 20.

Rosencranz[1] obtained wardrobe inventories from 25 college respondents in the spring of 1963. For each type of garment the average number owned by her respondents was greater than the average number owned by Von Konynenburg's respondents. Rosencranz obtained data on the entire wardrobe and the approximate cost of each type of garment. The average cost of the total wardrobe was $1513.33.

Garment	Average Number Owned
Coats	5.4
Dresses	8.7
Suits	1.4
Skirts	13.4
Blouses	14.5
Pullover sweaters	11.2
Cardigan sweaters	6.9
Slacks, jeans, skipants	2.9
Shorts, bermudas	3.3
Bathing suits	1.3
Shoes, footwear	10.3
Hats	1.8

table 20 Average number of garments owned by type of garment. Data: Kathleen Van Konynenburg. *A Study of Selected Clothing Practices of Cornell Junior Women.* M.S. Thesis, Cornell University, 1961, p. 19.

All of the inventory studies on both the high school and college girl confirm our casual observations that the skirt and blouse or skirt and sweater are practically a uniform for the adolescent; individual variation is seen primarily

---

[1] Unpublished data provided by M. L. Rosencranz.

in color and color combinations. As a class project, a student compared inventories reported by girls in beginning textile and clothing classes at one institution over a period of twenty-five years. Although the inventory forms varied over these years, thus making comparisons somewhat risky, it was nevertheless evident that the greatest change in college freshmen's clothing was the growth in popularity of separates and the increased number of garments in the wardrobe. The presentday freshman girl owns approximately the same number of dresses that her mother did twenty-five years ago, but, in addition, she owns a much larger number of separates.

GROOMING PRACTICES

We have no recent study of grooming practices. Silverman (50) in 1945 found, as might be expected, that cosmetics were used by girls more often on week ends or special occasions than for every day, and that they were used more frequently by the sixteen-year old than by the younger adolescent. One surprising result, however, was that sixteen-year-old girls used more cosmetics than eighteen-year-old girls. For example, 53 percent of the sixteen-year-olds wore nail polish daily, while only 40 percent of the 18-year-olds did. There are a number of possible explanations for this: it may reflect the age of greatest interest in personal appearance, that is, the girls at sixteen were at the peak of their interest in, and concern over, appearance, and by eighteen interest has started to drop somewhat; at sixteen girls may be just beginning to try out a variety of cosmetics and by eighteen have finished experimenting and may have decided against using some types of cosmetics; or the sixteen-year-old girls may be more anxious to be doing what they consider grown-up while the eighteen-year-old girls are more independent in their thinking.

This study was carried out a number of years ago and practices undoubtedly have changed greatly in the meantime. From casual observation, we would say that the change has primarily been in the age at which girls become interested in grooming and use of make-up. The age at which cosmetics are first used and the age at which they are used most frequently appears to have decreased since 1945, when Silverman's study was conducted.

SHOPPING PRACTICES: TEENAGERS AS CONSUMERS

Business is recognizing that teenagers are a growing market. About 15 million of them are spending nearly $10 billion a year[2] and a large share of this is spent on clothes and cosmetics. Although as we have seen, we have little information on the amount which the typical teenager spends on clothing we know that it is a great deal more than he had twenty or even ten years ago.

We have noted that the adolescent is breaking away from his family, and the greatest need and desire at this age seems to be the need to conform to the

---

[2] Talk by Alice Linn, Extension Clothing Specialist, Division of Home Economics Programs, United States Department of Agriculture at a meeting in Lewiston, Idaho, October 31, 1962.

peer group and to escape its ridicule. Barr (5) found conformity to be the most important factor in clothing choices of older adolescents.

Several studies have tried to answer the age-old question of whether a girl dresses to please members of her own sex or the opposite sex. Hurlock (24), in a study done over thirty years ago, reported that adolescent girls were more anxious to please their own sex than the opposite sex. Silverman (50) put the question in a different way, and found that the majority of girls wanted to choose clothes that appeal to boys. Both are probably accurate in saying they want to appear attractive to friends of both sexes.

Vener (60) demonstrated the impact an adolescent's peers has upon his clothing behavior by asking the adolescent respondents whom they would like to emulate in their dress. Nearly 58 percent chose a peer as the person they would most like to resemble in dress; 21 percent chose mass-media celebrities, such as movie stars or famous sports figures; 11.5 percent chose family members as models; and not quite 7 percent chose community or "world of work" models.

The desire to conform to the peer group may be the reason that among adolescents we find slavish following of fads and changing fashions. Wax suggests that the young adolescent girl follows fad and fashion because she is "experimenting with herself and has not yet developed a self-image with which she can be comfortable" [65:591]. He goes on to point out that the older person is more secure; she knows herself and her roles therefore, she can accept or reject fads and follow fashion at a distance.

The conclusion we would reach from this is that the peer group is the most important influence on the adolescent's clothing behavior. The adolescent, not yet an adult, is unsure of himself; he does not know just what his role in society is to be; at the same time he is breaking away from his family; therefore, he especially needs the approval of the peer group. Clothing and appearance are tangible ways in which he can hope to obtain this desired approval. Consequently, he chooses whatever others are wearing since he knows this will be acceptable to them.

Although the approval of the peer group may be very important to the adolescent, the mother plays an important part in the actual selection of clothing. Coleman (12), Dickins and Ferguson (14), Gillespie (17), Hoffman (20), Leonard (35), Hurst (26), Rosner (47), Ryan (48), Silverman (50), Vener and Hoffer (60), Waldron (62), and a study by the Department of Agriculture (58) all have investigated the question of who chooses the adolescent's clothes. The most comprehensive figures on this point are those from the study by the United States Department of Agriculture in which 1,751 girls were questioned as follows: "Which of these items do you and your mother *usually* shop for together?" and "Who *usually* makes the final decision about what to buy . . . you or your mother?" The replies are given in Table 21.

Items of Clothing	Shopping done by:				Final decision made by:			
	Daughter	*Mother*	*Both*	*Not Ascertained*	*Daughter*	*Mother*	*Both*	*Not Ascertaine*
				PERCENT				
Dresses	20	4	72	4	42	15	39	4
Skirts	36	3	57	4	54	10	32	4
Sweaters	43	7	46	4	58	10	26	6
Blouses	50	6	40	4	61	9	25	5
Rainwear	16	6	41	37	28	13	24	35
Slips and petticoats	48	13	35	4	57	14	24	5
Anklets	66	11	17	6	71	9	14	6

table 21 Table: *Teenage Girls Discuss Their Wardrobes and Their Attitudes toward Cotton and Other Fibers.* Marketing Research Report No. 155, Marketing Research Division, U.S. Dept. of Agr., 1957.

The other studies generally give the same picture, that is, the high-school girl usually is accompanied by her mother and consults her when shopping, but, as she grows older, she assumes more of the responsibility for choosing her own clothes. The study by the Department of Agriculture found that 12 percent of the fourteen-year-old girls compared with 32 percent of the seventeen-year-old girls usually shop alone for dresses, and 31 percent of the fourteen-year olds but 58 percent of the seventeen-year-old girls said that they have the "final say" on choosing dresses. Studies on girls in grades eleven and twelve report from 68 percent to 85 percent of the girls choosing their own clothes; one study says that 96 percent purchased at least some of their own wardrobe.

The Boys' Apparel Manufacturers Association and Scholastic Magazine cooperated in a study (57) which included buying habits of boys in their last three years of high school. They contacted 294 leaders from 107 high schools. For major items of clothing, 82 percent of the sophomores, 67 percent of the juniors and 50 percent of the seniors shopped with parents or relatives. By their senior year, 49 percent were shopping alone or with friends. For less expensive clothing items such as sweaters, shirts and ties, 57 to 79 percent shopped alone or with a companion. A vast majority reported differing with their parents during shopping trips, but, when this was so, the student usually was the one who made the final decision.

Vener (60) asked high-school boys and girls "Whose opinion counts most when you are deciding what to wear?" The respondents were asked to select only one from a list. The largest percentage (37.8) checked that mother was the most important influence; boys and girls of the same age were checked next most frequently (21.2 percent). Older brothers and sisters were found to be of greater influence in dress patterns than the father.

Data from studies of college girls give percentages of from 82 to 92 as representing the proportion of girls who choose their own clothing.

There is some evidence that the age at which they choose their own clothes may also vary with socioeconomic level or between cultural groups. Dickins and Ferguson (14) obtained results similar to the other studies for the white girls in their sample—(approximately three-quarters of the eleventh-grade girls made the decisions about the clothes they purchased); the Negro girls, on the other hand, more often reported that their mothers made the decisions (57 percent of the urban Negro girls and 68 percent of the rural Negro girls).

In studies by Baldwin (4), Lokken (36) and Ryan (48) the boys reported choosing their own clothes, or wanting to choose them, as frequently as girls. This is surprising in view of consumer studies indicating that most men's wear items are purchased by women. It is quite probable, in view of the importance of clothing to the youth, that the adolescent boy not only selects more of his own clothing than he has up to this age but also more than he will at any other age.

The evidence concerning whether or not the adolescent and his family plan before purchasing clothing articles is conflicting. The results of one study indicate no planning and that garments were purchased as needed (12), Lucas (37) found that 66 percent of her population (Negro girls in tenth, eleventh, and twelfth grades) purchased clothing whenever "they had the money." Another study says that 70 percent had a definite plan, and a third found that the amount of preplanning was influenced by the number of courses in homemaking.

The Department of Agriculture study shows that there is certainly planning and discussion concerning the purchase of individual items. Ninety-two percent of the girls and their mothers talk about clothing before purchasing. There is, naturally, more discussion of larger items while fewer talk over the more inexpensive items. The percentage of girls reporting that they discuss a given article with their mothers before purchasing can be seen in Table 22.

Percent of girls who usually discuss item before shopping	Clothing item discussed
80	Dresses
68	Skirts
59	Sweaters
53	Blouses
48	Slips and/or petticoats
44	Rainwear
29	Anklets

table 22   Data: *Teenage Girls Discuss Their Wardrobes and Their Attitudes toward Cotton and Other Fibers. Marketing Research* Report No. 155, U.S. Dept. Agr., 1957, p. 21.

The discussion nearly always included the price which should be paid for the garment. The questions discussed and the percentage of girls who reported discussing the topic are shown in Table 23. Apparently the mother often makes the final decision as to whether or not the girl may purchase an item and how much she should pay for it, while the girl makes the final decision on which garment she wants of those that meet the mother's qualifications. Lucas (37) also found that the majority of the mothers made the final decision as to how much should be spent for clothing.

Percent of girls who said they discussed given topic with mother.	Topic discussed by mother and daughter before selecting garment.
88	Price
81	Need for item
73	Whether it will wear well
70	Style
67	Ease of care
66	Material
50	Where to purchase garment
49	Color

table 23   Data: *Teenage Girls Discuss Their Wardrobes and Their Attitudes toward Cotton and Other Fibers*. Marketing Research Report No. 155, U.S. Dept. Agr. 1957 p. 24.

Who pays for the garment is also another area in which we find conflicting evidence. The relative number of girls reported to have a clothing allowance varies from 10.5 percent to 62 percent, and the number who earn part of their clothing money varies from 40 percent to 87 percent. These differences probably reflect differences in the way in which the questions are worded or the answers interpreted, rather than actual differences. It is very difficult to get and to present accurate data on this point because practices are so varied (see p. 250). These conflicting results demonstrate the need for exact definitions or complete detailed descriptions when studying the question of allowances.

Nearly 80 percent of the eleventh-grade girls in Ryan's study (49) reported that they purchased some of their clothes with their own money. Fewer girls had purchased slips than blouses with their own money. This would suggest that girls use their earnings to add extra garments to their wardrobes.

Dickins and Ferguson (14) found that most of the girls in their sample were given money to buy the specific items wanted. The percentage of Negro urban girls using money they had earned was considerably higher than for the other three groups (see Table 24).

Group	From allow- ance	From parents	From money earned	From someone outside family	From savings or other	More than one way	No report	Did not buy	Total girls
				PERCENT					NO.
White rural	8	43	29	2	2	1	*	14	289
White urban	11	32	30	5	4	3	*	14	551
Negro rural	6	48	26	4	0	4	1	11	163
Negro urban	6	38	42	2	*	3	*	9	217
Average	9	38	31	4	2	3	*	13	1220

* Less than 5 percent.

table 24 Way girl obtained money to purchase last item of clothing bought. From D. Dickins and V. Ferguson. *Practices and Preferences of Teen-Age Girls in the Selection of Blouses, Skirts, Dresses, and Sweaters.* State College, Miss.: Exper. Sta. Bull. 636, 1962, 32pp.

There are certain other aspects of shopping behavior on which the results from various studies are in agreement. It has generally been found that adolescents pay cash rather than use a charge account in the purchase of clothing. They shop more often in a department store than in any other type. Once the decision to purchase an item has been made, teenagers usually buy it on the first trip; that is, they do not do a great deal of comparative shopping. They seldom shop alone; they go either with their mothers or with friends.

Almost all adolescents enjoy window shopping (see Waldron), but the results differ as to the importance various media play in the decision making. One study says that 62 percent of the girls were influenced by such sources as radio, newspaper ads, and salesmen; another says that 35 percent of the girls *regularly* read fashion magazines.

Ryan (49) found that the eleventh-grade girls, as well as the eighth-grade girls, got their ideas on what to wear most frequently from their peers. Eighty-three percent of the eleventh graders reported this source of ideas as compared with 90 percent of the eighth graders. The greatest difference between the eighth and eleventh graders was in the increased use of magazines as a source of ideas with the older girls; 79 percent of the eleventh graders reported that they got ideas from magazines, while 46 percent of the eigth graders gave this reply. Sales people and store displays gave 55 percent of the older girls ideas on what to select, and 21 percent got ideas from their mothers. The Department of Agriculture study found that in the purchase of a *particular* dress or skirt, 28 percent were influenced by media such as magazines, television, newspapers, and so on, 26 percent said that stores or store windows were sources of ideas and 24 percent attributed the source of ideas to girl friends or other people.

Boys depend primarily on what their friends wear as a guide for their own choice. Lokken (36) found that advertising by the clothing industry had more influence on the twenty-one-year old than the fifteen-year old. Clerks in the store had little direct influence. Baldwin (4) also found that advertising media had little influence on boys.

In several studies, girls have been asked about the factors they considered when purchasing a garment or about the elements they deemed most important. Unfortunately, we do not have a classification of reasons which is generally accepted. Therefore, the results of various studies are not comparable. The results depend upon the list given the adolescent for checking or, in instances using open-ended questions, upon the classification used in coding the answers. From all studies, however, reasons related to the appearance of the garment are usually those given most frequently, while reasons connected with durability or wearing quality or quality of construction are at the bottom of the scale in importance. Fit is often listed as a most important reason (see Table 25), but whether fit is important because of appearance or because it makes the garment more comfortable has not been investigated.

Negro girls in the study by Dickins and Ferguson checked color as the most important feature in clothing significantly more often than did white girls (see Table 25). We do not know the cause of this great difference

Group	Color	Fit	In Fashion	Weave	Fiber	Becom- ingness	No Report	Total Girls
			PERCENT					NUMBER
White rural	9	56	6	0	2	27	0	289
White urban	5	53	7	0	1	33	1	551
Negro rural	37	43	7	1	1	9	3	163
Negro urban	28	43	2	1	2	23	2	217
Average	14	51	6	*	1	26	1	1220

* Less than 5 percent.

table 25 Features checked as most important in clothing they wear by white and Negro rural and urban girls. Data: D. Dickins and V. Ferguson, *Practices and Preferences of Teen-Age Girls in the Selection of Blouses, Skirts, Dresses and Sweaters.* Miss. Agr. Exper. Sta. Bull. 636, 1962, p. 9.

between the two groups, but there are several possible explanations. It may have been caused simply by an unknown accidental variable, for instance, the girls in the Negro school might have had a lesson on color recently, so that it was uppermost in their minds. It may reflect a racial or cultural difference in which the Negro groups had a greater love of color than the white groups. More probably, this difference may be related to the component becomingness. The white girls probably had little difficulty in obtaining recommendations for becomingness of colors; magazines, textbooks on selection, and even advertisements list colors which are said to be most becoming for various hair, eye, and skin colorings. The Negro girls, on the other hand, had almost no such sources, and, in addition, they have much greater variation in skin coloring. Therefore, the greatest problem for them in the selection of clothing is in choosing a color becoming to them. More research is needed to arrive at an explanation of the difference between the two groups of subjects. To find whether or not the difference is a real one, the strata of explanation as suggested in Chapter 7 should be separated.

Ryan (49) investigated the relative importance of various components of desirability in the selection of blouses. This study was concerned primarily with explanations at the second stratum, that is, the perceived properties of attributes, but, also one factor on the first stratum—price—was included. She found that the eleventh-grade girls in her sample considered the components in order of their importance in the selection of a blouse to be becomingness, price, comfort, beauty, durability, ease-of-care and "like friends wear." The girls in the sample of the United States Department of Agriculture study gave the following reasons for choosing the last skirt or dress they bought: style (60 percent), color or print (49 percent), the needs the item would fill (40 percent), fabric or some quality of the fabric (39 percent), becomingness (31 percent), and inexpensive or on sale (20 percent). (58:27.)

Warden (64) has shown that girls want their clothes to look fashionable and expensive. Comfort and serviceability, while approved aspects, would be sacrificed if necessary for style and fashion. Dunlap (13) asked girls in what area of clothing they would like help if the opportunity were given. The highest percentage (20 percent) said they would like help on determining what was becoming and almost as many said they were interested in obtaining information which would be useful in the selection and purchasing of clothes.

Other research has concentrated on the specific attributes of garments, that is, factors on the first stratum, which are preferred by adolescents. Specific preferences for color have been investigated in many studies such as Dickins and Ferguson, Pearson. One conclusion common to many studies is that, as girls grow older, they tend to reject the brighter colors and to choose neutral or pale colors. Of Silverman's group, 35 percent preferred neutral shades at twelve while 60 percent preferred them at eighteen. Macauley (39) also found decreasing interest in bright colors with increase in age. The colors most frequently chosen for wearing by the fourteen- to eighteen-year-olds questioned by Pearson (44) were in order of preference: light blue, pink, aqua, black, red, while orange and teal were not selected as a preferred color by any of the girls.

In fiber preferences both the USDA and the Dickins-Ferguson studies showed that adolescent girls prefer cotton to other fibers for summer skirts and blouses, everyday and dress-up dresses, winter blouses and everyday dresses, and anklets. They prefer nylon for dress-length slips and petticoats and wool for winter skirts, coats, and dress-up dresses.

Preferences in line and style are difficult to evaluate because they are subject to fashion changes and are mixed with the desire to conform, but some attempts on measuring the preferences for this attribute have been made. Pearson (44), for example, found that for the girls in her study, a tailored dress or suit was first choice, a skirt and blouse second with a clinging evening gown the last choice. How much of this is true preference, how much desire to conform to what was being worn that season at school and how much to ideas of appropriateness is impossible to say.

Baldwin (4) found that for boys, the importance of comfort and color increased from the age of fifteen to nineteen, while the relative importance of the style of the garment decreased. In purchasing garments, the boys considered the same factors as girls: style, color, price, fit, comfort, and need, while their mothers emphasized durability.

Adolescent Interest in Clothing and Attitudes and Motives Toward Clothing

CLOTHING AWARENESS AND EXTENT OF INTEREST

No research is needed to tell us that clothing and personal appearance are of great interest and concern to the adolescent of fifteen years and older as well as to the young adolescent. But why is it of such great interest to him? How important is it in relation to other areas of interest and concern? At what age is his interest greatest and when does it begin to lessen? What aspects of clothing intrigue him most? What are his attitudes toward clothing? How do his attitudes and interests relate to his concept of himself and to his clothing awareness or sensitivity to clothing in social life?

We have mentioned that during adolescence there are many changes, and necessary adjustments, and the adolescent tends to feel insecure. This insecurity makes boys and girls highly sensitive to criticism and they seek approval and acceptance. As they are breaking away from the family, they desire the approval of the peer group. This tends to develop within them a deep conservatism, a tendency to conform to what they know will be accepted. Since they think in concrete rather than abstract terms, they embrace clothing as a means of demonstrating their conformity. Therefore, they are greatly interested in clothing and greatly concerned with their own physical attractiveness.

The relatively great concern over their own appearance and interest in clothing has been verified by research. Symonds (56) in 1936 published the results of a study in which 411 boys and 418 girls ranked fifteen areas of concern in order of interest and then ranked them in order of being a personal problem. In 1957 Harris (18) repeated the same experiment with 1165 high school students. The items which they were asked to rank were: (1) health, (2) sex adjustments, (3) safety, (4) money, (5) mental hygiene, (6) study habits, (7) recreation, (8) personal and moral qualities, (9) home and family relationship, (10) manners and courtesy, (11) personal attractiveness, (12) daily schedule, (13) civic interests, (14) getting along with other people, and (15) philosophy of life. In both studies, the girls ranked personal attractiveness highest in interest. In 1935, they also ranked it highest as a problem, but by 1957 it had dropped to third place as area of greatest concern. Study habits and money were, by then, greater problems for the girls. The boys ranked personal attractiveness much lower as an area of interest; they put it eighth in 1935 and ninth out of fifteen in 1957. As a problem, it was somewhat higher than as an area of interest. In both years, it was the problem which was ranked as sixth in concern for them. The results of these studies may have been influenced somewhat by the wording of the various items. "Personal attractiveness" may have connotations of femininity and, therefore, was ranked lower in interest by the boys. They might have responded differently to such words as "good looking" or "handsome." These words, of course, would have been a poor choice as far as the girls were concerned. On the other hand, if different words were used for the boys and the girls then the researcher could not be sure they were equated. Personal attractiveness is, however, first in interest for adolescent girls and, at least, of some interest to boys. Both boys and girls also ranked it relatively high as an area of concern to them.

Vener (60) found that adolescents could be ranked on a 5-point scale according to their level of "sensitivity" to clothing in social life. This scale which he calls a measure of "clothing awareness" is closely related to clothing interest or attitude toward the importance of clothing. The items included in the clothing-awareness scale were:

> How much thought and attention do you think someone your age should give to clothing?
> Do you ever want to know whether other people like or dislike your clothes?
> I don't enjoy wearing my clothes unless my friends like them.
> How often do you pay attention to the clothes you wear? [p. 8]

Girls, by this measure, demonstrated greater clothing awareness than boys, but there were no group differences between the eighth, tenth, and twelfth-grade students. Vener concludes that by early adolescence the individual has already been made conscious of the importance of clothing in social life.

He also determined that the greater the general social confidence the lower the clothing awareness. This supports our hypothesis that the greater the self-confidence, the less the need for, and hence interest in, clothing. Furthermore, for the boys, at least, those who had greater clothing awareness were less likely to feel sentiments of clothing deprivation. Vener suggests that this may be an adjustive mechanism for the individual personality. The person who feels sentiments of clothing deprivation would experience extreme frustration if he also was highly interested in clothing or was high in clothing awareness. Another result of this study was that those individuals who were high on the clothing-awareness scale were those who were most sensitive to the feelings and opinions of others.

Anastasi and Miller (2) gave a group of 100 high school students pairs of favorable characteristics of persons. The students were asked to check the one in each pair they would prefer in classmates of their own sex. "Neat in appearance," "good looking," and "good dresser" were among these characteristics. The responses of boys and girls were compared, and also the responses of college preparatory students (high scholastic and high socioeconomic background) with those not in college preparatory course (low scholastic and low socioeconomic background). Of the 30 characteristics given, "has many friends" and "friendly" received the most votes for girls and boys combined. "Neat in appearance" was 13 in the list, "good looking" 20, while "good dresser" was 28. Only "wealthy" and "will not fight or argue" were lower on the list than "good dresser." "Good dresser" was chosen twice as often by the precollege girls as it was by any other group. This group tended to choose "good dresser" instead of "neat in appearance." Thus, the data showed that neat in appearance was a more important factor in prestige than "good dresser" and (except for precollege girls) more important than "good looking." The relatively low ranking of appearance of others as an item of interest or concern and the high ranking when related to themselves points to the aspect of clothing which is of primary interest to adolescents: seemingly they are not interested in appearance and clothing per se, but only interested in improving their *own* appearance.

A number of studies have found that adolescence is the period when clothes assume their greatest importance, but no one study has attempted to determine the specific age at which the greatest interest in clothes occurs. However, we can place the age at which there is the greatest interest in clothes within a fairly narrow age range by drawing upon the results of a number of studies. Stone and Barker (54) found that interest in adornment and personal attractiveness was greater in postmenarcheal girls when the groups were matched as to chronological age. The older adolescent (eighteen years) is more interested than the young adolescent (twelve

years) according to Silverman (50). As criteria for interest, she asked girls
if they would be willing to work part time to have money for clothes and
also if they would forego social events if they did not have appropriate
clothes. Ryan (48) found that interest was higher for the high school girl
than for the college girl. She used several questions from Rosencranz's (see
Chapter 5) test for interest in clothing as criteria. Boswell (8) determined
the age of greatest interest more exactly. She found that interest increases
during adolescence from the younger to the older and is highest at the
eighteen- to nineteen-year level. Combining the findings from these studies,
we would conclude that interest in clothing rises sharply from about twelve
to approximately eighteen years when it reaches its peak. Interest in clothes
for the self gradually declines after the individual reaches about eighteen.

The degree of interest in clothing varies with a number of environmental
factors. Boswell found that it varied with the number of siblings and with
the father's education and occupation. The greater the father's education
and the higher his occupation in a socioeconomic classification, the lower the
interest in clothing. The child who had a large number of brothers and
sisters tended to have the greatest interest and those with no siblings the
least interest. These results may be partially explained by the items from
which she obtained her measure of interest. The ten items which she used to
measure interest were:

1. Learning to buy clothes for the whole family.
2. How to launder, press and repair clothes.
3. Skills to make clothes fit.
4. When it is cheaper to buy and when to make clothes.
5. How to have plan to store clothes.
6. Selecting appropriate clothes.
7. Knowing my share of the clothing money.
8. How to glamorize "hand-me-downs."
9. How to assemble clothing needs.
10. How to cut cost of clothes and keep them good looking.

An examination of the list shows that some of the items by their nature
would be of less importance to those with high socioeconomic background. It
also may be true that some might be of less interest to the younger adolescent
because the mother had the responsibility referred to in the item. This might
be true despite the fact that the adolescent was just as anxious about clothes
and just as interested in them for himself as were those who checked a
particular item.

Baumgartner (6) found that college women ascribed more importance
to clothes than did college men. The college student who came from a
higher economic background was a member of a fraternity, participated in
a greater number of activities, and ascribed greater importance to clothes,

especially dress clothes, than did the less active student from a lower economic level. The relationships between socioeconomic level and interest in clothing are the reverse of those found by Boswell, but the nature of the questions asked can easily account for the difference. Baumgartner was investigating the interest of the adolescent in clothing for himself. Further environmental factors which lead to greater or lesser interest in clothing for the self were determined by Ryan (48). These have been reviewed in Chapter 5.

SPECIFIC ATTITUDES TOWARD IMPORTANCE OF CLOTHING

Silverman (50) found that girls thought appearance and clothing were positive assets in job getting, in eligibility to clubs, in attracting boys, and in a girl's chances for marriage. "Twenty-four percent believed they could judge people to a considerable degree from their appearance, 60 percent thought they could make some deductions from externals, while 16 percent rejected the idea that such judgments could be made. It is very likely that girls feel that they themselves are judged in the same fashion, and that this feeling plays a large part in motivating them toward attention to clothing and appearance" [p. 61]. Alexander (1) confirmed these results in that 20 percent of the high school girls from her sample indicated that clothes were important because they tended to evoke favorable behavior from others. A somewhat smaller percentage (15 percent) of boys volunteered this reason for considering clothes important, while only one percent of the adult men in the sample said that they thought clothing influenced the behavior of others toward the wearer.

The reasons adolescents give for the importance of clothing vary with age and also with sex. According to results obtained by Alexander (1) boys are more apt than girls to say that clothing is important because "you are judged by how you look." In an open-ended question on why it was important to be well dressed, over half of the high schools boys gave answers which fell within this category, while between a quarter and a third of the adolescent girls gave this answer (see Table 26). The percentage who indicated that clothing was important because it meant acceptance by the group was very high for high school students but dropped greatly for the college student. On the other hand, the college student was more apt to report that clothes were important because they gave a feeling of self-confidence and well-being. This reason was given by over half of all the adolescents and by 79 percent of the college girls. When we consider that these answers were volunteered to an open-ended question, it becomes obvious that this is an extremely important point to be kept in mind when considering adolescents' clothing, that is, the most important function of clothing for the adolescent is the feeling of self-confidence and security which conforming and attractive clothing give him.

Category	High School boys n = 120	High School girls n = 189	College girls n = 714
Physical appearance	2	5	12
Expression of Personality	12	10	11
Impression			
a) evoking favorable judgment	57	24	31
b) evoking favorable behavior	15	20	9
Acceptance	40	54	15
Status (indication of)	4	5	2
Personal satisfaction (self confidence)	57	54	79

table 26 Percentage distribution of responses to questions on the importance of being well dressed. Data: Olive N. Alexander, *A Pilot Investigation of the Motives Underlying the Desire to Feel Well Dressed at Various Age Levels.* M.S. Thesis, Cornell University, 1961, p. 35.

Motivational factors in the selection and wearing of clothing by tenth- and twelfth-grade girls was investigated by Evans (16). She classified the following four motivational forces: (1) desire to depend on and be like others, (2) desire to be independent of and different from others, (3) desire to compensate for blocking elsewhere, and (4) desire to be recognized by and as superior to others. For her group the desire to be independent and different from others was most important in the purchasing of clothing, but the desire to be recognized by and superior to others was most important in the wearing of clothing.

These results did not vary with the intelligence of the respondent nor with the parents' occupation or education. However, her sample was fairly homogeneous as far as family background was concerned and the author points out that differences might be found where backgrounds were more dissimilar. She did find differences due to age and popularity. The tenth graders were more dependent than twelfth graders on parents in their clothing purchasing and less of the tenth graders reported a desire for independence. The most popular students were the most independent in their clothing behavior and the less popular students conformed most to group clothing standards. This supports our theory that the individual who is generally popular and confident of his acceptance is less dependent upon clothing.

Attitudes Toward Adequacy and Feelings of Satisfaction with Appearance. High school students generally consider themselves as well dressed as the average in their group and are basically satisfied with their wardrobes. This has been shown in a number of studies (see Dickins and Ferguson, Warden, Rosner, Silverman, Ryan). The older adolescents, or college students, are less likely to rate themselves as average. Silverman (50) found that more of the older girls tended to rate themselves either above or below the average. In Ryan's study (48) more college girls rated themselves above average and fewer rated themselves below average. The results of this study given in Table 27 for high school and college students are typical of the results found in most of the studies. Dickins and Ferguson, for example, found that 90 percent of the high school girls in their sample felt as well dressed as most girls in school; this is only 2 percent less than the figures given for the high school girl in Table 27.

	Confidence in Clothing		
Item checked	*Percent of college girls checking*	*Percent of high school girls checking*	*Percent of high school boys checking*
Extremely well dressed	3.1	1.8	5.5
Better than average	30.8	4.0	9.0
About as well as average	63.8	91.9	84.6
Poorer than average	2.3	1.5	1.0
Very poorly dressed	0.0	0.0	0.0

table 27   Data: M. S. Ryan, *Psychological Effects of Clothing: Part II, Comparison of College Students With High School Students, Rural With Urban Students, and Boys With Girls.* Cornell Agr. Exper. Sta. Bull. No. 898, 1953, pp. 5 and 19.

Vener (60) also has noted that the higher the age grade, the less the tendency to express sentiments of clothing deprivation. He states that: "In order to develop such sentiments the individual must compare himself with others in respect to certain factors of dress and judge himself deprived in relation to these others" [p. 16]. Therefore, although his measure is not concerned with whether or not the respondent feels better dressed than the average; it is comparable to the lower half of the scale of other studies, in which the respondents compared themselves with the average. There were no significant differences between the sexes concerning sentiments of clothing deprivation in this study. Vener did find, as would be expected, that the higher the father's occupational status, the less likely the adolescent was to express feelings of clothing deprivation.

Roff (46) found that self-satisfaction in general, not just in clothing or appearance, gradually declines throughout the adolescent period but begins to rise slightly at the end of adolescence (defined as twenty years). The slight rise in general confidence at twenty is perhaps reflected in other studies in the larger percentage of college girls over high school girls who rated themselves as above average on "well-dressed." However, from Roff's results, we would predict that the younger adolescents would rate themselves below the average while the results generally show that they rate themselves as dressed as well as the average.

General dissatisfaction, rather than satisfaction, in appearance was reported by Kitamura (30). His subjects were Japanese boys, 135 of whom were attending high school and 128 were college students. The results analyzed by age are in Table 28.

	Appearance Rating				
Age	*Satisfied*	*Dissatisfied*	*Unsettled*	*Indifferent*	*No Answer*
	PERCENT				
13–14	2	8	2	88	0
15–16	5	28	17	48	2
17–18	23	26	29	21	1
19–20	12	32	41	14	1

table 28 Data: Seiro Kitamura. On the feelings of satisfaction and dissatisfaction with one's own appearance and disposition. *Tohoku Psychologia Folia.* XII(3–4), 1951, p. 73.

It can be seen from the table that there is a marked decline with age in the percentage feeling indifferent about their looks. This agrees with other studies that interest in appearance increases during adolescence. The column labeled "unsettled" refers to those who qualify their statements. That is, they are satisfied with their appearance in some ways or at some times and dissatisfied in other ways or at other times. The discrepancy between these results and those of Silverman, Ryan, and others may reflect a cultural difference. On the other hand, different methods may tap different factors. Only more experimentation will tell which is the reason for the discrepancy.

In another study, Ryan (48) compared the individual college girls' rating of her appearance with a group's rating of her appearance and her estimate of the group rating. Twenty-eight groups, each composed of eight college students, were used as subjects. There were four rating scales which had to do with appearance: (1) well dressed, (2) appearance of face, (3) appearance of figure, and (4) individuality in dress. The most common pattern of results was agreement between the girl's rating, the median of the group's rating, and her estimate of the group's rating. In other words, the individuals usually gave themselves the same rating as the group gave them.

They also tended to estimate the group's rating accurately. The girls from larger cities and from higher economic backgrounds tended to be rated higher (both by themselves and by the group) on the well-dressed scale than did girls from smaller towns or lower economic levels. On all of the rating scales, there was a highly significant relationship between an individual's interest in clothes and both her self-rating and the median group rating.

Satisfaction with one's wardrobe is related to a number of other factors. Ryan (48) found positive relationships between satisfaction with wardrobe and the number of garments in it, interest in clothing, choosing one's own clothes, and the size of the home town.

As we have seen, Vener found no significant differences between the sexes and feelings of clothing deprivation, but he did find that the higher the occupation of the father, the older the adolescent, and the greater the organizational activity, the less tendency there was for the adolescent to have feelings of clothing deprivation.

Baumgartner (6) found *no* relationship between satisfaction with their wardrobes and the sex of the students, fraternity membership, college in the university, amount of social participation, economic background, expenditure for clothing, or size of the home town. However, those who earned all of their own money for college were less satisfied with their wardrobes than those who did not need to earn their expenses.

There is a contradiction between the results of the Baumgartner and the Ryan studies on the relationship between the size of the home town and confidence in clothing. There is also a contradiction in that Ryan found satisfaction varied with the number of garments in the wardrobe, while Baumgartner found no significant relationship with expenditure for clothing. The differences in results of these two studies may be differences in the way the questions were asked or it may be due to differences in sample. Baumgartner's sample included both men and women from a state university in the Midwest, while Ryan's sample included just women from a university in the East, some of whom were in state colleges and some in the endowed colleges (that is, some obtained free tuition while others did not). These same explanations may account for differences between Vener's and the Baumgartner results on relationships between satisfaction with wardrobe or feelings of clothing deprivation, (1) the economic background of the respondent, and (2) social participation.

The Effects of Clothing on the Adolescent

Satisfaction or dissatisfaction with clothing probably has greater effects upon the mood and actions of the individual during adolescence than at any other period of his life. This follows naturally from his heightened interest in clothes and his anxiety to be accepted by his peers.

Above all else, the adolescent's self-confidence is affected by his evaluation of his own appearance. If he feels well-dressed he is more apt to be relaxed and confident in any social situation, while if he believes that he is poorly or inappropriately dressed he is ill at ease, self-conscious and worried about what others are thinking of him. Many writers both in fiction and autobiography have described the humiliation brought about by the wrong clothes.

Silverman (50) included two sets of statements in her questionnaire which related to this aspect of the psychology of clothing for the adolescent girl. One statement related to the negative side—feeling ill at ease or uncomfortable because of clothing. Over 50 percent reported that they sometimes felt uncomfortable because of their clothes and 11 percent said that they often felt ill at ease and did not have a good time because of their clothing. In response to statements on the positive side, 76 percent said that "knowing she had a good appearance gave a girl a great feeling of self-confidence."

Vener (60) examined the relationship between confidence in the social situation and feelings of clothing deprivation and found that the greater the social confidence, the less likely the individual was to express sentiments of clothing deprivation.

Ryan (48) asked high school girls and boys and college girls concerning the effects of feeling well or poorly dressed upon their mood and actions and upon their enjoyment of a specific occasion (that is, the last time they were on a date). Table 29 shows a comparison of the latter for the high school girls and college girls.

A difference in age seems to make a difference in the confidence in clothing and in its effect on the wearer. As a girl becomes older, she apparently

Item	College Girls	High School Girls
Worried, ill at ease	.8	10.6
Costume nondescript, felt uninteresting	.9	2.6
Uncomfortable, hampered	2.3	3.0
Comfortable, relaxed	15.6	15.5
Self-confident, forgot clothes	42.6	43.4
Looked well—gave a lift	31.8	12.8
No effect	5.8	11.7

table 29 Effects of clothing on enjoyment of specific occasion. Percentage distribution. Data: M. S. Ryan. *Psychological Effects of Clothing Part II. Comparison of College Students with High School Students.* Cornell Un. Agr. Exper. Sta. Bull. No. 898, 1953, p. 12.

is more confident of her appearance and is more happy because of it, while the younger adolescent is less confident and so more apt to be embarrassed or worried and ill at ease. On a specific occasion, 13 percent of the college girls and only 6 percent of the high school girls reported that they felt they looked well and so were talkative and "peppier." On the other hand, just 2 percent of the college girls, but nearly 12 percent of the high school girls, felt self-conscious about their clothes which made them quieter.

Results for high school boys were very similar to those for high school girls. The boys were embarrassed by their clothes just as often as the girls and were conscious of their clothes about the same proportion of the time. On the specific occasion, they were affected in approximately the same ways and as frequently as were the girls.

In another part of her study, Ryan (48) interviewed nearly 100 college girls. They were asked to recall a social event at which they felt extremely well dressed and a similar occasion at which they felt very poorly dressed. Over 96 percent were able to recall such occasions, and of these, 82 percent said their mood and enjoyment of the occasion were affected and over 58 percent said that their actions were affected. The girls were giving extreme examples, but the percentages are so high that they make it evident that clothing is an important factor in the enjoyment of a social situation.

The students described a variety of ways in which feeling especially well-dressed affected their moods. The most common effect, mentioned by nearly half of the group, was that they felt more confident and so they were relaxed, comfortable and at ease. The next largest group, composed of over one-third of the respondents, said that they were happier, gayer, in higher spirits, more light hearted or in a better mood. A few said they felt friendlier and several felt "slightly peacockish" and had a desire to show off. The most common effect of feeling well dressed on their actions was that they were more active participants in the event, that is, they moved about more among people, tried to meet people, were more talkative and better company. Others said that they were "more vivacious" or "peppier" or "gay." A few tried to call attention to themselves.

On describing the situation when they felt poorly dressed, the majority described their mood as "worried," "bothered," "ill at ease," "uncomfortable." Others reported an overawareness of their clothes, they spent most of the time "wondering what people thought" or "wondering if they were looking at me." A number also said that they were irritable. Many said they "wanted to go home," "to shrink," "to stay out of sight," or "to sit in the corner." This was shown very markedly in their reports of the effects on their actions—nearly all reported some sort of withdrawal from the group.

The slight withdrawal from the center of attention or active participation is much more common than the actual refusal to attend a social function. Silverman found that none of the younger adolescents but 31 percent of the eighteen-year-old girls had refused invitations because they did not have adequate or appropriate clothing. Approximately the same percentage of Ryan's group of high school girls reported that they had refused to go to social events because of clothing. The college girls were much less apt to refuse because of clothing, over 85 percent reported that they never refused for this reason. The difference here may be one of socio-economic background. The college girls, because they were from a higher economic group, may have always had more adequate clothing. Feeling well or poorly dressed may also influence the number of organizations which the adolescent joins. Vener found that the greater the adolescent's organizational activity the less his tendency to express sentiments of clothing deprivation.

SOCIAL PARTICIPATION AS RELATED TO CLOTHING

The amount of organizational participation is dependent upon the way others perceive the appearance of the adolescent, as well as upon his own feelings of being well or poorly dressed. In the chapter on early adolescence we reviewed a number of research articles which dealt with personal appearance as a factor in social acceptance. Several of these studies used older as well as younger adolescents. Cannon and Staples (10), for example, worked with boys and girls from senior as well as junior high schools and found that there was a significant relationship between appearance and acceptability for the senior high school girls. Kuhlen and Lee (31) also used twelfth graders as well as younger adolescents. When the quarter most popular twelfth graders were compared with the quarter least popular, 77 percent of the popular boys and 83 percent of the popular girls were characterized by the group as neat and clean; also 66 percent of the popular boys and 59 percent of the popular girls were good looking. All of these percentages are somewhat lower than they were for the ninth graders. This would suggest that looks are less noticeably important at the end of high school than they were during early adolescence. Appearance, however, does seem to be related to leadership at the senior high school level.

Silverman (50) asked teachers to evaluate their students on six aspects of appearance: (1) cleanliness of person and clothing, (2) taste in clothing, (3) grooming, (4) neatness, (5) appropriateness of clothing, and (6) bearing or poise in bodily carriage. The teachers rated each student on a five-point scale on each of these attributes of appearance. The composite appearance ratings were ranked in descending order and those cases falling in the upper and lower 25 percent of the distribution were compared. She found that the poor-appearance group had an average of 2.7 extracurricular activities over a three-year period while the good-appearance group had an average of 5.8 activities (50:77). The good-appearance group not only tended to be "joiners," but apparently they were more active in the groups they joined. The good-appearance group had held a total of 35 offices in the preceding three years and the poor appearance only 4. Although part of this might be accounted for simply because they were in more activities and so had more chances of becoming officers, the difference is greater than would be expected by chance.

The withdrawal from active participation in various social activities may be of even greater consequence than participation versus nonparticipation. One wonders how many adolescents have refused to volunteer in class, to recite, or to voice their ideas in clubs and groups because they did not wish to call attention to themselves. It is recognized that the person who speaks up once or twice in a group finds it easier to do so again, while the individual who has not become accustomed to speaking out finds it much more difficult to do so; thus the reactions from feeling poorly dressed may have lasting effects.

Research on the problem of active versus passive participation as related to clothing deprivation is extremely difficult; there are many variables which influence whether or not the adolescent actively participates and it is difficult to devise an experiment in which the clothing variable is isolated. One bit of research[1] points to a positive relationship between confidence in appearance and active participation in class discussion. The members of a high school class were asked to rate themselves and all of the other members of the class on appearance. An individuals' score for confidence in dress was obtained by comparing her rating of herself to the average of her ratings for the rest of the class. A measure of active participation was obtained by averaging the teacher's ratings of student participation in class discussions on two different occasions. All of the girls in the upper third of the class on participation felt that they were as well or better dressed than the average girl in the class. Those who rated themselves below the median rating tended to be in the lower third of the class on participation. These results might, of course, be due to a third factor which was not controlled. For example, it may be that the more intelligent student is the one who is both better dressed and participates more actively in class because she knows the answers. This study, while not conclusive, does set up a hypothesis which should be investigated. With the continued improvement in research techniques, such a problem may shortly be not only desirable but also feasible.

When we are discussing participation either in the number of activities attended or in the degree of active participation, we must remember that most studies are dealing with selected samples. We know, of course, that the college group is highly selected both on the socioeconomic scale and degree of intelli-

---

[1] Martha Miller and C. Swanson. Unpublished project for a graduate seminar at Cornell Univ.

gence. The high school group, also, is selected in that those of the lowest socio-economic group and lowest intelligence may have dropped out of school and so are not included in the sample. A newspaper columnist reports that one of the causes of quitting school is expense and lists clothing as one of the costs, but gives no figures on the incidence of this. Data of this sort should be obtainable and would be of value.

CLOTHING AND DELINQUENCY

There is belief that the adolescent's great interest and need for clothing may lead to or encourage delinquency. Hollingworth says that a "considerable amount of delinquency among adolescents, especially among girls, is directly traceable to the intense craving for the right clothes" [22:114]. Since clothing is, as we have seen, of such great importance to the adolescent, we would agree that it might very well be a contributing factor in delinquency.

There is also widespread belief in educational circles that confidence in clothing not only influences attendance and participation in extracurricular events, but that the type of clothing also effects the behavior of the adolescent. Numerous schools have instituted regulations for clothing or have encouraged the pupils to formulate "codes" which include suggestions for appropriate dress. Towley (59), for example, describes a school in which the student council voted "to reverse the trend in sloppy dress." He reports that today there's no question of improper dress, the students, especially the girls, like it much better, and the faculty believe behavior has improved with dress.

A newspaper report from Ottawa, Canada, describes student-sponsored "dress-up days," together with "official crackdown on ducktail haircuts, blue-jeans and heavy make-up." The high school principal says that "dress-up days have a good over-all effect; there is a definite relationship between good grooming and good behavior with discipline problems cut down when students dress up." The relationship between clothes and behavior in high school has been on the agenda for conventions of principals, discussed in many P.T.A. programs and in magazine articles.

Another interesting hypothesis is put forward in Langner (34). He suggests that juvenile delinquency is associated with certain types of clothes; juvenile gangs have certain jackets, sweaters, or emblems which identify members as belonging to the gang and from these adolescents derive a kind of courage. He feels that he is part of the gang, protected by it, and that others will hesitate to harm him when they see he is part of the gang. Thus, he dares to commit acts that he would not otherwise.

All of these are extremely plausible hypotheses, but they are as yet only hypotheses and not proven facts. Although many principals and teachers report that with improved dress there is improved behavior, we need more than this to prove that improvement in one leads to improvement in the other. The reporting teachers or principals may have been biased; because they expected that they would see improvement in behavior on dress-up days, they found it. Also, the students may have been better behaved because they thought they were being watched or observed in their dress-up clothes. While we think that even if these factors were controlled, we would still find improvement in behavior with better clothing and grooming, it needs to be proved.

THE EFFECT OF COLOR AND LINE ON MOOD AND ACTIONS

Another way in which clothing may affect the mood or actions of the adolescent is in the color, line, texture or style of the costume. In other words, a girl might feel equally well dressed in a slim gray wool dress and in a full-skirted red-taffeta dress, but her mood might be quite different in the two dresses, and because her mood was different we might find that her behavior was different. Very little work has been done on this phase of dress. Ryan (48) asked high school boys and girls and college girls if their mood was influenced by various colors, textures, and types of costume and if the answer was "yes," they were asked to give examples. The answers showed that 66 percent of the college girls, 40 percent of the high school girls, and 32 percent of the high school boys felt that their mood was affected by these factors. They said colors influenced their mood more often than the texture or type of costume. The most frequent examples given by both boys and girls were that bright colors, especially red, induced a gay mood. The principle difference between the examples given by the high school girl and the college girl was that the high school girl often said that black made her feel sad and depressed, while the college girl reported that she felt older and sophisticated in black. This method of attempting to determine the relationship between mood and color or type of costume is very crude, and, because each subject gave only one or two examples, we have no way of knowing the relative number of adolescents affected in the same way by specific colors, textures or styles. The results indicate, however, that this might be a field which would warrant further study.

We have reviewed some of the ways in which clothing may affect behavior. Let us now consider whether these are equally true for all adolescents or whether it varies from one adolescent to another. Obviously, the answer is that all adolescents are not alike in the effects of clothing upon their behavior. As we might expect, it varies first of all with their interest and attitudes about the importance of clothing. Those who think clothing is important because others will judge them on looks or because they will be more acceptable to others if well dressed are more likely to be affected than are those who think clothing is important for other reasons.

We have suggested earlier the hypothesis that the greater the individual's sense of security and social acceptance the less his need for, and interest in, clothes. It follows from this that he would be less affected by clothes. The high school football hero who knows he is accepted may be less conforming than the majority of students and not be disturbed by different clothing. If this theory is true, it may very well explain why clothing is of greater importance during adolescence than during other periods. We have noted that adolescence is a time of insecurity. It would therefore follow, according to this theory, that it would be a period of heightened interest in clothing and also a period in which clothes have a greater effect upon the individual. This theory would not only account for differences between individuals, but also why clothing is more important to a given individual on one occasion than another. The individual would be indifferent to what he wore with his own family or special gang in which he knew he was accepted. He would, however, be more affected by his clothes on occasions when he was not sure of his acceptance.

There is a bit of evidence to support this last hypothesis. A college student interviewed a number of her peers as they were dressing for dates. Each respondent was interviewed three to five different times over a period of several weeks. A girl felt concerned about her clothing, planned far ahead, worried more about what to wear, and so on, when she was dating a boy for the first time or when she was going to be with a group she didn't know well, was much less concerned and did not worry about what to wear when getting ready for a date with a boy she knew well. Van Konynenburg (61) also found that the college girl was apt to dress up more if she were attending an event where she would meet strangers. This theory concerning the relationship between general security and the effects of clothing should be put to experimental proof.

Fad and Fashion Leadership

We have noted that adolescents are more anxious to conform to their own group in matters of dress than any other age group. There is not only less deviation in dress, but there are more fads adopted by high school students than by any other group. Many of the fads are never even noticed by adults. It may be the buckling or unbuckling of a strap on the back of pants, the way socks are rolled, or when to wear or not to wear certain colors. For example, I was unaware that certain colors were completely taboo on certain days until my daughter asked what to wear to school. I suggested a certain outfit and in horror she said "but it's Monday so I can't wear green." (I may very likely have the day or the color wrong.) After my expression of surprise, she listed a number of such regulations which would not be apparent to the casual observer but which were rigidly followed by her peers.

It is surprising that since fads and fashion are so important a part of adolescent life, we do not have more research data on them, and on adolescent fashion leaders. We do have a few studies on fad and fashion leaders of the college age group and we have discussed Glickman's study of fashion leaders among early adolescent boys. However, I know of no important study of fad or fashion leaders pertaining to the senior high school age group.

Janney (27) conducted a very interesting study of fad and fashion leadership among college women. Several college girls were observers and reported on 67 clothing fads. These observers noted who started the fad and who did or did not follow it. The overwhelming majority didn't originate fads, but did follow them. Those who did not follow were in general insensitive and unskillful in other types of social situations. The originators of fads were members of prestige-bearing cliques and were generally leaders in other types of activities. They also tended to be popular with men. Different types of fads were originated by leaders from separate cliques and this disparity in type of fad seemed to be congruent to the clique's type of social activity. For example, those who started the bizarre fads were apt to be interested in dramatics and related activities. There were also a few girls who attempted to start fads but no one followed them, in fact, the observers reported that whenever these girls took up a fad, it was dropped by others.

Fashion leadership among college men was investigated by Sohn (51). The leaders in this study were determined by asking members of the seven fraternities having the highest prestige to name the students whose clothes they admired, and whom they would consult about clothes. The individuals who obtained the highest score did *not* seem to differ from others in the number of organizations they belonged to, the number of dates they had, size of home town, whether they had older brothers or were taller. The leaders tended to have a higher personal income but this was not a significant difference. The only difference which Sohn found between clothing leaders and nonleaders was that clothing leaders were more apt to be leaders in other ways. This supports Janney's results that fashion leaders are leaders in other areas as well.

Family Relationships Related to Clothing

There is apparently less conflict between parents and older adolescents than between parents and younger adolescents. Perhaps by fifteen, girls have sufficiently experimented with cosmetics, hair arrangements, and clothes and have developed better taste and judgment, thus giving parents less reason to nag. Perhaps by the time her daughter is fifteen, the mother has admitted to herself that her daughter is growing up and should have greater independence. Whatever the reason, we do find less conflict. Block (7), for example, found that none of the statements concerning conflict over clothing or appearance were checked by eleventh- and twelfth-grade students as disturbing to them. In general, she found that there was a decrease in the total number of conflicts between children and parents from the seventh through the tenth grade, but an increase in the eleventh and twelfth grades. However, the increased conflict between parents and older adolescents was apparently not over clothing or appearance.

Where conflicts exist, we have some indications of the cause. From the

Purdue Opinion Polls (45) we see that adolescents feel more strongly than parents that they should be allowed to choose their own clothes. The tenth-graders in Block's study reported that their mothers "complain about how I comb my hair." This was more often checked by the tenth graders as something which disturbed them than any of the 50 other statements. Frustrations among adolescents stem from parents imposing standards of dress which do not conform to the group, according to King (29), who investigated the role of clothing in family relationships of 25 families.

Mead (41) determined areas of disagreement between adolescent girls and their families by giving a questionnaire to 100 high school girls and their mothers. She found that the majority (greater for mothers than daughters) enjoyed shopping together and that they usually agreed on where to shop and what to buy. However, 90 percent of the mothers thought that their daughters wanted them along, while 50 percent of the girls preferred to shop either alone or with a friend. Mothers and daughters did not agree on the importance of 8 various factors in clothing. The mother placed quality, comfort and durability as most important with conformity least important. The girls, on the other hand, thought cost, conformity, quality and becomingness most important with quantity and ease of care least important. In the actual selection of a garment, however, mothers and daughters generally agreed on specific aspects. For example, there was general agreement on whether the garment fit well or did not fit. They also usually agreed on what was appropriate for a given occasion. It would appear from this study, that, although the mothers and daughters had different values these usually did not create conflicts in the actual selection of garments.

Relationship between Clothing Behavior and Personality

One reason adolescents give for the importance they place on clothing is that it is a means of expressing personality. As we have seen in Chapter 4, we have little research evidence to support the belief that the wearing of specific colors or styles is associated with definite personality traits. We do have evidence, however, that there are relationships between personality traits and broader clothing behaviors, attitudes toward clothing, or problems related to clothing in the adolescent.

Pearson (44) used the Bernreuter Personality Inventory Test as a measure of personality. She compared various scores from this test with preferences for lines and color in clothing and whether or not the individual was wearing becoming clothes at the interview. While there were no positive relationships between specific preferences and personality traits, she found that subjects having the greatest range of color preference tended to be well-balanced emotionally, extroverted, and dominated others, while those who concentrated their preference on the smallest range of colors tended to dislike solitude and to seek advice often. She also found that the group classified by the Bernreuter scale as being emotionally stable were more apt to be wearing becoming lines.

Silverman (50) used part of the Sheviakov and Friedberg questionnaire on "Interests and Activities" as a measure of personality of eleventh- and twelfth-grade girls. Ratings by teachers (see p. 293) were used as a measure of appearance. Comparing the top 25 percent in appearance with the lowest 25 percent, differences in personality between the groups were evident. The poor-appearance group showed greater dislike for items indicating leadership or the desire to occupy a position of prominence. This group also had a greater dislike for items relating to drama or fantasy and for interest in participation in activities with the same or opposite sex. In other words, the poor-appearance group apparently dislike, resent, or fear other people. At the same time, they have less regard for themselves. The good appearance group, on the other hand, showed that they enjoyed being with others and were interested in participating in activities with both the same and opposite sex. The good-appearance group also tended to be somewhat higher in intelligence.

Mohr (42) and Hollingworth (22) have both compared the intelligence of adolescents and their beauty. Mohr correlated the IQ and scholastic records of a group of college students with the way in which they were rated on beauty by students from another college. She found a positive, but very low, correlation between beauty and intelligence. Hollingworth found a positive relationship between beauty and intelligence; she asked judges to rate pictures on beauty of two groups of students—one highly intelligent and the other of average intelligence. These two studies and other research have shown that there is some correlation between appearance as rated by others and intelligence. Perhaps it is because both are related to good health, or some other factor; or it may be that greater intelligence leads individuals to be better groomed and thus improve their looks. Just what causes this relationship is still unknown.

Ryan (48) compared scores on the Bernreuter Personality Inventory with self and group ratings on appearance. There was a significant positive relationship between dominance and a high self rating on well dressed. There was also a slight tendency for those who scored high in self-confidence and in self-sufficiency to rate themselves as high on the well-dressed scale. The group's rating of a girl's appearance was not significantly related to any personality factors.

Bews, in another part of Ryan's study (48:III), gave the Rorschach test to a small sample of 10 girls, 5 of whom had shown a high interest in clothing and 5 very little interest. Since the sample was very small, the results are not conclusive and are merely suggestive. There were no indications of differences in severity of problems for the two groups but some differences in mode of adjustment. The low-interest group tended to be less swayed by emotion and less dependent upon the environment for stimulation, while the high-interest group seemed to be thrown more on the environment for its adjustment and tended to emphasize modes of adjustment closely related to overt patterning of behavior.

The relationship between personality and problems in clothing and appearance was studied by Stepat (52). She used the Washburn Social-Adjustment inventory, the Minnesota Personality Scale, the Mooney Problem Checklist and a clothing-problem checklist. Those who had the fewest problems in the clothing area also had the fewest problems in general, were better adjusted and had broader interests. Those who had a large number of problems in clothing were less well adjusted, often unhealthy, and were dissatisfied with their social life. There were few correlations between specific problems in the clothing area and specific problems in personality.

In the above studies several different "tests of personality" have been used. Obviously the results are influenced by the particular tests. Unfortunately, psychologists have not been able to devise a personality test as yet which is acceptable to all, nor one which repeated use has proven high in both reliability and validity. At this point, in reviewng any research in this area we must keep in mind that other personality tests might give varying results.

The only relationships established by research findings between personality and clothing have been of a very general nature, as given here. We do not know entirely which is cause and which effect. For example, the positive correlation between attractive looks and interest in social activities may be because both are caused by some third factor such as intelligence or socioeconomic background; or it may be that the high interest in social activities is caused by the attractive appearance because the attractive looking person has been accepted socially and so learned to enjoy them. On the other hand, it may be that the person who is interested in social activities has learned how to make herself or himself more attractive in appearance.

Bibliography

1. Alexander, Olive Ness. *A Pilot Investigation of the Motives Underlying the Desire to Feel Well-Dressed at Various Age Levels.* M.S. Thesis, Cornell Univer., 1961.
2. Anastasi, A., and Miller, S. Adolescent "prestige factors" in relation to scholastic and socioeconomic variables. *J. of Soc. Psychol.* 29, 1949, 43–50.
3. Baber, R. E. Some mate selection of standards of college students and their parents. *J. of Soc. Hygiene.* 22, 1936, 115–125.
4. Baldwin, Lois Madden. *A Study of Clothing Problems of the Teenage Boy.* M.S. Thesis, Virginia Polytechnic Inst., 1960.
5. Barr, E. DeYoung. A psychological analysis of fashion motivation. *Archives of Psychol.* 171, 1934.

6. Baumgartner, Charlotte W. *Factors Associated with Clothing Consumption Among College Freshmen.* Ph. D. Thesis, Ohio State Univer., 1961.
7. Block, Virginia Lee. Conflicts of adolescents with their mothers. *J. of Abn. Psychol.* 32, 1937, 193–206.
8. Boswell, Mary Middletown. *Background Variables Affecting the Clothing Interests of High School Girls in Metropolitan Groups.* M.S. Thesis, Texas State College, 1958.
9. Cadden, Vivian. Do clothes make the boy or girl? *Parent's Mag.* 32, 1957, 40–42+.
10. Cannon, K. L., Staples, R., and Carlson, I. Personal appearance as a factor in social acceptance. *J. of Home Ec.* 44, 1952, 710–713.
11. Chittenden, Gertrude, Murphy, M. N., Hamilton, A., Forrest, P. E., and Patterson, M. Developmental tasks: how we can help. *J. of Home Ec.* 45, 1953, 579–583.
12. Coleman, Frances. How high school girls buy clothing. *J. of Home Ec.* 31, 1939, 99–100.
13. Dunlap, Mabel. What high school girls want to know about their clothing. *Prac. Home. Ec.* 8, 1930, 139–140.
14. Dickins, Dorothy and Ferguson, V. *Practices and Preferences of Teen-Age Girls in the Selection of Blouses, Skirts, Dresses, and Sweaters.* State College, Miss.: Miss. Agr. Exper. Sta. Bull. 636, 1962, 32p.
15. Elliot, Grace L. *Understanding the Adolescent Girl.* New York: Holt, Rinehart and Winston, Inc., 1930, 134p.
16. Evans, Evelyn. Motivations underlying clothing selection and wearing. *J. of Home Ec.* 56, 1964, 739–743.
17. Gillespie, Vera. *The Clothing Buying Practices of a Group of High School Girls and Implications for Consumer Education in High School Classes in Massena, New York.* Unpublished study, Cornell Univer., 1941.
18. Harris, Dale B. Life problems and interests of adolescents in 1935 and 1957. *The School Rev.* 1959, 335–343.
19. Harris, Dale B. *Sex Differences in the Life Problems and Interests of Adolescents in 1935–57,* Chapter 8 in *The Adolescent—A Book of Readings,* by Seidman, Jerome, (ed.), New York: Holt, Rinehart and Winston, Inc., 1960.
20. Hoffman, Adeline. College clothing expenditures. *J. of Home Ec.* 52(8), 1960, 665–666.
21. Hollingworth, Leta S. The comparative beauty of the faces of highly intelligent adolescents. *J. of Genetic Psychol.* 47, 1935, 268–281.
22. Hollingworth, Leta S. *The Psychology of the Adolescent.* New York: Appleton-Century-Crofts, Inc., 1928, 259p.
23. Hoult, Thomas Ford. Experimental measurement of clothing as a factor in some social ratings of selected American men. *Amer. Soc. Rev.* 19, 1954, 324–328.
24. Hurlock, E. B. Motivation in fashion. *Archives of Psychol.* 111, 1929.
25. Hurlock, E. B. *Adolescent Development.* New York: McGraw-Hill Book Company, Inc., 1955, 590p.

26. Hurst, Patsy Ruth. *Factors Influencing the Clothing Buying Habits of Teenage Girls.* M.S. Thesis, Univer. of Okla., 1958.

27. Janney, J. E. Fad and fashion leadership among undergraduate women. *J. of Abn. Psychol.* 36, 1941, 275–278.

28. Johnson, Adelaide. The adolescent and his problems. *Amer. J. of Occup. Therapy.* 11(4), Part II, 1957, 255–261.

29. King, Bernice. *A Study of the Role of Clothing in Family Relationships in 25 Selected Families.* M.S. Thesis, Mich. State Univer., 1949.

30. Kitamura, Seiro. On the feelings of satisfaction and dissatisfaction with one's own appearance and disposition. *Tohoku Psychologica Folia.* XII(3–4), 1951, 67–81.

31. Kuhlen, R. G. and Lee, B. J. Personality characteristics and social acceptance in adolescence. *J. of Ed. Psychol.* 34, 1943, 321–340.

32. Kuhlen, R. G. *The Psychology of Adolescent Development.* New York: Harper & Row, Publishers, 1952, 675p.

33. Kuhlen, R. G. Sociometric status and personal problems of adolescents. *Sociometry.* 10, 1947, 122–132.

34. Langner, Lawrence. *The Importance of Wearing Clothes.* New York: Hastings House, 1959, 349p.

35. Leonard, Eugenie A. *Problems of Freshmen College Girls.* Bureau of Pub., Teachers College, Columbia Univer., 1932.

36. Lokken, D. E. *External Influences Affecting Clothing Worn by High School and College Men.* M.S. Thesis, Oregon State Univer., 1961.

37. Lucas, Hattie Thomas. *A Study of the Clothing Practices of a Group of Negro High School Girls and the Implications for Consumer Education in High School Clothing Classes in Newport News, Virginia.* M.S. Thesis, Cornell Univer., 1953.

38. Lynd, R. S., and Lynd, H. M. *Middletown: A Study in Contemporary American Culture.* New York: Harcourt, Brace & World, Inc., 1929, 550p.

39. Macaulay, E. Some notes on the attitude of children to dress. *Brit. J. Med Psychol.* 9, 1929, 150–158.

40. Mayer, Sister Marie Lawrence. Clothing inventories of 41 teenage girls. *J. of Home Ec.* 49(2), 1957, 124.

41. Mead, Marjorie Elaine. *Disagreements Between Adolescent Girls and Their Mothers Concerning Clothing.* M.S. Thesis, Iowa State College, 1957.

42. Mohr, Anna, and Lund, Frederick H. Beauty as related to intelligence and educational achievement. *J. of Soc. Psychol.* 4, 1933, 235–239.

43. O'Donnell, F. F. The adolescent and his clothes. *Parent's Mag.* 6, 1931, 20, 21, 51.

44. Pearson, Lois Helman. Teenagers' preferences in clothes. *J. of Home Ec.* 42, 1950, 801–802.

45. Remmers, H. H., and Radler, D. H. *The American Teenager.* Indianapolis: The Bobbs-Merrill Company, Inc., 1957, 267p.

46. Roff, Catherine. *The Self Concept in Adolescent Girls.* Ph.D. Thesis, Boston Univer., 1959.

47. Rosner, Ann. *A Survey of Clothing Preferences and Buying Practices of 100 Girls of Roosevelt High School in Chicago, Illinois.* M.S. Thesis, Mich. State College, 1954.

48. Ryan, Mary S. *Psychological Effects of Clothing: Part I, II, III, and IV.* Cornell Univer. Agr. Exper. Sta. Bull. 882, 898, 900, 905, 1952–54.

49. Ryan, Mary S. *Factors Relating to Satisfaction with Girls' Blouses and Slips: A Comparison of Mothers' and Adolescent Daughters' Opinions.* Cornell Univer. Agr. Exper. Sta. Bull. 1003, May, 1965.

50. Silverman, S. *Clothing and Appearance, Their Psychological Implications for Teen Age Girls.* New York: Bureau of Publications, Teachers College, Columbia Univer., 1945, 140p.

51. Sohn, Marjorie Ann. *Personal and Social Characteristics of Clothing Fashion Leaders Among Fraternity Men.* M.S. Thesis, Penna. State Univer., 1959.

52. Stepat, Dorothy. *A Study of Clothing and Appearance Problems in Relation to Some Aspects of Personality and Some Cultural Patterns in a Group of College Freshman Girls.* Ph.D. Thesis, New York Univer., 1949.

53. Stolz, Herbert S. How appearance affects personality. *Parent's Mag.* 17, 1942, 20–21, 34, 84.

54. Stone, C. P., and Barker, R. G. The attitudes and interests of pre-menarcheal and post-menarcheal girls. *J. of Genetic Psychol.* 54, 1939, 27–71.

55. Symonds, P. M. Sex differences in the life problems and interests of adolescents. *School and Soc.* 43, 1936, 751–752.

56. Symonds, P. M. Life problems and interests of adolescents. *The School Rev.* 44, 1936. 506–518.

57. Teen leaders and where they're leading. *Men's Wear.* July 10, 1964, 76.

58. *Teenage Girls Discuss Their Wardrobes, and Their Attitude Toward Cotton and Other Fibers.* Marketing Research Report, 155, U.S. Dept. of Agr., 1957.

59. Towley, Carl. Manners improve with change of dress. *Minn. J. of Ed.* 37, 1957, 25.

60. Vener, Arthur M., and Hoffer, Charles R. *Adolescent Orientations to Clothing.* Technical Bull. 270, Mich. State Univer., Agr. Exper. Sta., March 1959, 30p.

61. Van Konynenburg, Kathleen. *A Study of Selected Clothing Practices of Cornell Junior Women.* M.S. Thesis, Cornell Univer., 1961.

62. Waldron, Joyce Jean. *Clothing Buying Practices of the 11th and 12th Grade Girls of Wyandotte High School and the Opinions of the Girls and Their Mothers Regarding These Practices.* M.S. Thesis, Okla. State Univer., 1961.

63. Warden, Jessie. Some desires or goals for clothing of college women. *J. of Home Ec.* 49, 1957, 795.

64. Warden, Jessie. *Some Factors Affecting the Satisfaction and Dissatisfaction with Clothing of Women Students in the College of Education and*

the College of the Liberal Arts. Ph.D. Thesis, Penna. State Univer., 1955.

65. Wax, Murray. Themes in cosmetics and grooming. *Amer. J. of Soc.* 62(6), 1957, 588–593.

66. Zachry, Caroline, and Lighty, Margaret. *Emotion and Conduct in Adolescence.* New York: Appleton-Century-Crofts Co., Inc., 1940, 563p.

Chapter 14

Psychological Implications
of Clothing for the Elderly

We are skipping from the adolescent to the elderly with no specific mention of the greatest portion of the life cycle—the years between twenty and sixty-five. This is done, not because there are no differences in psychological implications of clothing within these years, but because there are so few research studies on the social-psychological aspects of clothing within this period. The material covered in Part I of this book is concerned mainly with adult years. Until we have studies which differentiate age groups within this broad period of life, we will need to use these general studies on psychology of clothing as applying to the entire period.

There is one study (5) on the late middle-aged group which deals with figure changes. In a sample of 361 women aged forty-five to sixty-five, over half of the respondents said that they had gained weight after reaching forty-five. An even higher percentage (64) checked an increased waistline. This was the figure change checked by the largest number of respondents, and, as we will see, it is even a greater problem for the woman over sixty-five.

We do have many research projects on various characteristics and factors pertaining to the elderly. According to Donahue (11), there were 90 listings on gerontology in the *Psychological Abstracts* for the years between 1940–45, while between 1950–55 there were 442 such listings—an increase of over 400 percent. This increase may be due in part to the increased number and severity of problems for the elderly, but probably it is primarily due to the great increase in the number of elderly persons in the population. The proportion of the population sixty-five years and older has more than doubled in the last fifty years. In 1900, 4.1 percent, and in 1957, 8.6 percent, of the population was over sixty-five; at the turn of the twentieth century the average length of life was forty-nine years, while by 1955 it had increased to seventy. (3) This expanded life span due to advances in the medical sciences has brought many new problems, some of which have implications for clothing. With a decrease in physical strength and energy, we must give thought to designing clothes which are easy to put on and take off and easy to care for; with changing bodily characteristics, it is necessary to solve the problem of fitting the mature figure and of designs and colors which are becoming to this age group; and with decreased earning power and hence income, we must consider the original cost and the maintenance cost.

The psychological needs to be met, at least in part by clothing, are fundamentally the same for the elderly as they were for other age groups. The elderly also need affection and opportunities for social contacts. They desire the approval of others and recognition of their personal dignity. They do not want to be singled out and pitied. As they have lost many of their old friends, they are increasingly lonely unless they make new friends.

Whatever the chronological age, the interests, attitudes and habits of earlier years will remain fundamentally the same. There is no sharp distinction between the middle-aged and the elderly; rather there is a gradual change in physical and psychological characteristics. The rate of change, however, varies for different individuals. We have only to compare friends and relatives of various chronological ages to see that this is true. A man in our neighborhood is ninety-three and yet he looks and acts like a man in his early sixties, or younger; he walks several miles each day, gardens in the summer, and ice skates in the winter. On the other hand, we all know of others who at sixty, or even younger look and act much older.

Just as there were physical changes from one younger age group to another, there are changes in physical characteristics as the individual grows older. These changes may either improve or detract from physical attractiveness. In our culture, which emphasizes the positive value of youth, we find many authors discussing the changes of advancing age as handicaps to be hidden or minimized. Some of these changes, however, may make the individual more, rather than less, attractive. Often the first and most obvious change is in color of the hair which usually turns to gray and then to white. This frequently is a positive factor; many people are more attractive with white hair.

Also, as individuals grow older, the face becomes more lined and wrinkled. This, again is not necessarily a detriment. These lines may give a pleasing character to a face which was bland and uninteresting with the smoothness of youth.

The figure usually changes in size and proportion as we grow older. There is often an increase in weight and a decrease in height. Weight gradually increases from the middle years to about the age of seventy when it begins to decrease.

The most difficult physical changes to adjust to are those related to general health—the loss of energy and vigor, stiffening of muscles, and sometimes the loss of hearing or eyesight.

Implications for Clothing of Physical Changes Due to Increasing Age

FIT

The body not only gains in weight after the middle years but the distribution of weight also shifts. The body fat tends to move slowly downward—the bust or chest becomes relatively smaller and the abdomen and hips larger. Often the waistline disappears entirely and the body becomes almost pear shaped. The shoulders become rounded and there is general bodily sagging. All of this creates serious problems in fitting, especially as the standard measurements for patterns are based upon measurements of younger women. Bartley and Warden (2) noted that three-fourths of the 47 elderly women whom they interviewed had a thickened waistline while nearly half had rounded shoulders. These respondents reported that the alterations most frequently needed in clothes were those in the length of the waistline. Tate and Glisson (28) report a study of 50 older women from a relatively high socioeconomic group. These women reported an enlarged waistline—mentioned by 72 percent—as the change most frequently causing difficulty in the purchase of clothes. The half-size dresses which have a larger waistline are a partial answer to the need. Bader (1) reports that 70 percent of her sample of 60 women ranging in age from sixty-five to ninety-three years wore half-size dresses. In spite of this, the most common alterations were changes in the waistline. Obviously there is need for information on the amount the waistline increases for the average women. This information should be made available for clothing manufacturers so that the elderly would have fewer problems in obtaining proper fit.

In addition to fit at the waistline, the shoulders often become rounded and there is a roll of fat at the base of the neck in back (sometimes called the widow's hump). These often cause difficulties in fitting; extra fullness is needed in the back, and the length between the neckline and the waistline usually needs to be increased if the garment is to hang correctly. Another problem due to shifting weight is the loss of fat in the upper arms. This causes an unattractive sagging of the flesh and an increase in wrinkles in this area which most women wish to hide. For this reason, many older women

*"I must be getting old—I'm beginning to select my shoes
for comfort and my sweaters for warmth."*

dislike short sleeves or sleeveless dresses and prefer a sleeve which covers the
arm to a point below the elbow.

EASE OF PUTTING ON AND TAKING OFF GARMENTS

With a decrease in energy and vigor and a stiffening of the muscles, even
those in relatively good health need garments which do not require extensive
stretching and reaching to put on or to fasten and unfasten. The Northeast
Regional Research project on consumer satisfaction noted that the component
of satisfaction mentioned most frequently by women over sixty-five was the
ease of getting a dress on or off (26). Gumpert says that "Two of the most
strenuous activities in the everyday life of the aged are getting dressed and
getting undressed" [17:72]. We noted when we were discussing the dressing
process in children (see p. 224) that dressing and undressing took more

energy than anything except the very strenuous activities. With the loss of the pliability and flexibility of youth, this becomes an even greater problem. In addition, many older people are afflicted with arthritis and other diseases of the joints and muscles which greatly increase the problem.

Dresses which open in the front are satisfactory in this respect. Larger armholes such as those for raglan sleeves are also easier to put on. A note in the *Reader's Digest* (14) describes underwear designed to be easier to put on and take off. Mrs. Odell, formerly successful in the advertising field, was paralyzed on one side by a stroke. She was unable to put on or take off her bra and girdle. Having read that there were 7 million disabled women in the United States, she decided to design underwear which they could manage by themselves. Working with designers from a lingerie company, she developed a bra utilizing Velcro nylon-tape fasteners instead of hooks and a slip with zipper opening in front. Such garments would be helpful not only for the disabled but for the elderly as well. Certainly this entire field is greatly in need of designers with creative imaginations.

PROBLEMS RELATED TO TEMPERATURE SENSATIONS

The older person has increased susceptibility to both heat and cold. The aging body loses its resiliency and power of adaptation and regulation. Part of the susceptibility, Gilbert (15) suggests, may be due to lowered basal metabolic rate and lessened muscular vigor. In addition, the elderly tend to move less and more slowly and thus do not have the warmth generated by movement.

There are also changes in the skin which lead to increased temperature sensitivity. There is a loss of a layer of subcutaneous fat which in the younger individual serves as a layer of insulation. The older person thus feels both the cold and heat more than the younger individual, thus clothing must be warmer in winter and cooler in summer. Sweaters, jackets or stoles which can be put on or removed with changes in temperature are a helpful answer to this problem.

BECOMINGNESS OF CLOTHING DEPENDENT ON PHYSICAL
CHANGES DUE TO AGE

With the change in color of hair and skin, the older person finds that some colors which formerly were unbecoming now are very becoming and of course the opposite is true. With gray or white hair, many women are attractive in colors which were unattractive on them before their hair turned. Those who had a ruddy complexion when young may have avoided reds and pinks because it seemed to emphasize the reds in their skin, but as they become older, the skin becomes paler and soft reds and pinks may be especially becoming. For others the skin may become more sallow as they grow older and so they are more limited in choices of colors. Because these changes in coloring are gradual, individuals often do not realize that they are taking place and that they might be more attractive if they chose other colors. Having lived many years with the idea that they "can" or "cannot" wear certain colors, it is difficult for the elderly to change their notions of what is becoming to them. I remember meeting an elderly woman who was very indignant with a sales clerk. The woman had asked for a red hat and the clerk had said that she did not have one, and even if she did she wouldn't sell it to the woman as it wouldn't look well on her. The woman replied that she had "always had a red hat" and left the store. The clerk, although tactless, was correct. The woman had greenish tones in her skin which the red emphasized. When I met her she was wearing a red dress and hat (presumably purchased in a store where the clerk was more tactful if less honest) and I was immediately repelled by her appearance. The woman had had black hair as a young woman and presumably a clear skin, and at that time red was probably especially becoming to her.

Certain lines and designs in clothing, as well as colors, differ in their becomingness for the elderly. We have mentioned that the body proportions change as the individual grows older. Dress designs which emphasize the waistline, for example, are not as attractive on the older figure as they were on the younger one. Plain unbroken expanses are less flattering to the large figure and severely tailored lines may emphasize wrinkles. For example, a high round jewel neckline may emphasize the wrinkles in the neck.

Clothing Practices and Behavior Related to Clothing

The individual sixty-five years of age and older is usually living on a lower income. Retirement in most cases has removed the income from full-time employment. As Reinicke (24) has pointed out, public social-insurance programs have virtually eliminated extreme poverty, yet they have provided only a modest amount of "discretionary buying power."

There is a sharp decline, both in the actual and the relative amount spent for clothing after the age of sixty-five. For those under sixty-five, 10.9 to 12.3 percent of the total budget is spent on clothing, but this drops to 8.8 percent for those sixty-five to seventy-five and to 7.8 percent for those over seventy-five (16:118).

Data from a 1952 survey in California show that clothing is the second most frequent unmet need for persons beyond the retirement age. (Medical care and drugs constitute the first unmet need.) The breakdown of this study showed that 14 percent had unmet needs of medical care and drugs, 12 percent of clothing. In comparison with these figures, only 4 percent were in need of household equipment and 3 percent had unmet housing needs. The unmet need for medical care and clothing may create difficulties in social adjustment. As Van Mering and Weniger have expressed it: "Their experience of being different or even deviant from the active younger people around them and their experience of growing more distant from the ongoingness of things can only *increase* if their needs for eye glasses, dentures, hearing aids, and adequate clothing remain unmet for long" [3:314].

The decline in the amount and proportion of the income spent for clothing is not entirely due to a drop in total income. The decline is seen even when income is held constant. That is, even if an older person can afford clothing, he buys less than someone younger. This is presumably because he goes out less socially, and also since he is physically less active, his clothes do not wear out as rapidly.

The decline is not specific to certain types of garments, but apparently is equally distributed over all parts of the wardrobe. Goldstein reports that "data for both males and females show that the relative amounts spent for particular items of clothing tend to be remarkably similar for all age groups" [16:131]. That is, the percentage spent for outerwear versus underwear does not show variation among different age groups. The only exceptions are that men tend to spend less for footwear as they grow older, and for women the relative amount spent for hosiery declines. These differences are in all likelihood caused by the decline in physical activity.

CLOTHING INVENTORIES

The United States Department of Agriculture's research on clothing inventories found that women over sixty had fewer of every type of garment than did the younger women (see Table 30). The men over sixty owned fewer than younger men of every type of garment except hats, caps, pajamas, nightshirts and bathrobes.

Undoubtedly research would show not only that the older age group owned fewer garments, but that the garments in their wardrobes were older.

	Age Group				
Item *(1)*	*Under 30* *(2)*	*30–39* *(3)*	*40–49* *(4)*	*50–59* *(5)*	*60 and* *over* *(6)*
	HUSBANDS				
Outer coats and outdoor jackets	5.0	5.6	5.3	4.9	4.3
Suits and suit equivalents*	5.5	4.9	4.9	4.7	4.3
Shirts and sweaters	27.6	24.7	21.0	18.8	14.2
Overalls and work trousers	4.7	4.3	3.9	3.5	2.4
Hats and caps	2.6	3.3	3.9	3.9	3.8
Shoes and boots	4.9	4.9	4.8	4.0	3.8
Socks	20.1	21.8	18.0	16.7	15.1
Pajamas, nightshirts, and bathrobes	3.3	4.0	4.3	4.4	4.3

	WIVES				
Outer coats and outdoor jackets	4.1	4.1	4.0	3.5	2.9
Dresses and suits	13.5	13.4	12.7	11.2	11.1
Blouses and sweaters	10.9	8.1	6.2	4.0	3.2
Skirts and slacks	4.2	3.1	2.2	1.0	.5
Shoes and boots	7.0	7.0	5.9	4.7	4.0
Hosiery	11.1	10.5	9.2	8.0	7.8
Pajamas, nightgowns, and robes	7.2	7.3	6.9	6.6	5.9

* Separate suit coats or sport jackets and separate dress trousers and slacks are each weighted one-half.

table 30   Grouped items: Average number of garments owned by husbands and wives in selected age groups. (Families without children or with one or two children aged to fifteen years.) Data: Family Clothing Inventories by Age, Minneapolis–St. Paul, Minn., 1949, USDA, January, 1951, p. 4.

Dodge (10) reports that of 196 older women interviewed, 50 percent had purchased a coat in the last year and paid between $25 and $49 for it. They bought, on the average, less than one better dress per year (for which they paid between $25 and $49) and one and a third housedresses for which they paid less than $6. Many reported receiving clothing as gifts. The older men interviewed in this study usually paid between $45 and $99.95 for a suit, and approximately 50 percent had purchased a suit in the last year. The men purchased an average of 1.22 shirts per year and paid between $3 and $3.95 for them. Many men reported that they received shirts as gifts. In this report, there is no indication of the sampling procedure. From the amounts spent and the number of articles purchased, we assume that the sample must have been selected from the higher socioeconomic levels. This assumption is substantiated by the fact that Dodge reports that almost a third reported no change in income in recent years.

SHOPPING PRACTICES

Much of our information on the shopping practices of the older age group comes from the study in Portland, Oregon, reported by Dodge (10). As we noted above, this study may have been based upon individuals from a relatively high socioeconomic group. Dodge studied the shopping patterns for apparel of the older age group by interviewing 196 women and 91 men. These older persons said that they did not travel to shop; 57 percent did not own cars and so were dependent on public transportation or conveniently located shopping centers. They disliked shopping by phone because they liked to see the merchandise they were considering; they most frequently shopped in department stores. The reasons given for shopping in a particular store in order of frequency were: (1) assortment of merchandise, (2) price, (3) quality, (4) availability, (5) convenience, and (6) habit.

Over 50 percent of this group reported that they preferred to shop alone. They indicated that they purchase more on impulse than they did in younger years. Over half of the group said that they enjoyed window shopping.

On the negative side, they felt that the salespeople were often indifferent to older people, and almost a third reported difficulty in finding apparel which fit and was the style they wanted.

As a part of this same study, merchants were asked about what they did to attract older customers. All of the merchants stated that they did not know what appeals to use for the older market, but most of them desired to obtain this information.

A second important research on the shopping practices of the elderly was carried out in Iowa City by Bader (1). In this study 60 active, ambulatory, socially participating women between sixty-five and ninety-three were interviewed. These women, the author reports, were above average in income, educational attainment, social participation, and professional position. About half of the women said they enjoyed shopping for clothing and half did not. Bader says that their attitudes toward the enjoyment of shopping for clothing is accurately summarized by the remark of one of the women who said "I like it less each year" [p. 4]. Reasons given for the declining amount of enjoyment in shopping for clothing included becoming tired easily, not wanting to spend the time shopping, not being able to find clothing they liked and which fit. Income seemed to be another important factor. When questioned about their relationships with salesclerks, almost all felt that they were treated courteously, but many said that they felt that salespeople preferred to help younger customers. Many said that they had favorite salespeople and several mentioned that older clerks were more helpful than young ones.

As in the research by Dodge, this project showed that women prefer to see the merchandise they are buying; only 9 of the 60 women reported buying clothing from a mail-order company and these were items not available in local stores. Probably for the same reason, these women did not desire a shopping service although the latter is partially explained by the fact that a quarter of the women had daughters who shopped for them.

While over 50 percent of the women in the Dodge study said they preferred to shop alone, over 60 percent in the Bader study said that they liked the advice of someone else when shopping for clothing. In most instances, they preferred the advice of a family member or friend. The discrepancy in results may be due to sample differences or to differences in the way in which questions were worded. It would be helpful if in future research this could be clarified and the results analyzed using finer age groupings. I would hypothesize that, as age increased beyond sixty-five, there would be an increase in the desire for advice. From casual observation, it seems to me that as women become older, they are less and less sure of their own judgment concerning fashion and becomingness.

Elements in the shopping situation which the older shoppers in Bader's study felt needed improvement were first of all chairs in the show room so that they could sit and rest. They preferred to have the sales personnel bring garments to them rather than having racks of dresses and coats which they had to look through themselves. They also would like better lighting, wider aisles, and more store directories.

The women were about equally divided as to whether they wanted special shops or departments for older women. They demonstrated by their answers that they desired smartly styled and better fitting clothes which did not set them apart from others. Some thought this might be accomplished better in separate facilities and others thought that it would not. As Dr. Jules Labarth has said: "If you called a shop 'The Old Ladies' Shop' who would ever buy in it?"[1]

USE AND CARE OF CLOTHING

We have almost no information on the use and care of clothing by the elderly. Bader, in the study reviewed above, found that all of the women dressed up when they went away from home. Around the home, two-thirds of them said that they wore cotton housedresses; over 20 percent wore old "good" dresses; and a very few wore the casual outfits such as skirts, slacks, or shorts and blouses common with the younger group.

In the Northeast Regional Research project (26), almost half of the older men reported that they wore dress or business shirts for church, organization meetings, social activities and other "appropriate" occasions, but only 15 percent indicated that they wore these shirts regularly. Comfort factors were the most frequent reasons given for wearing sport or work shirts for every day.

Although we have no research evidence to support the following statements, today's casual observation suggests that there are several ways in which the elderly differ from younger individuals in the use of clothing. In the first place, they continue habits in the use of clothing from their younger years. This is shown, for example, by elderly men in the wearing of suits rather than separate sport jackets and slacks. Older women seem to be much more apt to wear a hat than younger women. When these older women were young, hats were considered a necessary part of the costume for shopping or any social activity. At the present time, few younger women consider hats necessary for most activities.

Individuals past the retirement age seem to be more conservative in their clothing choices than younger people. They choose more subdued colors and

---

[1] Quotation furnished by M. L. Rosencranz.

more classic styles. This may be due in part to the fact that these are the only garments available in sizes which fit. It may also be due in part to lowered income; and may be because they expect conservative clothes to last longer. Even with larger income and greater variety of colors and styles available, it is probable that there would still be a tendency to select more conservative styles and colors.

There also seems to be a tendency for older people to wear more formal clothing. The emphasis upon the casual look is comparatively recent, and the elderly, partially through habit, continue to wear more formal clothing. There are other reasons, however. Older people want to make a good impression and wish to give a dignified appearance through more formal clothing.

We have almost no reliable information on differences in the care of garments between those sixty-five years and older and younger individuals. We would assume that with decrease in energy this would become more of a problem, but we have no evidence to support such a conclusion. On the other hand, most of the new developments in wash-and-wear fibers and finishes have come in recent years, and, out of habit, many of the elderly may not take advantage of these new developments. There is one bit of research evidence to support this last statement; the Northeast Regional Research project reports that: "More of the women sixty-five and older than those of fifty-four and younger washed their slips by hand and ironed them. Although these practices are time-consuming, it is interesting that these women did not consider their slips hard to care for" [26:51].

Attitudes toward Clothing and Clothing Preferences

Older men and women consider clothing important and feel that they should make an effort to be attractive and neat. Over 58 percent of the group interviewed by Bader (1) considered that clothing was just as important to them now as it ever had been, and 28 percent thought it was more important than when they were younger. Because older people are aware that some of the physical changes taking place detract from their appearance, they feel it is necessary for them to spend more time and effort on their clothing and grooming to be attractive. The young can get away with sloppy casual attire, but the man or woman over sixty who is not neatly dressed and well groomed arouses pity or contempt.

A pleasant appearance gives a lift to almost anyone and the elderly are no exception. A person who is dressed and groomed neatly and attractively is less likely to be filled with self-pity, and he is more sociable. Davis (8) notes, in reporting a study of social preferability and self-concept in the aged, that the self-concept of aged persons is influenced by their social relationships. In turn, social relationships are influenced by the self-concepts. Thus, the older person who feels that his appearance is acceptable is more likely to participate socially and, as he makes new friends and keeps in touch with old ones, his concept of himself is more positive.

We have mentioned that the elderly do not wish to be segregated or considered apart from others. They wish to conform to current fashions, at least to the extent that will prevent them from being singled out as different. Bader says:

> One of the unfavorable stereotypes of older people is that they are slow to accept fashion changes. There was not, however, in the Iowa City group, any indication of unwillingness to accept change, but there was evidence that the women were highly selective and deliberate in accepting fashion changes. This seems to indicate that there was serious judgment of what was suitable for them as older women and as individuals. The women in this study were, for the most part, interested in being attractively dressed in what was the best for them from the current fashions. There was a certain feeling of rebellion, not rebellion against aging, but against what aging seemed to mean to clothing designers, manufacturers, and merchandisers as evidenced in their offerings of poorly-designed, uninteresting, monotonous clothing in nondescript prints and unsuitable colors [1:6].

Ebling and Rosencranz (12) note that the majority of women in the older age group frequently looked at fashion magazines. They were interested in style changes and fashion shows. The rural women in their sample sewed more, read more fashion magazines than urban women, and they also had a stronger interest in clothing than had those from urban areas. This is contrary to research on adolescents and younger adults where we have found urban groups to be more interested in clothing than rural groups.

The Ebling and Rosencranz study also found relationships between social participation and the adequacy of the wardrobe. Women who attended fewer organizations more often stated that their clothing affected their feelings of ease at social gatherings and refused more invitations for lack of appropriate clothing than did those who participated socially to a greater extent. As with the younger groups, we do not know which is cause and which effect. It may be that the women who did not go out often had a limited wardrobe for this reason and therefore, felt more ill at ease when they did go out. On the other hand, it may have been that the woman who was unable to have an adequate wardrobe for economic or other reasons did not join as many organizations.

SPECIFIC PREFERENCES

There have been a number of studies on specific preferences in clothing for the elderly. The Northeast Regional project has dealt with consumer motivation of the elderly at what we have called the second stratum, or the perceived properties of a garment. In this study (26), the components of satisfaction with men's shirts and with women's slips and casual street dresses were investigated. The relative importance of the various components to over-all satisfaction with garments was measured by comparing the respondents' ratings of their favorite and their least-liked garment of a specific type. It was assumed that the greater the difference between the satisfaction ratings on the favorite and the least-liked garments, the greater the importance of that component's contribution to satisfaction with a garment. By this measure, becomingness was the most important component of satisfaction with shirts for men sixty-five and over, and durability and ease of care the least important of the components measured. For women over sixty-five, in slips, comfort and, in dresses, comfort and fit were the most important components of satisfaction and again durability and ease of care were the least important (26: supplement Table LIV, LV, and LVI). Since in this study the sample of older people varied in socioeconomic status as well as age from the younger groups, comparisons by age need to be interpreted with this in mind. It appears from the data, however, that durability is of little importance to the older respondents and of lesser importance for shirts and dresses than for slips. Perhaps this is because the elderly do not wear out garments. The influence of durability on satisfaction was greater for women of forty-five to fifty-four for slips than for other age groups. Fit of dresses was more important to women sixty-five and older than to other groups, perhaps because of their difficulty in finding dresses which fit. The importance of ease of care to satisfaction tended to decrease with increase in age of the respondent, but becomingness, by this measure was as important to the older age groups as it was to the younger groups.

Bartley and Warden report that:

Expressions concerning becomingness, comfort, and ease of donning made up most of the reasons for preferences of color and garment design in clothing worn while doing housework; while ease of donning, ease of care, and comfort were stated most frequently as being considered when purchasing work garments. . . . Expressions concerning becomingness made up most of the reasons for garment design and color preferences in garments selected to wear to church or social functions. In comparison, color, ease of care, and garment design were stated as being most frequently considered when purchasing dressy dresses [2:171].

Several studies have investigated the specific attributes (Stratum one) which are preferred by the older age group. The characteristics of the favorite dress for older women which emerges from these studies is a blue dress (either solid color or with a small print), with gored skirt, three-quarter sleeves, a V neckline with a collar and opening at least part of the way down the front. It should be simple—not "too fussy" in style and might be a dress with a jacket (see 1, 2, 4, 9, 12, and 26).

Blue has been found to be the favorite color for dresses in every study with older women on color preferences. Green is the next most popular. There is less agreement on the least-liked color; Decker (9) found it to be red-yellow, and Bivins (4) results showed that brown was the least liked with red next most disliked.

Preference for the less saturated colors, blue in particular, and for the V neckline are undoubtedly related to becomingness. These are attributes which most books on design and selection list as most becoming to the larger figure and to white hair. Women have probably found these design elements pleasing and therefore desirable.

The preference for a front opening is probably related to the ease of putting the dress on and taking it off.

Surprisingly, almost none of the studies has examined preference for fiber. An exception to this is the Bartley (2) study which noted that the typical garment worn while doing housework would probably be a cotton wash dress. In the Northeast Regional research project, a significant difference was found between women 65 and older and those under 54 in the fiber of the casual street dresses.

> Most of the dresses of the younger women were cotton; fiber blends were next; wool, third; and rayon, fourth. Only a few dresses were made of polyester, nylon, silk, or nonspecified fibers, and none of acetate. The fibers of the dresses belonging to the older respondents, in order of frequency, were: fiber blends, acetate, cotton, and rayon. The relatively large number of acetates found among the dresses of this group may reflect the market offerings for dresses in large sizes rather than a greater preference for acetate. [26:18]

We obviously need research on fiber preferences for this age group. As we have said, older women dislike having clothes which label them as belonging to a special group. If one of the chief differences between dresses designed for this group as contrasted with other groups is in the fiber, perhaps this is one of the causes of dissatisfaction with the choices on the market.

Other differences between the dresses of older and younger women in the Northeast Regional research were that the bodices of the younger women's dresses were fitted by means of darts, and fullness in the skirts was accomplished by pleats or gathers, while the dresses for older women more often had bodices fitted by means of tucks or methods other than darts, and the fullness in skirts was added by means of gores. These would seem to be differences between dresses for the age groups which would not affect the becomingness of the dress to older figures nor the ease of donning. Thought should be given, therefore, to whether or not these differences are desirable.

On the other hand, Bartley and Warden (2) found that 60 percent of the women in their sample said that they usually found the preferred fabrics, garment designs and colors in their sizes when shopping and were relatively satisfied with the clothing available in present-day markets. These results are in contrast to those from a number of other studies in which women over sixty-five complained of not being able to find stylish clothes with adequate fit.

Summary

The number and percentage of individuals over sixty-five in the population has increased greatly in recent years. Along with this increase we have a growing awareness of problems relating to this age group. Attempts have been made to investigate some of these problems in spite of particular difficulties in research methodology for this age group. The greatest difficulty in social-psychological research with the elderly is in obtaining a representative sample of individuals. Bader, for example, says:

> During the time the plans were being made for the study and the questions were being prepared for the interviews, work was also being done on the compilation of a list of names of women over sixty-five years of age residing in Iowa City, Iowa. Other researchers had reported that obtaining the names of persons over sixty-five years of age was difficult because there were few, if any, lists of names available. Just how difficult this would be was not realized until it was actually attempted. A list of six hundred names was finally compiled and the research group of sixty was drawn from this list [1 :4].

Similar difficulties were found in attempting to find a representative sample in the Northeast Regional research project. Some researchers have solved the problem by using only those older people in institutions. Others have used specific organizations such as the Golden Age Club or Senior Citizens. Obviously either of these methods yields a biased sample and therefore are adequate only when the research design does not call for a random sample.

Thought must also be given to the method of collecting data. Landis (22) points out that the questionnaire method is generally not feasible with the elderly. Older people often have bad eyesight or other handicaps and failing physical energy. They find it difficult to carry out any new or unusual task. Filling out a questionnaire thus may be difficult to accomplish and the returns may be poor. The questionnaires returned, furthermore, are likely to be from segments of the population which are most active and healthy, and so may be biased.

Personal interviews are much more feasible. Older people usually have the time and, as they are often lonely, they enjoy talking to new people. In interviewing this age group extra time must be allowed for each interview. Not only does the older individual wish to visit longer, but he is very apt to digress or wander from the topic being discussed.

In spite of these difficulties in research, we can make a number of valid statements concerning psychological implications of clothing for this age

The older individual is still interested in clothing and is motivated attractive to others. The need to make new friends may be even great in earlier years because of the loss of old friends; thus the older person wishes to have stylish clothes and not to be set apart in a separate group by different clothing.

The problems in dressing attractively are greater than they are for younger persons. In the first place, the older individuals are often retired and thus are living on a reduced income. This is partially relieved by the fact that the older group tends to be less active socially and so has less need for clothes. Also the group is less active physically, and so does not wear out clothing as rapidly.

In the second place there are physical changes in the body with advancing age which have implications for clothing. The most common change is in the thickening of the waist and hips in proportion to the chest and arms. This creates problems in fitting especially as most of the garments on the market are made from patterns standardized on young figures. Half-sizes are a partial answer to this need.

Other physical changes, such as the hair turning to white and the skin changing in color and becoming wrinkled, alter the colors and lines which are becoming. The older person prefers, probably because they are more becoming, the less saturated colors, especially the medium blues and greens. Sleeves which hide the upper arm and V necklines are also preferred, probably for the same reason.

The older person is not only less energetic but also often has stiffening of muscles and joints. Therefore, it is necessary to consider whether or not clothes are easy to put on and take off.

Physiological changes with advancing years make the older person more susceptible to temperature changes than the younger person. Sweaters, stoles, or jackets which can be put on or removed easily are therefore especially useful for the elder citizen.

Some of the preferences of the older group are being met by the market— half-size dresses are often found in blues and greens with matching jackets. The elderly shopper's greatest complaint is that she is unable to find stylish dresses that fit.

Bibliography

1. Bader, Iva M. An exploratory study of clothing problems and attitudes of a group older women in Iowa City. *Adding Life to Years.* Institute of Gerontology, State Univer. of Iowa, X supplement No. 10, 1963, 3–6.
2. Bartley, Lois and Warden, Jessie. Clothing preferences of women 65 and older. *J. of Home Ec.* 54(8), 1962, 716–717.

3. Birren, James E. *Handbook of Aging and the Individual—Psychological and Biological Aspects.* Chicago: University of Chicago Press, 1959, 897p.
4. Bivins, M. Consumer practices of older persons in selection, use and care of clothing. Unpublished pilot study at University of Conn., 1958.
5. Blair, Margaret Harris. Changes in appearance of women 45 to 65 years of age which affect use of ready-to-wear garments and commercial patterns. *J. of Home Ec.* 45(4), 1953, 248–250.
6. Boas, Ernst. *Add Life to Your Years.* New York: McBride Co., 1954, 271p.
7. Campbell, Zoe. Spending patterns of older persons. *Management Record.* 21, 1959, 85–87, 100–101.
8. Davis, Robert W. The relationship of social preferability to self-concept in an aged population. *J. of Gerontology.* 17, 1962, 431–436.
9. Decker, Patricia M. Color choices of older women; preferences or necessities? *J. of Retailing.* 39(4), 1963–64, 17–25.
10. Dodge, Robert E. Selling the older consumer. *J. of Retailing.* 34(2), 1958, 73–81, 100.
11. Donahue, Wilma. Psychologic research needs in gerontology. *J. of Gerontology.* 11, 1956, 196–203.
12. Ebeling, Maloa and Rosencranz, M. L. Social and personal aspects of clothing for older women. *J. of Home Ec.* 53(6), 1961, 464–465.
13. *Family Clothing Inventories by Age.* Minneapolis-St. Paul, Minn., 1949. Studies of family clothing supplies. Preliminary Report No. 3, Jan. 1951, U.S. Dept. of Agr. Bureau of Human Nutrition and Home Economics.
14. Fashion-able. *Reader's Digest.* Nov. 1964, 39.
15. Gilbert, Jeanne G. *Understanding Old Age.* New York: The Ronald Press Company, 1952, 402p.
16. Goldstein, Sidney. *Study of Consumer Expenditure—Incomes and Savings Consumption Patterns of the Aged.* Phila.: Univer. of Penna., 1960, Chap. 8, Clothing, 118–132.
17. Gumpert, Martin. *You Are Younger than You Think.* New York: Duell, Sloan & Pearce, Inc., 1944, 237p.
18. Gumpert, Martin. What age does to your skin and what you can do about it. *Lifetime Living.* 3, 1954, 41–42.
19. Havighurst, Robert J. Social and psychological needs of the aging. *Amer. Acad. of Polit. and Soc. Science.* 279, 1952, 11–17.
20. Hoffman, Adeline and Bader, Iva M. *Social Science Aspects of Clothing for Older Women. An Annotated Bibliography.* Iowa City: State Univer. of Iowa, Sept. 1964, 32p.
21. Hoffman, Adeline. Clothing problems and clothing behavior of older women. *Adding Life to Years.* Inst. of Gerontology, State Univer. of Iowa, IX No. 9, 1962, 3–6.
22. Landis, Judson T. Some observations on special problems encountered in studying the aged. *Amer. Soc. Rev.* X(3), 1945, 427–429.

23. Miller, Irene. Build a firm foundation. *Lifetime Living*. 3, Oct. 1954, 46–50.
24. Reinecke, John A. The "older" market—fact or fiction? *J. of Marketing*. 28(1), 1964, 60–64.
25. Rose, William G. *The Best is Yet to Be*. New York: Austin-Phelps, Inc., 1951, 148–157.
26. Ryan, M., Ayres, R., Carpenter, V., Densmore, B., Swanson, C., and Whitlock, M. *Consumer Satisfaction with Men's Shirts and with Women's Slips and Casual Street Dresses*. Part 1: Field Study in four communities in the Northeast. Cornell Univer. Agr. Exper. Sta. Bull. 984, July 1963. 43–52 and supplement, Tables LI–LVI.
27. Shipley, Suzanne and Rosencranz, M. L. Older women's clothing preferences. *J. of Home Ec.* 54(10), 1962, 854.
28. Tate, Mildred T. and Glisson, Oris. *Family Clothing*. New York: John Wiley & Sons, Inc., 1961, Chap. 15, 337–349.
29. Textiles and clothing for older people. *J. of Home Ec.* 54(10), 1962, 852.
30. Tudor, Marian. *Mr. Senior Citizen . . . Look Your Best*. Extension Service, N. Dakota State Univer., May 1962.
31. Tudor, Marian. *Mrs. Senior Citizen . . . Look Your Best*. Extension Service, N. Dakota State Univer., May 1962.
32. Wilson, Joy. Make-up tips for the mature woman. *Lifetime Living*. 1 and 2, 1952–53, 53–54.

Author Index

Subject Index